# McGRAW-HILL SERIES IN EDUCATION

HAROLD BENJAMIN, Consulting Editor

# SUCCESSFUL TEACHING

*The quality of the materials used in the manufacture of this book is governed by continued postwar shortages.*

*Selected Titles from*

# McGraw-Hill Series in Education

HAROLD BENJAMIN, *Consulting Editor*

○

# SUCCESSFUL TEACHING

## Its Psychological Principles

JAMES L. MURSELL

Teachers College, Columbia University

*First Edition*

THIRD IMPRESSION

New York                    London

McGRAW-HILL BOOK COMPANY, Inc.

1946

SUCCESSFUL TEACHING

*For* JEAN

# PREFACE

What must any teacher do if his pupils are to learn well and are to achieve lasting, usable, and meaningful results? This is the crucial problem with which this book is chiefly concerned.

The first step in writing this book began with applying the method of universal doubt. The author tried to wipe his mental slate clean, to suppose that nothing at all is known about what makes teaching successful. He attempted particularly to suppose that all methods—progressive, conventional, or otherwise—are equally unacceptable. This assumption was not too difficult, for it is quite clear that good teaching is not a very common thing. Thus, no method could be considered as answering the problem immediately.

Where, then, to start? There seemed only one possible point of departure. If there were any answer at all, it could only be found in what is known about the psychology of learning. True, our knowledge is not complete and does not go down to bedrock, but a great deal has been discovered, and we have a pretty good natural history of learning. Above all, there is a very striking and growing agreement among the best psychologists about the conditions of good learning. The author therefore undertook to find out the implications of this knowledge for the practice of teaching, beginning with as few preconceptions as possible.

The next step was to apply this body of knowledge about learning. It was obviously futile to say in effect to a teacher, "Here is what we know about learning. Now go ahead and use it." That procedure has been tried often enough, and it doesn't work out. Consequently, the author set about to refresh and extend his contacts with actual teaching. He reviewed his own experience, visited classrooms, conferred with teachers, worked with groups of student cadets, studied accounts of teaching situations and various recommended plans for teaching. He tried to do all this without preconceived ideas for or against and with only one question in mind. How does psychology bear on these situations? The author was looking for the bridge between our psychological knowledge and the practical teaching job.

The solution was not found in any set method. Learning sometimes seemed to go well and sometimes badly, almost irrespective of the particular method used. Moreover, many samples of teaching hardly seemed to represent any definable method at all, and such samples also might be good or bad.

The author found this bridge in a set of six principles. The more he looked at teaching and learning, the clearer it became that from the psychological standpoint certain crucial aspects attach to them. The learner's mind must work in the right kind of *context* if he is to learn well. He must set up the right kind of *focus*. The right kind of *social relationships* will help him enormously. To some extent he must work in his own *individual* way. Each particular job of learning must be a part of a *sequence* of developing power and insight. The right kind of *evaluation* is essential, for the learner needs to know how he is getting along and other people need to know it too. These six principles—context, focalization, socialization, individualization, sequence, and evaluation—comprise the author's bridge between psychology and the classroom.

In dealing with them, the first requirement was to find out what psychology has to say about each one. It can tell us a great deal. It can show quite definitely the general characteristics of *good* context, *good* focalization, *good* socialization, *good* individualization, *good* sequence, and *good* evaluation. It can show us how learning must be organized with respect to each principle if it is to yield the best results.

But a question still remains. Just exactly how does each of these principles work out on the job? Here the author came upon the idea of a hierarchy or scale of applications for each of the six. Take context, for example, which is always found in learning and teaching. Sometimes it is very poor (as, for instance, a dull, compact textbook), sometimes very good, sometimes intermediate in excellence. Thus, for each principle, one gets a hierarchy or scale by which actual teaching practices can be rated and arranged in an ascending order of excellence according to whatever psychology can tell us about how the principle in question ought to operate. Teaching cannot be seen simply as good or bad but exhibits varying degrees of excellence in six definite respects. So, for the teacher, the problem is not to practice any particular method, conventional or progressive, but to apply the six principles at the highest possible level.

Several additional explanatory comments now may be in order.

1. Teachers, supervisors, practice teachers, observers, or students of methodology can evaluate any job of teaching, actual or described, in terms of these principles. All of them can be seen operating in the teaching process, and the level on which they are operating can be estimated. And so a definite basis for forming a judgment and for indicating improvements is arrived at.

2. It is doubtful whether the author's set of principles is the only possible one. The only claim made is that they are definite, recognizable, and add up to a full, consistent account of the key aspects of teaching. Other sets might be developed. Motivation, for instance, does not appear in the author's scheme, although it might in another. It is omitted not because it is unimportant, but because, for the author, it does not represent a separate, recognizable aspect of teaching; it appears, rather, to be a result of all six principles. When these are applied at a high level, good motivation is the end product.

3. If a teacher applies these principles at a high level—*i.e.*, if he uses sound psychology—it will affect all his professional activities—particularly his preparation. Surprisingly enough, preparation has been badly handled in most books on teaching; it has been presented as routine daily lesson planning. Accordingly, a good deal of attention has been paid to this topic throughout the book, especially in the last chapter.

4. The issue of "one-man rule" versus classroom democracy is a very live one. The author's slant is that a teacher is not an autocrat nor a mere member of the learning group nor even in essence a director or a guide. He is an organizer, and he does a good job by applying specific principles of organization that are based on a sound general doctrine.

5. In emphasizing results, there is no conflict with those who emphasize child development, except when the latter is made an excuse for mere vagueness. Good learning is a primary agency for proper development, and good learning requires a proper developmental setting or sequence. No dividends, developmental or otherwise, accrue from bad learning.

6. This book deals with the problem of practical teaching. Of course, curriculum, administration, and an over-all philosophy are vital issues, all interrelated and connected with teaching. Moreover, with the decline of books and courses on general methods, the problem of teaching has been underemphasized of late. But after all, what is the use of the best curriculum, the most expert administration, the wisest philosophy, if teaching is so technically bad that it fails and potential learners simply do not learn?

JAMES L. MURSELL.

NEW YORK, N. Y.,
*June*, 1946.

# CONTENTS

xi

# CHAPTER 1

## SUCCESSFUL TEACHING: ITS MEANING

### THE CRITERION

Successful teaching is teaching that brings about effective learning. The decisive question is not what methods or procedures are employed, and whether they are old-fashioned or modern, time-tested or experimental, conventional or progressive. All such considerations may be important but none of them is ultimate, for they have to do with means, not ends. The ultimate criterion for success in teaching is—results!

This may perhaps seem so obvious as to be beyond all possible doubt. A person decides to take some lessons in golf or piano playing. As a return for the time and money invested, he wants an improvement in golf or piano playing, and the bigger the improvement for a given expenditure, the better he is pleased. A school conducts courses in algebra, French, or American history. The only assumption on which this makes sense is that the pupils are going to learn algebra, French, or American history, and the more they learn and the better they learn it in the time available, the better the courses have done what they were intended to do, which is a good working definition of success. Thus our criterion for success in teaching seems entirely harmonious with common sense.

Nevertheless it raises far-reaching and debatable issues which require considerable elucidation. Since the purpose of this book is to show how teaching must be managed in order to succeed in the sense indicated, it is very necessary to be as clear as possible from the outset about the meaning and implications of the criterion adopted.

**1. By what kind of results should the success of teaching be judged?** This is the first and perhaps the most obvious of all the numerous questions suggested by our criterion. It is closely related to the business of making the curriculum, an important part of which is to determine what the proper and desirable outcomes of education are. This book, however, does not deal with what are ordinarily thought of as curriculum problems as such. But if we look at the matter purely from the standpoint of teaching, which admittedly involves an abstraction but is possible and helpful nonetheless, it

1

immediately becomes clear that certain kinds of results are enormously more important than other kinds.    This is a distinction of great importance, because results of the former kind should always be regarded as the only true indicators of success.

Thus, results that are lasting are evidently far more important and significant than those that are transitory.    An investigation revealed that over a thousand college students in zoology, psychology, and chemistry did fairly well on objective tests given in June but had forgotten at least half that they knew when the tests were repeated in October.    Another investigation showed that college seniors lose an enormous proportion of the information they have acquired, or at least studied, during their school careers—such things as the meaning of an erg, an ohm, or a watt; the names of two substances used in making hydrogen; the velocity of light and sound; the date of the Hegira; the name of the American president during the Mexican war; or the main issue at the Council of Nicaea.    One might, of course, say with much justification that the loss of such material does not matter.    But after all, it was taught, and presumably with the idea that it would be retained.    One can easily imagine a teacher's placing great emphasis upon it, working hard to organize and present it well, driving his pupils to study it diligently, running a test to find out how well they had done so, and then congratulating himself on a satisfactory job when the showing was favorable.    This, however, would be a very unintelligent criterion if, as would almost certainly be the case, most of it disappeared in a short time and there was nothing else left.    Every teacher does well to consider, in connection with every lesson he presents, how much of it will still be in the learners' minds after a week, or a month, or a year, or ten years, or twenty years.    If he has the courage to do this, he is facing an extremely formidable challenge, but also a very healthy one, for it is the long pull that counts.[1]*

Again, results that a learner can use freely, flexibly, and confidently in a variety of situations are clearly far superior to those which he can only produce when he is given the right cue or asked the right question. A thousand out of twelve hundred ninth graders could handle algebraic operations such as multiplication, the use of brackets, the manipulation of fractions, and the solution of simple equations.    But out of that thousand, only a little over three hundred could find the value of $x$ in the equation

$$\frac{5}{2 - x} = \frac{3}{4 + x}$$

* This, like all similar numbers throughout, refers to the notes and references at the end of the chapter.

although not a single unfamiliar operation was involved.   Again, a grade-school group, most of whom could manage the four basic arithmetical operations when presented in standard and familiar form, were given the following problem: "Joseph rode on a merry-go-round 12 times.   Each ride cost him 3 cents.   How much did he pay for all his rides?"   The majority were helpless.   A few said they multiplied, but only because they noticed the word "times."   One child added, "Because there were lots of numbers."   And one reported thus: "If there are lots of numbers, I adds.   If there are only two numbers and lots of part [digits], I subtracts.   But if there are just two numbers and one littler than the other, it is hard.   I divides if they come out even, but if they don't, I multiply."   Here again, in both these cases, one can readily imagine a teacher working hard to get across the basic algebraic and arithmetical operations or skills.   But it would be a very ephemeral and delusive success, hardly worthy of the name.   And so once more every teacher does well to ask himself, in connection with every lesson he presents, whether the children are really able to use and apply what they are learning and to see its bearing upon unfamiliar situations, for these quite obviously are the kind of results that count.[2]

So there are some results which, on the basis of the merest common sense and without any theorizing whatever, cannot be considered as anything but unimportant, because they do not last and because they can be produced only on the one right occasion.   Both weaknesses flow from the same underlying defect.   Such results consist only of memorized words, without any real grasp of what the words convey.   Here and there some detail may stick in a learner's mind and be retained for a surprisingly long time.   But it is merely an inconsequential and useless psychological curiosity.   For the most part, after the lapse of a year, it is as though they had never been.   Such results cannot possibly be taken as the criterion for good teaching, and when it is oriented chiefly towards them, which all too often happens in fact and deed if not in word, then it is pointed toward failure.   Results of this kind, which do not enter into the personality of the learner, or shape his mental development, or affect his thinking, or influence his action, may properly be called *spurious*.

But there are results of a very different sort.   These appear when a child learns his mother tongue, when a student on a football squad learns the meaning of team loyalty, when mathematics is taught so that pupils grasp it as a method of thinking and analysis with endless implications and applications, when history is presented so as to convey a sense of the sweep and current bearings of past events, when the study of science yields an understanding of how explanations are elaborated and nature controlled by objective analysis. Such results last. They may not be retained with all their accompanying detail exactly as they were first acquired, but they establish lines of mental growth, and although they may be assimilated and transformed as deeper and wider understanding comes, they are never lost. And even the detail can easily be reconstituted and brushed up if desired. So, by the same token, they can be used in thought and action for the reason that they are not superficial or merely verbal but enter into the personality of the learner, influence his point of view and approach to things, and are richly meaningful for him. These are the kind of results by which the success of teaching must be judged and, in contrast to the others, they may be called *authentic*.

**2. Should teaching be judged by results in terms of the learning of subject matter or by results in terms of the development of pupils as persons?** This, in a sense, is a continuation of the previous question, but it opens up new considerations, and it brings to a focus one of the most crucial and earnestly debated of modern educational issues, on which it is altogether necessary to take a definite stand. Let us begin by putting the opposing arguments as completely and fairly as may be possible in a brief statement.

On the one hand it is contended that since human personality is far more important than any school subject, or indeed all the content of the curriculum put together, teachers should concentrate on the development of pupils as persons and accept this as the primary criterion of their success. Subject matter, indeed, is important, but it is only a means, and the development of personality is the end.

This position has been excellently expressed in the following words:

This self is emerging hour by hour as the child integrates his concepts, desires, and ways of thinking and acting around his ever-widening and ever-deepening life purposes. Such integration comes best through happy social living. The teacher's daily thoughts should dwell most about this process of happy living rather than about the child's expression of facts or mastery of specific techniques. Those are the little things, which though a part, should take their rightful very subordinate place in the large whole. Children themselves quickly recognize such differences. In a side room three little girls sit busily at work. One says to the others, "Does not the new girl in our room draw beautifully?" Then musing further, "But she is not a very good classmate to the rest of us yet." All continued to work. "Don't you know what I mean?" asks the talkative one. "Yes," and "Indeed yes," say the other two in surprised tones as they work calmly on.*

* Inga Olla Helseth, *Living in the Classroom*, p. 220, Edwards Bros., Inc., Ann Arbor, Mich., 1939.

Thus it is intimated that the efforts of the teacher should center not so much on curricular attainment as on the development of the right kind of personality which is far more important.

It may be interesting to remark that there is nothing new or novel about this doctrine. The famous theory of formal discipline or general mental training claimed precisely that Latin, Greek, mathematics, and pure science were not to be studied for their own sakes, but rather for the building up of certain powers and capacities, such as concentration, attentiveness, and the ability to think. The personal qualities that would commend themselves to an intelligent teacher of the classics a hundred years ago might be considerably different from those a modern progressive educator would think desirable. But the two would have very similar views about the relative importance of subject matter as such and the development of the pupil as a person.

So much for one side of the case. On the other hand it is argued that as a matter of fact the practical business of the school is and always has been to get the pupils to learn a stated curriculum. The school is fundamentally different from a general-welfare institution or a club or a clinic. It is an agency established and maintained by society to convey, particularly to young people, a body of content believed to be of great importance. In conveying this content and also in the general conduct of its affairs, it should no doubt have a constant concern for desirable personal qualities. Indeed the very purpose of conveying the stated content at all is to build them up. But they cannot and should not be the chief consideration in the day-by-day business of operating the school. The primary job which it has, apart from choosing the curriculum, is to get that curriculum well and truly learned. The success of its teaching can only be judged justly by how well it manages to get this done.

Such, then, is the issue. Desirable personal traits and qualities can certainly be considered results. So can subject-matter masteries. Which are we to choose? Which does our criterion indicate? On which should the success of teaching be judged? The answer is simple. We reject the alternative. To learn subject matter authentically, such traits as independence, initiative, creativeness, responsibility, cooperativeness, and the power to think and enjoy must be brought into play. The little girl who drew "beautifully" but who was "not yet a very good classmate" needed to learn to use her skill in a cooperative situation, and to do so would be good both for her skill and her growth as a person. On the other hand, when teaching evokes such traits as dependence, fear, insecurity, furtiveness, envy, and the tendency to get by no matter how, what happens to the subject matter? It is being learned, not as something that grips the pupil because it has a vital meaning for him, but at best as an external, superficial, mechanical routine. Nor is it true that a teacher can afford even relatively to neglect the learning of subject matter and concentrate chiefly on "happy living" in and of itself, for some of the most important and strengthening happiness in school comes from an awareness of increasing power with subject matter, and some of the most important and defeating unhappiness comes from a sense of laboring at an alien and meaningless routine, even though one does fairly well with it.

One might put the whole matter like this. A teacher should by all means be concerned with the pupil as a person, and should deal with him so that he develops as a person as well and completely as possible. But this is not quite all. The pupil in school is not a person without any further qualifications and specifications. He is a person with a job to do, a person who learns. If he is mishandled as a person he will not learn well. If he does not learn well he will be to that extent frustrated as a person. So the specific answer to the question at the head of this section is that the teacher must deal with the pupil as *a person who learns*, and that his work must be judged by the results which come from such dealings. The point is of such fundamental importance that a couple of concrete instances seem in order to make its meaning clearer.

The first is that of a certain high-school course in world history, which it is interesting to review from the standpoint of a student going through it. At the very beginning of the course, the student starts to gain a sense of the fascination and infinitely rich significance of the great story of the past. At first, assignments are sporadic, unsystematic, and different for different pupils. He himself, perhaps, is asked to look up a topic treated but slightly in the textbook, and to report to the class. His report, and those of other pupils, lead to stimulating discussions of the historic causes of present happenings. Little by little the chronological sequence of occurrences begins to establish itself in his mind, but it is always made meaningful by rich applications and many experiences of a revealing nature. For instance, he is helped to find readings which grip his interest and attention, and which dramatize great personalities and great events, and make them real. Before very long he may find himself working with a group of his fellow students to assemble, collate, and arrange for display a set of pictures bearing upon an important historical period. He himself, let us say, has strong literary inclinations, and he is encouraged to concentrate within reason upon the poetic masterpieces of the past, as revelations of how the men of long ago felt about the problems of their lives. Later on, when occasion serves, the whole class visits a historic site not too far away. There is careful preparation for the trip. Maps are made, notes are taken. And when the group returns there is much to discuss and collate. As the course draws to a close, the class undertakes to prepare and produce a historical pageant which calls for much hard and careful work. A textbook forms part of the material—used chiefly to keep the sequence straight, to round out the various topics, and to serve as a reference source—and for these purposes it is extensively utilized. Such, very briefly and with many omissions, is what happens, described in terms of the experience of one of the members of the class.

Notice that the whole business of learning history is organized in such a way as to emphasize and call for understanding, insight, initiative, and cooperation, and to develop appreciations and encourage creative tendencies. It is very certain that the course is an inspiring, stimulating, growth-producing personal experience. Our pupil learns a good deal about how to work effectively, how to cooperate with others, how to value and display initiative, and he gains deeper and broader appreciations and insights. All these are factors in his personal development; yet in a real sense they are subject-matter factors too, for they all come about in and through and because of the business of learning history. If one insists on asking whether history itself is well learned, the answer is in the affirmative. The *memoriter* results of the course have been found triumphantly to resist the test of time; and the pupils who have taken it have been shown to possess a markedly superior ability to see the relationship of history to what are ordinarily considered nonhistorical problems. Here is a clear case of the pupil being treated as a person who learns, and of the indivisibility of personal development and authentic subject-matter achievement.

A contrary instance is furnished by a history teacher in a certain high school who made a great feature of a remarkable system of penalties for mistakes during recitations. When a mistake occurred, she had a routine for assigning what she considered an appropriately long passage to be copied from the textbook after school. She was very lavish with these penalties and thought them a very valuable instrumentality for producing learning. Pupils were in a constant state of latent rebellion. Parents protested. But the teacher was wedded to her idea. She was contemptuous of all suggestions that it turned pupils against her, her subject, and schoolwork in general, that it was emotionally injurious, that it was antidemocratic. She insisted that it forced them to work hard at history which was the only important thing. Since she was on tenure and had the firm support of her superiors, nothing could be done.

This was bad teaching. One might say that it was bad because it developed various undesirable traits in the pupils, such as a tendency to cheat whenever they could, a delight in fooling the teacher, and numerous emotions of a decidedly unchristian kind. This was perfectly true, and also important. Yet common sense suggests that it was not quite enough. What about the history? The teacher was very proud of her results, and to be sure the pupils did seem to make a good showing on objective tests. But an ingenious committee of parents, acting on the suggestion of a malevolent professional educator among them, was able to show that these results were very transient *i.e.*, that the pupils forgot very fast, and that they developed such a negative slant towards history that they never willingly studied or read it again. That is what happens to subject matter when pupils are treated not as persons who learn but as receptacles into which material is to be crammed.

Thus the case seems clear. Teaching establishes its success in and through the production of authentic subject-matter results, which results are indistinguishably associated with desirable personal qualities. To learn something well and successfully is itself an inspiring and enlarging experience. And the material becomes nourishment for the mind and spirit. But when teaching does not bring about authentic results, when the best results it can show are spurious, even though they may be quite impressive when arrayed in a statistical tabulation, nothing can save it from failure. There is no nourishment, inspiration, or enlargement in routine and mechanical learning, and moreover it is a bad way to teach subject matter.

Thus the criticism which is being made today against a paramount emphasis on subject matter does not lie against subject matter as such, or subject matter effectively learned, but against the mechanical, routine, meaningless learning and teaching of it for the sake of spurious and superficial outcomes. And it is perfectly justified.

**3. Does our criterion indicate any particular plan or procedure or methodology by adopting which teaching may succeed?** No, it does not. In particular it does not indicate the kind of procedure of which people are likely to think first when they are told that the primary business of teaching is to get results. This is to determine precisely and carefully in advance just what results are wanted, to lay them out in some kind of orderly topical sequence, to teach them under the greatest possible pressure, to give long assignments, to pile on written work, to administer frequent and drastic tests, and to be very sparing of high marks. Practice of this kind seems very direct and sensible. Many teachers cling to it because they have never seen anything else, and cannot imagine a good job done in any other way. But as will be amply demonstrated later on, it leads to disappointment more often than not. Its tendency is to produce not authentic but spurious results, and even these are frequently very meager.

The work of a certain English headmistress shows how very differently teaching can be managed and still succeed in terms of our criterion. She decided to take personal charge of the music in her school. The school was situated in a district not quite in the slum category, but well down towards the poverty line. The children came from underprivileged homes, enjoyed very few opportunities for culture or intellectual or aesthetic stimulation, and lived in a meager and forbidding environment. The headmistress, who well understood the people with whom she had to deal, did not begin in the conventional way by laying out a sequential course of study in music. She had a very definite plan, but it was not that kind of a plan. She began by uncovering whatever interest the children had in music, and wherever she found some flax smoldering, no matter how dimly, she proceeded to fan it to a flame. For instance, she warmly encouraged creative endeavor whenever the least sign of it appeared. True, most of the early efforts would excite the pitying scorn of musical theorists, but she was dealing with children and learning, not with preconceived ideas. She encouraged the children to sing whatever they wished to sing and then helped them to discover other things that they might like still more to sing. A few of them could play a little, and these talents too were put into circulation instead of being buried in the ground. By the end of a couple of years these children were discovering music, and finding happiness and satisfaction in so doing. As to artistic standards, they were enjoying the best music of the ages, singing and playing the easier works of Bach, Haydn, and Mozart, and their efforts in the way of composition, some of it done individually, some in groups, were a credit to her and to them. In spite of all the limitations of her situation, personal and physical, she had a program and activity in music which would be a pride to the best-equipped and most favored elementary school in the United States. Results? Beyond all question. And achieved without one trace of conventional systematization.[3]

Clearly then we must not take our stated criterion as a starting point and jump to hasty conclusions about the right kind of procedure. The obvious thing to do is often the wrong thing. The reason is that good learning is a subtle and intricate affair, and often does not go as one would ordinarily expect. This is the reason why a direct, head-on drive for results, with all other considerations ignored, very often fails to get them, while a much more roundabout approach, seeming to lack systematization, apparently wasting time, taking account of all sorts of personal values, may succeed quite amazingly well. At the same time one must not infer that systematic teaching is always bad any more than that it is always good, or that developmental teaching of the kind done by the headmistress is under all circumstances and for all kinds of learners the most desirable. The truth is that the success of teaching cannot be defined in terms of procedure or methodology at all. The question is not what kind of method to use, fashionable or unfashionable, up-to-date or out-of-date, progressive or conventional, but rather what actual influences are being brought to bear upon the learner. For effective teaching is not a matter of choosing a certain method but of applying psychological principles which indicate how learning must proceed if it is to lead to fruitful and authentic results.

**4. Is our criterion fair to the teacher?** The criterion of authentic results, properly understood, is exceedingly exacting. It is one thing to get children to make a decent showing in daily recitation or in class-room tests, or even in examinations set by outside authorities like the College Entrance Board, or the New York State Regents, although even this is not as simple as falling off a log. But to get them to grasp what they learn so intimately, so personally, so adequately that they will remember it long and be able to use it in the concerns of living is a very different matter indeed. Yet this is precisely what teaching must do if it is to be called successful. This is precisely what our criterion means. Is it not, then, grossly unfair to the individual teacher? Is he not prevented from achieving results in this inclusive, ample, deep-going sense by all sorts of conditions and limitations over which he has no control?

What if his classes are enormously large, running perhaps to 50, 60, 70 or more pupils per period? What if he has to deal with hundreds of pupils each school day? What if he has to use a textbook that is ill-written and ill-planned? What if no facilities in the way of books and materials of various kinds are available? What if he is under the kind of supervision which makes him go along from topic to topic at a set tempo whether or not the pupils are hanging on or dropping off one by one by the wayside? No one familiar with the practical problems of schoolkeeping will deny that all these conditions exist, or that they are very limiting. And very often the individual teacher cannot do a great deal to change them.

What, then, can be said about it all? Two things, here and now. Firstly this. Failure is failure, whatever the reason, and whoever may be responsible. When a bridge falls down, it means that something was wrong with the construction, although if the engineer was supplied with defective and insufficient materials he may not be personally to blame. When a pupil does not learn as he could and should, it means that there is something the matter with the teaching, although the person in charge of the class may not be directly to blame for that something. It is sound and healthy to recognize this, for if all concerned were more urgently aware that it is their job to get authentic results, just as it is the job of an airplane factory to turn out good sound airplanes, they would be much less likely to sink back into complacency and tamely to tolerate conditions which make good results very difficult.

The second thing to say is this. A teacher who really knows his business, and who is willing to pay the price in devotion and toil and fatigue and aptitude to go on learning what is required to transact it properly—and the price is not a light one—can do a very great deal in spite of highly adverse conditions. Every teacher who really understands his job, and who has a vision of how much might be accomplished, will from time to time build dream castles of ideal schoolrooms and ideal schools. But he will not make these dreams an excuse for doing nothing in the meantime. The principles of teaching to be expounded in this book undoubtedly do indicate an ideal situation for their complete application. They undoubtedly imply a very great deal more than a log and a student and Mark Hopkins. But they are very far indeed from being without relevance to poverty-stricken rural schools, or to cramped city classrooms crowded with underprivileged children. And it will be shown that teachers in just such situations have achieved admirable things by their use. It is indeed very well to know what perfection is and to make it the goal of our hopes and endeavours. But it is very ill to resign ourselves to doing nothing until perfection is handed to us on a platter.

## THE SITUATION AND ITS CHALLENGE

If the criterion of results is courageously applied it becomes immediately apparent that an astonishing amount of the teaching that goes on in our schools is anything but successful. For contemplated results are not forthcoming, and this is true on a very large scale. This is the actual situation we face, and it constitutes an inescapable challenge to all conscientious teachers and to educational workers of every kind. Such a statement may seem extremely formidable, and so indeed it is. But it is borne out by a huge mass of thoroughly well-attested data, a few typical samples of which are here presented.

To begin with an early study, in 1873 the board of education of
Quincy, Mass., under the influence of Charles Francis Adams and
Colonel Parker, decided to investigate the results being obtained in the
town schools.   It had been the custom to examine the children at the
end of each year to determine promotions.   But the examinations
always scrupulously followed the textbooks they had studied, right
down to the very words.   Now it was to be different.   The children
were to be asked questions and set problems which would show
whether they had really mastered the subjects, rather than merely
memorized the textbooks.   The findings were deplorable.   Children
could read aloud passages they had practiced and almost memorized
but were helpless with unfamiliar ones.   They could do sums set in the
exact words of the textbook, but the easiest novelty defeated them.
They could spell lists of words from their primers, but their spelling in
their letters was very bad.   They put in much time at grammar, but
the effects were negligible in their written English.   Everything, in the
words of the investigating committee, was smatter, veneering, and
cram.   It is interesting to observe that the reorganization carried
through at Quincy was one of the first moves in the direction of what
is now called developmental teaching.[4]

Similar findings have been appearing ever since in connection with
almost every subject taught in the schools.   Take English composition,
for example.   In the schools of Gary, Ind., which are better than the
average, 93 per cent of seniors could be matched in writing ability by
an equal number of freshmen in the same school.   That is, only 7 per-
cent of all seniors could write better English than any freshman, in
spite of three additional years' study of the subject.   A survey made
by the University of Illinois goes even further, for it shows that many
seniors in the high schools of the state are no better in English composition than many children in the elementary schools.   Once again, it
has been found that 90 per cent of the words used by high-school
seniors in their compositions come from the thousand commonest words
in the language, that there is very little gain from the seventh to the
twelfth grade, and that college students do not seem to have a very
much better working vocabulary.   Of course the range of a person's
vocabulary is a limited indication but it is not an unimportant one; and
surely the teaching of English, if successful, ought to do something to
it between the seventh grade and senior year in college.[5]

Or again, take mathematics.   Workers in the Iowa State Department of Public Instruction have had much experience in giving tests to
large numbers of pupils, and what they have to say carries great weight.
A few years ago they put out a trial test in algebra.   It consisted of 62

items, most of them very simple and amounting indeed to what might be considered "minimum essentials." That is, a person unable to do most of the items simply had no grasp of algebra. The gross facts are shown in the table below. Notice that more than half of the thousands of pupils who took the test were unable to do as many as a quarter of the items. A study of the performance on individual ques-

ACHIEVEMENT ON AN ALGEBRA TEST BY 9,034 PUPILS

| Percentage Done Correctly Less Than | Percentage of All the Pupils |
| --- | --- |
| 10 | 12 |
| 20 | 37 |
| 25 | 52 |
| 30 | 72 |
| 40 | 93 |
| 70 | 99 |

tions adds to the depressing effect. One of the questions was: "A dealer sold a suit for $42, making a profit of 20 per cent. How many dollars did he make?" Five per cent of the pupils succeeded in getting it right. Another item which only 5 per cent managed was: "Solve the equation $C = ax - n$ for the ratio $1/x$." In another item a simple temperature graph was shown, and the question was: "At what hour of the day was the temperature shown in Fig. 2 approximately 8° below zero?" Seventy-three per cent failed to answer correctly. Yet again, the following rectangle was shown. Sixty-seven per cent succeeded when asked to write a formula for its perimeter, and 70 per cent could write the formula for its area. The figures look somewhat encourag-

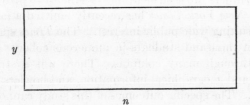

ing, but it is pointed out that this is really an elementary-school problem and that those who failed in it must have lacked the slightest grasp of the symbolism of algebra. To make the case even more complete, it should be remarked that the nine thousand or so pupils who made this deplorable showing came from the best high schools of the state, and that Iowa has a good educational standing among American states. It would be hard to find a more complete demonstration of the failure of instruction, or a more conclusive indictment of the organization of learning in the teaching of algebra.

The findings just cited are supported by many other investigations of the effectiveness with which mathematics is taught. One study reported that only 14 per cent of college freshmen who had taken plane geometry for entrance came up to the standard norm on a high-school test, that they displayed a striking lack of knowledge of definitions, theorems, and formulas, and a still more striking weakness in drawing conclusions from data. Also many college students are arithmetical cripples, almost 30 per cent of them having been found unable to do sums well within the capacity of the average eighth grader, and 15 per cent being unable to reason as well in arithmetical terms.[6]

Nor does science show up much better. A recognized standard test in chemistry was given to 731 high-school students who had taken one course in the subject, to 189 college students who had taken a year of chemistry in high school and a year of it in college, and to 57 college students who had taken a year of chemistry in college only. Differences between the three groups were negligible. Those having two years of chemistry showed up no better than those who had taken only one either in high school or college, and college chemistry produced no better results than high-school chemistry. Turning to physics, a test in this subject, dealing with mechanics and heat, was made up by a group of teachers. It contained what they believed their pupils ought to know after having studied the topics in their own classes. Very startling weaknesses were revealed. Knowledge of facts was shaky, and ability to deal with problems requiring thought and the application of knowledge was even worse.[7]

One other subject must be mentioned—American history—concerning which the *New York Times* has recently emitted a fanfare of publicity, with resulting wide public interest. The *Times* sponsored a test given to seven thousand students in numerous colleges and deplored the findings through many columns. There was a striking lack of chronological and geographical information, and howlers were remarkably frequent. The specific outcomes of this study cannot be accepted without reservation. The test was far from technically perfect. It overemphasized detail and centered unduly on the middle period of our history. The scoring key contained errors. And it may not always have been given under proper conditions. But in view of the facts already cited, which are only samples of the far larger number available, the only surprising thing about it was that so many people were surprised at the results.

A more careful and enlightening, though much less publicized investigation, tells the story even more impressively. A test containing simple facts in American history which, in the opinion of experienced teachers, a pupil might be expected to know, was given at successive levels in the schools. Upper-grade pupils who had taken the subject but once could produce 15 per cent of these facts. High-school pupils, after a second year devoted to content largely identical, had mastered 33 per cent of them. College students, after a third exposure, got 49 per cent of the answers right. Less than half learning, after three tours through the same territory![8]

Findings such as those just cited call for the serious and thoughtful attention of every educational worker. They reveal very clearly indeed a situation of profound and far-reaching significance.

1. In the first place, they are typical. They are in no sense selected for the sake of making a case. A multitude of similar findings, all of them corroborative, could very readily be cited. Even in the reports which have been mentioned here, many thousands of children from schools in widely separated parts of the country are involved. The situation they reveal is not of recent origin, since the investigations bearing on it go back to the very beginnings of educational research. So it is not true that teaching once used to get good and satisfactory results, but does so no longer. In all probability, too, the situation obtains in European as well as in American schools, although the available data are far more scanty. Nor is it limited to any subject, or to any level. It has been found on a very wide scale in every subject that has been investigated, and at every level from the lower grades to senior year in college.

2. The situation cannot possibly be dismissed as unimportant or illusory. One might possibly argue that human personality is more important than the material of the curriculum. This is no doubt quite true, but it does not meet the issue. Essential failure to deal with the problems and tasks that are presented to one, and with which one presumably tries to deal, cannot be a helpful influence in the mental and emotional and social growth of a human being. For instance, for the 9,034 young people reported on from the state of Iowa, algebra was in the main an experience of frustration rather than fulfillment. That is the clear and inescapable meaning of the test data. No doubt there are many influences in the school and the classroom which do make for the development of desirable personality. But those very learnings on which the school places its main emphasis, and which are supposed among other things to favor this very development, evidently do not. That is the essential point.

Again it might be argued that the study of the curricular subjects will train a pupil's mind, even though he does not master them very well. But this will not hold water, entirely apart from all the general arguments for and against the theory of mental training or formal discipline. Quite conceivably Latin might help one with English, algebra and geometry might teach one to think, science might help one to develop a sound outlook upon life. But if these things are to happen, surely the Latin, the algebra, the geometry, the science must be reasonably well learned. How can transfer take place if there is nothing to carry over? What value of any kind can there be in simply failing to grasp a subject? If the reader will resurvey the data just presented and ask himself how, on any conceivable argument, the kind and quality of work they reveal could be expected to train the mind, he will find only one possible answer.

Again it may be argued that the great majority of the pupils concerned undoubtedly passed their courses, and that perhaps 25 per cent passed them quite well—that is, with marks of A or B. Teachers' marks certainly do not reveal any such situation as that indicated, and therefore one might say it must be illusory. But it must be remembered that a teacher is in a position where he is bound to give passing marks to the great majority of his pupils, and good marks to quite a few, on pain of losing his job. A mark is based very largely on relative standing. It shows how much better or how much worse a pupil does in comparison with other pupils, not how well he does absolutely. And the whole force and point of such investigations as those cited is that they assume absolute, not relative standards. The question they ask is how well the pupil does in terms of mastery of the material itself. So it is the marks, and not the research data, which present the deceiving and illusory picture.

3. It might be argued that the school's expectations are fantastic and extravagant, so that the pupils cannot fulfill them, or learn what they are supposed to learn. This, however, cannot be maintained. Multitudes of these young people do very well in social situations, or athletic situations, or vocational situations, and the problems there are far from negligible. The learning that goes on even in a mediocre high-school orchestra is of an altogether different order from that in the average algebra class, and yet musical learning is not easy. Millions of these youngsters, too, have recently demonstrated that they can handle exceedingly tough problems in their training for war, which was at least as formidable a challenge as any that a school is likely to set up in its curriculum. One has only to look at such obvious facts as these to be reasonably sure, without any elaborate psychological investigation, that there is nothing radically wrong with the learning capacity of the great majority of young Americans and that the school curriculum is not intrinsically beyond their powers. Surely then, the

only possible conclusion is that there must be something radically wrong with the teaching.

4. It might be argued that the curriculum is wrongly organized, that it emphasizes the wrong things, that it contains the wrong kind of material, and so defeats the learner's mind.   Certainly when one sees a bright and lively sixteen-year-old girl on her way to school, carrying two rather uninviting-looking textbooks, one on geometry and the other on Latin, it is permissible to wonder why.   There may be a good answer, but at any rate the question is fair enough.   The structure and content of the curriculum, apart from its intrinsic difficulty, undoubtedly enters into the problem, but to discuss it is beyond the scope of this book.   However there is a relevant consideration here, just the same.   The kind of data which we have on hand, samples of which have been presented, indicate the sabotage of any curriculum. For bad learning extends far beyond the range of the old-line academic subjects which are presumably the villains of the piece.   What is the use of improving the curriculum if it is not going to be learned?   So although the situation may and probably does suggest that there is a problem centering in the curriculum, it indicates even more unmistakably that there is just as vital a problem centering in teaching.   For the best possible curriculum is reduced to an absurdity if the teaching is so bad that its contemplated results are, in fact, not forthcoming.

5. So to sum up, we face a situation which is an extremely urgent challenge for the improvement and reform of teaching.   It should be noticed that the case for improvement as here stated, does not rest on philosophical or theoretical grounds.   A good philosophic argument for reform can undoubtedly be made, and it is worth making because it serves as a comprehensive guide to endeavour.   But like the problem of the curriculum, the philosophy of education is beyond the scope of this book.   The case as here presented rests simply on ascertained and undeniable facts.   In a nutshell it is that teaching must obtain authentic results if it is to be considered successful, and that in a very great many instances such results are not forthcoming.

Once more, if the case for the improvement and reform of teaching as here presented does not rest on philosophic arguments, still less does it rest on partisan polemics.   Whenever the issue is raised, progressive education is almost sure to be trotted out either as bogey or angel; either as the ruination of our educational standards or else as their only salvation.   As a matter of fact, it is neither.   Many conservative persons are so distressed over progressivist proposals, which of course are numerous, ill-defined, and by no means always wise, that they dismiss the whole problem in a fit of impatience.   To the dispassionate student, however, it is immediately clear that the progressive attack upon established and conventional practice is directed not against established success but against widely demonstrated failure. The enormous majority of the young people whose attainments stand revealed in the investigations cited, and in many others that could be added, are the products of conventional education and never so much as saw a progressive school. So, although progressive education— which, to repeat, is a vague and ill-defined conception including a great deal of territory—may not have all the answers, this is very far from meaning that there is no problem. How can we get pupils to learn? How can we get them to achieve authentic results? How can we teach them in such a way that we can, in good conscience, consider our work a success? Those are the questions that stare us in the face, the situation being what it is. The purpose of this book is to indicate the answer.[9]

### Notes and References

*General References*

A discussion of the nature of teaching, considered as a broad and inclusive process, and of its relationship to psychology, will be found in James L. Mursell, *The Psychology of Secondary School Teaching*, rev. ed., Chap. 1, "How Psychology Can Help Us to Improve Teaching," W. W. Norton & Company, Inc., New York, 1939. An interesting discussion of the same topic, bearing particularly upon the teaching of typewriting but rich in general significance, is presented by William F. Book, "The Role of the Teacher in the Most Expeditious and Economical Learning," *Journal of Educational Psychology*, Vol. 1 (1910), pp. 183–199. A more general treatment of the functions and relationships of the teacher, which can readily be brought into contact with the treatment in the present chapter, will be found in Arthur D. Hollinshead, *Guidance in Democratic Living*, Chap. 8, "The Function of the Teacher," and Chap. 7, "The Relation of the Teacher to Her Group," D. Appleton-Century Company, Inc., New York, 1941. The issue of "dominance" by the teacher is here considered. The whole issue of subject matter, activity, and growth is illuminatingly discussed by Inga Olla Helseth, *Living in the Classroom*, pp. 297–309, Edwards Bros., Inc., Ann Arbor, Mich., 1939.

*References in the Text*

1. Sources of material cited on the retention of subject matter are Edward B. Greene, "The Retention of Information in College Courses," *Journal of Educational Research*, Vol. 24 (1931), pp. 261–272; and D. H. Eikenberry, "Permanence of High School Learning," *Journal of Educational Psychology*, Vol. 14 (1923), pp. 463–481.

2. Sources of material cited on the flexibility and usability of what has been learned are John P. Everett, *Fundamental Skills of Algebra*, Teachers College, Columbia University, Bureau of Publications, New York, 1928; and P. R. Stevenson, "Difficulties in Problem Solving," *Journal of Educational Research*, Vol. 11 (1925), pp. 25–103.

3. A full and very interesting account of the music program in the English school, well worth reading *in toto*, is presented by A Headmistress, "Experiment in Educating the Mind through the Body," *Hibbert Journal*, Vol. 31 (1933), pp. 217–233.

4. The reorganization at Quincy took place many years ago, but it foreshadowed many modern trends and the story is well worth reading. See Charles Francis Adams, *The New Departure in the Common Schools of Quincy*, Estes and Lauriat, Boston, 1881; also Lelia E. Patridge, *Quincy Methods*, Kellog Company, New York, 1885, which is the best and fullest account. For a brief statement refer to Edward H. Reisner, *The Evolution of the Common School*, The Macmillan Company, New York, 1930, see "Quincy" in alphabetical index.

5. Sources of the statements regarding English are S. A. Courtis, *The Gary Public Schools: Measurement of Classroom Products*, pp. 216–262, General Education Board, New York, 1919; *Report of the High School Visitor, University of Illinois*, 1919–1920, University of Illinois, Urbana, Ill., 1920; F. P. O'Brien, "The Vocabulary of High School Pupils in Written Composition," *Journal of Educational Research*, Vol. 11 (1925), pp. 344–350. For interesting comment on these studies see Edward W. Dolch, "The Measurement of High-school English," *Journal of Educational Research*, Vol. 4, (1921), pp. 279–286.

6. Sources of statements on mathematics are E. F. Lindquist, "The Gap between Promise and Fulfillment in Ninth-Grade Algebra," *School Review*, Vol. 42 (1934), pp. 762–771, which deals with the Iowa situation; William H. Lueck, "How Much Arithmetic and Algebra Do Students in First Year College Physics Really Know?" *School Science and Mathematics*, Vol. 32 (1932), pp. 998–1005; H. J. Arnold, "Arithmetical Abilities and Disabilities of College Students," *Elementary School Journal*, Vol. 31 (1930), pp. 259–270.

7. Sources of the statements on science are S. R. Powers, "A Comparison of the Achievements of High School and University Students in Certain Tasks in Chemistry," *Journal of Educational Research*, Vol. 6 (1922), pp. 332–343; Paul S. Miller, "A Qualitative Analysis of the Efficiency of Instruction in High-School Physics," *Journal of Educational Research*, Vol. 19 (1929), pp. 119–127.

8. For the *New York Times* American history exposé see files of the paper beginning April 4, 1943. Also see Erling Hunt, "The New York Times on American History," *Social Education*, Vol. 7 (1943), pp. 195–200, which is a highly competent and critical review of the controversy. The second study mentioned is J. C. Bell and D. F. McColum, "A Study of the Attainments of Pupils in United States History," *Journal of Educational Psychology*, Vol. 8 (1917), pp. 257–274.

9. For a much more comprehensive survey covering the studies referred to in the text and also a great many more similar of general tenor, see James L. Mursell, "The Defeat of the Schools," *Atlantic Monthly*, Vol. 163 (1929), pp. 353–361.

### Items for Discussion and Study

1. Can you suggest any basic criterion for successful teaching other than the one offered? What are some possible objections to the criterion of results?

2. Assemble from your own experience instances of meaningful learning and authentic results comparable to those presented. On the basis of your experience, do you agree that such learnings tend to be long and well retained?

3. Consider carefully the statement on pp. 4–5 that the teacher should think chiefly of "happy living" rather than of the child's "expression of facts and mastery of specific techniques." Which would you emphasize? Why? Is such a choice necessary? Can both be combined? How?

4. What idea about subject matter would be shared by an old-fashioned believer in formal discipline and a modern progressive educator? Would they be right or wrong?

5. Can you supplement from your own experience the instance given of learning being frustrated by bad personality relationships and influences?

6. Does the answer given to Question 3 as set up in the chapter on pp. 8–10 mean that any teaching procedure is as good as any other?

7. In the light of our analysis of what makes results authentic, why is the conventional plan for raising standards as described on pp. 8–9 evidently fallacious? Why is the plan of the English headmistress preferable?

8. Consider, list, and discuss some of the practical difficulties encountered by teachers in making learning meaningful and in getting authentic results. What attitude to such difficulties should a teacher take? Have you ever seen a teacher who managed largely to overcome such obstacles? Particularize.

9. Can you, from your own experience, find additional examples of bad learning in school similar to those presented in the chapter? How do you account for the difference between such learnings and the out-of-school achievements of the same persons?

10. Review the interpretation of the data revealing poor results as it is presented in this chapter. To what extent do you agree? Can you find any other important implications?

# SUCCESSFUL TEACHING: ITS PROBLEM

## TEACHING AS ORGANIZATION

*Teaching may best be defined as the organization of learning.* It follows, therefore, that the problem of successful teaching is to organize learning for authentic results. In the present chapter it will be shown how this problem has arisen in the practice of our American schools, how a long series of attempts have been made to solve it, and what kind of solution now seems to be emerging. In the following chapter it will be shown that there is a central working conception which must be embodied and realized in any promising solution. But first it is necessary to explain and illustrate the conception of teaching as essentially a business of organizing, since it is both somewhat novel and also of great importance in all our later discussions.

When a golf instructor takes on a pupil, he provides him with certain facilities usually consisting of a suitable room with proper lighting, a mat, a net, a few clubs, and some golf balls. He shows him how to stand, how to hold his club, how to swing. He coaches him for a stipulated time, advising him, putting him through the motions, criticizing his efforts, serving as a model. He makes an appointment with him for the next lesson. He suggests some independent practice in the meantime. What the instructor does is to organize his pupil's learning better than he could do it on his own account.

When a person enrolls in a correspondence-school course, he receives through the mail a pamphlet of instructions, a textbook, and a syllabus of assignments. He is expected to read the instructions and follow them out, and to take up the assignments one by one. As each is finished he mails it in, and soon receives it back with corrections and suggestions. From time to time there is a comprehensive review exercise of some kind, or a test, also to be mailed and returned, and also there may be one or two pep letters. The course usually ends with some sort of comprehensive culminating round up. Clearly what the school is paid to do is to organize the student's learning, presumably in a skillful and effective fashion.

When a distinguished university scholar delivers a series of lectures day by day to a class of students in a summer session, he is once more

# CHAPTER 2

## SUCCESSFUL TEACHING: ITS PROBLEM

### TEACHING AS ORGANIZATION

*Teaching may best be defined as the organization of learning.* It [ ]
lows, therefore, that the problem of successful teaching is to orga[ ]
learning for authentic results. In the present chapter it will be sh[ ]
how this problem has arisen in the practice of our American scho[ ]
how a long series of attempts have been made to solve it, and what k[ ]
of solution now seems to be emerging. In the following chapter it [ ]
be shown that there is a central working conception which must [ ]
embodied and realized in any promising solution. But first it is nec[ ]
sary to explain and illustrate the conception of teaching as essentia[ ]
a business of organizing, since it is both somewhat novel and also [ ]
great importance in all our later discussions.

When a golf instructor takes on a pupil, he provides him with ce[ ]
tain facilities usually consisting of a suitable room with proper lightin[ ]
a mat, a net, a few clubs, and some golf balls. He shows him how t[ ]
stand, how to hold his club, how to swing. He coaches him for [ ]
stipulated time, advising him, putting him through the motions, criti[ ]
cizing his efforts, serving as a model. He makes an appointment with
him for the next lesson. He suggests some independent practice in the
meantime. What the instructor does is to organize his pupil's learning
better than he could do it on his own account.

When a person enrolls in a correspondence-school course, he
receives through the mail a pamphlet of instructions, a textbook, and a
syllabus of assignments. He is expected to read the instructions and
follow them out, and to take up the assignments one by one. As each
is finished he mails it in, and soon receives it back with corrections and
suggestions. From time to time there is a comprehensive review
exercise of some kind, or a test, also to be mailed and returned, and
also there may be one or two pep letters. The course usually ends
with some sort of comprehensive culminating round up. Clearly what
the school is paid to do is to organize the student's learning, presumably
in a skillful and effective fashion.

When a distinguished university scholar delivers a series of lectures
day by day to a class of students in a summer session, he is once more

but what they all boiled down to, although it was not put in those words, was that she faced a problem of organization. The ordinary plan, which contemplates a fairly homogeneous and docile group of about thirty, clearly would not work. It was suggested that she might try decentralization, introducing a system of committees, or revolving class chairmanships, or elected monitorships, and giving the pupils a considerable and genuine sense of responsibility for what went on. Others, it was pointed out, had succeeded well by such policies in similar situations. Whether or not this was the right line of solution for this particular teacher, the point here is that her problem was to devise a pattern of organized learning, suitable for the individuals and the numbers involved, and suited also to her own personality.

These illustrations should make clear what is meant when teaching is defined as the organization of learning. This is a very precise characterization of the working realities of the process. It is distinctly preferable to the familiar definitions of teaching either as the *direction* or as the *guidance* of learning. It saves us from arguments about whether the teacher ought to guide or to direct—arguments that are somewhat futile since the truth is that he ought to do both. Direction and guidance by the teacher certainly occur in good teaching, but unless the words are stretched far beyond their usual meanings they do not cover nearly all that happens, and above all they do not go to the root of the practical problem.

One may think of teaching as the establishment of a situation in which it is hoped and believed that effective learning will take place. That situation is complicated and made up of many constituents. First of all there must be a learner, or more usually a group of learners, brought together in some fashion and classified in some way, as for instance by age, or brightness, or educational status. Then there must be facilities, including a stated time for meeting, stated periods, a convenient place, books and other printed materials on hand, maps, charts, instruments, tools, blackboards, stereopticons, motion-picture projectors, pianos, phonographs, and so on. Then there must be an orderly and understood procedure, which may be routine and regular or highly varied in character, for presenting, discussing, collating, and checking up on ideas and experiences. Then there must be some way of grading, or marking, or evaluating work done, so that all concerned, including the learners, will know how it is coming along. Within this extensive context the teacher will sometimes tell the pupils what to do, and sometimes help them to work out their own plans. So direction and guidance are among the constituent factors of the business, but very far from the only ones. This, in brief, is a picture of the situation to which the word "teaching" refers. All its various elements must be brought into relationship and built into an intelligible whole—that is, organized.

Or again, one may think of teaching as setting up a range of activities in the lives of a group of human beings, with the teacher as the focal point of the complex. These activities, again, are very varied and complicated. Some of them go on in the classroom, others in the study hall, others perhaps in small groups, others individually at home. They consist of asking and answering questions, listening to and offering explanations, working out problems, practicing skills, studying assignments, finding new things to read and reporting on them, engaging in discussions, writing papers, appreciating, enjoying, thinking, creating, and so on at great length. The teacher is closely in touch with some of these activities, perhaps offering suggestions only, perhaps giving help where help is needed, perhaps laying down definite instructions, and here again the elements of direction and guidance appear. But many of them, and indeed more than the teacher is apt to suppose, will arise out of the learner's own choice and volition, and be shaped up in competition with other activities in which he might engage. Any teacher will find it very interesting and suggestive to think of his work as setting up wave after wave of complicated, varied, far-reaching activity in the lives of his pupils. And teaching consists in the organization of these activities for the sake of learning.

## THREE APPLICATIONS: HOME STUDY, CLASS SIZE, AND TEACHER LEADERSHIP

By way of showing still further how well and realistically the conception of organization characterizes the working realities of teaching, it may be brought to bear on three very practical and pressing educational problems: those of home study, class size, and the role and leadership of the teacher.

**1. Home Study.** The question as to whether students should do their studying at home or at school is being actively debated today, and is a practical issue in many school systems. The arguments in the case have been well summarized as follows:

In favor of home study the following points have been made: (1) Parents want it. But to this it is replied that they want it chiefly for the sake of keeping children busy and out of the way. (2) There is insufficient time for adequate study during the school day. To this the answer is made that it is true only if the chief business of the school is to check up on the students' work. (3) It stimulates cooperation between home and school. But it is contended, and with much truth, that there are many better ways of promoting such cooperation.    (4) It favors independent work.   To this the answer is made that it might conceivably do so, but that whether it really does is extremely questionable.

The arguments against home study are (1) That it is not expertly guided, as study might be at school, (2) that it often in fact requires a pupil to study under disturbing conditions, (3) that it makes unhygienic demands upon his leisure time, (4) that it has a tendency to disturb home life, and (5) that it encourages the misuse of school time for purposes of merely checking up rather than teaching.[1]

It is clear that these arguments indicate a strong bias against study at home and in favor of study at school.   But they do not go to the root of the problem, which turns upon organization.   The question always is how to organize a pattern of varied activities in such a way that they will be most fruitful in bringing about good learning.   Evidently this includes the question as to where and when certain of these activities may best be carried on.   If a pupil is to read a stated passage in a stated book which is in his possession, then the best plan may be for him to do his reading where the book is normally kept and most commonly used because then he will not have to carry it to and fro and there will be less chance of his forgetting it.   This may well be at school.   If he is to hunt up some references for the sake of making a report to the class or writing a paper, he will presumably have to work in the school library or the city library, unless he has a home unusually well stocked with books.   If he is a member of a subcommittee of the class working together on some problem or topic for report, this in all probability indicates a school activity, unless the group can get together at somebody's home.   If class time has been used for the cooperative exploration, discussion, and elucidation of a problem, then it may be very profitable for the pupil to write out his individual impressions of what has been said while it is still fresh in his mind, and in some situation where he has leisure for careful reflection.   Whether this will be at home, at school, or elsewhere depends on circumstances.   If he is to share for a week in planning the family diet, the cooperation of his parents having been secured, and then to tell the class about the experience, the question as to where this must be done answers itself.

Thus the issue between home study and school study cannot be decided in a general way.   It all depends on how the entire pattern of activities in and through which learning is to take place has been planned.   The only answer is to make the most practical and convenient arrangements for this or that contemplated activity, taking into consideration time, place, and general conditions.   So the whole problem is simply one aspect of the organization of learning which is the essential business of teaching, and it must be considered and treated as such if it is to be handled intelligently.

**2. Class Size.**  The problem of class size, like that of home study, cannot be decided in the abstract.  Some things can be done with a small group which it would be folly to attempt with a large one.  Some of the measures which work out very well with a large group—such, for instance, as elected chairmanships or monitorships or subcommittee systems—would be not only needless but impeding with a small and intimate class.  When it is said that the ideal class size is about 25, this is a rash and indeed a meaningless statement; for one cannot tell what the ideal size may be unless one knows what is going to be done, and one cannot plan activities intelligently until one knows, amongst other things, about how many people will be involved.  This is true of a party, and it is also true of a class.  A big party will not do just the same things as a small one, but all may have a good time nevertheless.  A large class will not be handled just the same as a small one, but good learning may still go on, for it is quite untrue to say that large classes necessarily defeat teaching.  Nor is it true to say that large classes require more skill, for the first-rate handling of a small informal discussion group calls for great expertness and insight, although it may be less fatiguing than dealing with a mob of a hundred students.  The point is that large and small classes, like large and small parties, require different management.  And essentially both the party and the class presents a problem of organization.

**3. The Role of the Teacher.**  In discussions of the role of the teacher a choice is commonly presented between two alternatives, neither quite convincing.  What usually happens, it is said, is that the teacher behaves pretty much as an autocrat.  He is the source of all authority, the maker of all decisions.  He determines what is to be done, how it is to be done, and when it is to be done, and all that is left for the pupils is to obey.  He formulates all the plans and sees to it that the pupils carry them out.  He is able to impose his wishes and ideas because of his official position and because it is in his power to bring certain sanctions to bear.

This, it is argued, is just the way things ought not to be.  The policy is wrong, even vicious.  It is undemocratic.  It stifles initiative, cuts off all creative impulses, and reduces the learners to a state of sheer passivity.  A teacher might seem justified in imposing his wishes and ideas because he is certainly older and presumably wiser, more experienced, and more knowledgeable than his pupils.  But it is pointed out that however wise he may be he can hardly claim a monopoly of wisdom. The pupils' ideas, plans, wishes, and suggestions may also be excellent, and even though they may not be as good as those that the teacher could think up it may still be desirable to follow them, because they come from the learners themselves and so tend towards a healthy and effective learning situation. For these reasons, so the argument runs, it is wrong for the teacher to play the autocrat. It cannot be denied that there is considerable force in the contention.

But what is the alternative? It is that the teacher should behave simply as a member of the group, with no more rights, privileges, or powers than anybody else. The group, not the teacher, should formulate all plans and make all decisions. This policy, it is said, should be followed right through to the ultimate outcomes of its logic. The group should determine the content of the courses, and indeed of the curriculum, the activities to be undertaken, the learnings to be accomplished, the standards to be attained, and discipline should be entirely in its control. The teacher should never impose his own wishes and as a matter of principle should refrain from making plans in advance of the planning of the group. Clearly this is a very radical position, but it is maintained by responsible persons, and at least a few schools have gone almost all the way toward putting it into practice. Nevertheless it will strike most people as untenable.

Thus we seem to face alternatives both of which are unacceptable, and many a teacher and prospective teacher who earnestly desires to do what is best is likely to be troubled and confused. But the choice as stated is not necessary. The issue has not been properly defined. On the one hand the teacher is not properly an absolute autocrat. On the other hand he is not properly a humble participant. He is, precisely, an organizer. As a good organizer he will not center all authority in his own hands or insist on imposing his own wishes on everybody in every detail, unless some special or unusual occasion arises. On the other hand, he certainly will not function precisely like all other members of the group. He has a very special, responsible, and definite function—to enable the group to get things done. To accomplish this satisfactorily he needs all the wisdom, maturity, judgment, sympathy, knowledge, and skill that he can get, and he will use these assets as well as his official position for just this end. Certainly he opens the way for initiative and encourages the making and carrying out of good plans. But to do this well takes very expert organization, for initiative and good planning do not blossom forth by chance and are not the fruits of chaos. On the other hand, he cannot behave simply as a member of the group on a level with every other member and still perform his function, for this amounts to abdication. If he does, everything will go to pieces, and in the long run nobody will be benefited or satisfied. The stability and viability of the whole situation depend upon him, and he must use constant vigilance and skill and discreet authority to maintain them. This is always and everywhere the task of the organizer, which is precisely the task of the teacher.

## THE ATTEMPT TO IMPROVE TEACHING

### The Conventional Pattern of Teaching

The quest for better teaching procedures has been going on for a long time, and of course it is still proceeding. It has been, and still is, immensely strenuous, persevering, and widespread. In teacher training institutions, experimental and demonstration schools, and regular school systems throughout the country a vast amount of practical experimentation has been and is going forward, and a great many suggestions and plans have been proposed and tried out. It is of importance for the intelligent teacher to understand what is happening, but this is not easy, because the work is geographically very diffused, with different undertakings lacking relationship to one another, so that an impression of sheer chaos may readily be gained.

However considerable clarification may be attained if we think of this whole vast and widespread enterprise as a quest for a better way of organizing learning. Then the outlines of an orderly development become apparent. A conventional pattern of organization established itself in this country many years ago. It became almost universal and is still the one most commonly found. However its weaknesses became apparent to a point where it could no longer satisfy the conscience of the profession, and a search for something better began, following two chief lines. This search has not been coordinated or orderly, yet a long view enables us to see that it has evolved in a definite direction and that certain lessons have been learned. And today the general features of what we may hope to be a definitive solution are appearing.

The conventional plan of teaching is, in outline, as follows: The whole body of material to be learned is divided into blocks about large enough to be treated in either one or two school terms. These blocks are called courses. The courses in turn are subdivided into smaller blocks, considered suitable for treatment in one or at any rate a few class meetings. These smaller blocks are called lessons, or units, or some such name. Before each small block of material is dealt with in class the pupils are warned that it is coming up and are told to study it out of a textbook organized to parallel the sequence of the course. In class the main business is to ascertain whether this assigned study has in fact been done, and if so, how well. The technique employed is known as the recitation, which means the oral quizzing of the group. There may be a few review periods during the course, in which a number of lessons previously covered are brought up for reconsideration. There will almost certainly be several written tests of one kind or another. This is the textbook-assignment-recitation scheme of teaching which, with numerous minor and unessential variations, prevails in a majority of the classrooms of the United States.

So familiar is this mode of organization to many people and so little experience have they had, whether as pupils or teachers, with any feasible alternative, that they accept it as the inevitable and presumably the proper way to teach. To recite on lessons seems to them the ineluctable lot of any pupil in any school; to assign lessons and then to hear them the natural function of any teacher. Yet the plan is not a fiat of Providence, nor a product of logical necessity, but a man-made artifact brought about by a historical situation.

A hundred years ago the prevailing plan of teaching in the American common schools was very different. School was usually conducted in a single room, and in that room one teacher had to deal with an unclassified group of pupils of ages from about six to twenty and upwards, and also greatly varying in educational attainment. Here, as always, the practical problem was how to organize learning. The standard technique was to preserve order in the room, and to call up the pupils one by one to the teacher's desk. Arrived there, the child deposited on it the book he had been studying arranged so that the teacher could see it, turned his back, recited what he had learned, received whatever commendation or reprimand might come, and then returned to his seat for some more work while another pupil took his place. This was known as "backing one's book." It organized learning on a purely individual basis, and usually it was extremely inefficient.

As part of the great educational advance following the Civil War, there was introduced the graded system. The pupils in our schools were classified into groups on the criterion of chronological age. A grade meant a year, with the first grade beginning at the age of six. It is worth remarking that the graded system was once considered an extremely progressive arrangement. It brought about at least the semblance of orderly progress, and it gave the teacher a group of pupils reasonably homogeneous, at any rate in theory. For us the interesting point is that the graded system made the old individual method of teaching inappropriate, for now it became possible to teach the same thing to the entire group at the same time. Courses of study were prepared, textbooks were written, and standards were set with this in mind. The method of teaching was to assign lessons in planned sequence to the entire class or grade, and to do the checking up or reciting with the class as a whole instead of individually as was heretofore necessary. Thus the textbook-assignment-recitation pattern emerged, essentially as a transposition into a social context of the older practice of backing one's book.

Considered as a plan for the organization, the general character of the textbook-assignment-recitation plan is perfectly clear. It presents an orderly schedule of expected results, with a calendar date more or less rigidly set for each one of them. It involves the use of certain techniques to ascertain whether these results are in fact forthcoming. It warns the pupil in advance when the due date for a given job of learning is impending. But it puts the responsibility for carrying the job through, and for deciding on an appropriate method for so doing, entirely up to him. To be sure, some exceptionally good teachers may make suggestions about how to study when they give assignments, but this is known to be somewhat unusual and investigations have shown that it does not seem to help most of the pupils a great deal. And above all, it is not of the essence of the textbook-assignment-recitation scheme. The basic assumption of that scheme is that the learning process can be properly organized if the desired results are clearly formulated and if a systematic checkup is made to see whether they are forthcoming.

To anyone who has ever worked closely with and tried to help individual learners—a salutary experience recommended to every teacher who must deal with pupils largely en masse—this will seem a dubious proposition, to put it mildly. Here is a report of one such experience, turned in by a college senior named M in connection with his practice teaching. M had been assigned to work individually with S, a high school student who was having serious trouble with his history:

I looked up S's record in the guidance office, and he seems to have good average intelligence. I.Q. 102. As I got to know him he seemed bright enough. We had some interesting discussions of various topics, and he was quite keen. Had a craze for airplanes, has studied them thoroughly, knows a surprising lot about them. But when it comes to history, he seems to turn stupid. He brought me an assignment, and we talked it over, and he seemed to have no reasonable plan for handling it. Just meant to read it over and trust in luck. I suggested that he might try underlining the key items. He thought it a good idea. Next time we had a conference he showed me his book. Practically the whole chapter underlined! We discussed this and tried to see what was important and what was less important. He seemed to get the point and tried again, but it wasn't much better. Then we tried outlining. At first all he brought me was a mess of things he had jotted down. No notion of order or sequence. No selection at all. I suggested a regular system of heads and subheads, rather cut-and-dried, and I hesitated about it but thought it might help. But I don't think it helped much. The next two outlines he brought to me looked much better on the page, but when you got into them he wasn't a bit clear on the difference between a main item and a secondary one. Or on how the different topics hung together. Maybe if we had been able to keep on, we might have gotten somewhere. It seems to me that there must be something wrong with the way the work is set up, for S certainly can learn material as difficult as his history assignments.*

This is quite typical. Investigation has shown again and again that pupils are apt to work in the most inept and self-frustrating fashion. They seem unable to read with any clear purpose in mind, to recheck efficiently on what they have read once, to revise and polish and improve a piece of written English, to utilize and apply mathematical and scientific and artistic techniques, to collate and organize facts and draw conclusions from them, to practice physical skills economically and intelligently. Yet these are among the most essential processes by which authentic results are attained. Any teacher who will take the trouble to find out what his pupils are actually doing when they undertake to study an assignment will be left with little confidence in the system of announcing certain expected results and checking up on them as an effective means of organizing the learning process. Its prevalence is probably a chief reason for the widespread failure to learn, some of the evidence for which was cited in the previous chapter.

### Search for a Better Organization

The search for something better than the textbook-assignment-recitation pattern has moved along two chief lines. First there have been attempts to work out a better methodology, which means a better way of presenting the lesson, coupled with a more effective use of such devices as the question, the assignment, the textbook, the blackboard, and so on. Second, there have been attempts to make a fundamental change in the relationship between teacher and pupil, and in the pupil's basic activities. The possibilities, limitations, and meaning of both developments become apparent if we think of them as attempts to arrive at a better mode of organization.

1. Beginning with the quest for a better methodology, the first of our two lines of development and experimentation, the earliest and best known instance is the famous inductive-development lesson. It

* Unpublished report.

was originated by the German educator and psychologist Herbart, as part of a much wider scheme of reorganization. But it was lifted from its context by American students who visited Germany and brought it over here, where it was promoted as a cure-all. Essentially the idea was to lead the child's mind in a sequential movement from concrete experience and concrete data to the understanding of some general concept. To bring this about, the teacher was to plan the lesson in a series of steps. The first was *preparation*, the pupil being reminded of everyday experiences which bore upon the concept to be developed. Thus, if the lesson was on the condensation of vapor, attention would be called to the appearance of engine smoke on a cold day, or of one's breath, or of the steam at the spout of a kettle. Out of this would emerge the second step, the *statement of aim*. Under ideal conditions the preparatory work would so arouse the interest and curiosity of the learners that they themselves would ask how all this could be explained, and the question would constitute the aim for further work. Then came the *presentation*, in which new concrete material bearing on the concept was brought in, perhaps by demonstration, or a field trip, or by experiments, or by reading. Next came *comparison* and *abstraction*, which meant the reviewing and collating of all the data assembled so as to identify the common element running through it. Then came *generalization*, with the clear and explicit formulation of the concept and the fulfillment of the lesson aim. And the whole series terminated with *application*, in which the concept now explicitly formulated was brought to bear on new situations and problems.[2]

Another typical though much less well-known instance of an attempt to improve teaching by altering the mode of presentation of the lesson is the deductive-development lesson. Here the basic idea is to lead the pupil to apply general principles to a set of data and to draw appropriate conclusions. Once more a series of steps is involved. First would come the presentation of *data*. If, for example, the lesson was on the climate of the Andes, the data would consist of information about their location, altitude, etc., and about the general relationship of climate to geography. Next would come *assimilation*, with the general concepts brought to bear on the particular case. Next would come *inference*, and finally *verification*.[3]

Another and more recent plan, which has attracted much attention, is the so-called "mastery-unit technique." Material to be learned is set up in well-defined units, each to be studied to the level of mastery before passing on. The unit opens with a summary introduction presented in lecture form by the teacher. Then comes the study phase, in which pupils go to work on assigned material. Then comes discussion for the purpose of avoiding mere *memoriter* learning. Lastly comes recitation, in which the pupils demonstrate mastery.[4]

Besides these general methods supposed to be applicable to many subjects—of which there have been many others in addition to those described—various special methods designed for use in one particular subject have been devised. One of the most celebrated has been the direct method of teaching a foreign language, which turned upon avoidance of the vernacular, and required the use of very ingenious sequences and devices for the sake of doing everything in the foreign language from the very start. Again, the individual laboratory method in science is a fair instance of the same tendency. It is believed that the learner will grasp scientific ideas and techniques if he sets up, carries through, and records his own experiments, and do so better than if he reads about them or watches demonstrations.

Along with the development of these and many other methods has gone a concern for the better use of the devices of teaching. In conducting a recitation the teacher has been advised to formulate questions before calling on any individual pupil, to be sure that questions are brief and clear, not to use too many of them, and to insist on concise and definite answers. In making assignments the teacher should allow plenty of time to set them up carefully, should be sure to let the pupils know exactly what is expected of them, and should check up to be certain that instructions have been understood. In using the blackboard and visual materials the teacher should always have a definite point to put across, should take pains to have the presentation orderly, neat, and intelligible, and so forth. All this will show the direction taken in many serious and praiseworthy attempts to improve teaching.[5]

There is no doubt that many teachers have found suggestions and advice of this kind exceedingly helpful. In a general way it all makes sense. Above all, it gives one a definite scheme of action as one plans a lesson or conducts a class. One has a determinate series of steps to be followed, a determinate way of presenting one's material, and one knows that devices must be used just so.

As proposed patterns of organization, however, such methods suffer from two great defects—standardization and superficiality. (*a*) They are drawn up in advance of the material to be used and the learners to be taught. But a good plan must grow out of the actual situation and the actual job. The learners themselves, their development up to this point, their abilities, their interests, their group and individual responses, and also the contemplated learning in its actual setting all must be considered in any proper job of organizing. The resulting plan and the procedure into which it translates will most certainly be orderly, but it will not be a rigid stereotype. Much of the attractiveness of such methods as those we have discussed lies in their rigidity, because it makes them easy to understand and follow. But it is also one of their chief weaknesses. (b) Such methods are superficial in the sense that they take account of only some and not of all the aspects of the situation. They are plans for an orderly presentation rather than for a wide and varied range of activities carried on by a known group of persons, through which those persons learn. They are not schemes for the coordinated, purposeful, yet varied action of an actual group of human beings whose tendencies, both social and individual, are familiar to the organizer. Yet this is the only way in which action can be effectively organized, in teaching or anywhere else.

For these two reasons the various methods have, as a matter of fact, turned out disappointingly as means for bringing about better learning. When the acid test of results is applied, it seems to make surprisingly little difference what method is used, and in fact the novelties seem hardly better in this crucial respect than the textbook-assignment-recitation routine. The explanation is that the change is more apparent than real, and the stereotype is so general that it does not fit any situation very well or take adequate account of the essential factors which determine good learning.[6]

2. But also there have been attempts to improve teaching which involve a great deal more than a rearrangement of the modes of presentation and a better use of devices, and which go much deeper. What they imply is nothing less than a radical change in the relationship between teacher and pupil, and in the pattern of activities in and through which the pupil learns—ultimately a radical change in the management of the school and the conduct of education, although at first this was not clearly understood. The most conspicuous of these more far-reaching plans are the supervised-study movement, and the so-called "project method."

The supervised-study movement arose during the second decade of this century. It was based on a simple and intelligible yet far-reaching idea. The teacher should not merely assign and hear lessons. It was also his duty to help pupils to learn those lessons well. The commonest way of administering this idea was by the double divided period. Periods of double length were scheduled, one half being devoted to recitation, and the other half to studying the assignment under the supervision and with the assistance of the teacher. But there were a number of other plans and arrangements, and many subvariants of each of them.

Although supervised study in its various forms was tried out quite widely, it never fully lived up to expectations.   The reason usually given is that teachers might be able to conduct recitations well enough but did not know what to do when they were required to help pupils to learn.   This no doubt is true enough as far as it goes, but it is by no means the whole truth.   For supervised study implies a fundamental change in the relationship between teacher and taught.   The teacher ceases to be one who sits and hears lessons, and becomes a helper and guide.   The two functions do not readily or naturally combine.   If the teacher is to help the learner while he is in the very act of learning, why have the conventional lesson or recitation at all?   Is there not something anomalous in having a teacher help pupils on assignments and then turn round and quiz them?   Why not simply retain the study, and abandon everything else?   These are pertinent and inescapable questions, but the early proponents of supervised study were not prepared to face them.   Naturally enough, their minds were grooved in the convention of the textbook-assignment-recitation routine.   They assumed almost unwittingly that all study must be preparation for a recitation, and not merely learning.   The supervised-study movement as an organized attempt to improve teaching fell between two stools.   It really meant an abandonment of the standard practice of trying to control the learning process indirectly by formulating desired results and checking up on them, and the substitution of direct guidance of the learning process.   But neither its originators nor most of the practical school people who adopted it were able or willing to go all the way, or accept the full consequences of the proposal.[7]

Turning now to the project method, the very fact that it should have been so named is yet another proof of the inhibiting power of conventional notions.   For in essence it never was and is not a method at all, in the sense that inductive teaching, or deductive teaching, or the mastery technique, or the direct teaching of foreign languages are methods.   What it involved was not a mere change in the presentation of the lesson but a fundamental alteration in the activities of the learner.

The idea was taken over into general educational practice from manual arts, where a project meant simply and precisely a job of work undertaken by the pupil.   As soon as it was transplanted, its significance began to ramify and broaden so swiftly that definition became very difficult.   Projects could not be limited to manual undertakings. The production of a play, the planning and carrying out of a field trip, the writing of a poem or an essay or a musical composition, the enjoyment of a work of art, even the learning of some physical or intellectual skill or technique might quite properly be considered as a true project.

The only feasible way to define what was meant would be to say that any wholehearted "lifelike" activity was properly speaking a project. This, of course, was exceedingly sweeping, and the attempt at limitation by introducing the word "lifelike" was doomed to fail, for after all even the learning of the nine-times table or of a spelling list are parts of human life.

Nevertheless this very difficulty in making a tidy definition which would clearly differentiate between projects and nonprojects came from the very nature of the idea involved, and was evidence of its soundness. For the basic notion in the so-called "project method" is that the active purpose of the learner is a vital consideration. The learner himself must undertake the job, or he will not learn well. This means that one cannot identify a project by externals. One may visit a Latin class and find the pupils busily constructing a model of Ceasar's bridge across the Rhine. This looks like a project, but if they are doing it, not out of their own impulse and volition, not as a wholehearted activity, but merely to obey the requirements of a teacher, the appearance is deceptive. One may find a child studying the political history of ancient Athens, and this does not look like a project. But if he is doing so wholeheartedly and as an expression of his own purpose and desire, it is a project.

It has been said that every good project goes through a fourfold sequence of purposing, planning, executing, and judging. That is to say, the pupil (or with a group project, the pupils) determines upon an undertaking, plans it, carries it out, and evaluates its success and meaning. This has all the look of the step-wise sequences of presentation which were the essence of the methods previously described. As a matter of fact it is something entirely different. Purposing, planning, executing, and judging are not four steps each of which must be completed before the next is undertaken; they are simply four aspects of a continuous purposeful job, which may, to be sure, be quite clearly separated from each other, but which are far more likely to fuse indistinguishably. For the central idea of the project is purpose. The project method implies a basic alteration in the activities of the learner. Good learning will never be brought about merely by changing the mode of presentation of the lesson, no matter how reasonably, or by a more efficient use of classroom devices. Good learning is impossible without the aroused and directed will of the learner. The constructive contribution of the project method has been to emphasize this consideration, so obviously fruitful and vital for the proper organization of the learning process.[8]

## The Emerging Solution

Out of all this stress and stir and trial and failure and success has emerged, at any rate, the outline of a constructive and definitive solution to the problem of successful teaching.   Before that solution can be put fully into operation, a whole host of practical and challenging issues must be met.   There are two great causes of delay in meeting and dealing with these issues.   First there is the lack of courageous imagination among educators whose minds are cramped and fettered by the conception of the conventional school which has also been abundantly proves to be the ineffective school, and who have no clear and convincing picture of what a real teaching institution would look like or how it would work.   Second, there is the lack of intelligent support from the public, to whom schooling means a conventional routine barren of authentic results, and who are not aware of the advance in psychological knowledge which has made something far better entirely possible.   But at least we know how learning must be organized if it is to go well, and what the true operating principles of successful teaching must be.

A very careful and thorough student of current school practice has formulated the modern educational point of view which has been developing out of more than 50 years of experimentation and reflecion in the following words: "The true unit of educative experience is a realistic study of a problem and a cooperative, creative solution."* There might be some slight objection to this way of putting the matter, because it hardly seems to cover experiences in the way of appreciation and enjoyment which are highly important and can have a profound effect upon learning.   It might be better to say that learning should be organized in terms of undertakings which seem real and compelling and valuable to the learner, which engage his active purpose, which confront him with a significant challenge, and which lead to deeper and wider insights, more discriminating attitudes, and more adequate skills. This is the animating idea of the whole modern reshaping of teaching.

No school in the world has completely and satisfactorily translated this idea into practice, but many schools are well on the way toward doing so.   By examining what they do it is possible to discern with some degree of clarity and certainty the operating practices which become inevitable when we undertake to reorganize learning on this new basis.

* J. Wayne Wrightstone, *Appraisal of Experimental High School Practices*, p. 38, Teachers College, Columbia University, Bureau of Publications, New York, 1938.

1. *There must be profound changes in the patterns of learning and teaching.*

The old-time school set up teaching and learning in terms of numbers of narrow courses very loosely interrelated, if interrelated at all, and subdivided into still smaller blocks or units called lessons. The new school tends to substitute a much smaller number of broad fields or functional areas. An instance would be the cooperative study of a local slum region, taking a considerable part of a term, and a considerable part of the school day, and drawing in many teachers and many types of material conventionally distributed among separate courses.

In the old-time school the units of learning took the form of lessons which were the constituent elements of the courses, and these were decided upon irrespective of the interests and wishes of the learners. In the new school the tendency is for the learners to have an essential part in choosing and setting up the undertakings in and through which learning goes on. Thus the study of the slum area mentioned above would be cooperatively decided upon by teachers and pupils working together under the auspices of the school.

The old-time school drew a sharp distinction between curricular and extracurricular activities. The new school tends to regard any organized, fruitful, and significant undertaking as educationally important and valid, and to consider a pupil's achievement in connection with it as a proper part of his educational attainment.

The old-time school endeavoured to teach skills and abilities, such as mathematical and scientific techniques or the effective use of language, by means of specialized and isolated drills. The new school endeavours to develop such skills and abilities in close connection with the need to use them for satisfactory carrying out of significant undertakings, of which the study of the slum area mentioned above is again an example. The new school retains drill, but brings it into relationship with immediate use, and so breaks down its isolation.

2. *There must be profound changes in the motivation of learning.*

In the old-time school the problem of motivation was to induce the pupil energetically to attack tasks which were not of his choosing. The new school handles the problem of motivation by allowing and enabling pupils to have a cooperative share in choosing what they are to do.

In the old-time school, goals and standards were set by an authority entirely outside the pupil's range of control or choice, and he was under pressure to accept them and work toward them. The characteristic device for accomplishing this was the marking system. In the new school the significant undertaking in the selection of which the pupil had a share provides its own challenges and sets its own standards. The value of any individual's achievement is objectively determined by the situation itself.

The old-time school made great use of competition as a motivating force, and set up situations in which the individual pupil would strive chiefly to make a good record in comparison with his fellow pupils. The new school sets up situations in which pupils must accept coopera-tive responsibility for undertakings in the choice of which they them-selves have had a share, and which require joint achievement.

3. *There must be great changes in the social setting of learning.*

In the old-time school, class discipline meant a conventional type of classroom behavior, imposed from above and very little related to learning. In the new school, discipline becomes the orderly behavior of a group of people intent upon a joint undertaking. It arises directly out of what is being done, and so is part and parcel of the learning process.

In the old-time school, class discipline depended on controls and forces external to the group, and so was apt to go to pieces in circum-stances where these controls were withdrawn, *e.g.*, the absence of the teacher. In the new school the disciplinary control is inherent in the functional social situation where all are working towards a common purpose.

4. *There must be great changes in the chronological order in which topics and items are taken up and learned.*

In the old-time school the sequence of learning was determined by some sort of logical or quasi-logical arrangement of subject matter, each item or topic serving as background or preparation for those to come later. In the new school the placement of each item depends on its relationship to and its effect upon the mental and personal growth of the learner.

In the old-time school the sequence of the curriculum and the sequence of topics within the course were planned and decided entirely in advance and without any participation by the pupils. The same was true of the sequence of steps within the lesson. In the new school it is still the responsibility of the teacher to prepare thoroughly in advance and to develop careful plans, but the planning is flexible so that the actual sequence of the curriculum, the course, or the unit of learning can be modified by the cooperation and initiative of the learners.

5. *Along with these far-reaching changes in the organization of learn-ing there must inevitably go changes in the content to be learned.*

The old-time school was primarily concerned with transmitting the

cultural heritage.    The new school is primarily concerned in establishing understanding and control of present-day and immediate personal
and social needs and problems in such matters as health, civic relationships, the use of leisure time, and the like.    The cultural heritage is not
ignored, but instead of being transmitted for its own sake, it is brought
to bear on current living.

The old-time school made use of academic material exclusively.
The new school does not confine itself to intellectual or academic material, but draws upon the whole range of human experience—social,
aesthetic, ethical, manipulative.

The old-time school taught skills and abilities with a view to their
usefulness in adult life.    The new school teaches skills, facts, and
abilities for the sake of their immediate use in significant undertakings,
and their effect upon personal growth and development here and now.

The old-time school ignored the community in which it was placed
as a source of educative experience.    The new school encourages undertakings which involve the exploration of the local community and the
utilization of its resources.

The old-time school in the main used static materials, such as classi-
cal writings, history prior to modern times, and the long-established
portions of science and mathematics.    The new school continues to
utilize the great contributions of the past, but makes much use of
current materials which change with the changing times, including
materials collected by pupils and teachers as part of the process of
learning.

Such, in outline, are the most conspicuous differences between the
new education and the old.    It will be noted that once a fundamental
change is made in the organization of learning, everything in the structure and operation of the school undergoes alteration.[9]

If one asks whether an organization of learning in terms of fruitful
and significant undertakings which engage the purpose of the learners
is in fact superior to one in terms of the textbook-assignment-recitation
routine, the answer is yes.    Many comparisons have already been
made of the results achieved by the old and the new types of schools,
and they are consistently in favor of the latter.    To be sure, the advantage is not always and everywhere very great, but profound and comprehensive changes are not made adequately in a few years, nor is it
easy to find workers able to utilize the new learning situations for
what they are worth.    As the full practical implications of the reorganization become better understood and as the new modes of operation
reach maturity, it is reasonable to expect very much better results from
schooling.    The fact that children are already learning better and

getting better results in the new and reorganized schools is surely an earnest of further advance.[10]

## Notes and References

*General References*

For a fuller historical and systematic interpretation of the place of methodology in American education, see James L. Mursell, *Education for American Democracy*, Chap. 10, "The Problem of Teaching," W. W. Norton & Company, Inc., New York, 1943. For an epitome and general orientation on the problem of methodology see Stephen M. Corey and Walter S. Monroe, "Methods of Teaching," *Encyclopaedia of Educational Research*, pp. 231–725, The Macmillan Company, New York, 1941.

*References in the Text*

1. The summary of arguments for and against home study is derived from Robert W. Frederick, Clarence Ragsdale, and Rachel Salisbury, *Directing Learning*, pp. 145–161, D. Appleton-Century Company, Inc., New York, 1938.

2. The original source in America for the inductive-development lesson is C. A. McMurry and F. M. McMurry, *The Method of the Recitation*, The Macmillan Company, New York, 1900. See also William C. Bagley, *The Educative Process*, The Macmillan Company, New York, 1917.

3. A good account of the so-called "deductive-development lesson" may be found in William C. Bagley, *The Educative Process*, Chap. 20, The Macmillan Company, New York, 1917.

4. The basic book on the mastery-unit technique is Henry C. Morrison, *The Practice of Teaching in the Secondary School*, University of Chicago Press, Chicago, 1926. For a critical analysis of this and other methods see Roy O. Billett, *Fundamentals of Secondary School Teaching*, Chap. 16, Houghton Mifflin Company, Boston, 1940.

5. The reader interested in a further investigation of methodology, which has been such an important consideration in the training of teachers, should examine books such as the following: James H. Blackhurst, *Principles of Methods*, Des Moines, Ia., Iowa University Press, 1936; James E. Holley, *Modern Principles and the Elementary Teacher's Technique*, D. Appleton-Century Company, Inc., New York, 1928; William C. Ruediger, *Teaching Procedures*, Houghton Mifflin Company, Boston, 1932; M. J. Stormzand, *Progressive Methods of Teaching*, Houghton Mifflin Company, Boston, 1924; Gerald A. Yoakam and Robert Gilkey Simpson, *An Introduction to Teaching and Learning*, The Macmillan Company, New York, 1934.

6. For further references on methodology see bibliographies in the two titles listed above under General References. As a typical comparison between methods it may be interesting to read F. A. Riedel, "What if Anything Has Really Been Proved as to the Relative Effectiveness of Demonstration and Laboratory Methods in Science?" *School Science and Mathematics*, Vol. 28 (1927), pp. 512–519.

7. A good reference for those who wish to gain an over-all understanding of supervised study in actual practice is W. A. Brownell, *A Study of Supervised Study*, University of Illinois Press, Urbana, 1925; see also Cecile White Flemming, "Directing Study," *Encyclopaedia of Educational Research*, pp. 400–406, The Macmillan Company, New York, 1941.

8. For the project method the essential sources are William Herd Kilpatrick, *Foundations of Method*, Chap. 21, The Macmillan Company, New York, 1925; and William Herd Kilpatrick, "The Project Method," *Teachers College Record*, Vol. 19 (1918), pp. 319–325.

9. Extensive and interesting comparisons between the old and the new may be found in the following sources: J. Murray Lee and Doris M. Lee, *The Child and His Curriculum*, pp. 174–175, D. Appleton-Century Company, Inc., New York, 1940, to which the account in this book owes much, William H. Burton, *The Guidance of Learning Activities*, Chap. 8, D. Appleton-Century Company, Inc., New York, 1944. A basic source of great importance in making such comparisons is J. Wayne Wrightstone, *Appraisal of Experimental High School Practices*, Chaps. 1 and 2, Teachers College, Columbia University, Bureau of Publications, New York, 1938.

10. Studies in the comparative results attained by new and old schools have been fairly numerous. A good brief summary is Denton Geyer, "Reconstructing Education through Research," *American Educational Research Association, Official Report*, pp. 170–176, 1936. A much longer summary is J. Paul Leonard and Alvin C. Eurich, (eds.), *An Evaluation of Modern Education*, D. Appleton-Century Company, Inc., New York, 1942, in which Chaps. 2, 3, 4, 5, and 9 are particularly pertinent. Also see J. Wayne Wrightstone, *Appraisal of Experimental High School Practices*, Part II, Teachers College, Columbia University, Bureau of Publications, New York, 1938; also J. Wayne Wrightstone, *Appraisal of Newer Practices in Selected Public Schools*, Teachers College, Columbia University, Bureau of Publications, New York, 1935.

### Items for Discussion and Study

1. Make a factual analysis of two courses you have taken or are taking, choosing two which are very differently conducted, as organized plans for the promotion of learning. What are the operating factors in the situation, such as selection of students, textbooks, readings, syllabi, tests? How are they coordinated into the scheme of organization? Which are controlled by the teacher and which are not? How do guidance and direction enter in? Why does the word "organization" express the situation better than the two just mentioned?

2. Make an inventory, as complete and realistic as you can, of the activities which these two courses set going and maintain in the lives of the learners. Do these activities seem to you to favor effective learning and authentic results?

3. To what extent should the pupil organize his own learning? Does this mean self-teaching? Consider how to help him to do so. Is it ever possible for a pupil to organize his learning better than it is organized in a poorly conducted course in which he is enrolled?

4. Show how the introduction of the graded system brought about a change in the organization of learning.

5. Can you, from your own experience, find further illustrations of the great and central weakness of the textbook-assignment-recitation scheme?

6. Give an account of any other standard methods beside those described in the chapter.

7. Why have such methods appealed so strongly to teachers? Why is the very basis of their appeal also one of the great weaknesses?

8. Why is it not legitimate to classify supervised study or project teaching as methods?

9. Can you see any relationship between Wrightstone's statement quoted on p. 37 and the discussion of authentic results in Chap. 1? Can you see why this statement ultimately implies some such far-reaching reorganization as that described on pp. 38–41?

10. Analyze as far as you can the operating practices of some school with which you are familiar, to determine how its practices might be rated in the light of the contrast between new and old presented on pp. 38–41.

# CHAPTER 3

# SUCCESSFUL TEACHING—ITS ORIENTATION : CONTROLLING APPROACH

## MEANINGFUL LEARNING

So far we have been looking at endeavours to improve teaching, as it were from the outside. We have seen them as a series of undertakings, practical experiments, proposals, and plans which, taken together, amount to a search for better ways of organizing learning. But throughout our discussion an essential question has been implicit, which as yet has hardly been touched, and which must now be faced. What is it that all these experimenters and workers have been looking for? Is there some definable and recognizable type of organization which is essentially good, and which can be contrasted with another type essentially bad? This question is of great importance for the practical teacher. It is very valuable for him to know *what* has been and is being done in attempts to improve teaching, because this enables him to look at matters concretely. But it is just as valuable, if not more so, for him to understand *why* these things are done, because this enables him to discriminate between the hopeless and the hopeful, the bad and the good, both in the proposals and undertakings about which he learns, and in his own work too. What are the basic characteristics of a good organization of learning? What is the essential difference between a good organization and a bad one? These are the issues to which we are now to turn.

Essentially the difference is one of orientation. Just what it is can be seen by considering a couple of concrete illustrations from actual teaching practice and experience.

William was having the gravest kind of trouble with geometry. It might be possible, by dint of the probability curve and a good deal of charity, to give him a passing mark. But so far as getting any real and living grasp of the stuff was concerned, the only possible word was failure. William's father and his geometry teacher were both much concerned, for he was a bright enough boy. One day the father, rummaging in his son's room, happened upon an amazing discovery. He found a formidable-looking treatise on ballistics, between the pages of which were numerous pages covered with calculations in his son's handwriting.   Examination revealed that this mass of work evidently had to do with the small rifle which had been given to the boy as a birthday present some months ago, and in the use of which he had shown a passionate interest.

The father said nothing to William, but invited his teacher to the house for a quiet conference.   She arrived in considerable fear and trembling, which however proved needless.   The two of them examined the evidence, and finally the teacher exclaimed that the boy actually seemed to have taught himself more of certain kinds of mathematics than she knew herself.

This is as clear a contrast as one could well have between successful and unsuccessful learning.   What was the reason for the difference? It can be epitomized very concisely.   On the one hand learning that was highly meaningful to the learner, on the other hand learning that was not.   The particular instance points straight to a fundamental generalization.   The more meaningful the learning, the greater the promise of success.   The less meaningful the learning, the greater the probability of failure.

Again, consider well these two sentences, taken from a school textbook.

"On the seaward side of the mountains of Australia are dense hardwood forests.   Among the most valuable trees are the eucalyptus, sometimes known as gum trees."*

To many a child who meets this statement in his assignment, it will certainly be almost meaningless.   To start with, it will not matter to him.   He simply will not care one way or another about these remote mountains and woods.   Furthermore, it will be largely unintelligible, even though each separate word is simple enough.   If he happens to have been born and brought up in the great plains region, mountains and the seaward side of them will be at best vague and dubious images. If the word "hardwood" indicates anything in particular, he is a remarkable youngster.   And neither gum trees nor eucalyptus trees stand for anything in his experience or concern.   The whole proposition is verbalistic, and most tenuously related to anything that he cares about, or to anything that has played any part in his life.   What he has before him is simply a collection of words in a book.   Perhaps he is conscientious and does his best, but that best can hardly be more than an attempt to memorize the words.   And the memorization, even if far more thorough than it is at all likely to be, will still almost surely be transient and fleeting, for there is nothing in the statement that

* Quoted by Ernest Horn, *Methods of Instruction in the Social Sciences*, p. 60, Charles Scribner's Sons, New York, 1937.

puts down roots into his mental soil, the only way in which permanent retention can be accomplished.    Learning has been organized in a manner that points straight to failure.

Everyone interested in teaching would do well to ponder this simple illustration.    It is highly typical.    Learning situations of this kind occur by the thousand on every school day throughout the United States.    They instantly explain why so much teaching fails.    They may be hard to avoid, but that only amounts to saying that effective teaching is not easy to do, which is true enough.    But one straight, unprejudiced look at what actually goes on is quite enough to convince the observer that the bane of teaching is meager meaningfulness.    Thus the controlling orientation of good organization is towards meaningfulness.    *Learning is well organized when it is richly meaningful to the learner*.    The whole attempt to improve teaching is and must be a quest for just such patterns of organization.

## WHAT IS MEANINGFUL LEARNING:

A good way to start explaining what is meant by meaningful learning is to consider a few contrasting illustrations.    Two pairs of such illustrations are here presented, one pair from psychological experimentation, another from teaching situations.

Much of the early work on the psychology of learning dealt with the memorization and forgetting of nonsense syllables.    A typical nonsense syllable series might run as follows: def fud gak tig nup gel nad cim lon vid mos pel.    To learn this series well enough so that one could repeat it twice without error, which is the usual standard of the experimental work, would probably require somewhere around 12 repetitions. After the series had been learned up to this standard, forgetting would set in rapidly.    In a few days it would be possible to recall only a few of the syllables.    If one overlearned the series, continuing the repetitions after the standard of two perfect recitations had been reached, forgetting would be somewhat postponed and reduced, but not a great deal.    This is about as pure a case as one can find of almost meaningless learning.    And it is highly inefficient learning.    It takes a great deal of time and labor.    It does not last well.    And nothing one can do seems to make it last well.[1]

Such investigations contrast very sharply with experiments dealing with meaningful learning, of which the following is a good example. The investigator had college students study passages of difficult but meaningful prose, and then gave them tests to see if they could recognize the substance of what they had been studying, if it was expressed

in different words.   One of the passages they had to read went as
follows:

The accumulation of knowledge concerning the feeble-minded by the
dawn of the twentieth century had led to the clearly formulated conclusion
that the feeble-minded are incapable of self-directed lives.   Since then the
advance in diagnostic methods has resulted in the detection of higher grades of
feeble-mindedness; this in turn arouses hope on the part of many investigators
that the high grade feeble-minded at least may be capable of being educated
sufficiently to meet the demands of society.   On the other hand it has been
shown that only a pitifully small percentage of feeble-minded made good when
they are replaced in the community after being in an institution for the
feeble-minded.

A test item on this passage was: "Views on the educability of the
feeble-minded were less harmonious about 1900 than they have been
since that time."   It was supposed to be marked "false."   Clearly
this is a very different type of learning from that required by lists of
nonsense syllables.   And the contrast in efficiency is enormous.   Such
items could be learned on a single try and without any repetitions, and
the experimental subjects had lost nothing of what they had learned
at the end of 70 days.[2]

The same general contrast between the meaningful and the relatively meaningless is still more sharply and completely shown in the
following pair of lessons, both dealing with the same body of material,
the first scene of the first act of *Hamlet*.

The first lesson took up the assignment in the conventional fashion.
The text used was *Hamlet*, edited by L. A. Sherman, revised by H. Y.
Moffet, illustrated by A. Gladys Peck, and published in 1930 by The
Macmillan Company of New York.   The teacher asked questions
based on the text, and more particularly on the notes.   Where did
the action occur?   In the castle of Kronberg.   What can you tell
about that?   It was the strongest point of the coast defences of North-
east Seeland.   Why does the action take place here?   Because King
Claudius came to the throne under suspicion and needed protection
difficult to get in the royal palace.   "The rivals of my watch"—what
does that mean?   Partners of my watch.   "Give you good night"—
what is that short for?   God give you good night.   "Thou art a
scholar, speak to it (the ghost) Horatio"—why was Horatio to speak
to it?   Because a ghost cannot speak unless addressed first.   What
was the importance of Horatio being a scholar?   The ghost might be
specially influenced by Latin, a sacred language.   And so on.

The second and contrasting lesson on the same scene was conducted
by a lady who had some experience as an actress, and was a brilliant

reader.   There was some question and answer and discussion, but
everything focused on her use of this talent of hers.   She developed the
*mise en scène* most impressively—the darkling mist-enshrouded castle,
the sound of the sea, the chilly frightened soldiers groping about, the
emergence of the ghost.   She read excerpts from the play, interspersed
with comments of her own.   The class was enthralled.   One could
have heard the proverbial pin drop.

No one could observe these two teaching situations without being
certain of their comparative success.   The one concentrated on the
broad dramatic meaning which it was Shakespeare's intent to convey,
with its universal appeal and significance.   The other emphasized the
small historical and antiquarian details which he utilized as his vehicle,
the force of which cannot possibly be appreciated until the broad mes-
sage of the scene has been understood and felt.   As to results, it was
quite possible to believe that some of the boys and girls in the one class
would 20 years hence be reading and enjoying Shakespeare because of
what took place in that 40-minute period.   But it was difficult to
believe that the factual lesson would bring about much beyond partial
learning and quick forgetting.

These two pairs of illustrations provide a striking contrast.   There
are two instances in which the organized learning turns upon something
about which it is incredible that the learners concerned would care very
much, in which the whole emphasis is upon separate items and not upon
their interrelationships or wider bearings, and in which the task is
wholly or chiefly to retain these separate items.   Then there are two
instances in which the organized learning turns upon something which
might well strike the learners as important and worth while, in which
the emphasis is upon an essential core of relatedness which holds all
details together and unifies them, and in which the task is to become
more clearly aware of this vital and unifying core and of its wider
bearings.   On the one hand there is relatively meaningless learning.
On the other hand there is relatively meaningful learning.   To round
out the idea by at least a tentative definition, *learning is meaningful in
the proportion to which the situation or problem seems real or worth while
to the learner, to which its essential interrelatedness is emphasized, and
to which the learner's task is the apprehension of this interrelatedness or
unity*.

The careful reader will have noted that instead of speaking of
meaningless as contrasted with meaningful learning, the distinction
drawn is between less and more meaningful learning.   This is the correct way to think about the matter, and if it is remembered quite a
few confusions and difficulties will be avoided.   One cannot deny that

the textbook notes on Hamlet make some kind of sense, and that so far as they go they are intelligible.   But to most high-school pupils it will be a very limited kind of sense, although a Shakespearean scholar might see a great deal in it.   To revert to the textbook item on the Australian forests, this too makes sense.   To a lumberman proposing to set up in business in Australia it might be a very pertinent and pregnant and far-reaching sense, but again not to American high-school pupils.   Even the nonsense of syllables are not utterly nonsensical. There is a laboratory situation which makes the learner want to learn them.   They are made up of familiar letters, and their sound is similar to that of English syllables.   If one could invent a series of stimulus items conveyed by symbols nobody had ever seen before, and sounding like something nobody had ever heard before, one would recede a goodly distance toward unadulterated nonsense, but even then not the whole way.   The symbols and the sounds would still have some sort of pattern which could be grasped, some sort of relationship to familiar experience, and in the laboratory the subjects would still have an urge to learn them.   An experience in which meaning was reduced to absolute zero would be a contradiction, an impossibility.   It would be nothing at all, for there would be nothing upon which the mind could in any way take hold.   Thus totally meaningless learning is not possible.   At the very worst the pupils might after a fashion learn the item about the Australian forests by the mere sound and rhythm of the words, even if they knew no English.   In the same way it would be possible to learn the notes on *Hamlet* just as a parrot learns phrases.   And we know that the memorizing of nonsense syllables depends far more than is ordinarily realized upon the establishment of rhythms, groupings, and associations which, although they may be arbitrary, still tie the series more or less together.   So the point is precisely put by saying that the more meaningful a learning situation is, the better the learning is likely to go, and the more richly it promises authentic results.

Thus the basis of all successful teaching is to create situations as rich as possible in meaning for those who are to learn, to emphasize meanings as strongly and copiously as possible, and to lead learners to grasp them as the essential task.

## WHY TEACHING MUST EMPHASIZE MEANING

The reason why teaching that is to succeed—teaching that is to get authentic results—must center upon the promotion and organization of meaningful learning is that learning itself, in its very essence, is a process in and through which meanings are apprehended, clarified, and applied.   To ignore or obscure meanings, therefore, is to falsify the very process which teaching must effectively organize if it is to be successful. To do this would be as foolish as to try to make a good airplane while blandly ignoring the principles of aerodynamics.

The proposition that learning, in its very nature and essence, is the apprehension, clarification, and application of meaning is one of the most important, and for practical teachers decidedly one of the most fruitful of all the insights of modern psychology. The attempt to apply psychology to teaching has been going on now for well over a hundred years. For a long time it was hampered for the simple reason that there was not much psychology to apply. More recently, however, the trouble has been the emergence of apparently fundamental differences among psychologists. Various schools or sects have arisen, such as behaviorism with its emphasis on the conditioning of reflexes, associationism with its emphasis on the connection between stimulus and response and upon trial and error, dynamic psychology with its emphasis upon energy-output and will, *Gestalt* psychology with its emphasis upon the total pattern of experience and response, and numerous subvariants and combinations as well. Teachers in search of practical guidance have been somewhat in the position of engineers tackling the practical problem of building a bridge, and wondering in what type of physics they ought to believe.

The layman, always apt to find conflict spectacular and intriguing, has had his attention quite unduly drawn to these differences. But recently many of our best authorities have been pointing out that there is far more agreement than disagreement among psychologists, something that has long been clear to careful and impartial students of the research literature.

Differences, in the main, have been due to two chief causes. First, psychologists have dealt with widely varying research problems and situations. When some workers spend years of their lives studying the reactions of animals in finding how to escape from problem boxes, others in studying the conditioning of human and animal reflexes, others in studying the memorization of digits and nonsense syllables, and others again in investigating how human beings become able to solve problems and formulate concepts, it would be a miracle if they all seemed to speak the same language and say the same thing, especially as they are apt to lack time and energy to get together and see how all their lines of investigation converge. Then secondly, psychologists have developed and made much of special terms and concepts. Some, for instance, return again and again to the concept of connection or of "bonds" between stimulus and response, while others with equal persistence center their discussions around the concept of insight.    The careful workers among them have always been at pains scrupulously to define and qualify their basic concepts.    And when one examines their statements and reflects about what they really mean and really say, it becomes apparent that they are talking about different aspects of the same thing rather than exhibiting irreconcilable conflicts.    But once again a superficial impression is apt to be of sectarian strife.    So the appearance of difference is quite understandable, but very far from corresponding to reality, although to be sure there is not complete agreement and cannot be in a science where so much still remains unknown and unexplained.

Essential agreements among psychologists with regard to the nature of learning may briefly be summed up as follows:

All learning of all kinds is in essence a process which begins with a compelling problem, and proceeds towards its solution by the apprehension, clarification, and application of meaning.    This is true when an animal learns which door in the wall of a box leads to food.    The animal has before it a situation which is baffling but intriguing.    It deals with that situation by learning to perceive the right door in relationship to everything else as the key item in the situation and to act accordingly.    It is true when the knee-jerk reflex of a human being is conditioned to the sound of a bell.    Once again there is a situation artificially established in the laboratory that is baffling but at the same time "matters" to the learner.    And he meets it when the sound of the bell acquires a special prepotency among all the mass of incoming impressions, and is tied into a nexus of relationships.    It is true when a person memorizes a series of nonsense syllables; for the series never will be learned unless the learner wants to do so, and until all the syllables are tied together by rhythm or sound or some other coordinating factor.    It is true when a person acquires a motor ability such as skill at golf.    He is then faced with a motor problem, and he solves it by creating an intelligible pattern of action and accomodating it to the essential features of a physical situation.    And obviously it is true when a person learns to pick out the gist of a passage when he reads it, or to find the clue which enables him to solve a mathematical problem.

All learning of every kind, then, involves the following factors:

1. There must be a problem which the learner, human or animal, desires to solve, an obstacle or a difficulty with which he wishes to deal.    Put in other words this amounts to saying that there must be an aroused will to learn.

2. There must be an inner coherence or relatedness or intelligibility into which the learner seeks to penetrate since it offers the clue to the desired solution.    In some cases this may be apparent from the

very start, but often it is dimly and dubiously seen at first, and may even be no more than a hope.  But this search for the intelligible solution is a basic characteristic of all learning, and just as typical in the acquisition of a physical skill or of an appreciation as it is in the grasp of a pattern of ideas.  Always and everywhere the learning process is a search for and an endeavour to grasp an intelligibility often at the beginning extremely confused and obscure.

3. There must be an awareness that the clue has been found, the interrelationship apprehended—a sense that "this is it."  This may come all in a moment, or gradually, reluctantly, and with many recessions and confusions, but it is exactly what the claim to have learned something amounts to.  Learning, then, is understanding.  Learning is seeking, finding, and seeing the point.  Learning is problem solving, in the inclusive sense that when a person achieves a motor skill, or becomes able to appreciate a symphony or a poem, he has solved a problem and found a clue.  And it must be emphasized that this doctrine, this interpretation of the nature of learning, is not advocated by just one school of psychology, but has the authoritative backing of most if not all of them.

Where, then, does the difference lie between meaningful and what is often, though inexactly, called meaningless learning?  The answer is as follows:

1. It is possible to devise situations in which meanings are very obscure, or very remote, or very meager.  This is what happens when an elephant learns to stand on a tub, or when the iris reflex is conditioned to a sound, or when a person is set to memorize lists of digits or nonsense syllables, or when one practices for weeks on one small detail of the golf swing, or when one tries to get the bearings of a very difficult and elaborate exposition.  There is no strong urge to learn, and nothing very intelligible presents itself to the learner's attention. The consequence of situations like this is sure to be uneconomical and impeded learning.  Learning may even break down altogether, as when the elephant never masters his trick, or the conditioned reflex never appears, which latter is by no means uncommon.  At the best such learning requires some sort of external and artificial compulsion or incentive, and also many repetitions.  And no matter how long and hard the learner tries, the results are apt to be transient unless there are frequent reviews.  Note that although meaning may be obscure, or remote, or meager, it must be present to some extent or there will be no learning.

All these situations have certain definite and recognizable characteristics.

*a.* They are not deeply motivated.   The learner does not care very much.   He only learns because he finds himself in a position where he is more or less compelled to do so.   This happens in experiments on the conditioning of reflexes and the memorizing of nonsense syllables. The learner has consented to act as an experimental subject.   The experimenter helps him as much as possible by removing distractions and perhaps by offering incentives.   He is willing to do his best.   But the problem itself does not engage him, and it does not matter much to him whether he solves it or not.   It also happens when a pupil is working endlessly at some small detail of a motor skill.   He persists out of blind faith in his teacher, not because he himself sees the point.   Thus motivation is present, but it is not deep or compelling.

*b.* The kind of work the learner does tends to be a blind and mechanical going over and over of the same ground.   It cannot quite be described in strictness as repetition, for he does not go over the ground in exactly the same way each time.   But it is very different from the conscious search for a clue, or a relationship, or an understandable point, because intelligibility has been deliberately cancelled out as far as possible by breaking everything down into separate elements with a minimum of coherence or connection.

*c.* It tends towards a *memoriter,* or purely verbal, or superficial grasp of what is learned.   Here as always, things do come together in some sort of a coherent whole, or there would be no learning at all.   But it is a frail and feeble whole, as though the elements which make it up were stuck together with some sort of weak paste instead of being welded and integrated into one another.   This is why it so easily falls apart.

Again to repeat, such learning situations are thoroughly familiar in the psychological laboratory.   They have been established with both animal and human subjects, in connection with both motor and mental skills.   They are usually called situations involving meaningless learning.   But as we have seen, this is not quite accurate.   They should be spoken of as situations involving minimally meaningful learning.

2. It is possible to devise learning situations in which meaning is the manifest and central feature.   Instead of putting an animal in a mechanical problem box which he cannot possibly understand and does not want to understand anyhow, and in which all he can do is to scramble around, he may be, as it were, invited to use whatever sense he has. A hen or a rat may be set to learn which of a number of differently colored doors leads most directly to food.   An ape may be placed in a cage with a banana outside just out of reach, and be given a stick with which he can learn to scrape the fruit towards him.   A human

being may be put up against a series of wire puzzles, or a code, or an intriguing game which calls for the comprehension of a certain principle. Here everything goes very differently than in situations where meaning is at a minimum. There is of course still effort, but it is exploratory rather than repetitive. Once the vital clue has been found and the learning has been achieved, it is not readily forgotten. And sometimes success comes very abruptly and almost at once.

The characteristics of these situations also are clear and definite. (a) There is established at once or almost at once and from the start, the sense of a compelling and intriguing problem. The subject, animal or human, is aware of a problem that he wants to solve, and it grips and continues to grip him. Thus the learning is deeply rather than superficially motivated. (b) The whole process amounts to experimentation, often fumbling and hesitant but never quite merely mechanical, upon the intelligible problem featured in the situation. (c) The achieved learning does not take the form of a mechanical *memoriter* response, but of an established control brought about through understanding. Once again such situations have become familiar in psychological research, and their general character is well recognized.

It should be evident how all this bears upon teaching, whose central problem is the organization of learning, or the creation of situations in which good learning can go on. The classroom, just as much as the laboratory, can be the scene of situations in which meaning is reduced to a minimum, or in which it is played up as the central consideration. That the former makes for ineffectiveness and the latter for effectiveness is the testimony of a body of psychological research far too large and far to unanimous to be ignored. *A compelling and convincing problem, an intelligible rather than a routine approach, and a solution in terms of insight—that is the clearly indicated pattern of successful teaching. A problem so unconvincing and unreal that it must be forced upon the learner either by threats or artificial incentives, a treatment of it by dint of unintelligible effort, and an outcome that is merely a matter of routine memorization—that is the pattern of the kind of teaching that fails.* The one promises authentic results, the other promises spurious ones. Behind this conclusion is the weight of our achieved understanding of the learning process.[3]

### Notes and References

*General References*

An excellent concrete account of four teaching situations which will enrich and illustrate the contentions of the present chapter will be found in Inga Olla Helseth, *Living in the Classroom*, "Four Contrasts," pp. 7–25, Edwards Bros. Inc., Ann Arbor, Mich., 1939. It will be found interesting to compare Miss Helseth's analysis with that here presented. A more general but very illuminating and challenging reference is Ernest Horn, *Methods of Instruction in the Social Sciences*, Chap. 4, "The Problem of Meaning in the Social Sciences," Charles Scribner's Sons, New York, 1937.

*References in the Text*

1. The major source for experimental work on memory using the nonsense syllable technique is H. Ebbinghaus, *Ueber das Gedaechtnis*, Duncker & Humblot, Munich, 1885, translated by Ruger and Busenius with the title *Memory*, Teachers College, Columbia University, New York, 1913.

2. The material on meaningful learning is from H. B. English, E. L. Wellborn, and C. D. Killian, "Studies in Substance Memorization," *Journal of General Psychology*, Vol. 11 (1934), pp. 233–260.

3. On the major issue of the essential similarity of different schools of psychology the reader should consult the following sources: J. F. Dashiell, "A Survey and Synthesis of Learning Theories," *Psychological Bulletin*, Vol. 32 (1935), pp. 261–275, which is an extremely valuable statement, with very rich references, though difficult and condensed. *National Society for the Study of Education, 41st Yearbook*, Part I, 1942, is entirely devoted to the topic. Chaps. 1 to 7 inclusive are all important and will repay study. Chapter 7, "Reconciliation of Learning Theories," by T. R. McConnell is the summary chapter. A formulation simpler than any of the foregoing will be found in James L. Mursell, *Educational Psychology*, Chap. 6, W. W. Norton & Company, Inc., New York,

## Items for Discussion and Study

1. Bring together, discuss, and critically examine statements, assigned readings, problems, etc., from various subject-matter fields, appearing in textbooks, etc., which seem apt to be relatively meaningless to the pupils concerned. To what extent are such materials typical? How far do they explain the kind of failures to learn considered in Chap. 2?

2. Consider and discuss the specific respects in which relatively meaningless learning is inefficient. Can it be made efficient?

3. Is it possible decisively to determine how meaningful a job of learning is without knowing the learner's attitude to it?

4. May a learner be very eager to learn, and still find the task before him relatively meaningless?

5. Review the two previous questions in the light of one or more specific and actual jobs of learning which you yourself have found highly meaningful.

6. The three previous questions all deal with aspects of an issue which might be put as follows: Is the meaningfulness of learning determined by the nature of the task, or by the learner's mind? What do you think? What are the implications of your answer for the organization of learning?

7. What are the objections to drawing a distinction between meaningful and entirely meaningless learning?

8. Show, if necessary using the references at the end of the chapter, that many schools of psychology are in agreement as to the nature of learning. Why is this so important for practical teachers?

9. Points 1 and 2, on pp. 52 and 53 described characteristic situations in which learning is badly and well organized. Can you find parallel situations in school?

# CHAPTER 4

## SUCCESSFUL TEACHING—ITS ORIENTATION: SPECIFIC EMPHASES

### THE PATTERN OF MEANINGFUL LEARNING

Successful teaching turns upon the recognition, both in thought and action, of the truth that learning is essentially a meaningful rather than a mechanical process. On this psychologists of many different schools concur. It indicates unmistakably the general direction to follow in organizing learning effectively.

But psychological investigation carries far beyond this broad conception and can offer much more specific guidance to the teacher who wishes to do good work. It has revealed a number of specific aspects or emphases in the total pattern of meaningful learning, which make the general orientation more definite. (1) Learning is essentially purposive. It is meaningful in the sense that it "matters" to the learner. (2) The basic process of learning is one of exploration and discovery, not of routine repetition. (3) The outcome or result achieved by learning is always the emergence of insight, or understanding, or intelligible response. (4) That result is not tied to the situation in which it was achieved, but can be used also in other situations. The substance of these last three points is that learning is meaningful not only in the sense that it "matters" to the learner but also in the sense that it is intelligible and turns upon the so-called "higher mental processes," rather than upon the mechanical formation of connections. These are the two senses in which the word "meaningful" applies to learning, and they are intimately related, as we shall see. Such is the outline pattern of meaningful learning, and the more any learning exhibits these characteristics the more meaningful it is. Consequently the more effectively teaching establishes these conditions, the more successful it is likely to be.

### LEARNING IS PURPOSIVE

This is a consideration of primary importance for anyone who wishes to organize learning for successful and authentic outcomes. Learning absolutely requires an aroused and directed purpose, and without such purpose failure is sure.

56

The proposition has been recognized by psychologists for many years, and numerous research studies have confirmed it again and again. Those who wish to examine the experimental literature will find references to it at the close of this chapter. All that is necessary here, however, is to describe the findings of a single study which may fairly be said to rank as a classic. This is the work of Book and Norvell, who coined the phrase "The Will to Learn" as a title for their report.* Two groups of adults, as far as possible equal in learning ability, were selected. Both groups were set to learning a variety of tasks, each using the same number of repetitions. One group simply went through the repetitions without any particular motivation. The other group was specially motivated, chiefly by being informed systematically of the results of their efforts. The motivated group made strikingly better progress than the unmotivated group. The investigators took a special precaution against this superiority being due to some unrecognized influence, perhaps connected with the personalities of the learners. During the final third of the experiment the conditions were reversed. The hitherto unmotivated group was now motivated by the devices already used; and the hitherto motivated group now worked without the special incentives. The effect on achievement was immediate and unmistakable. With the reversal of the learning conditions, the relative achievement of the two groups was also reversed. Thus the conclusion was drawn that motivation is a powerful influence in making for rapid and effective learning. And the investigators sum up their opinion in the statement, "It is intense effort that educates." This single study epitomizes a great deal of the investigative work on the problem of purpose in learning.[1]

So far, all that has been established is that learning goes well when there is an aroused and directed purpose, and badly where there is none. This is obviously important, but the relationship between the will to learn and learning that is in the full sense meaningful has hardly been established. Later studies on the topic, however, make this clear. It has been pointed out that all the studies by psychologists of all schools recognize in one way or another that learning grows out of and is determined by a "field of complex motives."† And it is this field of complex motives that must be taken into account, shaped up, and brought to a focus by anyone who hopes to organize learning successfully.

Here are some concrete examples to show what the idea means.

* William F. Book and Lee Norvell, "The Will to Learn," *Pedagogical Seminary*, Vol. 29 (1922), pp. 305–362.

† J. F. Dashiell, "A Survey and Synthesis of Learning Theories," *Psychological Bulletin*, Vol. 32 (1935), pp. 261–275.

When an animal is put into a problem box, it is subject to quite a variety of impulses. It may simply lie down and go to sleep. If its master is near by, it may rub against the bars and make an affectionate demonstration. But the point of putting it into the box is to have it start learning how to get out. And so the motives must be manipulated and one made prepotent. This is usually done by seeing to it that the creature is hungry, and placing food outside where it can be seen and smelled. Again, when a human being sits down to go through the arduous and often unpleasant task of building up a conditioned reflex, he also is subject to the pull of motives far more varied than those of the animal in the box. He tends to notice the sights and sounds of the laboratory, the noises in the street, the demeanor and voice of the experimenter, and so on. He may be tempted to think about his future plans or something that has happened in the past, to make up an imaginary conversation, or to play a mental game. He is, so to speak, pulled this way and that, and here is the reason why experiments of this sort often fail. For he must be pulled in just one direction if the conditioned reflex is to appear. But this is very difficult because the conditioning of a reflex is intrinsically boring and even annoying. So all sorts of precautions and special conditions have to be set up—absolute quiet, absolute uniformity, steady lighting, absence of draughts, particular instructions to the subject to banish everything else from his mind. Even then failure is possible and not infrequent. When Pavlov worked with the conditioning of the reflexes of dogs, he found it necessary to confine the animals in special soundproof chambers and to handle them by remote control so that no human presence should set up distracting impulses. And even then the creatures were very apt simply to go to sleep! In a word, the setting of a conditioned reflex experiment must be arranged with the greatest care for the sake of shaping up and focusing the complex of motives on which the success or failure of the undertaking depends.

A very beautiful example of what the shaping up and focusing of motives can mean and do is found in one of the earliest experiments dealing with the more complex types of learning. Although the work was done nearly 50 years ago, the reports are still well worth reading. The task consisted of learning the "telegraphic language," or Morse code. Many of the experimental subjects were novices, but some of them were telegraphers of long experience. These operators however were mediocre. They had been unable to come up to the main-line rate in sending and receiving, and had resigned themselves to secondary branch-line jobs, in some cases for as long as 20 years. In the course of the research every one of these men increased his speed to well over the main-line rate. The experimental conditions operated to mobilize energy and will, and what had been despaired of was now accomplished.

What this impressive body of experimental findings inescapably conveys to the practical teacher is that an essential part of the job of organizing learning is to arouse and mobilize the will to learn. There can be no choice, no alternative. If this is not done, authentic results are impossible. But a great deal more is conveyed as well. It has been shown that the will to learn anything means that a priority has been established among the learner's life motives. He chooses to learn the particular thing in hand rather than to do something else. Now this priority can be established in many ways. The trick can be done after a fashion by pressure, by threats, by hard marking, by using penalties and rewards that have no intrinsic relationship to what is to be learned. But this is not a good way because it does not deeply and positively engage the motives which actuate the learner's living. He prefers to learn his lesson not because he wants to learn it but because he is afraid of unpleasantness, or at the most because he wants a good mark, or a privilege, or a commendation. These are the reasons why he gives up other things he would like to do. But such superficial motivation inevitably leads to superficial learning, to meager meaningfulness, to spurious results. The only kind of motivation which produces authentic results is one in which the task itself grips the learner, and seems to him more worth while than the other alternatives and the other competing choices of his life. Thus the teacher who wishes to succeed must not only be sure that the will to learn is aroused and mobilized. He must also consider very critically how this is being done. As our discussions continue, this crucial practical problem will be more and more clearly defined, and it will be shown that the proper mobilization of the will to learn depends upon the application of certain definite working principles of teaching.

This idea, though not always expressed with precision, is put forward in many ways by many educators. When it is said that pupils should learn in and through life situations, the critical student is conscious of an obvious difficulty. For what possible situation is other than a life situation, including the most formalized of drills, and for that matter the memorizing of nonsense syllables? What is really meant, however, is that anyone learns best when the whole pattern of his life motives is engaged, and this is perfectly true. Again there is the famous assertion that school work should be conducted in terms of wholehearted activity. Once more this means that it should be inte-

grated vitally with the whole scope of life motives and life values. A
third assertion, not infrequently made by progressive educators, is
that learning in school should never be imposed upon the learner by
some authority above or external to him but should always arise out
of his own free choice. Here, it may be, we have a trace of dubious
moralizing, and certainly the supporting claim that imposition and
authority are antipathetic to democracy is open to debate. But if the
proposition means that to tell a person out of hand to learn something
whether he wants to or not is a poor way to get him to want to do so,
and a good way to make the learning meaningless to him, then it
makes excellent sense. Instead of speaking of the will to learn, it
would be better to speak of willingness to learn or eagerness to learn,
and this means that the impulse to deal with the task must be a
mobilizing, a harnessing, a shaping up of life motives. And learning
is meaningful in proportion to the depth, power, and authenticity of the
life motives and life values which are engaged.[2]

This discussion of purpose may be brought to a head by applying
what has been said to the question of home study. A survey of the
amount of study done by 3,017 pupils in the Los Angeles schools showed
that on a daily basis 7 per cent did none, 12 per cent spent 15 minutes,
20 per cent spent half an hour, 16 per cent spent 45 minutes which was
the median, 17 per cent spent an hour, 14 per cent spent an hour and a
half, 12 per cent spent two hours, and 2 per cent spent more than two
hours. It is obvious that under these limiting conditions high achievement cannot be expected. What, then, to do about it? The way
toward an answer is to find out why pupils study so little, and this too
has been undertaken. Reasons given are that they fail to realize the
importance of schoolwork, that they feel permanent retention to be
impossible, that they are grade-minded, that they believe schoolwork
lacks value, that they have a general defeatist attitude. Now all this
boils down to just one thing. Schoolwork and school study have no
commanding place in the scheme of life motives and life values which
actuate these young people. Suggestions that they be reasoned with
and preached to, and that examples of successful men who worked hard
in school be held up before them are nothing better than preposterous.
A learning task convinces and attracts by its own intrinsic and manifest worth, or it never does so at all. The solution of the "problem"
of study so well revealed in these figures is not to pile on assignments
(which will surely be dodged or sabotaged) nor to scold and punish or
lecture and exhort. It is to organize learning in such a way as to get
a grip on the motives and impulses of the learner, which implies also
that it becomes richly meaningful to him.[3]

## LEARNING AS EXPLORATION AND DISCOVERY

Learning achieves authentic results by a process of exploration and discovery. It starts with the desire to reach a solution. It proceeds by an experimental, intelligible, varied attack in the endeavour to achieve the wished-for solution.

One of the most important things to remember in organizing learning is that it is not caused by brute repetition. There are abundant and convincing reasons in support of this proposition. (1) Nobody ever learns any skill or ability without making more wrong tries than right ones, except in the most unusual cases. If repetition were the cause of learning, surely the errors would be learned and the successes would not be. (2) The possibility of learning by what is called "negative practice" has been demonstrated. To mention one specific case, the persistent tendency to typewrite "hte" instead of "the" has been overcome by deliberately practicing "hte" instead of practicing the word in the right way. (3) There is not the least doubt that adjustments can be learned in one single experience. A person need only be laughed at once for a social gaff to get the point. He need only enjoy a view, or a poem, or a picture, or a piece of music once to remember it and wish to experience it again. (4) Lastly it is clear that a great deal of repetition goes on without producing any learning at all. Penmanship is a very good example, but there are plenty of others from everyday life. Indeed it has been shown experimentally that the degree of learning achieved has surprisingly little relationship to the number of repetitions.

Learning, then, is an affair of discovering and seeing the point that one wants to discover and see. What this means when applied to practical organization may be seen from the following instances. A supervisor reports as follows:

I've just come from the Dalke School. There one class is making a book to exchange with another school with whom they are corresponding, and I was interested in what I saw happening. One girl came up to the teacher with a beautifully spaced, neatly written page. "It took three rewritings to get that decent!" she exclaimed. The exclamation was triumphant in tone. "What do you think of this word?" asked another child as she pointed to a sentence. "I've tried five other words but I think I like this one best."*

One teacher of foreign languages said to his students, "Every time you look up a word in the dictionary in the back part of your reader, put a pencil dot before the word you look up!" The result is easily imagined. The keen

* Inga Olla Helseth, *Living in the Classroom*, p. 185, Edwards Bros., Inc., Ann Arbor, Mich., 1939.

student when he saw the dots accumulating before any word promptly memorized that word to save time. Similarly a child who needs a skill again and again in activities which he thinks of himself as continuing to do, masters those skills as he uses them. A second grade child who is handling money in the classroom community bank will insist on subtracting correctly as each case comes before him. A child who has seen that in the encyclopaedia can be found answers to his questions will gladly be shown how to use the encyclopaedia effectively as he proceeds to hunt information on item after item which challenges him personally. The little child learns the words he wishes to use in letters to Daddy who is a "travelling man." As he uses them, the facts of the multiplication combinations may be memorized willingly by a child who uses them often in play activities. This has proved to be done frequently even though the child knew that he could have the multiplication tables on hand for reference.*

A person improves his English style when he urgently wants to say something, and then goes experimentally to work to discover how to say it as clearly and satisfactorily as possible. A person strengthens his grasp of history when he has in mind some urgent problem, and proceeds to collect, collate, and winnow historical information and ideas bearing upon it. A person deepens his understanding of science or mathematics when he is confronted with some urgent challenge and delves into the resources of science or mathematics in order to meet it. The best learning anyone ever does is accomplished by exploration and discovery under the urge of strong desire.

All this is in contrast with the demonstrated futility of meaningless grind. One of the earliest educational demonstrations established it in connection with spelling. Spelling tests were given to about thirty thousand children from schools in many parts of the country, and it was found that pupils who were drilled in the subject for 50 minutes a day did no better than those who spent only ten minutes a day on it. By way of a more general demonstration, it has been shown again and again that children who are compelled to repeat a grade in the elementary school commonly do very little if at all better the second time. This calls to mind the investigation of American history previously mentioned, where three traverses of the same territory produced less than 50 per cent learning. The *New York Times* history exposé certainly revealed a disastrous state of affairs, but anyone who thinks it can be cured simply by more and harder pounding is deceiving himself and flying in the face of all the evidence. It is entirely unsound to organize learning simply for the sake of bringing about more repetition, for instance by setting up frequent reviews, or by trying to make children put in more time going over and over their assignments.[4]

* *Ibid.*, p. 192.

The real answer is to organize every job of learning as a meaningful undertaking. This is always what promises authentic and lasting results. Two thousand seven hundred and eighty-nine pupils from the seventh to the twelfth grade were given selections of prose which, although highly factual, were nevertheless interesting. They read these selections only once, which corresponds pretty well to the average home study procedure, after which they were given tests covering all essential content. After an interval of 30 days they were able to remember 52 per cent of the material, which is just about as much as is commonly retained one day after a series of nonsense syllables has been learned. Again, in the study of substance memorization to which reference has already been made, and in which there was perfect retention after 70 days, it was found that one single reading gave just as good and lasting a grasp of the meaning of the passages as did four readings. Finally, to move to quite a different sphere, exactly the same thing has been demonstrated in connection with music. It was found that some people took ten to twelve repetitions to memorize a musical theme, whereas others memorized it in one or two tries. The former memorized it note by note. The latter grasped it immediately as an interesting and intelligible whole, to be reshaped and corrected on a second hearing.

The evidence that meaning rather than repetition is the root cause of learning is nothing less than overwhelming. It is amazing that anyone who undertakes to teach, or has any interest in the proper management of teaching should not be aware of the proposition, or should doubt it for an instant. To insist on relying on drudge repetition in the quest for results is deliberately to fly in the face of some of the most positive psychological knowledge we possess.

This does not mean that hard work is needless, or that the sort of "once-over" preparation which is so characteristic of the study processes of many pupils is defensible. But the way to produce hard work that pays dividends in authentic results is not to increase pressure or amount but to change the whole mode of approach. A high-school pupil who reads over his history assignment just once and then quits, does so because he simply has no notion what to do if he reads it over again. So far as he is concerned it is just a matter of repeating and spending more time. There is no sense of a need for exploration, for becoming aware of relationships and refinements that were not apparent at a first survey. A college student who announces rather proudly that he can never revise a piece of written English is simply unaware of the problem of expressing oneself in the medium of language. To make him rewrite the job will get nowhere, for he will not know what to do about it.    What has to be done is to set up a challenge which demands the best possible expression, and which issues in urgent experimentation to achieve it.    There is nothing in our conception of learning which disallows hard work or long hours of toil.    In fact the clarification of meaning and the achievement of purpose call for a more exacting tax of effort than any meaningless drudgery.

Nor does anything that has been said in any way indicate that drill is either needless or improper.    What is not only needless but futile is drill divorced from purpose and lacking all the quality of exploration.    For the proper management of drill the following conditions are paramount.    (1) The learner himself must have a conscious desire and a conscious need for drill.    He must himself be aware that he lacks a certain skill or efficiency, and wish to achieve it.    (2) Drill should be set up not at the beginning of a unit or job of learning but far enough along so that the learner can be aware of what it is about, what it may be expected to do for him, and why it is a valuable tonic. (3) Since the intention of drill is to make a skill facile, smooth-running, and usable, and since the learner himself should be aware of this, it should be conducted in a brisk businesslike manner.    (4) It is always important that drill on any skill or ability should be in the exact form in which it is to be used.    The maintenance of the right pattern of response and the prevention of sloppiness are primary considerations. (5) At the end of a drill period there should always be reflection, self-criticism, self-assessment, and reorientation.    (6) Every effort should be made to have drill become increasingly self-chosen and self-directed by the learner.    In a word, drill should never be a languid, meaningless, pointless routine.    It should be—and if it is to be effective it must be—an exemplification of the purposeful process of exploration and discovery which is characteristic of all good learning.    For learning is not a process in which a set pathway is worn smooth, but rather one in which a terrain is explored until the best pathway is discovered.[5]

## ACHIEVEMENT AS UNDERSTANDING

Whenever learning goes effectively and really succeeds, its outcome is control brought about by understanding, or insight, or intelligible response.    It begins with a situation at once baffling and challenging. It proceeds with an experimental search for the right clue.    It culminates in a discovery of the right clue, a grasp of the essential meaning, a control of the situation, and hence a fulfillment of the actuating purpose.

As an illustration, consider what skill in tennis means.    The ball is in play, going over the net towards your opponent.    This means that your stroke has come off, but any feeling of exultation must be throttled down for it may throw you off your balance. Your opponent begins to run long before the ball touches the ground, and you yourself must begin to react at once to anticipate what he intends to do. The angle at which the ball is traveling indicates that he will be able to return it on his forehand, and he has a powerful forehand drive. This thought produces in you a tensing of the muscles, a special preparation, a qualm of anxiety, but again these must not be overdone. Then you perceive that a cross wind has altered its flight, so that he will not be in a position for a strong cross-court shot, and your physical, mental, and emotional preparation alters. He returns it with a high lob, and you set yourself and determine to keep cool while it soars through the air. So it goes. Clearly your success depends on picking out the key elements, the significant and determining elements in a complex and shifting situation. Skill in tennis actually consists of selective intelligence, or understanding, or insight in action. This is what you must acquire if your are to learn the game properly.

The contrasting and erroneous view of the nature of learning is that it is the establishment of a unique connection between an isolated stimulus and an isolated response. This would mean that in order to learn tennis all you would have to do would be to pick out the sight of the ball as an isolated stimulus, and then, as though a button were pressed, start a stereotyped series of movements. Of course, as everyone knows, such a state of things could never occur. One could never narrow down to the sight of the ball completely out of context, or respond with the same stereotyped stroke every time. It can be very roughly and remotely approximated by hitting a tennis ball against a wall, or by having a coach feed one shots all at the same angle. Work of this kind has its value, but only as a contribution to the altogether necessary ability to size up and respond to the moving situation on the court in a properly selective and meaningful manner.

It is doubtful whether any competent psychologist today would claim that the essential characteristic of learning is the mechanical establishment of connections between isolated stimuli and isolated responses. Such views have been maintained in the past, and in particular they have been attributed to Professor E. L. Thorndike. But years of added reflection and experimentation have revealed their fundamental inadequacy, and those who used to support them have changed their opinions. It has, however, been claimed recently that there are two quite different types or modes of learning, one consisting of connection-forming by sheer repetition, the other involving the higher mental processes, and having the character already described.

Animal learning, it is said, belongs to the former type, and characteristic human learning to the latter, although human beings also can
utilize the former type.   This would imply that there are properly two
basic modes for the organization of learning, one centering on isolated
drill and repetition, the other on the quest for meaning.   But this
distinction cannot be maintained in the face of obtained psychological
data.   Even the most artificial animal learning, even the most isolated
drill, even the conditioning of a reflex must have some glimmer of
meaning, or there will be no progress at all.   There are not two
kinds of learning, but only one kind, with its conditions more or
less well fulfilled.   There is not meaningful learning on the one hand
and meaningless learning on the other.   There is only learning more or
less meaningful, and so more or less excellent, successful, resultful.[6]

The point is of basic importance.   It implies that there are not certain portions of a subject—its fundamentals, or elements, or rudiments
—that must be learned as sheer routine before understanding and the
higher mental processes are brought to bear.   Rather what is required
is that all learning, right down to the most rudimentary, be conducted
in meaningful situations and pointed towards results in terms of understanding, insight, and the clarification of meaning.   This is the only
foundation for a successful organization.   Just what it involves may
be seen clearly from the following illustrations.

1. It has been long and widely believed that the routine study of
grammar is necessary as a basis for English expression, and that it will
improve English expression.   Evidence against this proposition, however, has piled up to a point where it must be considered overwhelming
and decisive.   It has been pointed out that a person approaches language study properly only when he is considering in one way or another
what he wants to say.   So the study of the structure of language should
be organized to aid him directly in saying better what he wants to say.

Thus instead of dealing with coordinate and subordinate clauses,
the emphasis shifts to the clear statement of thought.   A sentence
turned in by a pupil is placed on the board: "Mary plays a good game
of tennis and she makes excellent cake."   The class recognizes that
this is poor because the two statements are not related.   They suggest
that if the second statement ran "and she is also a good sportsman,"
the statement would be acceptable.   Again, instead of dealing with the
abstract technicalities of types of phrases—prepositional, appositive,
participial, gerundive—the emphasis should be on the combination of
ideas.   Three statements such as, "Mr. W. is our adviser.   He grasped
the seriousness of the situation.   He immediately called a meeting
of the officers," are obviously jerky and poorly graded, and the problem

is to reshape them in order to bring out their nuances of interrelationship. Again, instead of dealing with the concept of the sentence in terms of subject, predicate, and completeness of statement, the treatment can emphasize clarity and completeness in expressing ideas. Pupils are asked whether certain words leave one "up in the air," what is left out, and so forth. Thus the essentials of grammar are still taught, but they are placed in a meaningful setting and situation. There is a wish to say something, a process of exploration in discovering how to do so, and the culmination is an insight into the structure of language which brings the situation under control and the purpose to fulfillment.[7]

2. The teaching of punctuation, again, used to be organized as a process of memorizing numerous rules, some of the older books containing more than 150 of them. Usually it was very badly learned. Modern textbooks have reduced the rules to some 20, but this is still too much, and punctuation is still very badly learned. The key idea for reorganization is that punctuation is a system of symbols aiming to help the reader grasp the meaning, and that these symbols need indicate only three relationships—equality, dependence, and independence. Thus in the sentence, "If the hot weather continues there will be no crop," a comma is needed after "continues." The rule books say this is because the "if" clause is an introducing adverbial modifier; yet we have exactly such a clause in the sentence, "When we got to the mountains Dad let me drive," and no comma is needed. The need for a comma in the former sentence is that the reader needs to be shown where the break in the sense occurs. Again, a "loose modifier" must be set off by commas, not because it is an appositive or participial or prepositional phrase or a nonrestrictive relative clause or an adjectival phrase, as once more the rule books say, but simply because it introduces a needed delay in the forward movement of the sentence. The loose modifier in "My uncle, a great lover of horses, never fails to go to the Kentucky Derby," cries aloud to be set off by commas. So too, commas are needed between the parts of a compound sentence, not to conform to a rule but to avoid confusing adhesions. "Water lilies were floating in the spring and summer bunch berries reddened the overhanging knoll," needs a comma. "Prissy and Ivy made the beds and did the dishes," does not. Only three rules are needed in practical, *i.e.*, meaningful, punctuation. "(a) Separate sentences by periods, and use a comma or an 'and' to connect items working together in lists of two or more things. (b) If two statements combine in one sentence, use 'and,' 'but,' 'yet,' 'or,' 'nor,' etc., and a comma to prevent misreading. (c) Use a comma or a pair of commas to warn the reader of a

turn of thought." Thus here again we see that the outcome of a proper teaching and learning of punctuation is not a knowledge of routine rules but a comprehension of language relationships which enables one to control language situations.[8]

3. A chief reason why arithmetic is the "problem subject" in the grades is that the basic operations are organized as sets of unintelligible facts to be memorized by rote. Pupils are set to learn the hundred so-called "addition facts" as unintelligible data, and great care is taken to see that the learning is routine rather than meaningful. The order of learning is deliberately jumbled to avoid possibilities of inference. Thus $8 + 5$ and $8 + 6$ are not taught in sequence, because each is supposed to be memorized independently of the other. Again, if it turns out that a pupil has forgotten one of the addition facts, pains are taken to prevent his getting the answer by counting or figuring it out in his head. But this is basically unsound. Such a statement as $7 + 5 = 12$ is not really a fact at all. It is a generalization bringing together a whole mass of concrete experience and experimentation, and should be grasped as such. Present the pupil, for instance, with two groups of objects, one containing seven things and the other five. Let him take from the latter and add them to the former till he reaches ten. Then he discovers that $7 + 5$ is the same as $10 + 2$, each amounting to 12, and advances at least one step towards the clarification of numerical relationships as a technique for the control of experience. If anyone wants a concrete demonstration of the fallacy of believing that routine learning can be good of its kind and can provide a good basis for later meaningful learning, the disastrous results of arithmetic teaching which has built this belief into the texture of its organization should be sufficiently convincing.[9]

4. The same holds true of algebra. As so often happens, the trouble with this subject usually starts right at the beginning. Pupils never quite get through their heads the significance of using variable expressions such as $x$, $y$, and $z$. They are taught that these are unknown quantities which must always be translated into arithmetical terms, instead of concepts by means of which thinking can be made more systematic and powerful. They are given all sorts of rules for manipulating these alleged unknown quantities which they never really understand, and accordingly they handle them by pure routine. In algebra, as in all learning, the outcome must be comprehension if it is to be stable and effective.[10]

5. Science, again, should be organized not as a collection of facts and abstract formulations to be learned by routine, but rather in terms of cultivating the power to observe, to draw inferences from data, and

to grasp and apply concepts. The claim, sometimes put forward, that only children of superior intelligence are capable of a genuinely scientific mode of thought is not borne out by recent investigations. To be sure, the abler the individual the better he can think, and the more widely cognizant of meanings he can become. But even a young or a mediocre child must learn science in terms of understanding and insight or he will not learn it at all.[11]

6. The whole persistent problem of the organization of meaningful learning comes to a crux in connection with reading, which bulks so large in school study. The following sentences occur in a textbook description of colonial home life: "The big fireplace would be among the first things to attract attention. Above it, resting on the shelf or mantel, would be seen a candle, a clock, and one or two of the housewife's most beautiful plates. Within the fireplace, fastened to one side, would be the crane upon which a kettle was hanging over the blaze." This is an obviously inviting and concrete piece of writing, and one would think it readily understandable. But when a group of high-school students who had read it were asked to make sketches of their impression, no two of them agreed even on important items; only a few of the essentials were uniformly correct—the crane turned out to be a bird and the clock a "Big Ben." These students seemed to understand. Probably they thought they understood. But in fact they did not, and thus their learning was ineffective.

This immediately explains many failures in learning and teaching. It explains why a group of rural school teachers thought the United States Minister to China was a Presbyterian clergyman or a Catholic priest, and had equally fanciful notions in many other fields. It explains why only about half of 337 eighth graders knew that New York City is at the mouth of the Hudson, while 41 of them thought that the Pacific Ocean is the eastern boundary of the United States. It explains why more than a quarter of 1,264 college students, when asked to identify states on a blank map, could not recognize Vermont, Maryland, Arkansas, Connecticut, Kentucky, Arizona, West Virginia, Mississippi, Rhode Island, Oklahoma, Louisiana, New Mexico, Massachusetts, Alabama, and Wisconsin. These people had read about these matters many times. But they had never really grasped them in the only way anybody ever really grasps anything, and that is with their minds.

The first thought would be to make students work harder and longer, to drill with more precision and more energy, to test more frequently and more scrupulously, to grade more parsimoniously. Such measures alone are very unlikely to produce appreciably better learning, although hard work and precision most certainly have their place. For instance, it has been shown that children may be able to recite definitions of capes, bays, peninsulas, inlets, and so on, and to do so quite well, but still be unable to identify these geographical phenomena on a relief map. Why, then, merely try to make them recite a little better? To be sure, one cannot learn well without hard work. Grind, no doubt, is necessary. But it is also necessary to have something to grind at besides mere words. The only grinding process worth anything is one that progressively reveals the clarity and luster of the jewel called meaning.

Reading, in fact, is essentially a process of reasoning, and must be treated as such if it is to go effectively. The constant direction of effort must be towards understanding, not towards memorization. As one reads, and as one learns, it is necessary to be sure that one comprehends. For comprehension, insight, understanding, intelligible response is always the desired outcome of learning that is organized as it ought to be.[12]

## GOOD LEARNING TRANSFERS

Whenever learning in one context or situation affects learning in another context or situation, transfer of training is said to take place. The phrase has become fixed in educational literature and will be used here, although it is a bad one, since the word "training" has a much narrower connotation than the word "learning." But what is worse than any defective phraseology is the extreme narrowness with which the problem and significance of transfer is ordinarily discussed. Usually it is supposed to have to do simply with the effect of one school subject on another—the influence of Latin on English or French, of grammar on composition, of algebra on geometry, of geometry on formal logic, and so forth. This greatly obscures the importance of the whole question, which is fundamental in connection with the organization of learning. For all good learning transfers. One never practices hitting a golf ball at a net, or memorizes a recipe from a cookbook, or studies the grammatical structure of a foreign language, or works at logarithms, or indeed undertakes any job of learning without at least the hope that what one acquires in practice will be usable in some new and different situation. If this usability, this applicability, actually appears, one concludes that practice has to some extent succeeded. If not, then practice has failed. Transfer is always the hope of learning, and when learning is well organized it takes place.

The simplest and most everyday illustrations readily make clear how fundamental the problem is for the work of the teacher. Consider, for instance, the following.

A friend of mine, visiting a school, was asked to examine a young class in geography. She said, "Suppose you should dig a hole in the ground hundreds of feet deep, how should you find it at the bottom—warmer or colder than on top?" None of the class replying, the teacher said: "I'm sure they know, but I think you don't ask the question quite rightly. Let me try." So taking the book, she asked: "In what condition is the interior of the globe?" and received the immediate answer from half the class at once: "The interior of the globe is in a condition of igneous fusion."*

In other words, the visitor raised the issue of transfer and demonstrated that it had not taken place, and the learning stood condemned. Always the failure of transfer means the failure of learning. This happens when the date 1812 does not connect the Anglo-American war with the simultaneously occurring invasion of Russia by Napoleon; when a class in algebra can handle a problem expressed in $xyz$ but cannot handle it when expressed in $pqr$; when a pupil can recite a geometrical theorem so long as the triangle concerned is called $ABC$ but not when it is called $XYZ$; when a child can display a recitation knowledge of a principle of grammar but fails to employ it when he writes a theme; when a pupil demonstrates that he has memorized the salient facts about the dictatorship of Sulla but has not the slightest notion of their relevance to the career of Mussolini. These may be regarded as failures either of transfer or of effective learning, for here are simply two ways of looking at the same thing. As a matter of fact, too, the meager amount of transfer continually found between even closely related school subjects is once again a sweeping demonstration that learning is not going as it should. When algebra only helps a little with physics, when Latin only helps a little with French, when grammar only helps a little with English composition—and all these propositions have been amply demonstrated—then the only possible conclusion is that learning in algebra and Latin and grammar is badly organized and ineffective. Algebra ought to help with physics, Latin ought to help with French, grammar ought to help with English composition—and to help not a little but a great deal. Why then do they not? Surely because we partition off these studies as separate subjects or courses. We organize learning in narrow subdivisions and then feel nonplussed when the consequence is narrow and relatively inapplicable achievement, and results are shown to be spurious.

* William James, *Talks to Teachers*, p. 150, Henry Holt and Company, Inc., New York, 1899.

As so often happens, there is substantial agreement among psychologists as to what conditions are necessary to bring about transfer, in spite of seemingly different terminologies.   Some have insisted that transfer requires the presence of "identical elements" in the two situations; elements in common, for instance, between Latin and French, or algebra and physics, or grammar and composition.   This of course is quite true as far as it goes.   If it were possible to devise two sequences of learning which had absolutely nothing in common, not even the basic techniques and patterns of the learning process itself, it would be incredible that one of them could affect the other in any way.   But the mere existence of identical elements is very far from guaranteeing that transfer will actually take place.   These identities must also be perceived and understood, and so another school of psychologists has insisted that transfer is brought about by generalization.   One must grasp the general meaning of Latin if it is to carry over to French or to anything else.   So also with algebra, with grammar, or with any other study.   Why these two accounts should ever have been thought conflicting is something of a puzzle.   Presumably we have to thank metaphysically minded mischief-makers who are more interested in digging up extreme statements on either side and exhibiting them out of context than in a constructive analysis helpful to practical persons.

The simple truth is that transfer depends upon identical elements that are comprehended; that is, upon meaning.   Meaningful learning, as we have seen, is learning which begins when the learner urgently wants to get hold of a situation and proceeds to do so by a process of clarification and understanding.   And the more meaningful the learning, the more apparent and widely ramifying are its implications.   This is simply another way of saying that the more meaningful the learning the more widely and certainly it transfers.   The children who could not tell whether the bottom of a deep hole would be hotter or cooler than the top had first of all never really cared about what "igneous fusion" meant, and secondly had never really understood what it meant, the two failures going together.   The pupils who enter first-year physics and seem to have utterly forgotten their previous algebra, because of the novel terminology and symbolism of the new subject, never had a real urge to grapple with algebra and so never really understood it, so that at the best they acquired a parrotlike routine command of its techniques.

This piece of alleged English was turned in by a student as a translation of a Latin passage.   "L. Lucullus was able to remedy a part of this grave war and disaster by your united order part of the army was sent away and part handed over to M. Glabrio because you follow the manner shown by the example."* It is obvious that convulsive efforts of this kind cannot by any stretch of the imagination help a person's English style, in spite of the alleged beneficent influence of Latin upon the use of English. But the real point is that nobody would turn out such gibberish if he were studying Latin with a real urge and coming to understand what he was learning.

All such failures of transfer, then, are due to a defective organization of learning, an organization which continually stresses routine memorization rather than vital comprehension, and which ignores the vital consideration of the engagement of the learner's motives. One does not come to comprehend a geometrical theorem, or a scientific principle, or a grammatical rule by learning it off by heart and reciting it on the following day. One comprehends it only by urgently seeking for and grasping its implied relationships to other theorems and principles and rules, and its applications to actual concrete instances and experiences. One does not comprehend Latin by hacking out translations good enough to win a passing mark from a teacher who must pass 90 per cent of the class or lose his job. One comes to understand Latin or any other language when one runs into statements in it or wants to use it for statements of one's own which it is necessary to grasp or to make correctly. And as to drill, whether on a mental or a physical skill, exactly the same principle holds true. As a blind routine it is exceedingly ineffective for the reason that it does not yield transfer, i.e., it does not really help in acquiring the contemplated skill. But as a consciously selected procedure pointed towards the achievement of a desired goal and integrally related to it, drill is both highly valuable and altogether indispensable.[13]

Certain words of Horace Mann, written some hundred years ago, are well worth the thoughtful attention of every modern teacher.

All pupils of average ability who have been properly taught should have a command, not merely of the particular fact, or the general statement of a truth or principle, but also of its connection, relations, and applications. This is the circumstance which gives pertinency and significance to their distinctive appellation—textbooks. They are books containing texts. These texts the teacher is to expound. Each one of them should be the foundation of a discourse or a series of discourses. This is teaching. Hearing recitations from a book is not teaching. It is the exposition of the principle contained in the book; showing its connection with life, with action, with duty; making it the nucleus around which to gather all related facts and all collateral principles—

* George R. Miller and Thomas H. Briggs, "The Effect of Latin on English Translations," *School Review*, Vol. 31 (1923), pp. 256–262.

it is this, and this only, which can appropriately be called teaching. All short of this is mere journey-work, rude mechanical labor and drudgery.*

Horace Mann's confidence in "exposition" indicates a very imperfect realization of the difficulties of the problem of organizing meaningful learning, but his statement of the issue is admirable.

Modern teachers, too, recognize the paramount importance of the problem. Indeed, no teacher can think seriously about his work without coming face to face with it. Fourteen hundred and seventeen teachers of history, responding to a check list of 71 classroom difficulties in handling the subject, rate failure to think very high, and find as their chief complaint that pupils try to remember rather than to understand, that they merely accept the words of the textbook, and that they neglect to collate and compare events, persons, and causes.

That the problem, although cogent, is found baffling perhaps hardly needs demonstration, yet the following reported response throws the point into high and interesting relief.

Science courses commonly include as one of the major objectives, "the ability to do scientific thinking." Twenty-six teachers visited were asked the question, How do you train pupils to do scientific thinking? The answers were of four types: (1) the study of science results automatically in this ability because of the nature of the subject matter of science; (2) it is not possible to train a pupil to think; (3) we had a lesson on that last week, or we will have a lesson on that next week; (4) the pupils learn the method by watching the procedure of the teacher.

Thus we see that although the problem is urgent and indeed fundamental, and although it is well recognized as such, many teachers seem at a loss to handle it. To organize meaningful learning is the basis of all successful teaching, and we are now to turn to the working principles on which that organization depends.[14]

### Notes and References

*General References*

Edward L. Thorndike, "Education for Initiative and Originality," *Teachers College Record*, Vol. 17 (1916), pp. 405–416, will be found well worth careful consideration. James L. Mursell, *The Psychology of Secondary School Teaching*, Chap. 2, "The Learning Process" and Chap. 3, "The Controls and Conditions of Learning and Their Application to Instruction," W. W. Norton & Company, Inc., New York, rev. ed., 1939, presents a fuller analysis of learning.

*References in the Text*

1. Besides the study by Book and Norvell referred to in the text, the following investigations dealing with the will to learn will be found instructive: William F.

* Otis W. Caldwell and Stuart A. Courtis, *Then and Now in Education*, p. 18, World Book Company, Yonkers-on-Hudson, N.Y., 1924.

Book, "How to Develop Interest in One's Tasks and Work," *Journal of Educational Psychology*, Vol. 18 (1927), pp. 1–10; F. B. Knight and H. H. Remmers, "Fluctuations in Mental Production When Motivation Is the Main Variable," *Journal of Applied Psychology*, Vol. 7 (1923), pp. 209–223; Percival M. Symonds, "Practice vs. Motivation," *Journal of Educational Psychology*, Vol. 20 (1929), pp. 19–35.

2. For a forceful critique of "authoritarianism" and "imposition" in education see E. Thomas Hopkins, *Interaction*, D. C. Heath and Company, Boston, 1941. Chapter 4 will be found particularly repaying.

3. Data on amount of home study cited are by Louis T. Jones, "The Problem of Home Study," *California Journal of Secondary Education*, Vol. 11 (1936), pp. 448–451. Jones' findings are discussed together with the problem in general by Robert W. Frederick, Clarence E. Ragsdale, and Rachel Salisbury, *Directing Learning*, D. Appleton-Century Company, Inc., New York, 1938.

4. The general issue of repetition as a cause of learning is discussed by James L. Mursell, *The Psychology of Secondary School Teaching*, rev. ed., pp. 71–75, W. W. Norton & Company, Inc., New York, 1939. Its true role and meaning is most illuminatingly considered by E. P. Guthrie, "Conditioning: A Theory of Learning in Terms of Stimulus, Response, and Association," *National Society for the Study of Education: 41st Yearbook*, Part I, Chap. 1, 1942. The spelling investigation is by J. M. Rice, "The Futility of the Spelling Grind, *Forum*, Vol. 23 (1897), pp. 163–172, 409–419. The report caused a furore when it first appeared, and is still worth reading. An excellent source of material on the effects of grade repetition is Hollis L. Caswell, *Education in the Elementary School*, pp. 248–260, American Book Company, New York, 1942.

5. The study of the effect of a single reading is A. G. Dietze and George Ellis Jones, "Factual Memory of Secondary School Pupils for a Short Article Which They Read a Single Time," *Journal of Educational Psychology*, Vol. 22 (1931), pp. 586–598. The investigation of musical memory is Kate Gordon, "Some Tests on the Memorizing of Musical Themes," *Journal of Experimental Psychology*, Vol. 2 (1917), pp. 93–99. For a discussion of drill closely related to yet somewhat differing from that here presented see Inga Olla Helseth, *Living in the Classroom*, pp. 204–205, Edwards Bros., Inc., Ann Arbor, Mich., 1939.

6. For an authoritative presentation of the true "connectionist" position see Arthur I. Gates, "Connectionism: Present Concepts and Interpretations," *National Society for the Study of Education: 41st Yearbook*, Part I, Chap. 4, 1942.

7. For a fuller account of the reorganization of grammar along the lines indicated see Ellen Frogner, "Grammar Approach versus Thought Approach in Teaching Sentence Structure," *English Journal*, Vol. 28 (1939), pp. 518–526.

8. For a fuller account of the reorganization of punctuation see Rachel Salisbury, "The Psychology of Punctuation," *English Journal*, Vol. 28 (1939) pp. 794–806.

9. The reorganization of arithmetic in terms of meaningful learning is treated by William A. Brownell, "Psychological Considerations in the Learning and Teaching of Arithmetic," *National Council of Teachers of Mathematics: 10th Yearbook*, pp. 1–31, 1935; also much more elaborately in his *The Development of Children's Number Ideas in the Primary Grades*, University of Chicago Press, Chicago, 1928.

10. For an admirable discussion of alleged lower and higher types of learning with specific reference to algebra see E. L. Thorndike, "The Abilities Involved in Algebraic Computation and in Problem Solving," *School and Society*, Vol. 15 (1922), pp. 191–193. The meaningful treatment of algebraic processes, including addition, is treated by John P. Everett, *Fundamental Skills of Algebra*, Teachers College,

Columbia University, Bureau of Publications, New York, 1928. This study has had considerable influence on teaching.

11. The pessimistic view of science teaching is presented by M. Louise Nichols, "The High School Student and Scientific Method," *Journal of Educational Psychology*, Vol. 20 (1929), pp. 196–204. Of particular value in this article is the description of how scientific thinking can be taught to those the author believes able to learn it.

12. For the inability of pupils to identify geographical phenomona see T. J. Eskridge, *Growth in Understanding of Geographic Terms in Grades IV to VI*, Duke University Press, Durham, N.C., 1939. Two very repaying articles dealing with reading as analogous to reasoning and problem solving, both by E. L. Thorndike, are "The Psychology of Thinking in the Case of Reasoning," *Psychological Review*, Vol. 24 (1916), pp. 220–234, and "Reading as Reasoning: A Study of Mistakes in Paragraph Reading," *Journal of Educational Psychology*, Vol. 8 (1917), pp. 323–332.

13. For general discussions of transfer see Pedro Tamesis Orata, *The Theory of Identical Elements*, Ohio State University Press, Columbus, Ohio, 1928; also his "Transfer of Training and Educational Pseudo-Science," *Mathematics Teacher*, Vol. 27 (1935), pp. 265–289. A very suggestive and interesting article is E. L. Thorndike, "The Effect of Changed Data upon Reasoning," *Journal of Experimental Psychology*, Vol. 5 (1922), pp. 33–38.

14. The study of difficulties in history teaching, which well repays reading, is Franklyn P. Wirth, "Classroom Difficulties in the Teaching of History," *Historical Outlook*, Vol. 22 (1931), pp. 115–118. The statement on the teaching of scientific thinking is from Wilbur L. Beauchamp, *Instruction in Science*, National Survey of Secondary Education Monograph No. 22, U.S. Office of Education Bulletin No. 17, p. 57. The entire discussion is important.

For those who wish to make a broad though perhaps somewhat technical comparison between the position on learning here defended with others, a study of Charles H. Judd, *Education as Cultivation of the Higher Mental Processes*, The Macmillan Company, New York, 1936, will be profitable. Judd argues for the recognition of two kinds of learning—routine and meaningful. His contentions should be compared with those of Dashiell and the authors of the *National Society for the Study of Education: 41st Yearbook*, to which frequent references have already been made.

### Items for Discussion and Study

1. Make as realistic an appraisal as you can of the actual motives which have led some student you know (possibly yourself) to study some given assignment. To what extent were deep and controlling "life motives" involved?

2. Contrast the kind of learning that goes on in the following situations: (a) A football squad learning a new play. (b) A soldier learning to advance under fire with maximum effectiveness. (c) A high-school student studying the origins of the Constitution. Could the differences be described as differences in meaningfulness?

3. Granted that many high-school students spend little time in study and that this makes good achievement impossible, would the best way to increase the effectiveness of learning be simply to require them to spend more time?

4. What is the real meaning of the proposition that learning goes on best in "life situations"? Why is the expression confusing?

5. Progressive educators often insist that tasks should not be "imposed" on pupils. Discuss. Can you find both truth and error in the claim?

6. What commonly accepted practices for the raising of standards are clearly invalid if repetition is not a cause of learning? Does this imply that hard work can be eliminated without disadvantage?

7. Describe and discuss promising measures for raising standards of achievement in various subjects, and for getting better results in the light of the proposition that effective learning is always the emergence of understanding.

8. What is the relationship between the idea that repetition causes learning and the conception of learning as the connecting of a response with a stimulus?

9. Show by concrete illustrations from your own experience that "all good learning transfers," and that we always practice for transfer.

10. What does the meagerness of transfer between school subjects indicate?

11. How does the conception of meaningful learning reconcile the two theories of transfer as due to identical elements and to generalization?

12. In what way is motivation a factor in producing transfer? Consider some practical implications for teaching.

13. How do learning situations such as those described under heading 2, Chap. 3 (pp. 53–54), favor transfer?

14. Why is Horace Mann's confidence in exposition in the citation on p. 73 ill-founded? What substitutes would you suggest?

# CHAPTER 5

## THE PRINCIPLE OF CONTEXT AND THE ORGANIZATION OF LEARNING

### THE PRINCIPLE OF CONTEXT

A boy studying the unit Parallel and Perpendicular Lines in plane geometry was meeting with little success. He was unable to solve the problems assigned. He was unable to develop proofs. It seemed that the materials in the text were not real to him. They were removed from his sphere of interest. He had a poor record in other classes. He bore the stamp of school failure and had difficulty in keeping his name on the eligibility list for football. Teachers spoke of his lack of intelligence and interest in school. This boy was told that he might select his own materials for study and that he would receive credit for all work done, whether indicated in the assignment outlined for the class or not. The only requirement was that his work must be focused on an understanding of parallel and perpendicular lines. He studied the football field. He drew diagrams showing parallel yard lines. He showed that corresponding angles on the football field are equal. These were simple materials but they did focus on understanding of parallel and perpendicular lines in geometry and they were real to this boy. It was the height of the football season. He was a member of the school team. Football to him was life. The materials he brought to the instructor from this phase of activity interesting to him were of his own choosing. He felt a personal interest and this soon carried over into other spheres of activity. Soon he began to solve exercises of equal difficulty with those worked by other members of the class. He never developed into a strong student of mathematics, but his work was satisfactory, and his attitude, application, and initiative were all commendable.*

Here is a concrete exemplification of a principle essential for the effective organization of meaningful learning, upon the proper application of which often depends the success of teaching. *Meaningful learning must proceed in a context exemplifying the meanings involved.* This expresses, in its most general form, the basic *principle of context.*

It is extremely likely that the instructor who handled this difficult case so well proceeded simply and solely by the light of his own good common sense, and was not aware that he was bringing to bear one of

---

* William G. Carr and John Waage, *The Lesson Assignment*, pp. 53–54, Stanford University Press, Calif., 1931.

the fundamental and universal principles of all successful teaching. Like all sound educational ideas, this one is certainly harmonious with common sense. It can hardly fail to appeal to practical teachers, once they understand it. Many of them put it into operation, at any rate from time to time, almost as a matter of course.

Yet there is great value in setting it up explicitly and in studying it with care and deliberation. The principle of context is far too vital to be left to chance, or to haphazard and unsystematic use. It is one of the most important guides we have to success in teaching. Everyone interested in teaching should understand why it is important and what its practical application involves. One of the most striking characteristics of modern teaching is the tendency to use this principle more and more consciously, extensively, and skillfully. Many of the changes in pedagogical manners and methods which have occurred over the past twenty years, and which sometimes seem to be superficial or merely capricious, at once become understandable as attempts to utilize context more effectively. Every teacher, in planning his work, should without fail take this principle into account and consider how best to apply it. Every teacher who thinks his work is not "getting across," and not yielding the sort of results for which he hopes, should ask himself, among other things, whether he is utilizing this principle as he should, for here may well be the cause of the trouble. And anyone who wishes to evaluate either an actual observed job or a described scheme of teaching should, among other things, explicitly consider to what extent and how it makes use of the principle of context, making it one criterion for judgment and appraisal.

## THE CHARACTERISTICS OF GOOD CONTEXT

The broad formulation of the principle of context which has just been presented is no doubt understandable enough, and not at all likely to arouse disagreement. But as it stands it is quite insufficient to show how the principle should and should not be applied in practical teaching situations. Indeed if it were allowed to remain without any further explanation and particularization, it would amount to little more than a truism. No learning of any kind could possibly go on in the abstract and without any setting whatsoever. A child might be told to memorize the spelling of a list of words not one of which he understood. But still the printed list and the spelling book would constitute a context of a sort, albeit a very inadequate and unhelpful one. The boy in the instance cited above was not studying parallels and perpendiculars completely out of context while he was failing to learn geometry, but in a context which did him very little good—that, namely, which was established by the textbook-assignment-recitation routine. Clearly, then, certain questions present themselves. What is the difference between an ineffective and an effective context? How and under what conditions does the context, or setting, of a job of learning have a beneficial effect upon it? How is the principle of context specifically related to the organization of learning?

The answers in general are implied in what has already been said about the nature of learning as a meaningful process, which is the fundamental working concept of all successful teaching. But the precise and specific nature of those answers becomes clear in the light of a number of investigations whose outcome and bearings well deserve the attention of every practical teacher, because of their very pointed relationship to his everyday problems.

**1. The Acquisition of Concepts.** First there is a group of investigations having to do with the acquisition of concepts. They center about two studies which are of particular importance, and these we shall specially consider, although there are many others also.

In the first of these, 12 series each containing 12 Chinese characters, samples of which are shown below, were presented to the experimental subjects. Each series had an element in common which appeared in every one of the 12 items in it, and also was given a nonsense-syllable name. Items from the various series were presented in random order, and not sequentially, and the experimenter watched to see how soon his subjects would become aware that certain of these items were held together by a common element or concept.

The second of the two key studies required the subjects to take part in a game with the experimenter as opponent. A number of matches were placed between them, from which they were to draw in turn. The number of matches in the pile was varied, and so were the numbers each player might draw. Sometimes the game was played under the condition that each side might draw either one or two each time. Or the draw might be one or three; or one or four; or one, two, or three; or three or four; and so on. The player who drew the last remaining match won.   The subject was always allowed to make the first draw, and if he played correctly he could win under almost all the varying conditions.   If, owing to the total number of matches or the conditions of the draw the first player could not certainly win, which occasionally happened, he could be aware of this from the start of the game so long as he understood the principle involved.   The point of the experiment was to see how the subject would come to grasp the principle by means of which he could usually win, and which would in any case tell him whether he could win or not.   Here too, clearly, the evolution and grasp of a concept was involved.

Certainly the problem of how to get concepts properly learned, upon, which these investigations bear, is one that faces every working teacher every day.   It may seem that, like many other psychological studies, these are somewhat remote from practical teaching, the reason of course being that, like any other experiments, they must be closely controlled and therefore require somewhat artificial situations.   Nevertheless, the outcomes are highly pertinent and significant.   These outcomes serve to carry further the exposition of the principle of context, and to reveal the differences between a good and a bad setting for learning.

1. *First and foremost, and above all, a good context for learning must be one with which the learner dynamically and strongly interacts.*

It must engage his interest, his will, his active purpose.   This was the essential difference between the textbook and the football field in the case of the boy who was falling down in his geometry.

This is brought out very clearly in the studies on the acquisition of concepts.   As the author of one of them expresses it, the attitude of the learner must be that of a participant, not a spectator.   In the investigation using Chinese characters, the subjects had to search and experiment actively, and it was found that mere presentation of the material was quite ineffective.   In the study using the match-drawing game, the sense of a goal close at hand and almost realized had a marked influence, and in particular it was found that demonstration by the experimenter did not help.

2. *The acquisition of a concept requires a context of actual concrete experience.*

On this the two investigations mentioned, and also various supporting and subsidiary studies, emphatically agree.   All of them show that it is not enough to have an idea explained in words.   What tends to happen then is that it is not understood, so that a verbal response is established instead of a concept being formed.   To be really understood it must be grasped in terms of actual concrete application and exemplification.

This is a point of the utmost importance. Such words as bay, acre, element, heat, equality, democracy, are bandied about in American classrooms with the greatest freedom. It is constantly assumed that if children can manipulate them as linguistic entities with a conventional and expected appropriateness, they know what they are talking about. Pupils are asked to name the chief bays on the Atlantic coast, to give a definition of the geographic term "bay," to compute the number of acres in a tract of land measuring a thousand feet by a thousand feet, to decide whether water is an element and why, to give its specific heat, to decide whether democracy is possible without equality, and so forth. When they falter or fail, teachers are apt to lay the blame on poor memory, or insufficient intelligence, or lack of industriousness, or else to be sheerly and simply baffled. But in a very great many cases the trouble is that the learnings proposed and inaugurated have been set up without any concrete context. When children reveal that they think justice is "a court," or "the courthouse," or "to be kind," or "to be honest," that to them an adverb is "a word ending in ly," or that they consider multiplication as meaning "to make bigger," or that they have absolutely no mental picture whatsoever of an acre or a square mile, any confident and correct manipulation of these concepts is hopelessly impossible, for the simple reason that they are not grasped. And they can be grasped only in terms of direct concrete experience.

This point that a good context is concrete may seem different from the preceding one which was that a good context must be dynamically compelling. But it is closely related to it. Human beings have a very limited capacity for working with and manipulating abstract ideas in verbal or symbolic form. The highly developed specialist and scholar can do it to some extent, but even he needs the control exercised by some precise technique such as mathematics, and he constantly needs to come back to concrete reality if he is to keep his feet on the ground and avoid flagrant absurdities, as the whole evolution of experimental science very clearly shows. So the real point of a concrete context is that it gives the learner something to work and experiment with, something that can command his will and energy, and still keep his processes under control.

3. *The concrete and dynamically compelling experiences in and through which concepts are acquired should be simple, and they should be copious.*

This is another point on which the research studies are in agreement. It is positively established that a general notion is better, more surely, and more firmly grasped by means of simple instances rather than complicated ones. Also a large number of varying instances will tend to produce better and surer learning than is likely to occur with only a few.   Here again is a practical and very important point.

A great deal of laboratory work in science teaching violates this requirement.   It organizes learning in a setting of concrete experience. But that experience is so complicated and difficult that it constitutes a problem in itself, and the pupil has to concentrate so hard on the manipulative technique and the detailed instructions that he misses the scientific principle.   Moreover the number of such experiments is usually far too small.   One often looks through mathematics textbooks in which there are not nearly enough simple applications to give the children a good chance to get rules and definitions properly through their heads, and those that are given are apt to be anything but concrete.   The same is often true of the teaching of the principles of syntax in the ordinary grammatical approach to a foreign language. The acquisition of a general idea is gravely hampered unless it is done in a context that is not only concrete but also simple and abundant. Anything else means ill-organized learning.

This idea, once more, is closely tied up to the requirement that context be dynamically compelling.   A simple and abundant context gives the learner plenty to work and experiment with, and also a stimulating sense of getting somewhere, of succeeding, of coming to see the point. One effect of a limited context is that it tends to bring about learning which does not transfer.   A father once tried to teach his young child the concept "square."   To do so he used the top of a square box as an illustration—or in our terminology, as the context for the learning. The child seemed to catch the idea quite well.   Then, when company was present, the father decided to show his offspring off.   So he held up a square piece of paper, and asked the child if it was square.   He got the answer, "no"!   The concept was tied up to the particular illustration, and could not be dissociated from it.   This sort of thing happens all the time in practical teaching.   The rule, the idea, the generalization is tied up to one or two examples, all pretty much of the same kind.   So long as the setting is constant, it can be produced very well.   But the moment a new context, or a new set of relationships is introduced, it is not there.   The answer is not to give more explanations in words, but more abundant simple context.

This idea has innumerable and very fruitful applications.   The case of the boy at Harrow School in England who was horrified at the sight of a pauper's funeral, and devoted his life thereafter to the amelioration of conditions among the poor is an exact example of context that was both concrete and highly dynamic.   Or again, to read about slum conditions in a textbook is learning organized at its least promising level. To go and see them as members of a class adds something, for at least the experience is concrete. To discuss, analyze, and chart what one has seen adds something more, for now one begins to work with the material. But to participate in some plan for their improvement is best of all, and brings the concepts and ideas to life as nothing else can.

All this casts some doubt upon the rather stilted and artificial number games sometimes used in arithmetic, and the personifications used in grammar and elsewhere, with parts of speech represented as animals, and so forth. The context so organized is concrete, but it is dynamically feeble. The learner can hardly take it seriously or work with it dynamically.

On the other hand, games certainly can be used in teaching, if it is remembered that one of their chief purposes is to supply suitable context. Here is an illustration of a game called "Explorers."

The map may be desk size with paper boats and flags, or floor size with cork ships and cloth flags, or yard size with wooden vessels and many properties. Color one flag for each explorer before you begin playing. Make it the color of the flag of the country for which the explorer sailed. Make a large map of the world and trace thereon the routes taken by the explorers. Write questions at points along the route such as Whence? Why? Result? When? Prepare pictures of their flags and their ships. Color them and cut out each one. Get some small corks and cut a little slit in the top of each cork. Then stick each flag and each ship on a cork so that it will stand up.

When all of your ships and flags are stuck in corks and your map is made, you're ready to play. There can be as many players as there are ships and flags. If only a few people want to play they divide the ships and flags equally.

(1) Each places his ship at the place on the map from which the explorer (named on the ship) set sail. (2) Each player in turn tries to answer the first question on his route. If he can answer it correctly he moves his ship to the next question. If he does not know the answer he must stay at the starting point until his turn comes again. (3) After one has had a turn, all the others take turns, one after another. Only those who know the answers to their questions can move up. (4) When all the players have had one turn the first has his second turn. If he can answer the question, he tries to move his boat up to the next question also. (5) All the players continue to have turns in order. (6) The game continues until a ship finally lands in its proper place.

The player must stick up the flag of the country which gets claim to the land because of that explorer. If the player puts up the wrong flag he's out. If there is one player for every ship then the winner of the game is the first person through. If only a few people play, then the winner is the person who can put up the most flags.*

* Inga Olla Helseth, *Living in the Classroom*, pp. 290–291, Edwards Bros., Inc., Ann Arbor, Mich., 1939.

It is clear that such a game, reasonably well though not ideally, fulfills the essential conditions of concreteness, copiousness, simplicity, and dynamic attractiveness at least for young children.

In the same way the old-fashioned object lesson, the museum visit, the field trip, the display of pictures or motion pictures all amount to the organization of a concrete context for learning. But this alone is not enough. It is also essential that the learner do something about these items of context, responding to them actively, experimentally, purposefully. If he behaves as a mere spectator, the concreteness of the experience will certainly not guarantee good learning.[1]

**2. The Learning of Operations or Processes.** Here again we have a large body of experimental work which reveals the same characteristics of a good context as those already mentioned. In the teaching of mathematics trouble very often starts at the time when children are first introduced to simple addition, and becomes steadily more serious and baffling as they move onward through arithmetic to algebra, dealing with more and more abstract and complicated operations. It is well understood and recognized that one chief source of difficulty is that a child is so often set to learning the operations without any sufficient concrete context with which he can work and experiment and which is capable of commanding his will and effort, that all he really acquires is a set of uncomprehended verbalizations. Then further progress in mathematics is not a process of increasing clarification and control, as it should be, but of increasing bewilderment and helplessness. When a six-year-old child seems quite well able to count up to ten, but cannot indicate how many dots there are in the following :: :: :, or when he can tell you that four and four are eight, but must count one by one to find out how many dots there are in the following :: ::., then he is being groomed for mathematical failure. Later on, in the ninth grade, it will appear that he can tell the answer when he is required to add $15a + 7a - 5a$, or to solve the equation $2x = 10$, but that he is defeated by expressions such as $18x + 3x - 16x + 4x = 18$, although not a single new process is involved. If his teacher is not too calloused to be surprised at anything, he may feel some puzzlement over the phenomenon and may wonder if the prescription may not be more drill, or a more astute technique of instruction in how to think, or possibly even a remedial course. But the trouble is that this child has never quite known what he was talking about in mathematics, and has understood less and less the further he went. Possibly a remedial course might be in order, but the idea of it should be to correct not some mysterious defect in the pupil but the damage done by badly organized learning. If the fundamental processes had been rooted in dynamic, concrete, abundant experience from the very first, then the succession of operations and manipulations from simple addition on would have been found manageable enough, instead of looking like an ever more tangled thicket of unintelligible rules and procedures.

Judd has put the matter in this way:

> The mental steps involved in the intelligent use of numerals for purposes of addition are as follows: (1) The individual learns that a single symbol may be used to represent a group of concrete objects. (2) He learns by actual manipulation of concrete objects how two groups can be combined in order to make a single new group. (3) He learns, through experiences with groups of concrete objects which he rearranges, rules of combination in which he has confidence. (4) He learns that the rules of combinations with which he has become acquainted in the concrete can be applied to symbols and that the memory of these rules releases him from the necessity of verifying the results at which he arrives in particular cases.*[2]

**3. Problem Solving.** Here is a typical textbook algebra problem. "A father promised his son a gift of $500 on the day that the son would be half as old as he. Their ages now are 35 and 10 respectively. How many years will the son have to wait for his gift?" This, clearly, is an attempt to organize a concrete setting for the study of equations of the first degree, instead of simply presenting stimuli such as $(35 + x)/2 = 10 + x$ and working to bring about the response $x = 15$. (This happens to be the equation involved in the above problem.) So far it is very praiseworthy, and seems to be a psychologically sound move, at least in principle. Yet pupils commonly find such verbal problems very difficult, to an extent where final tests in algebra courses have to be made up so that a pupil can pass even if he skips all the problems. Context, then, in these instances, seems to accentuate rather than alleviate the trouble. Why should this be?

The reason is that ordinary verbal problems, such as are found in most mathematics textbooks, involve two very grave weaknesses in the organization of learning. First, they have a spurious—that is, a merely described—rather than an actual concreteness. The fathers, children, trains, bathtubs, merchants, and so forth talked about are merely pawns in the game of mathematical manipulation. Second, and as a closely related consequence, they completely and obviously lack dynamic appeal to young people. So to solve them can bring no advantage. Failing to do so need cause no chagrin. It simply makes no intrinsic difference at all, save insofar as a mark may be concerned. One glance at a few typical verbal problems establishes this beyond a reasonable doubt.

* Charles H. Judd, *Education as Cultivation of the Higher Mental Processes*, pp. 56–57, The Macmillan Company, New York, 1936.

As to the kind of problems that ought to be used, one investigation at least gives a hint, though it is very far from developing a satisfactory answer. Questionnaires about the type and choice of verbal problems were sent out to groups of teachers and groups of pupils. The teachers felt that those dealing with business, economics, and personal finance were of paramount importance. The pupils, however, gave the highest possible rating for importance to those dealing with the activities of youth. Quite possibly, in the cosmic process, an economic issue is more important than a football game, although one cannot be sure. But it is quite certain that the football game makes a far more effective context for learning for most high-school students. And ordinary verbal problems are poor vehicles for mathematical learning because they set up abstract, unconvincing context.

It is interesting to compare this diagnosis with alleged difficulties in connection with verbal problems as reported in some of the research studies. One of the most frequently mentioned is "lack of reasoning ability." But this has the look of dubious mysticism, for the same pupil who is baffled by the $500 gift will achieve prodigies of contriving to get to and from a party. Reasoning ability seems to depend a good deal on what one has to reason about. Another often mentioned difficulty is "lack of systematic attack," and many earnest efforts have been made to remedy the defect, such as supplying lists of questions which the pupil is to ask himself—what is "given," what is to be proved, what is represented by $x$, and so on. But we may find our failing pupil remarkably systematic when it comes to something that matters to him, such as figuring up how long he must save to be able to buy a bicycle. So, once more, the nature of the context seems to be the determining consideration. Then again, "poor reading ability" is often cited as an obstacle. But it must be remembered that our pupil is being asked to read competently a brief, compact, technically phrased statement about something in which he does not and cannot feel the slightest interest, and which is often intrinsically absurd, like trying to fill a bathtub with the plug out. In such a setting good reading is not apt to flourish. Thus every one of these diagnoses, carefully analyzed, points to abstract and unconvincing context as the root of the trouble.

The studies on problem solving and its psychology very strongly imply the necessity for concrete and dynamically appealing context in other ways also. A large group of children were tested on a series of arithmetical problems, a typical example being: "Find the amount of a bill for 3½ yards of material at 40 cents a yard, and for 10 yards at 80 cents a yard." Many of them engaged in sheer random calculation, and there were no less than 80 wrong modes of approach, only 18 of which showed the slightest gleam of comprehension. To try to teach systematic analysis or the techniques of problem solving to children in terms of such material is almost certainly futile. But if they had to tackle the job of actually making purchases with their own money, very different results would probably be forthcoming.

Or again, consider the significance of verification in connection with computation and problem solving. Many teachers treat it as a sort of tag or appendix and have pupils verify their answers when they happen to think of it, and because supervisors and books on methodology say they should. But it is a vital factor in well-organized learning. When a child emerges from a mass of figuring with the discovery that $x$ equals $57\frac{1}{2}$ people, or $123\frac{3}{4}$ children, the remedy is not to have him review his calculations, but to understand what he is about. If he were dealing with concrete material which really made a difference to him, such blindness would be impossible, and verification would go along with problem solving and computing as part and parcel of it, which it should be.

It has been said that there are two main troubles with the organization of learning in most courses in algebra, and the statement applies to other subjects also. First, the fundamental operations are taught in isolation, whereas they should be taught in connection with their actual uses. Second, too many problems are introduced and these are superficially treated, whereas a much smaller number of problems each discussed, considered, and studied very thoroughly would be far preferable.

Let us consider just what this indicates, particularly the second point. We wish, let us say, to teach quadratic equations in and through their application to problematic situations. With a little ingenuity it will be easy enough to think up a whole series of conventional problems calling for their use. Most of these problems, however, will be no more than mere puzzles, lacking any trace of concrete reality, and often quite silly if taken seriously. Everything we know indicates that they will not do the learner much good. But to devise actual concrete problems, in which the learner will get a chance to manipulate, to measure, to compute, and to be checked up by ineluctable reality, is far from easy. Where are they to be found? The answer is that a few such problems amply treated and fully and experimentally explored will do more to reveal to the learner the true inwardness of quadratics than all the verbalizations the wit of the teacher can excogitate. It may seem that the demand for fewer problems is exactly contrary to the idea of copious and abundant context.

But a few problems of the right kind will offer an immensely richer context than a great many of the purely verbal variety. Thus once more, with the learning of problem solving, the evident need is a context that is dynamically compelling, concrete, simple and abundant.[3]

**4. Theme Writing.** It has long been recognized that the choice of a topic within the child's experience is a vital point in theme writing, though like so many other sound psychological considerations this one is frequently ignored in practice. More than 20 years ago it was found that the same children will do a better job on the topic How I Learned a Lesson, than when required to express themselves on A Snowball Fight on Slatter's Hill. The same consideration probably applies to the sanity of Hamlet and the exact motivation of Brutus and Mark Antony, typical theme subjects, and very remote ones. Formal investigation, indeed, is hardly needed to establish the contention. It is one of the commonplace pieces of advice given to ambitious writers who wish to coin money from the magazines that they had better deal with material close at hand and interesting and familiar to them.

Good writing, moreover, is purposive. It springs from the wish to tell somebody else something that one finds important. One learns to write best in a setting where such purposes are evoked. Such is the testimony of newspaper reporters who say that they get more of the inwardness of using English from a month's experience than from many courses in composition. And the same principle applies to school work also. Two hundred and seventy-five pupils from the seventh to the twelfth grades were divided into two sections. One was given standard instruction in English composition for five months. For the other, special arrangements were made. There was emphasis on presenting ideas to an audience rather than to the teacher. Some of the best work was put on display in the town library. Opportunity and encouragement for the personal choice of topics was given. In other words, there was a radical change in context. During the five months the seventh graders in the special group made two years normal progress, the eighth graders a year and a half, and the twelfth graders one year. The change in context, and particularly its dynamic character, did far more than strenuous blue-penciling, grammatical analysis, the study of rhetorical forms and paragraph organization, and the rest of the conventional apparatus of teaching composition. Such procedures have their uses, but only in a proper setting. Normal progress in theme writing, moreover, is progress with learning badly organized, with meager and unconvincing context, and with purpose fixed mainly on satisfying the teacher.[4]

**5. Reading.** The research material indicating the paramount importance of effective context in connection with reading is so conclusive, so significant, and yet so voluminous that while the subject must be mentioned, the brevity of the reference will make an adequate account impossible.

Children read the following passage: "You need a coal range in winter for kitchen warmth and for continuous hot-water supply, but in summer when you want a cool kitchen, a gas range is better." Then they were asked: "What effect has the use of a gas range instead of a coal range on the temperature of the kitchen?" A fairly characteristic answer was: "A cool kitchen is used for a gas range." This is the sort of reading that goes on in thousands and even millions of homes where youngsters are trying to "get" their school assignment. It amply and immediately explains the failure of a great deal of teaching. What is the remedy? More hard work and longer hours of study? Surely a dubious expedient if nothing else is to be done, for wrongly directed effort is apt to do little except increase trouble. The author of the study in which the above result was reported says, and very truly, that the child who made the response simply noticed certain words at haphazard, without attending to their interrelationships and relative emphases. The failure was a failure of reasoning. But the practical question is how to get children to reason better when they read. If in this particular case the young readers had come from farm homes on the great plains, with broiling summers and icy winters, the problem would have solved itself and the absurdity would have been avoided.

The materials for reading presented to children in school are full of expressions which seem understandable and are not. Tests given to groups of children have shown this very clearly. When they read that there were few newspapers in the country in 1775, they took this to mean anywhere from one to six hundred. When they read that in the early national period travel was slow, this meant to them that the trip from New York to Boston would take anywhere from two days to two months. When they read that Greenland is covered with a thick icecap, this meant an icecap anywhere from one inch to "thousands of feet" thick. And an area of ten square miles was interpreted variously as corresponding to the size of Washington Park, or of the state of Iowa. What sort of thinking, what sort of learning, what sort of results, what sort of real education can possibly be derived from reading such as this? What, again, is the remedy? Should school textbooks be written in a quasi-legal style, in which every possible misinterpretation is meticulously anticipated? Obviously not. Should one establish remedial reading clinics at all levels above perhaps the fifth grade? This too seems questionable, for it would surely be better to eliminate the causes of the disease rather than to spend time and money trying to cure it after it has taken hold. Should one institute more systematic work on the technique of reading? Possibly so. But there will be no certain improvement so long as children in school must read masses of material remote from experience and foreign to purpose and interest. Such reading will never be well done. The only satisfactory remedy is to organize a concrete and dynamic context in terms of which the process of reading goes on.

The problem also arises in connection with so-called "appreciative reading." A very familiar and much-used poetic selection is the following:

> The Assyrian came down like the wolf on the fold;
> And his cohorts were gleaming in purple and gold;
> And the sheen of their spears was like stars on the sea,
> When the blue wave rolls nightly on deep Galillee.

A reconstruction of responses to questions revealed that an able ninth grader understood the passage about as follows: "The Assyrian, that is somebody, came down like a wolf on the fold, and something he had on was gleaming in purple and gold, and the something of their spears was like stars on the sea when something happens to the waves at night." An inferior pupil understood it thus: "The Assyrians came like wolves at night, crossing the rolling waves of the sea of Galillee. And his weapons were gleaming like purple and gold; and the sharpness of the spears was like the sea of stars seen by Galileo." What sort of literary appreciation is likely to develop on such foundations? And yet once again, what is the remedy? More and better notes? This is hardly promising, for the apparatus of exposition can grow so cumbersome that it creates a problem of its own. The only recourse is to escape altogether, by hook or by crook, from the cycle of verbalization, and to evoke the direct visualization which the lines express. It is not necessary to know just what a cohort was, or just how many soldiers it contained, or even whether it really was a unit of the Assyrian army, so long as the word calls up some reasonably valid picture. If this happens, then once and for all there will be banished the idea that possibly it means a pair of pants.[5]

## SYSTEMATIZATION NOT ENOUGH

One of the commonest policies adopted in teaching with the hope of getting better results is systematization. The material to be learned is laid out in an orderly manner, and careful explanations as to just what to do are given with the intention of helping the learner to work more effectively.

The three general methods described earlier—the inductive lesson, the deductive lesson, and the mastery-unit technique—are essentially attempts to systematize learning, or at least that is how they usually work out in practice. Many textbooks contain various aids to study, such as summaries, previews, and questions, which have the same purpose. Many conscientious teachers do a great deal of work along the same line, by trying to give assignments very clearly, spending considerable time in questioning and discussing to be sure that everything is well understood, organizing a careful sequence of tests, calling for tentative topics, outlines, and bibliographies well in advance when a theme is to be written, and so on. Many other instances will doubtless occur to the reader.

One ambitious proposal of the kind consists of a set of questions which a pupil tackling a geometry "original" is supposed to ask himself.

(1) What kind of relation is to be proved? (2) Is there any part of the figure about which we know two or more facts? (3) Draw the figure. (4) State what relations are given. (5) State what relations are to be proved. (6) What is the link that may connect (4) and (5)? (7) Test the latter conclusion. (8) If true, write the proof and if not consider other suggestions. (9) Is the proof as a whole correct and in the briefest form? (10) Which step was omitted if the result was incorrect? (11) Which lead was futile?

This example shows, about as clearly as anything can, just what systematization is supposed to accomplish. It is based on what, superficially at least, seems a very reasonable hypothesis. There is no doubt that the good student really does raise and answer for himself various questions as he goes along, or that he tends to work in an orderly fashion. Then why not transform a poor student into a better one, or strengthen the weak points of a good student, by regularizing such practices and insisting upon them? Specifically, the hypothesis is that well-organized learning is systematic and orderly learning.

This, however, is only half true. As a matter of fact, even very careful and strenuous endeavours to systematize learning often lead to very disconcerting and surprising failure, when judged by the criterion of results. It has already been pointed out that the effect of a change of methodology as a single independent factor is likely to be negligible. But also there are some specific investigations which point in the same direction and clearly indicate that systematization in and of itself is always a frail reed.

A class of university students in American history was divided into three groups of comparable ability. The first group was given three definite written exercises each week. The second was given one such exercise each week. The third was given none. The exercises consisted of writing the story of the election of 1860, listing the members of Lincoln's cabinet, and suchlike. At the end of ten weeks, objective tests were given to the whole class. There was virtually no difference at all in the achievement of the three groups, and some evidence that the work of the abler students had been hampered by the heavy written work. Consider the enormous waste of time, on the part of teacher and students alike, which such a showing indicates. In the same way supervised study often fails to yield the results which might, a priori, be anticipated. A ninth-grade class in English was divided into two equally able sections, one of which was run on the double divided period plan, with the extra period devoted to supervised study in English composition. There was some gain over the section in which the students did their own studying in their own way, but not a great deal. And many individual pupils seemed to get no benefit at all. So too the systematic use of practice exercises and of workbooks, and the transformation of the class into a study laboratory in charge of the teacher are all practices that are far from guaranteeing the improvement in results at which they are aimed. The same is true of "How to Study" courses heavily emphasizing clerical details and orderly procedure, as many of them do.

Thus it is very clear that one cannot place much reliance on systematization and nothing else if one wishes to bring about better learning. The studies cited in this chapter, particularly those on the acquisition of concepts, suggest at least part of the reason. It was found that merely to tell the learner in advance what he was to discover helped surprisingly little. He had to work it out by his own purposes, and by experimentation, exploration, and discovery in a rich, concrete, copious context. There, undoubtedly, is part of the solution.

A question often asked by practical teachers is whether an inductive or a deductive organization is preferable. Should one begin by stating the concept or general idea and then reinforce it by applications? Or should one begin with concrete data and build up to the generalization? So far as can be gathered from the research material, it makes no very great difference. One need not, indeed one should not, be wedded to either plan as a cut-and-dried procedure. The distinction between the inductive and the deductive treatment seems to be unreal psychologically. Always the point is to organize learning in a context of the right kind, made intelligible by whatever explanations and discretions seem apt to help the learner to see the point, or rather to help him find it for himself.

The plain truth is that one cannot transform learning that is poor because of its meager meaningfulness into good learning merely by systematizing it. Everything that has been said about the psychology of learning in these pages should make this evident. All that is apt to be accomplished is a more systematic verbalization. This is by no means to decry systematic endeavour, or to say that good work can be done in a hit-or-miss or slovenly fashion, as will become very clear in connection with the principle of focus. But an effective and orderly method of work is an effect rather than a cause. It is a product of the learner's own purpose, and of his awareness of emerging meanings. When imposed as a routine for handling situations which are very poor in meaning, it cannot be effective. Systematization without proper context cannot yield a good organization of learning.[6]

## SUMMARY AND INTERPRETATION

The relationship of what has been said in this chapter to the basic conception of meaningful learning is probably evident to the reader, but there is some value in stating it briefly and explicitly. The problematic situation that embodies the task of learning must be stated in terms of a context which is important and compelling to the learner, and which engages his active participant purpose. It must be stated in terms of a context which, by its concreteness, copiousness, and manageability gives the greatest possible scope for experimentation, exploration, and discovery, leads towards control through understanding and insight, and facilitates transfer.

How naturally the principle of context harmonizes with the insights and impulses of a vital teacher is very well shown by the following passage from a work of fiction.

She knew how to teach; she knew how to awaken interest. At the South London School she had initiated debates, clubs, visits, excursions to the houses of Parliament, the London County Council, the National Portrait Gallery, the Tower of London, the Becontree estate; she had organized amateur housing surveys, and open-air performances of Euripides (in translation); she had supervised parents' conversaziones, "cabinet meetings," essay competitions, inquiries into public morals or imperial finance. Her official subjects were history and civics, but all roads led to her Rome—an inexhaustible curiosity about the contemporary world and its inhabitants.*

* Winifred Holtby, *South Riding*, p. 54, The Macmillan Company, New York, 1936.

## Notes and References

*General References on Context (Chaps. 5 and 6)*

Inga Olla Helseth, *Living in the Classroom*, Chap. 12, "The Environment of Things," Edwards Bros., Inc., Ann Arbor, Mich., 1939. "Community Resources in Rural Schools," *National Education Association, Yearbook*, 1939. Ernest Horn, *Methods of Instruction in the Social Sciences*, Chap. 5, Charles Scribner's Sons, New York, 1937.

*References in the Text*

1. The two basic studies on concept formation are Clark L. Hull, "Quantitative Aspects of the Evolution of Concepts," *Psychological Monographs*, Vol. 28, no. 1, whole No. 123 (1920), which utilizes the Chinese characters, and John C. Peterson, "The Higher Mental Processes in Learning," *Psychological Monographs*, Vol. 28, No. 7, whole No. 129 (1920), which utilizes the match-drawing game. Supplementary studies on the problem are Kenneth L. Smoke, "Negative Instances in Concept Learning," *Journal of Experimental Psychology*, Vol. 16 (1933), pp. 583–588, which deals with the Hull investigation; and R. H. Waters, "The Influence of Tuition upon Ideational Learning," *Journal of General Psychology*, Vol. 1 (1928), pp. 534–549, which deals with the Peterson study. An excellent summary with illuminating comments dealing with the work of Hull is found in Arthur I. Gates, Arthur T. Jersild, T. R. McConnell, and Robert Challman, *Educational Psychology*, pp. 447ff, The Macmillan Company, New York, 1942.

2. For an extended treatment of the teaching of arithmetical operations in terms of meaning see W. A. Brownell, *The Development of Children's Number Ideas in the Primary Grades*, University of Chicago Press, Chicago, 1928. For a briefer treatment from substantially the same viewpoint see Charles H. Judd, *Education as Cultivation of the Higher Mental Processes*, Chap. 4, "The Number System and Symbolic Thinking," The Macmillan Company, New York, 1936. Much material indicating difficulty of transfer in algebraic operations will be found in John P. Everett, *Fundamental Skills of Algebra*, Teachers College, Columbia University, Bureau of Publications, New York, 1928.

3. Typical and revealing investigations of problem solving, its difficulties and general psychological bearings will be found in the following: Jesse Jerome Powell, *A Study of Problem Material in High School Algebra*, Teachers College, Columbia University, Bureau of Publications, New York, 1929; Orlie H. Clem and Bertha Adams Hendershot, "Difficulties Involved in Solving Verbal Problems in Algebra," *Journal of Educational Research*, Vol. 11 (1925), pp. 95–103; Winona M. Perry, *A Study in the Psychology of Learning Geometry*, Teachers College, Columbia University, Bureau of Publications, New York, 1925; Walter S. Monroe, *How Pupils Solve Problems in Arithmetic*, University of Illinois Press, Urbana, 1929.

4. The basic study which revealed the influence of choice of topic is Earl Hudelson, "English Composition, Its Aims and Measurement," *National Society for the Study of Education: 22nd Yearbook*, Part I, 1923. This reports the development of the Hudelson composition scale. Also see R. L. Lyman, "Summary of Investigations Relating to Grammar, Language, and Composition," *Supplementary Education Monographs, School Review and Elementary School Journal*, No. 36, University of Chicago Press, Chicago, 1929, which contains much source material. The report on the successful teaching of composition is by F. P. O'Brien, "An

Experiment in Supervision of English," *Kansas Studies in Education*, Vol. 1, No. 6; *Bulletin of the University of Kansas*, Vol. 27, No. 12 (1926).

5. For the essential nature of reading see E. L. Thorndike, "Psychology of Thinking in the Case of Reading," *Psychological Review*, Vol. 24 (1916), pp. 220–234. For the problem of meaning particularly in appreciative reading, see T. W. H. Irion, *Comprehension Difficulties of Ninth Grade Students in the Study of Literature*, Teachers College, Columbia University, Bureau of Publications, New York, 1925.

6. Two investigations dealing with attempts to systematize learning and the kind of results achieved, to which reference is made in the text, are Fred H. Gorman and DeWitt S. Morgan, "A Study of the Effects of Definite Written Exercises upon Learning in a Course in American History," *Cooperative Studies in Secondary Education, Indiana University School of Education Bulletin*, Vol. 6, No. 4, pp. 80–90, (1930); J. W. Heckert, "The Effects of Supervised Study on English," *Journal of Educational Research*, Vol. 5 (1922), pp. 368–380. The questions for geometrical problem solving are developed in Winona M. Perry, *A Study of the Psychology of Learning in Geometry*, Teachers College, Columbia University, Bureau of Publications, New York, 1925. A book which heavily emphasizes systematization for improved results is H. B. Reed, *Psychology of Elementary School Subjects*, Ginn and Company, Boston, 1938, an examination of which will provide many instructive instances.

### Items for Discussion and Study

*In connection with this chapter there are two primary suggestions for discussion and study to which special attention is called. They will recur in connection with Chaps. 7, 9, 11, 13, and 15.*

A. Consider the characteristics of a good context as stated in the present chapter in connection with the citation from Wrightstone in Chap. 2, p. 37. Why is a good context important in giving the learner a genuine sense of a problem? Consider the issue broadly, for Wrightstone's statement epitomizes our basic conception of meaningful learning. Work out your discussion with concrete instances of good context from teaching situations you have read about, managed yourself, observed, or participated in as a learner.

B. Collect and record a number of instances of the use of context from teaching situations you have read about, managed yourself as teacher, observed, or participated in as a learner. Analyze and evaluate them on the basis of the characteristics of good context presented in this chapter.

Since similar suggestions are made for study in connection with each of the principles of teaching considered in these pages, it would be well to record the data and the results of discussion on the above points in a notebook or card file, and to do the same with each of the subsequent principles, so that a cumulative body of material is built up.

1. Could an enterprising pupil organize a good context for himself, even if it were not provided in the organization of some course he was taking? Consider how this might be done in connection with some specific school subject, such as algebra, chemistry, American history, etc.

2. In what way and to what extent does *Life* magazine exemplify the characteristics of a good context? Substitute or add other pictorial magazines if you desire.

3. What would be the ideal context for the study of principles of teaching, of educational psychology, of tests and measurements? How would the teaching of these subjects have to be reorganized to provide it?

4. How is it that a mature and advanced scholar seems able to work and learn well in his specialty with very little concrete context, and, in fact, in the main with a verbal context only? Is he really able to do so? Do the characteristics of good context hold true in such situations?

5. What would happen to an algebra course that was reorganized in terms of concrete and appealing problems?

6. Mail-order equipment, *e.g.*, a refrigerator, is often delivered dissassembled and with a set of quite abstruse directions for assembling. Show how the act of assembling it leads to an understanding of the directions, and how this exemplifies the characteristics of a good context. Can you think of other such examples from daily life?

7. Collect and discuss examples of attempts to improve learning by the systematization of teaching, *e.g.*, by elaborate syllabi, sequences of tests, fixed dates for reports, etc. Why is this type of organization alone not likely to yield improved results?

8. Have you ever encountered learning organized in the way indicated in the citation from Holtby, p. 94? Particularize and discuss.

# CHAPTER 6

## THE PRINCIPLE OF CONTEXT AND THE APPRAISAL OF TEACHING

### HIEARCHY OF APPLICATIONS

There is presented below a hierarchy showing degrees of excellence in the management of context, on which any given teaching situation can be approximately located. Before passing on to consider the various levels indicated, a few comments need to be made. A similar hierarchy or scale is presented in connection with each of the six principles to be considered, and the points discussed here apply to all of them, with some minor modifications.

### PRINCIPLE OF CONTEXT: HIERARCHY

I  Textbook only

II  Textbook together with collateral or supplementary readings in general of somewhat similar type, academic in character and aiming at further exposition

III  Nonacademic and current materials, such as magazine articles, newspaper clippings, advertising items, brochures, poems, and so forth. May be accompanied by either or both of the foregoing or not

IV  Graphic materials such as pictures, movies, maps, charts, tables, graphs, "visual aids" generally, also phonograph recordings. May be accompanied by any or all the foregoing

V  Demonstrations, museum trips, excursions, presentations by visiting "experts," *e.g.*, traffic policemen, fire wardens, etc., in general, chances to observe phenomena and events more or less in natural setting. May be accompanied by any or all of the foregoing

VI  Personal, social, community undertakings, either in school or out. May be accompanied by any or all of the foregoing

1. There is no such thing as learning without any context at all. Every teacher organizes it to some degree, more or less consciously, more or less effectively. The only question is how well he does so. Modern teaching makes a great deal of the principle of context, and one of its greatest contributions is the discovery of ways and means of applying the principle in the best possible way. Such teaching is often

98

considered different in kind from the routine of textbook assignments and recitations which are the staple organization of the conventional school. But the difference is only one of degree. No teacher can possibly ignore the principle of context, and in fact no teacher ever does. Every teacher tries to apply it in his work, sometimes clumsily and stupidly, sometimes with keen and imaginative insight, and between the worst and the best exemplifications there can be identified a series of levels of increasing excellence and adequacy. Thus the teacher accustomed only to the textbook-assignment-recitation routine should not think that developmental teaching belongs to a wholly different universe. On the contrary, developmental teaching undertakes to apply at a high level of adequacy a principle which ordinary textbook teaching applies at a low level. Also it may well be that even the most able teacher in the most excellent school cannot invariably apply the principle of context in the most ideal fashion. Again, an able teacher in a very limited and restrictive school may feel that he cannot operate at a very high level on the scale. Still it is very valuable for any such teacher to see what placement may properly be indicated for his work, and to be aware that a fundamental principle is involved, which should be brought to bear as effectively as possible.

2. It will often happen that a given instance of teaching cannot be exactly placed on the scale. In some respects its management of context may be superior, in others inferior. This is because a teaching situation is very complex, and full of subtle and not always consistent values. Thus a teacher may rely upon the textbook and the recitation as the staples of his business, and yet from time to time introduce rich and fascinating applications and illustrations, or even remarkably good projects. But this does not mean that the hierarchy is useless or invalid. The flux of reality always at some point defeats every classification whatsoever, but classification and analysis are extremely useful for all that. So the hierarchy of applications of the principle of context provides an extremely serviceable clue for the analysis of any teaching situation, whether observed, or described, or actually carried on by the person who does the analyzing, even though the situation in question may not correspond in all its aspects to any one of the levels indicated.

3. A point which has already been emphasized and which will be stressed frequently in these pages, may well be mentioned here. In the evaluation of teaching, the fundamental question is not one of methodology in the ordinary sense. Teaching stands or falls not by the choice or "proper" use of this or that method, but by the extent to which it manages to organize meaningful learning. A teacher can best

improve his work, not by following more meticulously the indicated steps of some method, or the indicated procedure for using some device, but by understanding and correcting the weaknesses in his plan for organizing learning. The value of a study of teaching in terms of psychological principles, such as that undertaken here, is that it isolates the key points of organization and thus facilitates analysis and improvement. One such key point is the principle of context.

4. This leads to a fourth comment which may seem hardly necessary. The principle of context is by no means the only criterion and guide for successful teaching. A teaching situation may exploit context in a promising manner, but may be a failure because some other equally vital principle is being disregarded or misapplied. Then all one can say is that it shows possibilities but could be bettered by changes in a definite and designated direction.

So much for a general exposition of the significance and utility of the hierarchy. It is now time to turn to characterizations of the various steps or levels.

### THE FIRST LEVEL

Consider first a textbook-recitation lesson in American history, taught to a tenth-grade group. The teacher announced the topic at the beginning of the period—The Rise and Influence of Slavery. The assignment was Chap. 13 from *The Making of Our United States,** entitled "The Shadow of Slavery." The chapter traces the slavery issue from the beginning of the national period to the outbreak of the Civil War. The material is broken down into 11 sections, headed in boldface type. Questions for thought and discussion are interspersed in the text. The chapter begins with a paragraph setting up the topic and ends with a summary, both of them in boldface type. At the close there is a text review consisting of numerous detailed questions, a list of seven important dates, a list of names and terms, and lists of further readings. Besides this there is a considerable amount of visual material—two small-scale maps showing the presidential elections of 1848 and 1860; black-and-white pictures of the St. Augustine slave market and of Lincoln's arrival in Washington for his first inaugural; small portraits of Garrison, Taylor, Fillmore, Pierce, Buchanan, Stowe, and John Brown; and a reproduction of the heading of Garrison's *Liberator*.

The 50-minute period was devoted, in the main, to oral questions on the content of the chapter, interspersed with some discussion and exposition. Ten minutes were devoted to writing on some of the text review questions in the book. It was clear that the textbook as it

* R. O. Hughes, Allyn & Bacon, Boston, new ed., 1943.

stood was the main instrumentality for the organization of learning, and in spite of certain excellences, it is woefully inadequate for such a purpose. It provides an exceedingly insufficient context for learning, consisting almost entirely of exposition and narrative, both highly condensed and matter-of-fact, helped out with certain devices or aids intended to help the student to read more effectively. The value of the numerous small portraits is especially open to question. The lists of additional readings, of course, open up certain possibilities. But neither these nor the graphic materials were utilized in any way in the lesson observed. An enterprising teacher might have made them starting points for far-reaching and repaying activities. The general impression left by the lesson was one of dutiful but somewhat bored reciting on material which certainly had not been vitalized by its treatment.

In summary, then, the points of criticism were these. (1) The context lacked dynamic appeal and had the general character of a lesson to be learned under compulsion. For a scholar, or perhaps for an advanced university student majoring in history, the material might be useful, interesting, and calculated to evoke dynamic participation, since it amounted to a well-organized quick summary. But that it could have any such values for high-school students in the tenth grade seems incredible. (2) The context was predominantly verbal and nothing was done in the lesson to alleviate this defect. There were signs of an attempt to introduce material of a different kind through illustrations, but they were not effective, and no use was made of the pictures in the book, as was perhaps inevitable considering their character. (3) The context was meager and, on the whole, quite difficult for, though the vocabulary of the book is not excessive, it is compactly written and hard to handle. The author evidently tried to meet this defect by providing lists of readings, some of them academic and some not. But they were not used in the teaching, nor was current relevant material introduced by the teacher.

The organized learning situation emphatically did not have the character of a compelling problem in a vital setting, leading to exploration, discovery, and understanding. On the contrary, it turned on the building up of limited verbal responses to verbal stimuli, out of touch with the life motives of the learners except that they were under pressure to do the job. There was no direct evidence of what came of it all, but it is almost certain that authentic results were not forthcoming. Read in the converse, these criticisms indicate, point by point, what a vital teacher might do to rectify such a situation.

Another lesson, somewhat similar in general type, but in a certain respect better, proceeded as follows.   The subject again was American history, but this time in the sixth grade.   The lesson in this case ran over two school days as an organized pattern of activities.   The teacher introduced it as follows: "We will take the next chapter for tomorrow. It is on The Building of the Erie Canal.   Have you got that written down?"   Then followed some checking up and talk to and fro.   Then she continued, "Now take down these questions: (1) When was the Erie Canal started?   (2) When was it completed?   (3) What did De Witt Clinton have to do with the building of the Erie Canal?   (4) How much did it cost to build?   (5) Where was it built?   (6) Who invented the telegraph?   (7) When was it invented?"   After this the pupils spent the rest of the period in study.   Next day they were to recite in the conventional manner.*

Here was a very clear, businesslike, definite organization of learning. This at least is something, and indeed considerably more than one always finds.   The teacher at any rate knew what she wanted the pupils to know.   But she inaugurated a very bad learning-teaching situation for all that.   They were set to work to identify certain stimuli and certain responses, to establish connections between them, and to keep them connected for 24 hours.   Had they any mental picture of the Erie Canal?   Of the country it traversed?   Any notion of the picturesque life that centered about it?   Of the issues it raised?   Of their modern counterparts?   Did the name De Witt Clinton have much more significance for them than a set of nonsense syllables? Might not the same be true of the inventor of the telegraph?   Did the two featured dates tie together any significant body of experience and reference?   Evidently all these and similar questions must be answered in the negative.   All the learning was narrowly grooved, and context was reduced to a minimum both in amount and significance.   Again there was no sense of a compelling problem, no opportunity for exploration, discovery, and the achievement of understanding.   All the criticisms of the preceding instance apply here.   This is an interesting and instructive example of teaching, because it shows so very clearly that an organized plan of learning may be very definite and yet very defective.

### THE SECOND AND THIRD LEVELS

The most obvious move towards a recognition of the principle of context at least a little better than that in the two preceding instances

* This was an observed demonstration lesson based on an assignment cited by Gerald A. Yoakam, *The Improvement of the Assignment*, p. 30, The Macmillan Company, New York, 1933.

is to go beyond the use of a single textbook and to introduce collateral reading, or supplementary reading, or references, either optional or required. Here is a fairly typical example.

In a fourth-grade sequence in geography, there was the topic, The Importance of the Soil. The following references were given: F. M. McMurry and A. E. Perkins, *Elementary Geography*, pp. 1–8; J. F. Chamberlain, *How We Are Sheltered*, pp. 1–11; A. G. Keller and A. O. Bishop, *Commercial and Industrial Geography*, pp. 291–297. The following problems were set up as guides for study and discussion. (1) Why is the soil an important factor in the life of every boy and girl? (2) What does the soil provide for? (3) Which is the more important, shelter or clothing? (4) What special kind of shelter does our country require? (6) How many of the materials for food, shelter, and clothing come from the soil? (7) What are the people who raise things from the soil called? (8) Which occupation is called the greatest in the world? (9) Why? Then followed certain study directions, calling for the systematic reading of the textbook and one of the reference books, the latter for "as long as time permits."

It is extremely probable that the average observer, and quite possibly the average supervisor, making a judgment in terms of externals and fashions rather than exacting analysis, might consider this decidedly better teaching than the two former instances. At least a gesture has been made in the direction of a context wider than an assigned passage in a single compendious textbook. Moreover, the questions, in appearance at least, are not brutally factual, and undoubtedly open up avenues for discussion and exploration, although it seems a little far-fetched to invite children to choose between clothing and shelter. But if we fix our attention on the results to be achieved, and on the psychological organization necessary to achieve them—the two key points in all teaching—it is very doubtful whether the improvement really amounts to much.

True, there is a wider context, but it is of exactly the same kind, both as to content and dynamics. It consists of more readings of an expository and informational type. More of the same, in other words! And on examination one finds that the pupil is to react to it and deal with it exactly as he would react to and deal with a reading in a textbook. For the "problems" which have so much the look of true "thought questions" are all answered in the readings, so that they become nothing more nor less than study guides. The whole assumption on which this organization is built is that learning consists of identifying prepotent stimuli and establishing the "correct" responses to them. How much good would this wider context do a city-bred child who had hardly seen a farm, never met a farmer, and was none too sure that milk comes from cows and eggs from chickens? How clearly would it establish in his mind a valid concept corresponding to the decidedly tricky word "soil"?

It is interesting also to note how cautiously and halfheartedly even this very conservatively expanded context is introduced. The children are to read in "one" of the "reference books" for "as long as time permits." In other words, anything beyond the text is an extravagance, nice if it can be managed, but holding only a low priority. Unfortunately where this kind of contextual material is concerned, such tepidness is all too well justified.

Contrast the foregoing items with the following reading list from a fourth-grade unit on Exploration, dealing with Columbus, Magellan, Drake, Meriwether, Clark, etc. Prose items included *The Story of Tonty* by Mary Hartwell Catherwood, *The Treasure Finders* by Oliver Clay, *The White Conquerors* by Kirk Monroe, and suchlike. Poetry included *Columbus* by Joaquin Miller, *Hope* by William Dean Howells, *Pioneers* by Hamlin Garland, and so forth. From the standpoint of the principle of context this is a much improved though still not ideal list, for the following reasons: (1) Much of it is intrinsically interesting and vital. This means that it tends to evoke a definite and strong participant response very different from the reaction elicited by condensed informational or expository passages. (2) Much of it possesses the quality of concreteness. True, it still consists of words. But words used for concrete portrayals, specific narrative, and imaginative construction have a very different effect from words used for abstract exposition and argument. There is something here to work with, something which the mind can grasp and utilize, something which opens up opportunities for comparison, discussion, thought, and exploration. All in all we have here a context which, although still verbal, nevertheless still differs both in content and dynamics from that offered in cases like the previous one.

A considerable attempt has been made to advocate what is called "extensive reading" as contrasted with "intensive reading" as a favorable factor in the organization of learning. The term is none too exact, but its general meaning is perhaps fairly clear. The average textbook is definitely set up for the sake of intensive reading. It is exceedingly compact. It treats each topic briefly. It contains a good deal of material per page, which means precisely a meager context for what is to be learned. And it presupposes that the reader will study it minutely and intensively, giving careful attention to each and every point, and even to each and every sentence. A passage set up for extensive reading reverses these conditions. It is longer. It contains much less material per page and is generally more diluted. And it presupposes a more facile and less analytic type of reading. There is some evidence that when the same material is set up first intensively and then extensively, the average reader, and particularly the average young reader, will get more from the latter and remember it better.

So far so good. But what the advocacy of extensive reading seems to amount to in actual practice is simply more collateral, without any particular discrimination as to the kind of collateral. Yet the whole implication of the principle of context is that the mere increase of collateral, or its introduction where none has been used before (which happens to be the situation in a great many schools and courses), will not do a great deal to lead to more success in teaching—that is, to better results. The kind of collateral, and the reactions and impulses it evokes are the vital points.

Stories, novels, plays, bulletins, magazine articles, newspaper clippings, advertisements, commercial and government brochures, railroad and steamboat and air-line timetables, and current items generally can make admirable contextual material. The reason is that they tend strongly in the direction of the concrete, the specific, the actual, the immediate. They possess the quality of reality, rather than being formulations of theory or catalogues of facts. Also they lend themselves to participant discussion, study, and action on the part of the pupils. It is naïve to expect pupils, either as individuals, or as subgroups, or as a class group *in toto* to get much excited about or to dig eagerly into some bald textbook statement of the conservation issue under Theodore Roosevelt. But these effects, which every teacher desires, can be induced by using current material of various kinds, dealing let us say with Jackson Hole and the conservation problem in the Tetons, particularly if the pupils are encouraged to discover items for themselves and bring them to school for display and comment. And it should be understood that excitement and a tendency to dig are prime conditions for effective learning, and that their arousal is a far surer sign of a teacher's success than the most dutifully meticulous use of some apparatus of study aids designed to increase the digestibility of an essentially indigestible textbook chapter.

The point is this. Collateral should not be considered as a load, or a fashion, or something that for some vague reason ought to appear in the syllabus. All reading should be considered as a context for learning, and its organization should be subject to the principle of context as we have come to understand it. The difference between the kind of organization at the second and the third level of hierarchy very clearly exemplifies the characteristics of a good context as developed in the preceding chapter. On both the second and the third levels there is a definite attempt to provide a more abundant setting. In the former case, however, the material is abstract and often quite difficult. In the latter, it tends towards concreteness without however completely arriving, and is usually easier. But the decisive difference is in the dynamic values of the context. Very few students in school will become excited or fascinated by an academic disquisition. But they may well become excited and fascinated by a historical novel or a scientific exposition related to problems with which they have to do. In the one case life motives and values are not likely to be evoked with any force. In the other case they may well be. There can be no question which favors the better learning, because the difference is between not much caring about what one reads, and really caring, and so wishing to discuss, and collate, and explore, and understand.[1]

## THE FOURTH AND FIFTH LEVELS

A further advance in the organization of effective context is the use of visual materials such as maps, graphs, still pictures, motion pictures, specimens and samples, and also demonstrations to be watched by the learners. The idea is an old one. The first illustrated schoolbook was the Latin text, *Orbis Pictus*, by John Amos Comenius, published in 1658. The pictures were of familiar scenes, one for example representing a barber shop, giving the Latin words for the various objects shown—the hair, the barber, the chair, and so on. Thus the illustrations were closely related to the contemplated learning, which is more than can be said for the pictorial content of many more modern textbooks. As a matter of fact, no textbook can begin to do justice to the graphic materials now available from a great many sources, such as the Federal and state governments, commercial and industrial concerns, travel bureaus, magazines, and so on almost endlessly, as well as companies producing commercial and educational films. An immense wealth of such material exists, and every teacher should to some extent familiarize himself with it, so as to be able to make his own selections, and perhaps more importantly, so as to be able to guide and assist pupils in making theirs.

Such material has many uses and can be built into the sequence of learning and teaching in many ways. Its employment for introducing a new topic, as a source of information, and for review has been suggested. But one should avoid the idea that there are only a few right ways of using it, and that it belongs only at certain specified points in a lesson development. What is necessary always is to use it in such a way that learners will really learn from it—in such a way that it becomes an effective context in which the learning process proceeds. It should throw into relief and dramatize an intriguing problem, and give opportunity and incentive for discovery, exploration, and understanding.[2]

There should be no need to say that visual material ought never to be regarded merely as entertainment, or as a filler. But the very fact that it has entertainment value gives it great possibilities as a dynamic and convincing context for learning. The great danger is that although it may not be treated as pure entertainment, pupils will respond to it in the main as passive spectators. Teachers should understand that when this happens the effectiveness of visual material as a factor in the organization of learning is greatly reduced, perhaps even nullified. When pupils look at a motion picture, or have still pictures or graphs or maps brought before them, or observe a demonstration experiment, it is necessary that they should be actively and attentively participating in an active experience, or the visual material will have a relationship to learning hardly closer than those pictures of Greek and Roman ruins which still adorn the walls of many a classroom.

A few concrete instances will do more than much exposition to show how such participant attitudes can be established. The first is a demonstration lesson in eleventh-grade chemistry, to begin with a case in which mere spectatorship would seem to be at a premium. The teacher, however, successfully overcame the danger by effectively dramatizing the whole procedure. The topic was the synthesizing of hydrogen and oxygen to form water. A large U tube containing mercury was produced and set on the bench. It was connected to a faucet from which oxygen was piped. Slowly the level of the mercury fell in one leg of the tube and rose in the other. Then the inflow was stopped, the apparatus was connected with the hydrogen outlet, and the process continued. When approximately proper proportions were shown on the graduated scale on the tube, the gas faucet was disconnected and the mixture was detonated by an electric spark. Through all this the class was paying a fascinated attention much more commonly found in a motion picture theatre than in a science classroom. No observer could doubt that effective learning was going on, or that the teacher had captured the imagination and enchained the motives of the young people. He did it exactly as a motion-picture director does it, by skillfully though unobtrusively manipulating the dramatic values, by having everything ready and workable, by using suitable equipment which was easy to watch and which played up just what he wanted to emphasize. When one compares this with the sort of learning apt to be induced by a typical expository paragraph on the composition of water in the ordinary textbook, one is left without any possible question as to the importance of a compelling and concrete context as a factor in organizing learning for authentic results.

In handling even rather commonplace visual materials much can be done to foster participant attitudes and effective learning by dramatizing the point to be brought out. But often learning can be organized in such a way that pupils take an altogether more active part, by studying, discussing, or commenting upon visual material, by selecting it themselves, or by actually developing it themselves. Thus a fourth-grade group spent 20 minutes examining a large wall map of the United States, and carrying on a discussion about where their parents and grandparents had lived, and where some of their relatives were now living. The reader should notice how simple and obvious this procedure was. The teacher introduced it without the slightest fuss or parade, or any suggestion of doing anything new or remarkable. It transformed the whole learning pattern from passive absorption and fact finding into active participation.

Again, an undertaking into which a second-grade group was led was to cut out from a pile of old illustrated magazines pictures which conveyed the meaning of such words as sovereign, wharf, reef, tempest, and so forth. The pictorial material was concrete. The search for it involved active participation rather than mere spectatorship. There was exploration, discovery, and understanding—the whole authentic pattern of meaningful learning. Note once more how easily and naturally all this was done. All that was needed was enough imagination, forethought, and energy on the part of the teacher to think of the pile of magazines and to have them on hand, and enough understanding of what makes learning go well to use them properly.

A somewhat more ambitious plan was followed in an eighth-grade unit on Elizabethan England. The description is taken from the report of a student observer.

Particularly good were student-drawn color sketches of typical costumes of the day, all of them very well done for the age. The research on clothing seemed to have been done on a rather scientific basis, with each sketch pointing out the various items of clothing by their contemporary names. This was probably done to aid in understanding of these words, which usually mean nothing to students reading fiction or history of any period other than their own. All the bulletin board space was taken up with either student drawings or leaves from a very comprehensive picture book on Elizabethan England. All were informative and none was repetitious, none hung up just as a reward for good work or to show off the best artists in the class. Although the class I observed included no direct mention of these wall decorations (sic!), I gathered that costume work was part of the report of the "committee on costumes" within the class, and was hung to permit the other students to observe more closely. Similarly, drawings of typical furniture and house plans were the work of committees devoted to these phases of the life of the times.

Extended comment is certainly not necessary. Actually to develop visual materials of this kind, in company with fellow pupils who are carrying through similar enterprises, obviously avoids the bane of mere spectatorship. Again it may be worth while to note the naturalness and ease of the plan, carried out with no self-conscious parade of integration of art and history, but simply as a good job of organizing a context for learning.

Examples of this kind emerge into those in which the organized context carries definitely beyond the classroom and the school, which is the distinguishing mark of the fifth level indicated in the hierarchy. Thus in a certain school it is a frequent practice to invite the local traffic policeman to discuss safety problems, and the local game warden to discuss wildlife and its conservation. One might say that the outside world is brought concretely, convincingly, and impressively into relationship with school experience and school learning. Or again, children are often taken to observe at first hand great engineering undertakings, park developments, slum areas, museum collections, and the like.

### THE SIXTH LEVEL

Many of the instances we have been considering merge into cases where the organization of context proceeds in and through undertakings planned and carried out by the children in cooperation with the teacher. Here the following description of the work of the Ojai School, situated in the valley of the same name in California, is full of suggestions:

Conspicuous in the Ojai valley and in the country adjacent are certain geographical and geological formations which cannot fail to impress even the most casual observer. Different types of mountains of quite considerable height . . . surround the valley; strata are found at every conceivable angle, from vertical to horizontal positions, with anticlines, synclines, fault lines, and overturned folds. Fossils are abundant in many easily accessible places.

The marvelous sculpturing by water, alluvial fans, wave-cut terraces, canyons, and valleys, flood plains, etc., may be observed from the very school grounds, or at only a short distance from it. The whole environment is, so to speak, an open book with marvelous illustrations, where he who wishes may read. Here is a unique opportunity for a first hand study of many of the features which make up the world landscape, an opportunity to get away from words, symbols, and diagrams, and to deal directly with reality.

In the Ojai environment the interrelation between the country itself and the manner in which man makes his living is direct and obvious. Irrigation, farming, grazing, the cultivation of oranges, apricots, almonds, etc., the oil wells—all represent man's economic response to this environment, its natural features, soil, and climate.

On the basis of the data collected the children are encouraged to formulate their own tentative theories as to the origin and formation of the things seen, and to bring these theories before the class for discussion. Questions brought up in the class discussion, points argued, usually send the children back for still closer observation. Then when their minds are full of what they have seen, when they have a number of well stated problems to grapple with, when their whole attitude is one of genuine and eager curiosity, then and not until then, are the children allowed to turn to the textbooks, to geographical and mining reports, to maps, in fact to everything available that has been said or done by scientific men who have already examined the field before them.

This means a reversal of the ordinary teaching process which introduces the textbook first, and subordinates the out-of-doors to the secondary position of illustrating and explaining the textbook; a reversal also in the fact that the children, and not the teacher, are apt to ask questions, questions which may sometimes be very perplexing to the teacher.

Our Saturdays are usually given over to field trips, but excursions extending over two or even three days have been planned for. Each child is in the field as an original investigator, taking notes and making sketches, using compass, maps, hammer, and clinometer. On our excursions, the work is carried on by the group of children selected for the topic or phase of the work in which he is most interested or for which he has peculiar advantages in gaining information. The method of the working out of each project and its ultimate result are finally laid before the whole group for discussion. This brings the purpose and motive of each investigator to their final realization. The report to the group takes the form of informal talks, maps, sketches, diagrams, and photographs of everything that has been done. . . .

The topics selected for investigation are: Alluvial Fans, with the fan on which the Thacher School is located as a type; Sedimentation and Erosion, Mountain Making—sedimentation, formation of rocks, earth movements, folding, faulting, earthquakes; Irrigation—underground water, wells, reservoirs, tunnels, flumes and check dams; Oil Industry—relation to rock structure, drilling methods; Organic Cultivation—relation to temperature and access to water.*

The whole complex of organizational principles upon which the effectiveness of learning and the success of teaching depend is here illustrated. But the attention of the reader is specially invited to the

* A. Gordon Melvin, *Methods for New Schools*, pp. 238–240, The John Day Company, New York, 1941.

applications of the principle of context.    Clearly we have here a setting which is concrete, abundant, readily apprehended, and dynamically compelling.    And learning is deliberately organized to take advantage of it in every possible way, and to capitalize the values and opportunities it offers.    It may seem that the Ojai School systematically advocates an inductive rather than a deductive organization, but such a formalized interpretation seems to miss the main point.    The rich and and convincing use of context, the avoidance of verbalization, the employment of an emphasis upon concrete and convincing experience is the real issue.    Just how or when expository material in textbooks or works of reference is introduced does not much matter so long as it is not allowed to disturb these essential values, or to become a substitute for them.    Also it might seem that the school is entirely committed to developing a curriculum based on the interests of the children. In a sense, this is quite true, but the foundation of the program is not interest in the sense of spontaneous or cultivated whim.    What is done is to project the children into the concrete and abundant environment, and to organize for and with them enough freedom of choice so that they learn in and through genuine participation.

The almost endless possibilities for organizing effective context in connection with any type of learning are indicated by the following suggestions in the fields of science and arithmetic.

For children between the ages of 10 and 12, undertakings of the kinds listed below are found effective in connection with science.

1. *Instruments*.  We read and discuss thermometer readings; we use magnifying glass and microscope; we make and use a sundial; we experiment with a magnet; we keep weather reports; we make and use a simple telescope; we use a siphon.

2. *Gardens*.  We make a garden on the school grounds, raise flowers and vegetables, harvest them; we make a rock garden in the classroom on sand table or window shelf; we propagate plants by seed, bulb, cutting, and leaf; we learn the names of common flowers and vegetables; we take home seed, plants, and cuttings; we learn how to transplant plants; we raise plants by chemi-culture.

3. *Live Things*.  We bring our pets to school; we maintain and observe an ant nest; we collect caterpillars and observe them; we raise silk worms and reel off the silk; we raise baby birds; we observe and record bird life in our neighbourhood; we observe frogs and toads.

4. *Miscellaneous*.  We collect materials having a scientific interest for us— rocks, minerals, leaves, feathers, shells, seeds, woods—and make containers to hold them; we label our specimens; we visit the planetarium and make sky graphs and charts; we visit museums; we read science magazines; we study cloud forms; we study water—its constructive and destructive effects; we

study the seasons; we make bird baths and feed birds; we make bird books; we experiment with different kinds of soils; we maintain an effective (not static) science table.*

Again, in the field of skills, mostly arithmetical, the following:

We lay out the school yard into game areas; we weigh and measure each other; we keep growth records; we make health rules; we collect and discuss menus; we organize teams in physical education; we act as umpires at games of other classes; we prepare a map of the school yard for the principal; we take good care of physical education equipment and of all tools in daily use.

We draw maps and floor plans to scale; we solve arithmetic problems arising in our units of work; we review number combinations, fundamental processes, and simple fractions; we learn to use decimals and simple denominate numbers; we solve problems within our experience; we learn to use the ruler; we make change accurately.†

As some indication of the great range of possibilities for context, here is a catalogue of experiences involving the use of number.

1. *Experiences involving counting.* (*a*) Finding the number of children present in the room, the number absent, the number of chairs needed for a group, the number going to picnic or party. (*b*) Finding the number of people in each child's family. (*c*) Finding the ages of members of the class. (*d*) Distributing and counting school materials. (*e*) Passing and counting books and papers. (*f*) Finding the number of pages in books. (*g*) Using numbers to designate reams, sheets, papers in a book or chapters in a book. (*h*) Learning the system of house numbering.

2. *Experiences involving computation.* (*a*) Mailing letters and packages. (*b*) Finding cost of materials in making jelly. (*c*) Planning Christmas presents within a certain sum. (*d*) Ordering seeds or bulbs from catalogue. (*e*) Making maps of school neighborhood. (*f*) Holding picnic lunches or parties. (*g*) Financing school newspapers through sales, subscriptions, advertisements. (*h*) Making and using calendars. (*i*) Keeping a pet rabbit in school involving certain costs. (*j*) Calculating amount of material needed in making pillow, doll dress. (*k*) Writing money orders. (*l*) Making maps of school grounds. (*m*) Measuring amount of materials needed for various garments. (*n*) Improving or altering buildings or grounds, such as measuring for new floor, amount of lumber required, computing costs. (*o*) Laying out courts or fields in handball, tennis, volleyball, basketball.

3. *Experiences in buying and selling.* (*a*) Paying carfare when going upon an excursion. (*b*) Buying personal school supplies from store. (*c*) Computing cost of own school lunches. (*d*) Ordering midmorning lunch and checking money. (*e*) Planning weekly order of milk and crackers. (*f*) Computing cost of materials used in school activities. (*g*) Buying food for school

* Robert H. Lane, *The Teacher in the Modern Elementary School*, p. 115, Houghton Mifflin Company, Boston, 1941.

† *Ibid.*, p. 117.

pets. (*h*) Selecting least expensive and most serviceable materials for school activities. (*i*) Using real money on excursions and in shopping. (*j*) Buying and selling of groceries, milk, meat, fruit, and vegetables, and comparing cost of groceries at different stores. (*k*) Using money in buying for class needs. (*l*) Purchasing or requisitioning class supplies. (*m*) Buying furniture or equipment for various rooms. (*n*) Computing cost of supplies for school newspapers. (*o*) Collecting Red Cross or other contributions. (*p*) Selling tickets for school entertainments.

4. *Experiences in using standard measures.* (*a*) Using dry and liquid measures in actual measurements of material. (*b*) Finding how many cups of milk in a quart. (*c*) Weighing done in playing store. (*d*) Using a recipe for quantity cooking, as in planning a party. (*e*) Measuring heights. (*f*) Using measures in recipes. (*g*) Reading meters. (*h*) Measuring in woodwork, weaving, gardening. (*i*) Telling time. (*j*) Telling time of intermissions, classes. (*k*) Reading stop watch. (*l*) Computing length of school periods. (*m*) Estimating time required for trip and cost of transport, etc. (*n*) Scoring arithmetic and spelling papers. (*o*) Comparing individual and class scores. (*p*) Finding pupil and class averages. (*q*) Making graphs to show progress.

5. *Experiences in keeping records.* (*a*) Observing and recording the number of clear and cloudy days a week, a month. (*b*) Keeping data on the room calendar. (*c*) Keeping attendance records. (*d*) Keeping records of temperature indoors and out. (*e*) Keeping weather records in temperature and barometer readings.

6. *Experiences in keeping scores in games.* (*a*) Keeping scores in games and contests. (*b*) Figuring game scores, basketball percentages. (*c*) Measuring distances for races, high and broad jumps.*

Such lists of activities and experiences can manifestly be built up in connection with any field of study, and furnish a mine of material from which a highly effective context can be organized.

Nor should personal contacts be neglected in organizing context. Children may well be encouraged to seek information and explanation from workers in various fields—farmers, traffic policemen, railroad engineers, oil drillers, prospectors, and so on indefinitely. It is impossible, even in a far longer treatment than this, to exhaust all possibilities. But if the teacher once sees clearly the importance of seeking materials suitable for a dynamic and concrete context, and persists in his quest, he will be rewarded with never-ending opportunity and unfailing interest.[3]

## ADMINISTRATIVE IMPLICATIONS

The real difficulties which stand in the way of a full application of the principle of context are practical rather than theoretical. For it

* A. Gordon Melvin, *Methods for New Schools*, pp. 30–32, The John Day Company, New York, 1941.

involves changes in the management of education which, if carried to their logical conclusion, are neither slight nor simple. An individual teacher who understands what needs to be done to make learning effective, and who has reasonable freedom of action, can by dint of energy and initiative accomplish a great deal. But in a great many ways he is hampered and limited by the practice of the conventional school which, as an organized environment for learning, provides a very narrow and insufficient setting. From the standpoint of the principle of context as applied to administration, the following changes are indicated:

1. The classroom should be planned and set up as an environment which facilitates a wide variety of activities, undertakings, and experiences. It has been suggested that the room be planned to provide centers or areas as follows:

An art center—easels, calcimine, brushes, etc. A clay table—an oilcloth covered table equipped with clay jar and tools for making pottery. A music table—materials for rhythm band in primary grades and for home made musical instruments in upper grades. A workbench—equipped with simple tools for wood and metal. A library corner—table generously equipped for free reading adjacent to well stocked bookshelves. A gas plate, sink, and cupboard for simple cooking experiences. A science table—room for growing plants, for plant experiments, for collections and other museum materials. A games table, equipped with checkerboards and other simple games for relaxation and pleasure. A small portable stage for oral English, simple dramatizations, and radio broadcasts. A typing table, equipped with one or more portable or standard typewriters. A bulletin board, in all primary rooms, for room notices, exhibits, world events, items, etc. A simple playhouse, which will permit children to rearrange the several rooms quickly and easily. Provision for block play, blocks and storage space when blocks are not needed.*

No doubt to many teachers this will seem like proposing to bring down heaven to earth, so far removed is it from what can actually be had. But the recommendations are cited to show what a transformation in the conventional setup is implied when we talk about effective learning and authentic results in general, or about the principle of context in particular.[4]

2. Another consideration of great importance is the availability of material and equipment. A school well organized on sound psychological principles will maintain a materials bureau containing books, samples, slides, pictures, maps, motion-picture film and equipment, handicraft articles, files of bulletins, clippings from the press and from

* Robert H. Lane, *The Teacher in the Modern Elementary School*, p. 130, Houghton Mifflin Company, Boston, 1941.

magazines, and so forth. Such a materials bureau should not be hived off by itself simply as a service unit, but should be treated as far as possible as a cooperative undertaking in which the administrative officers of the system, the teachers, and the children all take an interest, and into which flow contributions from many sources including the work of the pupils. By way of comment it may here be remarked that one significant test of the professional alertness of any teacher is his continuing interest in vital teaching materials, and his persistence and seriousness in collecting them for his work.

3. School and community relationships are very important in the organization of a proper context for learning. Undertakings involving community contacts will often be desirable. As with any and every vital enterprise, these can at any time cause a certain amount of trouble. Teachers and administrative officers need not be too much dismayed if some criticism occasionally arises, for the only sure way to avoid it is to do nothing at all. But if a proper teaching situation is to be maintained, confidence on the part of the clientele must be a continuing concern so that opportunities will open up, and so that some valuable enterprise will not be wrecked by misunderstandings and objections on the part of the public.

4. In the timing of learning, adherence to the calendar must give way to qualitative achievement. It is just as impossible to organize meaningful learning on a rigid schedule as it is to make a plant grow in accordance with a set timetable. What is required by the principle of context is a simplification of the school day, which should not be broken up arbitrarily into short periods, and much flexibility in the arrangement for the school term and year.

When we come to consider other principles for the organization of learning, still further administrative implications will appear. Thus the marking system as ordinarily administered certainly does not make for good learning and authentic results. But for the moment our concern is with the principle of context only. And it is apparant that a far-reaching transformation of the school and its working arrangements is involved. But what else could one expect? The school was never built up as an institution around a sound technology of learning, and it is in many ways a clumsy and inept mechanism, as its achieved results very clearly show. The kind of changes here proposed are not for the sake of some vague theory but for the promotion of better learning and more adequate outcomes. Our psychology shows clearly enough how such outcomes may be obtained and such learning brought about. And the technological problem is to apply this knowledge to the running of the school.

## Notes and References*

1. An excellent source, with many concrete instances of assignment of various types, which are good material for analysis and appraisal, is Gerald A. Yoakam, *The Improvement of the Assignment*, The Macmillan Company, New York, 1933. Further good illustrative material abounds in William G. Carr and John Waage, *The Lesson Assignment*, Stanford University Press, Stanford University, Calif., 1931.   Much of the material in these two sources is of a conventional and quite limited type.   The chief study on extensive reading is Carter V. Good, *The Supplementary Reading Assignment*, Warwick and York, Baltimore, 1927, which also contains good bibliographies.

2. A valuable reference on visual aids, which can be used to round out the discussion in the text is Harry G. McKown and Alvin B. Hughes, *Audio-visual Aids to Instruction*, McGraw-Hill Book Company, Inc., New York, 1940.

3. For many concrete instances of context at a high level see the following: Robert H. Lane, *The Teacher in the Modern Elementary School*, Houghton Mifflin Company, Boston, 1941; J. Murray Lee and Doris M. Lee, *The Child and His Curriculum*, D. Appleton-Century Company, Inc., New York, 1940; A. Gordon Melvin, *Methods for New Schools*, The John Day Company, New York, 1941; James S. Tippett, *Schools for a Growing Democracy*, Ginn and Company, Boston, 1936.

4. Practical suggestions on physical reorganization, with pictures, are given by Robert H. Lane, *op. cit.*, Chaps. 4 and 6.   Suggestions for collecting and filing source material are offered by William H. Burton, *The Guidance of Learning Activities*, pp. 257–261, D. Appleton-Century Company, Inc., New York, 1944.

## Items for Discussion and Study

*In connection with this chapter there is a primary suggestion for discussion and study, related to the second of the two primary suggestions presented in connection with Chap. 5.   A suggestion similar to what follows will recur in connection with Chaps. 8, 10, 12, 14, and 16.*

Review the material assembled in connection with suggestion B, Chap. 5. Add to it, if you desire, from observation, reading, and experience either as a pupil or a teacher.   You have before you a number of concrete illustrations of context, and analyses of them on the basis of the general characteristics of a good context.   Now bring each of them into relationship with the hierarchy of applications of the principle of context, using it as a tool of analysis.

Once more it is suggested that you retain the results of this analysis, which may be repeated in connection with each succeeding principle of teaching.

1. Why will class discussion and thought questions generally go better and mean more on a background of concrete rather than purely verbal context?

2. Take the examples of teaching presented in this chapter, up to and including those on the third level, and consider how they might be improved from the standpoint of context.   What changes in the organization of the course would be involved, *e.g.*, timing of the topics?

3. Is collateral reading advisable?   Why?   To make the course harder?   How should it be selected?   Should it be the same for all pupils?   Should pupils be allowed to suggest such readings?

* For general references on context see Chap. 5.

4. Investigate and list sources of graphic materials that might be of use in your own teaching.   Begin building a card file of such sources, indicating addresses, type and cost of materials, etc.   Consider particularly sources of free material, such as the various agencies of the federal government.   Consult your local librarian for assistance.

5. Select a given lesson or topic which might be taught on the grade level in which you are interested.   Go through the files of the illustrated magazines and, if possible, clip or at least notate items that might be used as context.   How would you use them?   What advantages might come from their use?

6. To what extent can motion pictures be used as a learning context?

7. Consider how the various examples on pp. 107–109 exemplify the characteristics of good context as formulated in the preceding chapter.

8. Develop lists of activities and experiences related to other subjects similar to those presented for science on pp. 111–112 and for arithmetic on pp. 112–113.

9. If you are in contact with a school system as an observer or a practice teacher, investigate (a) the availability of teaching materials (Is there, for example, a curriculum depository?).   (b) the possibility of using community resources such as art museums, public library, trips to factories, cooperative undertakings, etc. (Is there any regular system or arrangement to facilitate such uses?).

# CHAPTER 7

## THE PRINCIPLE OF FOCUS AND THE ORGANIZATION OF LEARNING

### THE PRINCIPLES OF FOCUS

Consider the contrast between the two following lessons, both dealing with the theorem of Pythagoras.

In the first lesson the teacher assigned the theorem for home study, which simply meant that the pupils would have to do their best to learn it for themselves out of the book. It was laid out as follows.

*Theorem:* The square on the hypotenuse of a right triangle is equal to the sum of the squares on the legs.

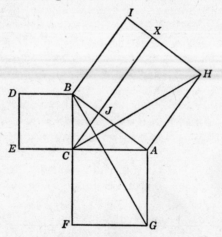

*Given:* *ABC* is a right triangle, right angle at *C*.

*To prove:* that the square *BE* + square *CG* = square *BH*

*Proof:* Let *BCED, CFGA, AHIB* be squares constructed on the sides *a, b, c,* respectively. Draw *CX* parallel to *AH* meeting *AB* and *HI* in *J* and *X* respectively. Draw *CH* and *BG*.

Then in

$$\triangle\!\!\!\!\triangle\ HAC \text{ and } BAG$$
$$\angle\, HAC = \angle\, BAG$$
$$AG = AC$$
$$AH = AB$$

$$\therefore$$

$$\triangle HAC = \triangle BAG$$

118

But the area of the square $AGFC$ = twice area of $\triangle BAG$. Also area of the rectangle $AJXH$ = twice area of $\triangle HAC$. $\therefore$ area of square $AGFC$ = area of rectangle $AJXH$.

In like manner it may be proved that the area of square $BCED$ = area of rectangle $BJXI$

Hence, by adding we have the area of the square $AHIB$ equal to the area of square $BCED$ plus area of square $CFGA$; that is,

$$\text{square } BE = \text{square } CG + \text{square } BH.$$

This was the material assigned for home study. Part of the next day's class meeting was devoted to reciting on it. Specifically this meant that the teacher drew the figure on the board, following suggestions made by different members of the class. Then the various steps of the proof were elicited by questions directed to individual pupils, some managing to answer correctly, others failing. The teacher asked for the reasons behind the various steps of the proof—the congruence of the two triangles, the relationship between the areas of the triangles and the rectangles. When one or two children were unable to explain, others were called upon to clear up the point. This process of recitation and discussion took about twenty minutes. Ten minutes were then spent on a few application exercises dictated by the teacher, which consisted of computing the area of the square on the hypotenuse when the lengths of the legs were given. The children worked out these exercises and passed their papers to their neighbors who corrected them in accordance with answers read out by the teacher.

In the second lesson the theorem was not in the first place assigned for home study at all. The triangle $ABC$ was placed on the board, and the children were told in informal language that the square on one side (indicated by pointing and sketching) was equal to the sum of the squares on the other two (similarly indicated). Then they were invited to consider how one might prove such a proposition. In particular they were asked to try to think out what the nub, or key, or one essential step of such a proof would have to be. They were given a short time, which turned out to be about ten minutes, to consider the matter, to try to work it out with pencil and paper, and to discuss it with their classmates if they wished. Then suggestions were requested. They came quite abundantly, and were freely criticized. The period was more than half over before the idea of drawing the construction line $CX$ presented itself, and the point of the two rectangles into which the square $AHIB$ was then divided began to emerge. After quite a bit of talk to and fro and roundabout, the idea of triangles began to float in the group mind. If it could be shown that these two rectangles were equal in area to the squares on the smaller sides of the triangle *ABC*, the demonstration would be achieved. Several members of the class simultaneously saw that the congruence of the triangles presented the necessary and sought-for link. So far everything had been in entirely informal language, and the period was about up. For work at home the teacher assigned the job of writing up the proof carefully and exactly, with each step and each assumption clearly indicated. The results were brought to class next day, criticized and discussed, and finally compared with the statement of the proof in three different textbooks.

Here evidently are two sharply different patterns of learning. The first group were put up against a body of material every detail of which was about as important as every other detail, so far as they were concerned. Their job was simply to assimilate everything that appeared on the page. The learning of the second group, on the contrary, was organized about a focal item which was of preponderant importance. Their first job was to discover the key or clue of the proof, and most of their time was spent in searching for and finding it. So far as the first group was concerned, the proof had no key or clue at all, and was simply so many inches of printed matter. No one who observed the two lessons could possibly doubt which was the more effective. In the first class there was a conventional polite languor. In the second there was an eager, almost combative interest as the proof developed with some of the compelling power of a good drama. The two lessons differ in many respects. There are contrasts in the distribution of activities between school and home, in the uses to which the group situation was put. But the key difference from which all others flowed—the difference that made one lesson almost certainly a success and the other almost certainly a failure in achieving lasting and authentic results— was that in one case there was a good focus, and in the other there was not.

Here then is exemplified the *principle of focus*, the second of the six principles in terms of which learning must be organized if teaching is to succeed. *Meaningful and effective learning must be organized about a focus.*

Every experienced student and observer knows how much teaching there is which simply wanders all over the map. The class is called to order, announcements are made, themes are discussed and returned, a checkup is run on yesterday's assignment, the next assignment is given, the bell rings, the period ends. Sometimes an exceedingly promising context may have been established, as when a class comes together the day after a museum trip or an important and striking school assembly, and yet all that is done is to chat about it in a pleasant and desultory fashion. The spectacle of unfocalized teaching is exceedingly common, and it occurs far too often even in the most enlightened schools. For one highly pertinent and just criticism of a good deal of modern teaching is that while it has gone far in the direction of applying the principle of context, it has not always succeeded so well with the principle of focalization.

No extensive research is needed to convince any observer that unfocalized learning of the kind so often seen is most unlikely to be effective. He can get his evidence by watching the boys and girls, for it is all too evident that in such circumstances they are not getting much of anywhere. Focalization is a most important criterion of successful teaching, for the reason that it is a vital condition of effective learning.

## THE CHARACTERISTICS OF A GOOD FOCUS

The general idea that if a job of learning is to go through well it must have a focus is so obviously reasonable and sensible that no one is likely to question it, although plenty of teaching does not seem to embody it any too well. But just how a good working focus improves learning, and just what one ought to have in mind in seeking to establish it are by no means self-evident. So the next thing must be to clear up these two points.

The importance of focalization, its effect upon the learning process, and the conditions of its proper operation are all to be understood in terms of the conception of meaningful learning. There is, however, a considerable body of psychological research which shows the relationship between the general point of view already explained in these pages, and the specific problem under consideration. This research translates into some very valuable guiding ideas for the practical teacher, and serves to show how the principle of focus, which so far has been stated only in the most general way, must be brought to bear upon the successful organization of learning.

**1. Focus Mobilizes Purpose.** The sources of will and purpose are in the context. Their canalization into will and purpose depend upon the focus. Set up learning in a context of activities which exemplify and evoke the compelling motives and determining values of the learner's life. Shape learning towards those insights which will make the activities successful.

Dynamically considered, the learning process is like a river. The waters trickle and seep from a thousand small springs and muskegs and boglands. The little streams move and thrust, but at first they are feeble and easily stopped and absorbed. Gradually they coalesce, find direction, circumvent or overcome obstacles, and gather power. The true source of energy which leads to the effective and meaningful learning of an abstraction of a generalization is an emerging awareness that it is a tool by which the determining motives of the learner's living may better fulfill themselves.

This is why a boy will learn to box better if he learns it to defeat a bully rather than in general.   It is why he will learn typewriting better if he learns it to get out the school paper rather than in general.   It is why a man will learn algebra and trigonometry fantastically faster than he did in school if and when he needs these abstract techniques to become a competent navigator.   Here is the key to the true use and treatment of systematization in teaching.   Merely to have a systematic plan is not enough.   Merely to have rich and compelling experience is not enough.   Learning turns upon the systematization *of experience*, not on systematization alone.   Context generates motive, focus mobilizes it.

Here too is the reason why abstract learning seems to generate an impulse of its own—why mathematics as such, or history as such, or linguistics as such, or any other field of intellectual achievement can become interesting and compelling in its own right.   The explanation is by no means that some new force or impetus called "curiosity," or "pure intellectual interest" enters the dynamic pattern.   As a scholar progresses in his field he does not lose all contact with the solid earth and turn into a creature capable of being nourished by thin air. He becomes more and more widely and richly aware of the ramifications and endless significance of the abstractions which seem so formidably remote to the layman.   All the motives and values of his living are pulled into the process of exploration, and his advance is by a psychological process different in degree and competence indeed, but identical in kind with that by which the little child comes to grasp and understand the general truth that two and two make four.

Not even the most unenlightened of schools can possibly be indifferent to the dynamics of learning.   Such a school assuredly endeavors to direct motivation and arouse purpose.   It does so by rewards, penalties, deprivation of privileges, and the marking system.   Some educators talk as though these measures did not involve "life motives," or were not relevant in any way to the determining pattern of values by which young people live.   Of course this is not true.   But the trouble is, in part at least, that impulsions so aroused are not germane to the desired learning.   To be specific, one does not learn to write good English because of a threat of being kept in after school.   One learns to write good English by trying to say something to somebody, and doing it as well and intelligently as one possibly can.   The former motive is irrelevant and the latter relevant to the learning. In the former case we have badly organized learning, meager and spurious results, and a partial or complete failure of teaching.

A sixth-grade group, under the guidance of their teacher, undertook to plan and publish a class newspaper. There was a very eager discussion of methods and techniques for collating material, of the form and style of the news stories and other items, of problems of format, and so forth. Within the context of this undertaking many focuses for learning established themselves—questions of grammar, style, organization, spelling, calligraphy, and so on. These focuses were highly effective because the children were set and ready to learn. They were, so to speak, in a very teachable condition. The enthusiasm, eagerness, drive, and interest generated by the dynamic context made the focal learnings very important and repaying, so they were tackled with zest, and well and swiftly accomplished. Yet these are the very learnings set up in the ordinary course in English composition which moves languidly towards indifferent results, and in which irrelevant rewards and penalties furnish a motivation which cannot flow from its narrow and unappealing context.

It has been remarked that children are interested in people such as foreigners or heroes or celebrities, in places, in the natural world, in adventures, in tools and machines, in making things with their hands, in the beautiful, the mystical, the bizarre, the unusual.* The "scientific" adequacy of this catalogue need not concern us at all, for at any rate it is not ill-chosen. And it brings to light a vital point. Among the natural interests and concerns of childhood no one has identified a wish to learn things out of textbooks. Yet the organized disciplines known as natural science, social science, mathematics, art, and the rest, which the textbooks embody, are without question the most potent instrumentalities civilized man has developed for the control of his environment and the shaping of his life. If one wishes to think competently about nature, one must think as the scientist thinks. If one wishes to think competently about society one must use the categories and techniques of the social scientist. If one wishes to understand the past one must see it from the viewpoint of the historian. If one wishes to deal with beauty one must use the tools of the artist. These are the best ways of understanding that the mind of man has devised, and it is a choice between them and unenlightenment. How, then, bridge the gap between the natural interests and concerns of the child and these uninviting yet essential impera-

* Robert H. Lane, *The Teacher in the Modern Elementary School*, pp. 96–98, Houghton Mifflin Company, Boston, 1941.

tives?   This is the very heart of the problem of teaching.   There is only one answer.   Utilize natural interests as a context which is meaningful because it is compelling and concrete, and in that context set up foci of understanding which derive their force from their contact with the immediate, but which lead beyond it towards that systematic comprehension which is the very stuff and end of the disciplines themselves. Everything we know of the nature of learning indicates that this is the pattern of organization which spells successful teaching.[1]

**2. Focalization Gives Form and Unity to Learning.**   The idea that form or unity is one of the most important characteristics of well-organized learning has been growing clearer in psychological thought for many years.   At first, and for a long time, the problem was set up as turning on the difference between learning "by wholes" and "by parts."   If one wishes to memorize a list of nonsense syllables, or a poem, or a prose paragraph, would it be better to break it up into small segments to be learned one by one, or to deal with it *in toto?*   Most of the early experiments decisively recommended the latter.   Learning by the "whole method," which in effect meant going through the material from start to finish whenever one worked at it, brought about very decided economies in the total time consumed by the learning, even though the separate sittings might be longer, and also in the total number of repetitions required, and produced longer retention.   The "whole method" was not easy to apply, and took a good deal of self-confidence, because in the early stages one might feel that one was not getting anything at all.   Consequently, unguided learners rarely adopted it, and tended to break down a job of learning into small part-wise units so that they could see a tangible result quickly.   But still, when a person managed himself well enough to use it, the studies indicated that he would gain marked benefits.

Much of this early experimental work was entirely valid.*   But when attempts were made to apply it literally to practical learning and teaching of the kind that went on in school rather than in the laboratory, some decidedly odd conclusions were indicated.   To many teachers it seemed that two inferences were involved.   (1) A large unit is always better and more efficient than a small one.   (2) The best way to learn anything is always to begin at the beginning and go right through to the end, and to do so every time.   The former idea, however, is certainly not implied in the experimental work, which dealt with the wholeness of the material and not its length.   And the latter, although it may be all right under special experimental controls, is hardly feasible in the classroom or in studying assignments.

* Some of it was technically unsound due to imperfect experimental controls.

From the very start of the investigations, however, certain findings had been appearing, which ought to have been warnings that the wrong practical inferences were being drawn. The superiority of the whole method was far greater with sense material than with nonsense material. With relatively meaningless material the "part method" or some variant of it was often found better. And recently still more qualifications have been brought out. The superiority of the "whole method" is greater with bright than with dull children. It is greater with easy than with difficult material. And one may get practically the full benefit of the "whole method" by beginning with a good preview or synopsis and then learning partwise.

Clearly then, something more is involved than setting up large units and always practicing them from start to finish. The inference that it is always best to learn in big gulps is a great and dangerous oversimplification. Indeed, careful investigations have shown that the alleged "whole method" is by no means so uniformly superior as it was once supposed to be. Note the word "alleged" whole method. For very often what has looked like a wholewise approach to a job of learning has really been nothing of the kind. Frequently what the learner was really trying to do was to assimilate a large unit which, so far as he was concerned, had no inner unity at all, and which therefore could not be called a "whole" in terms of his experience and awareness. A list of nonsense syllables, or a very complicated prose paragraph, or a passage far beyond the learner's intelligence simply did not constitute an effectively functioning whole at all for him. So his apparently wholewise learning was fictitious.

From all this lengthy and slowly clarifying research a most important practical conclusion has emerged. It is that the great necessity must be, not to organize learning in large units or to work always from beginning to end, but to organize it so that the learner will see interrelationships, or the pattern, or the plan in what he is trying to learn. A student, in connection with his tutorial work, had to study a very complicated 200-page monograph. It was full of statistical tables, graphs, and references, and packed with detailed reports of investigations. He made exceedingly heavy weather. He would toil away at a page or two until it seemed to him that he had grasped it, and then go on to the next section, only to find that he had lost his hold upon what he had just been studying. Finally, after much labor, he did manage to get some notion of what the monograph was all about, but only after plodding through it time after time, and making notes which ran almost to a quarter the length of the text. Now this was very badly organized learning. It was partwise learning of a very vicious kind.

But to tell him that he ought to read through the whole thing from start to finish and keep on doing so would have been a mockery, not a remedy.   What he obviously needed was some sort of a clue, so that when each new point, or table, or research report appeared, he could grasp its relationship to everything else, and see at least dimly how it carried the argument forward.   He did, in the long run, find such a clue, but only after much toil and sweat; and not till it was found did he begin to do a decent job of comprehending the monograph.

This is entirely harmonious with an investigation that showed the whole method to be superior under certain conditions but not under others.   When the material used was poetry which had a strong rhythm and a definite story and which was not particularly difficult, learning went well not so much because of the "whole method" as such, as because the clue was there.   The learner could see how the poem fitted together, and he was helped along also by the strong rhythm.   But when the poem was very difficult, abstract, and relatively nonrhythmical, then the learning went badly in spite of using the whole method.

Thus an effective focus for learning must have the characteristic of a good clue which gives the learner a sense of direction, and enables him to see at least dimly the relationship of one thing to another, and to recognize that the job before him has form and order.   Notice how beautifully this kind of focalization worked out in the second of the two geometry lessons described at the opening of this chapter.   The learning was set up as a search for the nub of the proof.   This in itself brought form and order into the enterprise, even before the crucial discovery was made.   There was a nub, a key point, a central relationship, and it must be sought and found.   As yet one did not know what it was.   But the very assumption that it must be there, that it must be found, and that the first job was to find it, gave order to the whole undertaking.   Suggestions and comments, some of them pretty wild, were not merely random remarks.   They were all felt to be attempts to converge on something.   There was a sense of "getting warm."   The time and effort spent in class and the time and effort spent at home and their distribution, at once had a rationale.   They were not spent in a particular way because the teacher said so, but because the emerging structure of the situation demanded it.   There was an awareness of orderly progress, and at the end an awareness of a convincing solution, all dependent on the establishment of the right kind of focus.

Compared with this the learning organized in the first lesson was hardly focalized at all.   The pupils were told to learn the proof of the theorem.   They knew from experience that next day they would have to recite on it. But it did nothing whatsoever to shape up or give form to the learning process itself. Perhaps if they had all been mature and experienced mathematical students they would have known how to focalize properly on a new proof all by themselves. But it is perfectly certain that high-school pupils in general will not be able to do any such thing without help. What happened was an attempt at undifferentiated swallowing, and only a teacher who is unfamiliar with the clear practical lessons of applied psychology would be surprised if the results were meager and transitory.

Again, a group of teachers were planning a unit on insects in the ninth grade in general science. They had in mind what, in the terminology of this book, would be called an effective application of the principle of context. They intended to utilize not merely a textbook but also still and motion pictures and interesting readings of many kinds. Also they were making provision for observation, collection, mounting, and display of insects. Furthermore it was their intention to invite the cooperative choices of the pupils, instead of determining everything rigidly in advance, so that genuine purpose might be engaged. But still they were not satisfied. They felt that much of the material and many of the ideas they were developing were good, but that the unit was just one thing after another, and that there was no clear reason for including or excluding this item or that. One of these teachers had the thought to inquire of a distinguished scientist what, in his judgment, was the most important single big idea about insects. His reply was: "That man is continually fighting them for control of the earth." Never mind whether this suggestion was entirely valid and defensible. Note its transforming effect upon the unit. At once it became an orderly, coordinated whole, instead of a grab bag of miscellaneous bits and pieces which it might be nice to do or interesting to know. There was a reason for inclusions and exclusions, and for a certain order of treatment. Moreover that reason, that rationale, could be just as clear to the learners as it was to the teachers. As they worked into the unit they could be aware that it was an ordered universe instead of a chaotic attic-full of odds and ends. And this was brought about by finding and establishing a proper focus.

There are two different yet closely related senses in which a good focus unifies and coordinates learning, and it is important to be clear about both of them. The point has already been touched on, but it has so many practical applications in the classroom, and contributes so significantly to an understanding of what good teaching is that it must be explicitly considered.

1. First, a good focus coordinates and unifies learning *in the*

*learner's mind as a single centralized purposeful job.*   It enables him to see where he is going, how far he has come, what must still be done, and how the various considerations before him hang together.   It coordinates the job by setting up a unitary goal.   When a pupil sits down and opens his geometry textbook in order to study the Pythagorean theorem, this very important sense of direction, relationship, and clear goal is apt to be absent or quite feeble.   He does not quite know what learning or "mastering" the theorem amounts to, and so he spends what seems a reasonable time on it and hopes for the best, since he cannot tell for sure whether he has really learned it properly or not.   Then he comes to class next day, and it turns out that his studying has not been successful.   The teacher is apt to put the blame on laziness, or dullness, or a vague something called failure to think. But the real trouble is that a poorly focalized job of learning has been set up.

Learning organized about discovering the nub of the proof is in strong contrast to this.   The learner now has a clue to follow and a goal in mind, and he can tell very well whether he is sticking to it or losing it.   He may run into blind alleys, but since he has a sense of direction he is able to retrace his steps, and is not merely confused and baffled. He may try out experiments along this line or that line; but even if for the time being he gets nowhere, he sees the relationship of all such attempts to one another and to the job as a whole.   And above all he knows perfectly well when he has succeeded.

2. Again, a good focus unifies and coordinates learning by unifying and coordinating *the activities, individual and social, in and through which the learning goes on.*   This is the objective counterpart of the unification which goes on in the learner's mind and purposes.   In the first of the two geometry lessons there was no real reason for the arranged distribution of activities.   The studying could have been done just as well and perhaps better in school.   The oral quizzing of the recitation could have been abandoned and a written test substituted.   In the second lesson, however, there was a very real reason indeed for the pattern of activities.   A thread or clue was being discovered and followed up.   This called for group thinking when a group was present.   And then the results of this thinking were licked into shape individually.   All this orderly setup came about because of the establishment of an effective focus.

In a great many teaching situations the pattern of activities through which the pupils are supposed to learn is clearly pointless.   Questions are asked round the class, and each child gets perhaps three in a period. What is he doing the rest of the time?   One typical suggestion is to try to trick the child into thinking he may be pounced on at any moment. But this does not work out well, and is less than honest. The real answer is to transform the ordinary quiz recitation into active group discussion and thinking which draws everybody in even though he is not talking. But to do so a clear and compelling focus must be set up, so that everyone is aware that he is really contributing to a joint enterprise. Again, the way to handle the distribution of activities between home and school is to focalize the learning in such a way that it must be so managed if the learners are to get anywhere. Again, one sometimes sees a class reading a poem around stanza by stanza, or an act of a play speech by speech. But this is apt to be completely pointless, and just a way of filling in time. If the class were engaged in appreciating the poem on some clear and mutually agreed upon criterion, with everyone contributing as best he could by his reading, or if they were engaged in selecting a cast for the production of the play, then the pattern of activities would be unified and coordinated, and would look like sense. And this, of course, means focalization.

From time to time in this book teaching situations will be described in which activities are enormously diverse, and in which every pupil seems to be doing something different from anyone else. Such situations can involve supremely well-organized learning, but only when all the differences are held together by a potent unity. In cases of this kind the core of the learning is usually not something laid out in advance, but something that develops as a common contribution made from diverse sources. Always if this is to happen, there must be a powerful focalization, so that however far afield any individual or subgroup may go, and whatever tangents he may follow, he is always aware of the relevance of what he is doing to the central unity.[2]

**3. Focalization Organizes Learning As a Quest for Insight.** All good learning is a process in which the learner comes to discover and apprehend the nub, or common denominator, or central clue in a complicated situation, and is able to control the situation through insight or understanding. In the experiment in match drawing described in Chap. 5, the game itself with the pile of matches and the varying draws was the situation. The learner was from the first made aware that a formula could be found which would enable him to win almost always, and to know in advance when he might not be able to. This was the focus which fixed his attention and efforts on the discovery of the needed rationale. Again, when a child is endeavouring to express himself clearly in written language, his ability to control the situation depends in part upon his coming to understand that in most instances a transitive verb "governs" the accusative case. Or again, in certain situations, the technique or skill of algebraic addition may be the central nub of the problem, and the skill must be grasped in and through understanding before the problem can be solved and the situation handled.   These are all instances where the central intelligible control is intellectual, but the same pattern of learning appears in the acquisition of motor abilities.   A person practices golf in a wide range of different contexts—at the net, on the practice tee, on the course, with various clubs, with and without an instructor present.   What he is trying to do is to discover, to feel his way towards, an intelligible sequence of action known as the golf swing, which must first emerge and then become established.   Thus the control of any situation whatsoever depends upon grasping a central core of intelligibility—in effect, an intelligible formula.   Effective learning is the process in and through which this central element is discovered and firmly grasped.   And it is such a central intelligible element which always constitutes the proper focus for learning.

An instance from practical teaching illustrates this point very well. Six more or less interlocking projects were devised in connection with which children were to learn to manage fractions.   The first project was a candy sale to raise money for the second project, which was a mothers' party.   Then baskets were planned for two needy families. Then a luncheon was prepared for the first grade.   Then a quilt was made for a children's hospital.   Then a teachers' luncheon was planned and served.   The children decided that they would need five dollars for the mothers' party which was the second project, and they got it by the candy sale.   So they had to figure the profit per pound of candy, and how much they must make and sell in order to obtain the sum they required.   In this connection it was necessary for them to buy materials up to certain amounts, to study recipes, to translate cupfuls into pounds, and so fourth.   At the end of this and all other projects, the results were summarized on the board.   For instance, after the candy sale the following were among the items that were written up.   "1. Our estimated cost of materials for $33\frac{1}{3}$ pounds of candy was $4.63. . . . 4. The total amount spent for the materials for the candy sale was $3.82. . . . 6. On Wednesday the orders filled amounted to $49\frac{9}{16}$ pounds. . . . "   A great many analogous "fraction situations" appeared as the six projects went on.   These insights, emerging out of the situations, and necessary for their control, were the focuses of the learning.   Here was the central core of meaning or intelligibility which underlay the specific operations and manipulations.

A frequent and by no means wholly unjustified criticism of much modern teaching turns on this issue of focalization.   Worthwhile, intriguing, wholehearted activities are developed. Admirable contexts for learning are established. But because of defective focalization, learning, or at any rate the right kind of learning, does not take place.

Thus Carleton Washburne draws a distinction between what he calls "*ad hoc* projects," and "omnibus projects." The six undertakings just described would be *ad hoc* projects, because they are deliberately designed to provide a setting for the teaching and learning of fractions, and such work he considers justifiable. An omnibus project, however, is an inclusive group activity which undertakes to do the whole job of educating, without however any definite intention in advance to convey any specific learning of subject matter. A group of children, for instance, may spend a great deal of time getting out a school paper and, as Washburne points out, they may learn a good deal about typesetting, but not so much about English or spelling. The work at the Ojai school which was mentioned in the preceding chapter, as described, certainly turns on omnibus rather than *ad hoc* projects, and science, mathematics, social science, and so forth are certainly learned in a manner that is not systematically planned in advance.

There is no doubt that the omnibus project does involve a serious problem of focalization. It can easily run off the tracks and degenerate into nothing more than happy living with a minimum of serious and valuable learning. But experience decidedly indicates that it can be handled as a successful organized pattern of learning and teaching, and when it does it yields excellent and superior results because of its vitality. The *ad hoc* project is unquestionably easier to handle but the danger is that it may work out simply as an imposed scheme of activity which does not elicit or express the purpose of the learner, and which then ceases to be a project at all except in name. As to the criticism that the omnibus project leads to ill-balanced, poorly rounded, incomplete, unsystematic learning, and that it leaves all kinds of gaps in the pupil's achievement, this is by no means as serious as it sounds. The conventional school is dedicated to complete and well-rounded preparation in its organized patterns of learning, but as we have seen it is very far indeed from accomplishing anything of the sort. Indeed there is good reason to doubt whether a complete, well-rounded grasp is possible at all for young learners. It seems to be something towards which one moves in the course of mental growth, rather than something with which one begins. Compared with such an ideal, vitality and reality of learning and the genuine evocation of purpose seem enormously more important. And these the omnibus project is better calculated to promote than any other learning-teaching pattern.

By way of passing comment it is interesting to notice here once again that the illuminating approach to teaching is not in terms of methodology but of psychological principles. When we have a vital context and well-established focuses we have the conditions for good learning, whether the plan happens to be called an omnibus project, or an *ad hoc* project, or something else.

Judd, too, has raised substantially the same criticism as that brought forward by Washburne.

It is a fundamental mistake to overlook the advantages of systematic thinking. In their zeal for correlation many teachers devote themselves over-energetically to taking numbers out of their systematic arithmetical connection and placing them in other connections. Thus, the fraction $\frac{1}{2}$ is part of the number scheme. It may also be an important element in a cooking lesson, as when one learns how to divide a cupful or a quart into two equal parts. Many thinkers regard it as a true example of systematization of experience to bring the fraction $\frac{1}{2}$ into the cooking lesson, but fail to recognize that there is even more training in systematic analysis and synthesis in relating $\frac{1}{2}$ to $\frac{1}{4}$ or $\frac{1}{6}$.*

And he goes on to apply the same considerations to other subjects, as for instance when teachers relate historical events to their geographical setting, but not to chronology, and so forth.

LONGITUDINAL AND TRANSVERSE CORRELATION*

|  | Transverse | Transverse | Transverse |
|---|---|---|---|
| Longitudinal.. | Numbers and number sequences | Addition, subtraction, multiplication, and division | Fractions |
|  | Populations of cities and counties | Calculating in bookkeeping | Pints and quarts in cooking |
|  | Dates showing sequence of historical events | Solutions of formulas in science | Inches and feet in shop projects |

* Judd, *op. cit.*, p. 176.

There is no doubt that the issue here raised must be given the most serious consideration by everybody who wishes to improve teaching and learning in our schools. Judd follows it up further by drawing an interesting distinction between what he calls transverse and longitudinal correlation. A transverse correlation, as will be seen from the table below, is one in which an item is considered in its abstract or

* Charles H. Judd, *Education as Cultivation of the Higher Mental Processes*, pp. 176–177, The Macmillan Company, New York, 1936.

systematic relations, numbers as related to the fundamental processes, processes as related to fractions, and so on. A longitudinal correlation is one in which an item is related to its concrete applications.

Since the issue is fundamental, let us try to state just as clearly as possible the position regarding it which is indicated by the analysis presented in these pages. (1) What is usually called subject matter, and what Judd calls transverse correlation, is of paramount importance. In the instance of the projects described above, the fractions are more important than the candy sale, if only for the very good reason that they transfer far more widely and give a far broader and more efficient control of behavior. No one wants to make up a school curriculum out of candy sales, mothers' parties, typesetting, and how to plan trips to Boulder Dam. (2) Complete and well-rounded understanding is the end result of years of mental growth, and even after many years and long scholarly labors final completeness is never attained. It is not the starting point of learning. The conventional school has persistently tried to carry learning along in a complete and well-rounded fashion step by step, and it has conspicuously failed. There is no reason to believe that this can ever be done. Far better begin with vital learning, although it may be fragmentary and disjointed, and work towards completeness by an evolutionary process. (3) Judd's two kinds of correlation are not comparable, and to give them the same name is very misleading. They refer to two quite different psychological functions. Longitudinal correlation means context. Transverse correlation means focus. There is no question of a choice of one against the other. Both must be properly handled if we are to have good learning. (4) Any good learning situation requires a dynamic, unifying, clarifying focus in a rich and compelling context. This is never easy to organize, and perhaps the difficulty is at a maximum in the omnibus project. But that is where the reward is at its maximum too, and the thing certainly can be done. In any case, the issue should never be stated as one of methodology, but as the proper application of psychological principles in the organization of learning.[3]

### Notes and References

1. The statement regarding children's interests is made by Robert H. Lane, *The Teacher in the Modern Elementary School*, pp. 96–98, Houghton Mifflin Company, Boston, 1941. For an illuminating treatment of the whole topic, and particularly for a discussion of the importance of the systematic "disciplines" and the dynamic problems implied, see Ernest Horn, *Methods of Instruction in the Social Studies*, Chap. 4, Charles Scribner's Sons, New York, 1937.

2. For important references on the role of form in learning, see G. Katona, *Organizing and Memorizing*, Columbia University Press, New York, 1940; also

J. P. Guilford, "The Role of Form in Learning," *Journal of Educational Psychology*, Vol. 18 (1927), pp. 415–425. For general interpretations of the whole-part problem see G. O. McGeoch, "The Whole-Part Problem," *Psychological Bulletin*, Vol. 28 (1931), pp. 715–716; G. O. McGeoch, "Revaluation of the Whole and Part Problem of Learning," *Journal of Educational Research*, Vol. 26 (1932), pp. 1–5; Mary V. Seagoe, "A Revaluation of the Whole Part Problem," *Journal of Educational Psychology*, Vol. 27 (1936), pp. 537–545. Experimental reports of particular significance for teaching are Milton Jensen and Agnes Lemaire, "Ten Experiments on Whole and Part Learning," *Journal of Educational Psychology*, Vol. 28 (1937), pp. 37–54; G. O. McGeoch, "The Intelligence Quotient as a Factor in the Whole and Part Problem," *Journal of Experimental Psychology*, Vol. 14 (1931), pp. 333–358; Mary V. Seagoe, "Influence of the Degree of Wholeness on Whole-Part Learning," *Journal of Experimental Psychology*, Vol. 19 (1936), pp. 763–768; Mary V. Seagoe, "Additional Laboratory Experiments on Qualitative Wholes," *Journal of Experimental Psychology*, Vol. 20 (1937), pp. 155–168; Mary L. Northway, "The Nature of 'Difficulty' with Reference to a Study of 'Whole Part' Learning," *British Journal of Psychology*, Vol. 27 (1937), pp. 339–403; E. W. Sawdon, "Should Children Learn Poems in Wholes or in Parts?," *Forum of Education*, Vol. 3 (1927), pp. 182–197. The two last deal with the sort of learnings set up in school, and the last with previewing. Also for over-all summaries and interpretations, see James L. Mursell, *Educational Psychology*, pp. 191–196, W. W. Norton & Company, Inc., New York, 1939; and Arthur I. Gates, Arthur T. Jersild, T. R. McConnell, and Robert Challman, *Educational Psychology*, pp. 377–389, The Macmillan Company, New York, 1942.

3. Criticism of the omnibus project is made by Carleton Washburne, *A Living Philosophy of Education*, Chap. 24, The John Day Company, New York, 1940. The reference to Judd made in the text is worth careful study. The projects mentioned are described in detail by Charlotte Mapes and Henry Harap, "Six Activity Units in Fractions," *Curriculum Laboratory Bulletin*, No. 33, George Peabody College for Teachers, Nashville, Tenn., 1933.

### Items for Discussion and Study

*Refer to the two opening suggestions for discussion and study in connection with Chap. 5. Follow them out in connection with the principle of focalization. Retain the outcomes in your notebook or card file.*

1. From your own experience show how the establishment of a proper focus or point of attack in a job of learning gives rise to a stimulating sense of emerging success. Does this help learning? What are some implications for teaching?

2. The job of covering a certain amount of ground in a textbook or in collateral reading it apt to be dull and therefore poorly done. Prepare some concrete instances from history, social studies, natural science, etc., showing how much the same body of content becomes interesting if organized around a good focus or focuses.

3. Take several sample chapters or units as presented in some available school textbooks. How is the material held together or unified? Is the focus such that it will immediately challenge the learner's mind? If not, can you suggest ways and means of bringing this about?

4. What value do you find in beginning a new lesson or topic with a preview?

5. Does the effect of a play, a poem, a story, a movie in any way depend upon focus?

6. Show with concrete illustrations how good group discipline is related to focalization.

7. Assemble, either by checking through this book (do not confine yourself to this chapter) or from other sources including your own experience, instances of teaching situations where all pupils do not do the same thing at the same time, and show that though there is no uniformity, there may still be a fine unity if there is a proper focus.

8. Show with detailed analysis why children are likely to learn abstract ideas and processes better in situations such as those on pp. 109$ff$ than if the ideas and processes are taught without any particular application.

9. How serious is it if there are gaps in a pupil's systematic grasp of a subject, so long as he really understands and grasps those parts of it and those ideas with which he actually works?

10. Much is made today of integrated or experience or activity teaching. Is it possible in such situations to evoke precise ideas, skills, and knowledge?

11. In organizing a job of teaching would it be better first to decide on the focuses and then build context around them, or to set up projects and let the focuses emerge from them?   Is there a middle ground?

# CHAPTER 8

## THE PRINCIPLE OF FOCALIZATION AND THE APPRAISAL OF TEACHING

### HIERARCHY OF APPLICATIONS

The principle of focalization can be brought to bear upon the practical problems of teaching by means of the hierarchy of scale here presented. As always, the various levels indicated are not categories into which all instances of teaching can be precisely and exclusively fitted. This scale, like all the rest, is simply an instrument of analysis and appraisal, to be used in dealing with described proposals, plans, and methods, in giving precision and direction to classroom observations, and in reaching judgments of one's own work and its merits and defects. The principle itself, of course, is of universal applicability. To be sure it is possible for activities in and out of class, presumably intended to bring about learning, to have no discernible focus whatsoever, and still to masquerade under the name of teaching. Sometimes one encounters such a situation, but it is chaotic and quite futile. Almost invariably every teacher at least intends to establish a working focus. Clearly then it is important for him to understand how this is done at its best, and also what precise criticisms lie against less successful attempts, and why they are apt to defeat the central purpose of all teaching, which is to bring about effective learning and authentic results. This is what the hierarchy, and the exposition of it that follows, is intended to make plain.

### PRINCIPLE OF FOCALIZATION: HIERARCHY

I   Learner's task defined by page assignment in textbook, by exercises to be completed, etc. Simple, crude, uniform organization of learning, routine in character

II   Focus established by announced topic, together with page or chapter references, etc. Lends itself to more extensive and varied learning patterns, but again chiefly an information-getting memorizing process

III   Focus established by setting up broad concept to be comprehended or problem to be solved; may or may not have to do with current experience; makes for still more varied learning patterns, and tends to break away from routines and memorization

IV  Focus established as a concept to be understood, a problem to be solved, a skill to be acquired in order successfully to carry on some undertaking in progress

## THE FIRST LEVEL

In a wide survey made some years ago to ascertain existing practice, it was found that by far the most common way of establishing and defining a focus for learning was to make textbook assignments by page.* The situation has probably not altered very greatly at the present time.

**1. Appraisal.** The critical analysis which must be made of this type of organization is uniformly negative. Nevertheless, there are several reasons why it repays careful consideration. A psychological analysis of any kind of teaching is illuminating because it helps one to discriminate between good and bad in terms of principles and reasons. Again, a type of teaching so common as this certainly should be conscientiously scrutinized. And thirdly, a careful analysis, although prevailingly negative, shows what must be done to bring about improvement.

The organization of learning by page assignments without topical indications is no doubt the easiest and most convenient practice, requiring a minimum of thought and trouble from the teacher. But it is exceedingly defective. It provides a very poor context. Also it violates all the primary conditions for establishing of a good focus for learning.

1. In the first place, it makes for a type of learning without unity or form. The mind-set of the pupil is simply toward "covering" the indicated material, and the business of the teacher is to ascertain whether this has been done. But to cover a given number of pages is the vaguest kind of an undertaking. Exactly what is the learner supposed to get out of it? Neither he nor the teacher can surely know. There is nothing to indicate relative importance, no emphasis upon interrelationships, no central core. All that is possible is undifferentiated study pointing toward haphazard and undifferentiated reciting on items that happen to come to mind. So at the very best, organization by means of page assignments is not likely to unify or structuralize the task of learning. And sometimes one finds a teacher who does not even trouble to assign a stint of pages all dealing with a single major topic, because he is chiefly concerned with covering the proper amount of ground, or keeping up with the schedule.

Moreover this very poorly organized mind-set, favored by a focus

* William C. Carr and John Waage, *The Lesson Assignment*, pp. 18ff, Stanford University Press, Stanford University, Calif., 1931.

consisting of page assignments, expresses itself in a crudely organized pattern of learning activities, for both the individual and the group. Thus homework simply means getting the required pages, and classwork simply means reciting on them, and that is how the job of learning goes.    Compare this with the very intelligent distribution of activities between home and school in the geometry lesson described on page 119, where the pupils thought through a problem together in class and put it into a formal statement individually at home.    This possibility entirely depended on establishing a genuine problematic focus, and could not be done with a focalization on a page assignment, which leaves nothing to be done at home except to study the pages and nothing to be done in class except demonstrate how well the material in them is retained.    Once again, one often finds excellent teaching situations in which different members of the class do different things, and where the central core of the learning is built out of their varying contributions.    Examples of such practice will be found on pages 177–179.    But again, this calls for a strong focus to hold everything together and to unify the job.    With a page-assignment focus it virtually cannot be done, because the only thing indicated is for everybody to go through the same stint.    One reason why so many teachers find it hard to realize that good, sound work can permit and even encourage differentiated doings by different members of the class without a sacrifice of unity is that they have never seen anything but a low level of focalization which creates an entirely undifferentiated mind-set, and reciprocally a dead uniformity in the pattern of learning activities.

2. In the second place, this type of organization strongly favors a learning pattern of routine memorization, rather than the search for and discovery of a central core of intelligibility.    To be sure, even the "covering" of ten assigned pages in a textbook is not wholly devoid of meaningfulness, for without it learning would not be possible at all. But it is a greatly limited and impoverished meaningfulness, and in particular the process of discovery and clarification which is so central in learning becomes nothing more than discovering what is in those ten pages.    Teachers of history or science who complain that their pupils read and study and recite but do not think, have themselves very largely to blame if they cling to this type of organization.    The pupils think, but only after a fashion, and in a direction which the teacher does not desire or anticipate.    They do not think very much about history or science because the situation is not arranged to induce them to do so.    But they are quite apt to think about how most conveniently to cover the ten pages so as to satisfy the teacher at the following day's recitation.

3. In the third place, the dynamics of this pattern of learning are almost sure to be feeble. The basic conditions of purposive learning are falsified. The context does not generate impulse, and there is nothing in the focus to mobilize it. If teaching were not so persistently regarded as a remote and dehumanized routine, fundamentally different from the ordinary doings of everyday life, this would be perfectly obvious. What sort of response would one get from the public if, in advertising, a play were announced as covering pages 112–197 in a certain edition of Shakespeare? Yet it is very certain that what makes for bad dynamics in the one situation will do so in the other, even if the latter is teaching, about which there is nothing sacrosanct and special.

**2. Steps toward Improved Practice.** A teacher who has been accustomed to setting up work by page assignments, or who has to use a course of study or conform to supervisory regulations which use the practice, can nearly always make considerable improvements if he wishes to do so. Moreover he can go a considerable distance without introducing revolutionary changes. The thing for him to do is to understand the defects of this type of focalization, from the standpoint of the psychology of learning, and then set out to correct them as far as his situation permits.

It will not do much good simply to try to make the assignments more clearly, to repeat them several times, to put them on the blackboard, to make sure that the pupils have heard them and understood them correctly and have written them down. No doubt one of the reasons why learning goes amiss is that the teacher does not take enough precautions to make certain that the pupils really know what they are supposed to do. But focalization by page assignments is intrinsically defective, and a bad practice cannot be turned into a good one by making it more businesslike.

What the teacher must by all means do is to study the assignment himself with care, and to turn it over in his mind until it ceases to be a body of material to be covered, and becomes a set of items grouped about a central unifying core. He may sometimes have to take some liberties with the course of study, combining or subdividing indicated lessons, but usually this is not impossible or forbidden. Then and not till then is it shaped up for teaching, because then the learning can be unified and coordinated. In making the assignment, the teacher can discuss with the class the central point to be developed instead of merely emphasizing the pages they are to read. He can help them to see how to read the prescribed material to bring out the focus. He can consider by himself and also with them how the core idea or theme relates to other matters, including current interests and experiences. He can suggest that different members of the class consider and work up this or that special aspect of the matter, and then report back to the group as a whole. And the class meetings when the assignment is taken up need no longer have the character of undifferentiated quiz recitations but rather of group thinking and learning, because a genuine problem has been set up.

Probably a teacher who starts working along this line will at first transform page assignments into topical assignments, though with increasing experience and confidence he may find himself developing problems and even projects. This leads to a consideration of the second level of the hierarchy.

### THE SECOND LEVEL

The use of topics as focuses for learning is a not inconsiderable step in advance, and can be a great one if their potential weaknesses are understood and avoided. It is important to do this, because topical organization is gaining currency today with the wide popularity of so-called "units," many of which are simply topics rechristened.

**1. Appraisal.** The topical form of organization can be used with good effect, *but only if it is treated as an instrumentality for good and meaningful learning*. The danger always is that the topic will be treated as a mere convenient subdivision in the course of study, a sort of category in a filing system, a grab bag of odds and ends of information very loosely interconnected. This criticism is at least to some extent illustrated by the lesson on The Shadow of Slavery described on pages 100, as an examination of the actual pages in the text will show.

Such topics as The Properties of Gases, Life in Ancient Athens, How We Got Our Constitution, Communication, or The Novel—and all five are taken from recent courses of study—are open to question. Good teaching and well-organized learning may be possible within the areas thus blocked out, but the names themselves do not suggest it. They would, presumably, be acceptable titles for articles in an encyclopaedia. But is good learning really favored by putting a sort of psychological fence around gases, or Athenian life, or communication, or the novel, with the idea of tilling the ground thus enclosed? It may be, but on the other hand it may not be; and the most that one can say is that these topics must justify themselves by something more convincing than their names.

Considering the topic as a possible focus for learning, there are three questions to be asked about it.

1. Does it stand for a real, effective, functional unity? Often it

does not.  When a certain course of study was examined and the teachers using it were interrogated, it turned out that the unit on Life in Ancient Athens was nothing more nor less than a few centuries of Greek history under another name.  This is far from being an atypical instance, and not nearly so extreme as the case of a summary unit on the Civil War, which undertook to deal with its cost in lives, its cost in money, its effect on business, on immigration, and on the status of women, and its permanent benefits.  Such a range of material is fantastic, and to hold it together in the learner's mind would take a miracle.  Clearly this is focalization only in name.  As summations under subject headings such units may be justifiable enough.  But as unified, bounded, internally interconnected learning undertakings they are preposterous.

Always in teaching, the important consideration is not how subject matter is classified but what happens in the learner's mind, and what pattern of learning activities is induced.  The ordinary topic tends to produce an undifferentiated, unselective mind-set, rather than to establish the urgent priorities on which good learning depends.  The job to be done is simply to get as much as possible of what is included, and the pattern of activities is controlled by this consideration.

All this is well illustrated in connection with an observed lesson on the thirteenth century.  It was handled with somewhat more than usual competence, for the teacher had much freedom with her material and was not compelled to a slavish adherence to a textbook.  The teacher began by saying that this morning the group would try to get a picture of the thirteenth century, which they had been studying. Such was the not unambitious focus.  The "getting of a picture" seemed to promise something, but the enormous and vague spread of the topic was ominously suggestive of the grab bag or the encyclopaedia, and so it turned out.  For the getting of the picture proved to mean rather desultory chat, in which various features of thirteenth-century history, such as the expansion of the Papacy, the evolution of the cities, the growth of commerce, and the fading of feudalism were suggested by individuals in the class, jotted rather casually on the blackboard, and talked about for a few minutes each.  This was clearly spurious focalization, and as one watched and listened to the pupils it became evident that learning was very languidly organized.  There was no pulling together of context, no sense of emerging meanings and insights, no positive dynamic.  Only the pupil actually talking seemed to be interested or attentive, and attentiveness steadily slumped as the period went on.  The teacher gave every evidence of thinking wholly about her material, and not at all about what was going on in the minds of the learners.   Presumably she trusted to the Almighty to get them to learn and to gain some benefit from this picture of the thirteenth century.   Certainly she did little enough about it by dint of conscious and planned organization.

2. The second question to be asked about any proposed topic is this. Does it lead to a type of study in which the learner progressively discovers and clarifies a central intelligible idea, or to one in which he merely memorizes certain data?   It is pointed toward the achievement of insight or toward routine learning?   With the great majority of topics and units in actual use, the former alternative is all too clearly involved.

One may, of course, try to define very clearly just what the pupils ought to know within the topic.   But what they ought to know is exceedingly apt to turn out as nothing more than what the teacher thinks they ought to memorize for the sake of a recitation or a test, rather than what they ought to understand.   This is well illustrated in the lesson described on pages 101–102, in which certain specific directions for study were included in the topical assignment on the Erie Canal.   Questions, directions, and study aids of this kind are not infrequently used, but in general one can hardly say that they do much to improve the focalization.   Their actual function is to delimit the topic, and to show the pupils what they had better memorize, and what they can safely ignore.   One of the practical objections made to utilizing them is that pupils will pay no attention to anything not mentioned in the questions and study aids, which is just what one might expect. For they are very far from transforming *memoriter* learning into discovery and clarification in which all relevant considerations have their importance and claim their due share of attention.   On the contrary, they amount merely to instructions from the teacher or the textbook writer about how to point up memorizing.

The mastery-unit organization elaborated by Henry C. Morrison, to which reference has already been made, is usually considered a novel and distinctive method, involving a principle unique to itself, whether that principle is acceptable or not.   In reality, however, it amounts to a plan for carrying the idea of aids and directions for study and highly specific assignments to its ultimate logical conclusion.   It was built on the assumption that no topic was suitable as an instrumentality for learning or teaching until it had been analyzed to a point where one could say just what a learner must grasp if he was to master it.   Quite an elaborate process of focalization was provided in the initial stage of teaching the unit, for it was the teacher's business to start by presenting to the learner the gist or essence of what was to be mastered, after which he went on to study the material either in or out of school or both.   But in actual practice the initial presentation amounted simply to a summary preview in lecture form, outlining the main ideas and their sequence.   Presumably this might do something to regularize study and to avoid a good deal of aimless floundering. But it pointed straight towards study procedures of the *memoriter* type, and the mastery of the topic usually proved to be no more than knowing a fair amount about it.

A great deal of topical or unit organization undoubtedly suffers from this defect.   It is often recommended that a certain more or less fixed learning-teaching sequence be followed, falling roughly into four steps variously named.   The first is a preview which sets the stage or establishes the focus.   The second is a study sequence.   The third is a period of recitation and class discussion.   And the fourth is a testing period.   This is a very orderly looking scheme, but one should not estimate its psychological values and limitations by external appearance only.

Bluntly, the question is this: Are we trying to get our pupils to think, or to memorize?   Many of the standard schemes for conducting the sequence of a unit by dividing it into steps or stages undoubtedly contemplate the latter.   They are plans for making memorization, retention, and recitation orderly and businesslike.   But if this is all they do, they are not likely to improve learning a great deal.

3. The third point to raise about any topic, considered as an instrumentality for the organization of learning is: Does it engage, point up, and mobilize purpose?   And here again the danger is that we may be trying to operate with a block of material perhaps well enough suited to go into a single folder in a filing system, but quite unrelated to the normal processes of the human mind or the normal concerns of young Americans.

**2.  Steps toward Improved Practice.**   Many topics, as handed down by curriculum committees, educational experts, and builders of courses of study, need a great deal of working over before they are likely to be effective in the organization of learning.   What has already been said by way of appraisal indicates pretty clearly the dangers to avoid and the values to seek.   But to indicate how the topical organization may be effectively handled, two actual instances may serve to sharpen up the analysis.

The first is the example mentioned on page 127 in which a topical unit on Insects was transformed by being built around the issue of whether insects or human beings would ultimately control the earth. This at once suggests a pattern of thinking and activity which would certainly be highly coordinated, but not necessarily laid down like a blueprint, or set up in predetermined stages. There could be a great wealth of exploration, investigation, reading, discussion, and reflection. A common core of understanding could evolve out of the various contributions and suggestions of the different pupils. Vital processes of individual and group thinking could be inaugurated, and though cut-and-dried conclusions and specific items of information as indicated in the course of study might not come from it, genuine learning certainly could. Thus when a focus authentically centering upon insight and understanding is established, learning can be well coordinated without the sort of tidy arrangement of steps and stages often recommended for the sequence of a unit.

The second illustration is provided by the work of an imaginative New England teacher. The state course of study required her to teach the unit Pioneer Life. As an instrumentality for getting her pupils to do some real learning it seems not to have struck her any too favorably. But here a piece of luck presented itself, and she had the wit to take advantage of it when it came.

An ingenious boy brought a novel nutcracker to school in the form of an old pestle. Through discussion regarding the improvised tool we made the discovery that some of the homes of the children harbored many articles of similar interest. By showing the children pictures of various antiques portrayed in books and magazines, the children became aware of the existence of such items as the following in their homes or about their premises: a blanket chest which was kept in the cellar to store tools, an old sea chest which was being used for a woodbox, several real old iron kettles that had been thrown away, two old charcoal irons that the children used for toys, some candle moulds, pewter pieces, a warming pan, an old pine cradle, an old foot stove, a butter churn, several spinning wheels, a pair of old saddle bags, handmade clothespins, some rare old books, two old wooden shoe lasts, a well-preserved sampler made in 1771, a powder horn, an old fireplace oven, some fine pieces of old blown glass, and many other articles of account running through the colonial period.[*]

This, to be sure, must be considered an extension in the way of more significant context. But it was a great deal more than a mere enrichment of the topic. Actually it transformed it. The actual learning, irrespective of the announced subject, centered upon understanding and to some extent emotionally realizing the lives of people in the

[*] J. Murray Lee and Doris M. Lee, *The Child and His Curriculum*, pp. 201–202, D. Appleton-Century Company, Inc., New York, 1940, who cite it from W. S. Dakin, *Units of Work Developed by Pupils of Intermediate Grades, Connecticut Rural Schools*, State Department of Education, Hartford, Conn., mimeographed bulletin, 1934.

locality during pioneer days. The teacher did not put her new focus into words, presumably because she hesitated to infringe upon the sacred state course of study. But she established it, just the same. And it had all the three aspects of excellence. It brought unity and form into the mental processes and the learning activities of her pupils. It pointed straight toward insight and understanding. And it aroused interest and mobilized purpose.

A distinction is often drawn between subject-matter topics or units, and experience topics or units. Europe in the Thirteenth Century would belong to the former category, and The Water Supply to the latter. Much fierce debate has raged around this alleged contrast, with some protagonists insisting that subject-matter topics are educationally undesirable while experience topics are desirable, and others taking the opposite view. The whole argument, however, misses the essential point. One does not transform badly organized learning into well-organized learning simply by setting up different things to learn. The lesson on the Thirteenth Century described above was a poorly organized job. So was an observed lesson on The Water Supply, in which all that the pupils did was to study two brochures and recite upon them. Either of them could have been made over into a good job, but to do so would have taken profound changes.

This points immediately to the conclusion to be drawn from this entire discussion of topical organization. A topic tends to be a classification of material rather than an effective agency for shaping up the learning process. As such it constitutes a poor focus. To be effective, a topic must usually be reshaped and indeed transformed, in some such way as was done by the enterprising teacher from Connecticut. It must be unified. It must be brought to center upon insight. It must become dynamically compelling. This usually means that it is altered into something that is hardly a topic at all in the ordinary meaning of the word. The advantage of the term "unit" is that it can apply to something quite different from the topic, for while all topics may be considered units, not all units are topics in the sense of being containersful of material. This gives the term its flexibility, but also involves a certain danger. For it can mean almost anything at all, which is equivalent to nothing. Thus a teacher may be using what can be called a unit organization and actually be organizing learning all the way from very well to very badly.

### THE THIRD LEVEL

A third and more highly developed type of focalization is found when work is set up in terms of concepts to be understood or problems to be investigated or solved.   This again is becoming more and more common in advanced practice, so it needs to be carefully considered.

**1. Appraisal.**   The following is an instance of problematic organization set up in connection with topical subdivisions.

> *Topic I—Water*
> Unit 1—Major concept.   The continuance of life upon the earth is dependent upon the water cycle.
> *A.* Minor concept.   Water is one of the necessities of life.
>> 1. Problem.   How do animals use water?   Why?   (*a*) With food and drink; (*b*) for bathing; (*c*) as a home.
>> 2. Problem.   How do plants use water?   Why?   (*a*) As food-manufacturing material; (*b*) as a home.
>> 3. How do you use water?   Why?   (*a*) With food and drink; (*b*) for cleaning and bathing.
> *B.* Minor concept.   Water occurs in a variety of forms, on the earth and in the atmosphere.
>> 1. Problem.   How does water get into the atmosphere?   (*a*) Evaporation from bodies of water, land, and set surfaces.   (Call for pupils' experiences.)   Experiment 1. What causes water to evaporate?   (*b*) From air exhaled by living things.*

Obviously this is an entirely different type of organization from a mere blocking out of material in a series of convenient topical units. It is directed deliberately at the mental processes of the learner, and it emphasizes thought, understanding, and the achievement of insight rather than the memorization of data.   It seems to offer admirable teaching opportunities, and the kind of focalization likely to be effective.

Its value, however, depends on the way it is used.   This may be clearly seen by considering the example given above.   In particular, the focal points of learning, which are defined by the major and minor concepts, need to be apprehended in terms of rich and varied context and application.   For example, the question, "How do animals use water?" should point toward the accumulation of a considerable wealth of observation, reading, and recorded experience brought together by the initiative and interest of the pupils, and thus varying from year to year.   Certainly the effectiveness of the focuses would be considerably reduced if not entirely neutralized if they were projected simply on a basis of standardized textbook assignments.   Indeed their character as problems to be investigated, on which turns their psychological value, would be lost.   There should be much time and attention

---

* An excerpt from a more extensively quoted course of study cited by Roy O. Billett, *Fundamentals of Secondary School Teaching*, pp. 263–264, Houghton Mifflin Company, Boston, 1940.

devoted to developing, eliciting, and recording the experiences of the pupils with regard to the water cycle, which is the central unifying idea. It should be possible to handle each section and subsection very flexibly, spending as long on each one as might appear repaying, and combining and recombining them with much freedom. As a skeletal scheme for learning through thinking, the plan as set forth has much promise, but the fulfillment of that promise would depend upon the living flesh with which the skeleton was covered.

Another instance generally similar in type is provided by an experimental course in plane geometry set up in connection with a controlled investigation. In this course constant emphasis was placed upon the nature of postulational thinking, the importance of defining key words and phrases, the processes of generalizing from data, reasoning by analogy, and detecting implicit assumptions, on the nature of indirect proof, and the significance of inverses and converses. This is in marked contrast to the ordinary treatment of geometry, which sets up theorems, definitions, and so on to be memorized, and problems illustrating and applying them to be worked out. In other words, there was a shift in the organization of the focuses.

In the ordinary geometry course focalization is chiefly on the theorems and other data as presented in the textbook. In the reorganized course the emphasis shifted to the processes of reflection and analysis involved in the theorems, problems, and other material of plane geometry. How ineffective the conventional arrangement is becomes evident when we remember that the study of geometry as ordinarily conducted, yields very little transfer and has a very slight effect upon the capacity to reason on nongeometrical topics. This is exactly what one might expect from learning organized about focuses which do not bring about any functional unity, which do not turn upon the evocation of insight, and which do not mobilize purpose and will. The experimental course, on the other hand, showed a very striking transfer to general reasoning, which again is what one expects from a focalization centering not on routine but on intelligibility.

Once more, however, as with the previous example, it should be emphasized that a focalization of this kind involves a more far-reaching transformation of teaching than may be apparent at the first glance. If it amounts to nothing more than an empty and abstract systematization, it is not likely to get very far. A course in geometry so organized cannot and should not proceed at the same regular and predetermined speed as one which set up a daily or weekly ration of theorems, postulates, definitions, and problems, and proceeds without any realistic concern for the learning that actually goes on. If one takes the position that all learning worthy of the name is essentially a process of discovering general meanings in a context that is itself real and compelling, and proposes to build a scheme of organization embodying the belief, then one must take the consequences, and these are both serious and far-reaching.   A process of vital thinking cannot be stereotyped, although it can be organized.   It cannot be done up in a series of neat bundles, each to be dealt with on a nicely planned and exactly foreseen schedule.   It cannot be projected on a precisely predetermined background of experiment, reading, or experience.   This is thoroughly sound psychology, and it is born out by the experience of every person who has ever learned in terms of clarification and reflection.   If teaching is organized in such a way as to bilk or ignore these admittedly formidable consequences, then in spite of all protestations and all appearances it relapses into the kind of routine organization whose failure has been demonstrated in practice again and again.

**2. Steps toward Improved Practice.**   Here again, as was the case with topical organization, the proper and superior handling of problem-concept organization is pretty well indicated in the appraisal that has been presented.   The great point is never to think that a problem set up in a textbook or a course of study or enunciated by a teacher will function as such in the minds of the learners unless careful and deliberate measures are taken to make it do so.   The learners themselves must be aware of the pull of the problem, or see the concept emerging and coordinating experience, or the focalization fails.   The problem-concept focuses in the unit on water, which were cited above, are opportunities, not fulfillments, and they will not automatically bring about superior learning and authentic results.   This is why it may often be more effective to accept and use problems coming from the pupils themselves, in preference to the more clearly stated and more significant formulations of some author, because the sense of reality and urgency is the key to the learning situation.   This too, is why any problem-concept formulation almost certainly needs working over, setting up in a rich and concrete and compelling context, and why time must be taken to discuss the focuses with the pupils in order to bring about the proper mind-set.

### THE FOURTH LEVEL

The essential difference between the third and the fourth types of focalization is that in the latter the focus is established with greater flexibility, and more closely related to and directly derived from the immediate sequence of activity in progress.   Careful preparation and planning is assuredly essential for good teaching, but when it is so elaborate, so detailed, and worked out so far in advance and at such a distance from the immediacies of the situation as the problem-concept scheme mentioned above it readily defeats its own purpose. The great and central necessity always is to bring about meaningful learning, and to do this one needs to be free to take advantage of what the pupils are thinking, talking about, and doing, and of what interests them at the present moment. A plan which makes this difficult also makes it difficult to organize meaningful learning and effective focalization.

The following is a very instructive illustration, for it has to do with a thoroughly commonplace classroom situation, and shows how the teacher partly succeeded and partly failed in capitalizing on it. A class period in twelfth-grade chemistry began with the return of a set of test papers, which had been corrected in red pencil. Properly considered, the return of a test is a true teaching-learning situation, and by no manner of means a routine chore, for powerful motives are engaged, and a highly dynamic context is at once established. This was certainly so in the case under consideration. Every member of the class was alert, interested, eager, and in effect highly teachable. The teacher was evidently aware of the opportunity, and had anticipated it. In some respects he used it well; in others not so well. He proceeded to concentrate on certain questions which had been missed by most or all of the pupils. One of them was: "Does every atom of iron weigh the same?" He propounded it, and there was an immediate and impressively noticeable pause for reflection. A mass of previously incoherent experience was by way of being pulled together. The challenge of an insight to be achieved dominated the minds of the group. The drive to achieve it was manifestly present. That is, an admirable focus had been established. But the teacher threw away the opportunity he had created by answering the question himself! It had all the effect of being told how a story finishes. With the next question, however, he did considerably better. It was: "Will a substance weigh more or less in a vacuum?" Again there was the pause, the hesitation. But now the teacher added to the drama of the focus by introducing a new and concrete context. He had ready on the bench a bell jar inside which was a spring balance carrying an object and indicating its weight, and he proceeded to exhaust the air from it, amid fascinated attention. The vacuum was created, the balance moved, the solution of the problem emerged, there was a brief discussion to bring out its general import. As one watched the pupils, one had the irrefutable impression that something had been unforgettably learned and that a scientific insight had been carried a stage further.  Then he dealt with the question: "Is ammonium oxylate more soluble than calcium oxylate?"  And now his tactics were different, although the psychological principle was the same.  This, he insisted, was not a memory question, because the class had been doing experiments with these two substances.  It had been, however, very poorly answered.  He called to the minds of the pupils the relevant experiments, and referred to their written reports on them.  These were looked up on the spot, and proved to have been badly formulated.  There was discussion, self-criticism, clarification, and a solution.  A focus had been established which unified and brought into order a body of previously incoherent experience, which challenged insight and understanding, and which commanded interest.

The main points to notice are the extreme casualness of the procedure and also the strong impression that authentic and lasting results were being obtained.  One wondered if this teacher were conscious that he was applying a highly important and fundamental principle of good and meaningful learning.  Quite possibly he was not, for he virtually threw away one golden opportunity.  A possible criticism might be that he did not exploit the others as extensively as he could, and would have done better still to spend more time on the questions so well handled.  Yet it was a display of extremely skillful teaching, and its success turned on the very precise and adequate application of the principle of focalization.

Another performance by the same teacher with the same class still further reinforced the impression of remarkable ease and casualness combined with remarkable psychological know-how.  About 20 minutes before the end of the final period of the forenoon, which had so far been devoted to other matters, the question of the refraction of light by a prism came up.  It seemed to emerge almost accidentally, yet suddenly there it was, in the very center of everybody's attention.  The teacher proceeded to establish an extremely concrete and dynamic context by going to his storage cabinet, producing a prism, a spotlight, and a screen, and manipulating and setting them up, to the accompaniment of a running fire of comment and discussion back and forth with the pupils.  The build-up could hardly have been more effective.  An admirable focalization was established.  Every pupil was interested almost to the point of breathlessness.  An achievable insight beckoned just one step ahead.  Then the bell rang.  There was a unanimous groan, followed by pleas to the teacher to complete the demonstration.  No, he said, it was time for his lunch.  And with that he brought the period to a close and hurried forth!

There is an excellent illustration of what the art of teaching really means. It does not turn upon added precision, definiteness, and clarity in making page assignments out of a textbook, or in substituting a topical organization instead of a pagewise one, or in working out elaborate plans in advance for handling a sequence of concepts to be understood and problems to be solved. That art, or at any rate a very important element in it, consists in knowing that a real teaching opportunity is an opportunity to dramatize and focalize understanding and insight, and in the ability to take advantage of such opportunities when they occur, and to promote their occurrence. A teacher who has become master of this portion of his skill will not be happy with a course of study in which jobs of learning are defined by textbook pages, but he will be able to do something with it. He will prefer a topical organization, but even this he will not like too well, though again he will be able to find opportunities in it. A concept-problem organization will please him better, although he will suspect the cut-and-dried letter of the law. But what he will like best of all will be to promote significant and appealing activities which he knows to offer rich chances for meaningful learning.

Quite a few additional examples of focalization at a high level have already been given in these pages, and the reader will find it instructive to reconsider them. There is the case of teaching English expression by emphasizing the clear statement of thought rather than by the memorization of grammatical rules, as described on pages 66–67. There is the case of teaching punctuation as a system of symbols to assist the reader to grasp meanings, as described on pages 67–68. There is the case of teaching elementary arithmetic with emphasis upon the understanding of numerical relationships rather than upon the memorizing of addition facts and so forth, as described on page 68. In all these instances, the learning centers upon a core of intelligibility embedded in a range of experience, which makes it understandable and brings it under control. In them all three characteristics of an excellent focus for learning are present.

To go back to the two examples cited above, in which successful teaching arose out of the skillful handling of an entirely commonplace classroom situation, it is highly instructive to put them side by side with another, in which there was a very ambitious and striking reorganization, with a complete abandonment of conventional school practice. Superficially the two instances look very different, but in essence they are closely similar, for both involved and exemplified the selfsame psychological principles. Here, as so often, we are reminded of a consideration which it is highly important to understand and remember. The excellence of teaching does not depend on externals, or conventions, or methods, but on the way in which learning is organized, and on the application of psychological principles.

The case now to be considered consisted of a study of textiles by a fifth-grade group.   It was an extremely rich, complex, and far-reaching project, carried on for a period of six months.   At the opening of the school year the fifth-grade group concerned became interested in the textile industry, which was the main one in the locality, because of an exhibit at one of the near-by mills.   In this way the undertaking got started, under the guidance of the teacher in charge.   In the early stages of the work pieces of cloth of different kinds were brought to school, studied, discussed, and classified.   Children contributed family experiences from parents who were employed at the local mills.   Books were read, reports and articles collected, experts were interviewed. Before long four basic types of textiles were identified—silk, cotton, linen, wool—which involved the emergence of one of the numerous focal learnings.   Then the children began to find out where different basic materials were grown, and why.   Geography was studied.   Subgroups reported to the class on various types of textiles.   Problems relating to the import and export of textiles arose and were followed up, involving a study of simple economics.   Many experiments were set up, including the testing of textiles with water, the effect of various dyes, and burning different kinds of cloth to note the kind of ash formed.   Color relationships and mixtures of dyes were studied.   Old spreads were brought to class, examined, and discussed.   An old lady, long a local resident, was invited and came to school to tell the children about weaving in former times.   Price problems were studied, including differences between wholesale and retail rates, and involving the examination of commercial catalogues.   Mothproofing, and many kindred topics were brought under consideration.

This, of course, was one of Washburne's "omnibus" projects, and it disposes of the claim that such organization is not compatible with good learning.   The list of outcomes derived from this undertaking is impressive and extensive.   The children gained skill in construction and in manual arts.   In connection with reading, they learned how to use tables of contents, how to skim, how to outline for central thought. In connection with written English, they learned such things as how to write a compact business letter and how to develop a good economical sequence in making a useful and readable report; also the legibility of their handwriting improved.   Mathematical skills included fractions, finding the price per bale from the price per pound, comparing costs, finding and using averages, and so on.   All these learnings emerged as meaningful focuses in a rich, concrete, dynamically compelling context. The undertaking looks infinitely more ambitious and radical than the return of test papers in twelfth-grade chemistry. But the psychological factors at work were the same in both cases.

Yet another instance, which might perhaps be considered midway between the two, is furnished by an eighth-grade core course. School opened late in September, and by the end of November series of reports from subgroups of the class, dealing with topics in or germane to American history were coming in and being reported to the class as a whole. Such a situation, where some of the children undertake to tell the others about what they have been studying and discovering, is exceedingly apt to degenerate into a flabby, dull, profitless routine, if not into actual farce and disorder. However, the group reporting on November 30 saved the day nobly, and did as good a job of teaching as one could wish to see. (Undoubtedly the teacher himself had plenty to do with their success, but he kept most discreetly in the background.) They were reporting on isms in American history and American life, and they started by putting on the board the following chart or scale, running from left to right:

Anarchy Communism Socialism Liberalism Republicanism Nazism

This schematization served as an excellent focus. There was universal, eager, even violent discussion throughout the class. Some revisions were forced upon the originating group. Materials previously studied, magazine articles, newspaper stories, radio addresses, and informal comments were brought to mind. Thus a great body of context was shaped up and unified, certain insights undoubtedly emerged although the legitimacy of this or indeed any such linear arrangement of "isms" was very properly challenged, and a powerful dynamic was elicited.

At the risk of being somewhat repetitious it is worth while to point out carefully just how the conditions of good focalization are fulfilled in the examples just presented.

1. In every case the learning process was given form and order. It was not an affair of pounding in a number of items, not vitally related to one another, and each of equal importance. There was an awareness of priority, of a central thread or clue which brought everything else into relationship. This had for its obverse a pattern of learning activities which were well coordinated although, particularly in the instance of the unit on textiles, they were exceedingly varied. There was never a predetermined series of steps or stages, but all the activities of groups and individuals were held together because of the coordinating and unifying clue that ran through them.

2. The organization of learning turned primarily upon the quest for insight and understanding. What was set up was not a body of material to be memorized, but a range of experience to be comprehended and controlled.

3. Purpose and the will to learn were effectively mobilized. The life values and motives of the learners were evoked and enlisted. To put the point otherwise, the motivation was positive rather than negative, a matter of interest rather than compulsion. To some it might seem that the unit on textiles is a peculiarly admirable example of teaching, for the reason that so much of the planning was actually done by the pupils, and because they made so many of the decisions. In fact, provisions were made to encourage them to do so, by setting up committees, calling for suggestions and discussing them when offered, and so forth. All this is apt to win high praise in certain quarters as a laudable exemplification of democracy. Perhaps indeed it is. But still it is important not to confuse the issue. The point always is that if a focus is to inaugurate effective motivation it is very desirable for the learners to share in setting it up so that it can embody purposes which are really their own. This can be done by a committee system or some such ambitious plan. But it was also achieved excellently by the science teacher, and in the simplest kind of way. The sort of organization exemplified in the unit on textiles can be just as much of a fetish as the inductive-development lesson. Always the great necessity is to penetrate beneath the outward forms of procedure, to the psychological processes actually operating. And a good focus is one that mobilizes the genuine and authentic purposes of the learners, whatever the particular means used to bring this about.

## FOCALIZATION AND PLANNING

All that has been said about the principle of focalization goes to show that it must bulk large in the planning done by any teacher who wishes to succeed. What is known as lesson planning or preparation very often amounts to little more than laying out enough doings to fill the period, while at the same time staying with the sequence determined by the textbook or the course of study. The routine business including announcements, questions on the previous assignment, some scheme for blackboard work, a short written test, the assignment for the following day—these are the kinds of items which the conscientious teacher wishes to get in hand overnight as he considers the job before him. He will know what to do. The pupils will be kept busy. Disciplinary troubles will be held to a minimum. There will be no complaints. Things will move along smoothly.

Without wishing to disparage earnest efforts it is necessary to say that this is very inadequate. With such planning the machine may run well, but the chances of effective learning are not good. The point, by all manner of means, is to plan focuses rather than lessons, unless by a lesson one means a unified job of learning and teaching rather than a loosely hung sequence of doings long enough to occupy about 50 minutes. The difference is vital, and the required condition is by no means hard to fulfill, so long as one has it in mind. A few examples will show just what is involved.

A sixth-grade chorus, meeting out of school hours under the direction of an enthusiastic teacher, was observed. The children began to learn the famous and beautiful round, *Dona Nobis Pacem*. They progressed quite well, and the teacher in charge directed their efforts very earnestly. She called constant attention to the right notes, and also to wrong notes, when and as they occurred. This was a fairly good focus, but no more. The attention of the learners was concentrated on correctness, which is well enough as far as it goes. But why correctness? Why the right notes? Surely because of their appropriateness, their beauty, their expressiveness. Here was the core of meaning which needed to be dug out. What went on was by no means discreditable but one got the distinct impression that the teacher had decided on the particular song chosen without giving any consideration to amount to anything to the psychological processes involved, which of course were the key to the whole situation. If she had directed the attention and effort of the group constantly to the beauty, the expressiveness, the significance of the words and the music—which could readily have been done, and which, in a world at war, cried aloud to be done with this particular song which is a prayer for peace—a creditable job would have been transformed into a first-rate one. A more impressive result would have been forthcoming, and a deeper and more lasting impression made on the young minds.

Again, a sixth-grade group was observed during a period when they were reporting on and discussing a recent museum trip. Once more, one gained the unavoidable impression that the teacher had thought of this as a good and appropriate way of filling in a period, without considering the psychological factors which it was his business to organize. What happened was that one child after another reported vaguely and uninterestingly on what he or she had seen, done, or missed. Interspersed with these statements there was a good deal of pleasant but desultory chat. It was so clearly pointless, so clearly lacking in focus, that before long the teacher became disturbed. He suggested that individuals volunteer to make statements, while the rest listened carefully, after which they were to criticize them for form and content. There was the germ of a very good idea here, but alas, only the germ. It did not work out. Criticism for form and content needs pointing up, sharpening up, organizing. And this was not done. So the period dragged on to a resultless close, pretty much a waste of time, unless one considers mild boredom relaxing and thus propitious to mental health.

A closely similar spectacle was presented by a tenth-grade class in English. They spent the period (and obviously this was the teacher's inspiration as to what to do) in reading around one by one the second act of the play, *Abe Lincoln in Illinois*. One was left wondering why they did it. Each pupil in turn read a speech, the rest dawdling, doodling, and occasionally whispering, and paying attention only when the moment to be vocal approached. There were a few giggles when a boy read one of the Lincoln speeches commenting on his own appearance in most unflattering terms. There was a good deal of fumbling and stumbling over words. One gathered that there was some intention to produce the play later on, which would certainly have suggested focalization having to do with the selection of the caste, the advisability of cuts, and so forth. But nothing of the sort was done. Perhaps the teacher had been too tired on the previous evening to think with any care about what he wanted the pupils to learn from the experience, and how they might best be brought to learn it.

Nevertheless, one must not jump too hastily at the conclusion that focalization is lacking simply because the teaching seems casual or easy or unhurried. A second-grade group was visited shortly before Thanksgiving. They were sitting in a semicircle on the floor, chatting so informally that at first it seemed as though no significant learning could possibly be going on. But as one watched and listened, it became apparent that there was considerable method in the informality. The talk circled here and there, and began to center on Thanksgiving. The Pilgrims were mentioned. Who were they? It developed that they came over on the *Mayflower*. It was a sailing ship. Why a sailing ship? Something was said about their hardships. Why, then, did they come at all? One of the children mentioned freedom of worship. At once the teacher made a pounce. What did that mean? The occasion ended by the suggestion that the little pupils ask their parents about Thanksgiving, and talk more about it next day. Nothing could have been less formal. Nothing could have been more apparently easygoing. Yet the characteristic pattern of a unifying and meaningful focus or series of focuses in an engaging context was present. Perhaps the only criticism was that the focal theme was held a little too long for such young children.   But there was an indubitable impression of genuine learning and successful teaching.

Innumerable illustrations could be given of the application, misuse, and ignoring of the principle of focalization, for occasions in which it occurs or ought to occur arise in every teaching situation.   The idea is essentially simple and intelligible, and a very real factor in teaching skill is to grasp it, to learn how to plan for it, and to capitalize opportunities for its use when these arise unforseen.

### Items for Discussion and Study

*Refer to the opening suggestion for discussion and study in connection with Chap.6, of course substituting Chap. 7 for Chap. 5.   Follow it out in connection with the principle of focalization.   Retain the outcomes in your notebook or card file.*

1. Take a school textbook and from it lay out an assignment simply by pages. Then consider very carefully and realistically just what you are asking the learners to do.   Is good learning probable?

2. Reconsider this same assignment.   Follow the suggestions on pp. 139–140. See if you can work out a better focus and a better organization.

3. Apply the criticisms of topical organization here presented to a number of instances taken from school textbooks, courses of study, etc.

4. Reconsider the topics you used in the above question.   Try to decide what pupils of some given grade level ought to know about them.   Can you tell?

5. A frequent criticism of study guides, study questions, etc., is that pupils who use them will ignore everything in the material to which they do not refer. How serious is this criticism?   Can the condition be overcome?

6. To what extent did the general science unit on Insects, after it had been reorganized, meet the conditions of good focus stated in Chap. 7?

7. Work over some of the topics assembled in connection with Question 3 above, and see if you can organize them about better foci.

8. Work over the problem-concept unit on Water, pp. 146–147 and show how you would reorganize it for effective learning, considering both context and focuses.

9. Following on the last question, can you suggest specific measures, such as group reports, demonstrations, field trips, etc., which might lead to the developing of problem-concept focuses from the actual on-going process?

# CHAPTER 9

## THE PRINCIPLE OF SOCIALIZATION AND THE ORGANIZATION OF LEARNING

For nearly three weeks George had been working hard at his report for his eighth-grade core course. It had to do with home life in New York City about the year 1820. The topic had not exactly been assigned by the teacher, nor had George chosen it wholly on his own initiative. It had been decided upon, along with many other topics, as a result of discussions in which the teacher, the whole class, and naturally George himself had shared, and which were all intended to supply background for an assembly program they were to put on later in the year. His report, moreover, was not to be just handed in to the teacher, but submitted to the class. He felt a real responsibility for it, and had been anxious to do as well as he could. He had hunted up books of reference and old magazines. He had visited the Museum of the City of New York several times, and had many interesting things to tell about what he had seen there. The Museum offered photographs for sale, and he had purchased some of them, and requested that the school reflectoscope be on hand in the classroom so that he might show a few. He had rewritten his report several times, reorganizing what he had to say so that it might be clearer, and doing his best to polish up the style. Now he was facing his big occasion and presenting his findings to his classmates. He met with an interested response. There were a few questions and comments which helped him to see where his presentation might have been improved. Also some suggestions came up which, as it turned out, sent him back to look for more material. There could be no doubt that both George himself and also his fellow pupils were doing some richly meaningful and very effective learning. Nor could there be any doubt that the effectiveness and meaningful quality of the learning was due, in no small measure. to the intelligently handled social situation in which it took place.

In this particular instance a general proposition is involved. *The meaningfulness and effectiveness of learning depends to an important extent upon the social setting in which it is done.* Here is the third basic psychological principle of successful teaching—the *principle of socialization.*

Like all the rest of the principles of teaching here being considered, this one is both soundly based on psychological findings, and also quite in keeping with common sense and common experience.  Very little of the best learning goes on in complete solitude.  The expert and highly specialized research worker seeks contacts with others whose background, training, and interests are similar to his own—if not face to face, at least by mail; if not from day to day, at least on not too infrequent occasions.  The creative artist, who seems so lonely and remote as he elaborates his works—and this, of course, is a learning process too—nearly always seeks some constructive human association, immediate or prospective or both.  The very persistence and vitality of scholarly and professional organizations, whose members may come from great distances for discussion and mutual stimulation, are good evidence that learning is not by nature a purely solitary preoccupation and that the learner in the very act and process of learning behaves always as a social being.

There is an idea, not usually made explicit but prevalent nonetheless, that the socializing influence of a school should be considered apart from the knowledge, skill, and insight which it tries to impart. Very often such a separation does exist, up to a point, although it is not usually as marked as people easily suppose and can never in the nature of the case be absolute.  A child from a crude, underprivileged home comes to school for the first time.  The social situation makes a very forceful impact upon him.  He quickly begins to find out that he must behave himself according to certain standards, that he must make many new accommodations to strange children and to strange adults. Also he quickly discovers, as one of the striking aspects of this new society of which he has become a member, that in it people are learning to read and actually reading.  His own learning to read is just as really part and parcel of his accommodation to the social setting, and just as deeply colored by it, as his learning to arrive on time, or to answer courteously when asked a question.  Several years later on, when he is in high school, the amount and seriousness of his study will depend a very great deal upon the social fashions of the institution, and will in considerable measure be an expression of its social atmosphere.

So it is a very grave error to suppose that the social setting of the school or the class is irrelevant to the learning that goes on.  On the contrary, social influences are woven inextricably into the very texture of the learning.  They may affect it favorably, or they may affect it unfavorably, but affect it they certainly will.  This is the reason why every teacher who wishes to work with good success needs to understand the social conditions that favor effective learning, and to contrast them with those that make for ineffective learning, and in general to know how to apply in his endeavors the principle of socialization.

## CHARACTERISTICS OF GOOD SOCIALIZATION

Specific research dealing with the relationship of social patterns and influences to the learning process is not as copious as that having to do with the other principles of teaching discussed in these pages. This seems somewhat strange, for almost all teaching is group teaching, and the most ordinary observation shows that the effect of the social setting is potent and continuous. Nevertheless, enough material exists to make possible a reasonably secure and practically helpful analysis.

1. **Social Facilitation.** It is known that there exists a definite factor called "social facilitation." An individual will do many tasks better when he does them in a group of similarly occupied workers than when he does them alone. The mere presence of such a group tends to produce more speed when speed is wanted, more care when care is emphasized, more accuracy when accuracy is emphasized. This gain, due to the presence of a group is known as a "social increment." It is greatest when all members of the group can readily see what the others are doing. Moreover, social facilitation is favored when the group works without any kind of restriction or disturbance. Thus the mere presence of a teacher has been found, under certain circumstances, to bring about a reduction of the social increment. The psychological mechanisms of social facilitation are not understood, but its reality is well established. A coacting group constitutes a dynamic influence upon the performance of its members by its mere existence and example.[1]

These findings are of appreciable, albeit limited practical significance. There is no doubt that one of the skills of successful teaching is to employ from time to time what may be called "social momentum." A good illustration is class chorus work in the teaching of a foreign language, which is of proved effectiveness. The technique of the teacher consists in manipulating the situation so that everybody is drawn in, so that everybody is aware by sight and hearing of what everybody else is doing. His job is best done when he starts the ball rolling, and then lets things alone. Work in rhythmics, too, can and should exemplify social facilitation, although many other factors are involved. A great many drill sequences can yield considerable social increment in efficiency if skillfully handled with the idea in mind. There is every reason why the group opportunities of the school and the classroom should, from time to time, be deliberately exploited in such ways.   Effective management turns upon establishing a parallel momentum, dramatizing it, and then letting it alone without nagging or disturbance.

**2. Incentives.**   A considerable number of investigations have been made upon the effect of incentives upon learning and achievement. All of them are in substantial agreement, and they throw considerable further light on the kind of personal and social relationships that should be maintained in a learning situation.   The points which have been brought out are all of practical significance and can readily find application in the well-conducted classroom

1.  In the first place it is well established that some kind of recognition for work done and effort made is always better than none at all. One might think that this would hardly need saying, and that mere common sense would indicate as much without any kind of experimental or statistical proof.   Yet it happens often enough that papers and tests are returned, verbal answers received, and initiative displayed without a word of recognition or commendation by the teacher.   This is a very serious weakness in the organization of learning, for it has been shown again and again that the learner definitely benefits by gaining some notion of the impression he has made.   A not unimportant factor in successful teaching is the regular practice of giving him some such notion.

2.  Positive incentives are more effective than negative incentives. Praise for success gets better results than blame for failure.   Pleasant requests and suggestions bring about better learning and better achievement than scoldings.   It has been shown in the experimental work that the immediate values of positive incentives are appreciably greater than those of negative incentives, but that their cumulative effect when brought to bear over a period of time is very much greater. A pleasant social atmosphere and pleasant personal relations tend to build up achievement and to influence learning more and more favorably when they are maintained and the longer they last.   Scolding, harshness, sarcasm, and blame for failure have some immediate effect, but that effect tends to die out with the passage of time.

3.  Scolding, sarcasm, and ridicule are very vicious types of negative incentives.   Their consistent use indicates a definitely bad management of the learning situation.   Where criticism is indicated, it should be calm, unhurried, and above all considerate.   Moreover, positive and definite prohibitions are more effective than threats.

The importance of these considerations comes from the ascertained fact that in a great many classrooms negative incentives preponderate. Of course there is no argument whatsoever for insincerity, or for sentimental gush over work that is poor and that the pupil himself pretty well knows to be poor, or for toleration of unruly and outrageous conduct. But a teacher ought to be able to avoid such obvious blunders and follies and still maintain a consistently helpful, kindly, and positive attitude. The point is to organize the social aspects of the learning situation so that the group of people working and living together in the classroom, among whom of course the teacher is the key member, is consistently set in the direction of recognizing and rewarding success. There should be a fixed policy of permitting and encouraging individuals and small groups to display initiative, achievement, and endeavour for the commendation of those present. It is often a very excellent and successful plan to arrange that a pupil who is in difficulties shall be helped by one or more of his classmates. This calls for wise and tactful management, but there are recorded cases where it has had a remarkable and transforming effect upon the achievement of the individual concerned, and has greatly benefited the morale of the entire group.

In summary, the thing to remember is that whenever a group of people is brought together and at work on a common undertaking, powerful forces are brought into operation. These forces can be channeled in a favorable direction by making personal relationships pleasant, by adopting a policy of recognizing worthy endeavour and achievement, and by permeating the entire situation with a friendly spirit. And the crucial personal relationships are by all means those between the teacher and the individual pupil, and the teacher and the group. Such advice may have somewhat the look of sentimentality, but as a matter of fact it is thoroughly realistic and based on sound evidence. It indicates the line to be taken by anyone who wishes to do an effective job of organizing learning.[2]

**3. The Democratic Group.** Some remarkable research findings have been reported in recent years showing that a group democratically organized and conducted has a markedly better effect upon the learning and achievement of its members than a group autocratically organized and conducted. The words "democratic" and "autocratic," which have been used in several of the research studies, are probably not the best that could be chosen. They are none too precise, and they imply so much in the way of approval and condemnation that their employment almost begs the question at issue. It is most unlikely that, with things as they are in the world today, any American educator would deliberately recommend that classroom situations should be autocratically handled.

What has been shown is this. We have the best kind of working

and learning situation when a group of people feel that they have
undertaken something because of their own initiative and desire, when
they accept a joint responsibility for seeing the job through and for
doing it as well as possible, when they themselves feel a joint and individual responsibility for good order and for working conditions that
favor achievement, and when the person in charge takes an objective
"man-to-man" attitute towards them as a person who is there to see
that things go as well as they can and to help with the enterprise in
hand.   We have a definitely inferior working and learning situation
when the group proceed chiefly for the reason that the person in charge
tells them to, and when the working and learning procedures and the
general group behavior are determined chiefly by his orders.   It has
been shown that the latter, or "autocratic" situation tends to develop
undue aggressiveness on the part of some members of the group, both
toward one another and toward the leader; that in others it tends to
develop undue submissiveness and solitariness; and that in general it
leads to less effective action and achievement.

These conclusions have been confirmed very strikingly, and indeed
have been amplified by work done in the field of industrial psychology.
It has been shown in a series of experiments that an improvement in the
morale of small groups of workers boosted their rate of production
sensationally.   A good working morale was found to depend on pretty
much the same factors that have already been mentioned.   Real participation in planning was very important, with the workers feeling
that their opinions and wishes would not only get a hearing, but have
an actual effect on what was done.   A consistently friendly and considerate personal and social atmosphere played a large part also.
Variations in tasks, and avoidance of monotony had a considerable
influence.   And another factor was the promotion of a team spirit and
a sense of mutual responsibility in the working groups.   It was very
impressively shown that a good participant or "democratic" morale
had much more effect upon productivity than various factors more
usually considered by efficiency experts—such as better lighting, a
respacing of rest periods, or special incentive pay.   Indeed it was
shown that insofar as such measures had any appreciable effect, it was
because of their influence upon morale itself.

Thus the importance of a "democratic" classroom situation is no
mere fancy, nor is it based on sentimentalism, or on any far-fetched
philosophy.   It is a highly significant factor in the realistic organization of learning for the sake of authentic results.   Yet there is good
reason to believe that it is deplorably ignored by a great many teachers.
This is indicated by two very important and careful studies which have

received wide attention. Both present a picture of autocratic rather than democratic management as typical in the classrooms of the United States. They show that teachers are extremely alert to, and concentrate heavily upon, offences against an imposed pattern of behavior which is expected of the pupils. The good child is one who conforms and obeys, the bad child is one who does not. There is a strong tendency to overlook initiative, leadership, the disposition to think for oneself or to find one's own solutions, and in general to consider such active qualities and characteristics of no great importance. Problems of discipline are thought of as having to do chiefly with talking in class, disturbing others, making noises, attracting attention, and so forth, rather than with the positive promotion of creative and cooperative patterns of group activity. And the most common means of dealing with these discipline problems, and of controlling behavior is by censure, scolding, sarcasm, ridicule, threats, and deprivations such as change of seat, or being sent to stand in the corner or to the principal's office, or denial of privileges. Such measures, be it noted, are of exactly the kind calculated to impair the effectiveness of learning and compromise the success of teaching.[3]

## INTERPRETATIONS

It needs to be said with a good deal of emphasis that the establishment of a democratic or participant group situation in the classroom calls for a great deal more than good intentions and a general amiability. Every teacher and every prospective teacher ought to understand this clearly. What is required is deliberate, conscious, skillful organization.

1. There is, for instance, the problem of leadership within the group. One survey revealed that, in free discussion, a quarter of the pupils did two-thirds of the talking, that the voluntary self-initiated assertive remarks of the most loquacious were 16 times as numerous as those of the least loquacious, and that the best informed pupils were not the ones who talked the most. The exact figures and specific comparisons would no doubt vary, but situations of this kind unquestionably present themselves in many a classroom. What, then, to do? It is hardly enough to advise the teacher to put a damper on the chatterboxes and to encourage the diffident and the silent. This is very difficult to accomplish. It has many obvious disadvantages. And at best it is no more than a palliative, for the root of the trouble lies in the manner in which the social learning situation is set up.

Free discussion is no cure-all and has no magic power. Loosely conducted with a group of 30, 40, or more children among whom are a few big and ready talkers, it can be very stultifying.   It needs to be organized, stage-managed, shaped up in advance—with certain individuals and groups asked to carry a responsibility, and with certain well-considered techniques adopted to hold everything in line.   Moreover it is very far indeed from being the only or the typical pattern of democratic or participant group behavior.   One may, for instance, set up small group or individual reports, the systematic collection of suggestions looking toward the solution of a problem, arrangements for mutual assistance, and the keeping of minutes recording the class activities for the day.   Skillful and imaginative variation of the patterns of social behavior in the group of learners will do much more to uncover and render operative the talents and capacities for special leadership among the group than an undifferentiated adherence to free talk carried on in the class as a whole.   One should always remember that what is important is the sense of a joint task adopted by an act of choice and will, and a sense of common responsibility for it.   These are the essentials of the democratic situation, rather than some more or less superficial and conventional pattern of action.

2. The interesting suggestion has been made that friendship relations may profitably be recognized in the classroom.   This was managed by asking each child in the group to write down the names of his three to five best friends, after which a friendship diagram of the group was worked out.   Equipped with such a diagram, there are quite a number of things a teacher can do about it.   He can provide opportunities for the development of friendly relationships by moving an isolated individual surrounded by a closely-knit group, by seeing to it that potential friendship groups are brought together on committees or in clubs, by getting a retiring or isolated or friendless child to look out for someone else or help a newcomer, and so forth.   He can build social skills and personal acceptability particularly in isolated individuals, perhaps by coaching some unpopular rebel in decent manners, or by tactful suggestions about clothing, or by promoting achievement in some game which would enable the friendless person to shine on the playground.   He can build individual self-confidence, as in one case where the most isolated child in the room was (by behind-the-scenes arrangement) asked to do work for the principal who professed to be much pleased and permitted him to choose a special treat for his classmates, or as in another case when a teacher retained in his room the eight most isolated children when the rest were being moved owing to reorganization, and gave them special status and responsibility with the new incoming group.

What, it may be asked, has all this to do with reading, writing, arithmetic, the social studies, art, and music? What has it to do with results? The answer is: A great deal! It is one of many admirable and imaginative ways of putting into actual practical application the findings we have been outlining from the social psychology of learning and achievement. This particular approach is not specially or universally recommended. But it should help teachers and prospective teachers to see what is meant by saying that a favorable social atmosphere is not to be created by good intentions and pleading talk, but that it depends upon planning and organizing. One great reason why teachers often lack such an atmosphere in their classrooms—and its absence is a constant drag upon success and a brake on the attainment of results—is simply that they never take the trouble to think about it or work for it.

3. It should be noted that all the findings on the influence of the social setting upon learning and achievement seem clearly to imply that cooperation is preferable to competition. The direct evidence on this point is not decisive, due to technical limitations in the investigations, but the inference seems inescapable. Competitive relationships have been and still are the mainstay in the social aspects of conventional teaching. We have, it is true, discarded the spelling bee, and the practice of having pupils shift seats up and down, toward or away from the "head of the class" as they answer recitation questions. But the marking system is little more than a statistical sophistication of these devices. Some predetermined scheme of distribution makes it inevitable that each pupil's mark will depend upon the relationship of his performance to that of everybody else, and thus throws him into competition with his fellows.* As an autocratic technique for dividing and ruling, this is admirably judged, for the teacher becomes the donor of rationed rewards desired by every individual. But it directly contravenes the kind of group relationships and spirit which, on the basis of all we know, most favor effective learning. A pleasant social atmosphere, friendly personal relationships, pleasure in the achievement and success of others, joint responsibility, mutual helpfulness, and team spirit are the distinctive characteristics of the well-managed classroom and of well-organized learning.

4. The entire problem of social management is directly and intimately related to the main theme of this book—the conception of

* A predetermined scheme of distribution means a decision to allot a certain percentage of each mark, as for instance 5 per cent of A's, 20 per cent B's, 50 per cent C's, 20 per cent D's, 5 per cent F's. Then each individual's mark depends not on the absolute worth of his work, but on how it compares or ranks with that of the entire group.

meaningful learning.   One cannot democratize meaningless routine.
One can only impose it.   If the assignment is to study pages 59 to 68
in the textbook, or to cover the material in Chap. 20 dealing with the
presidency of General Grant, the chances for genuine and joint responsibility and endeavour have been obliterated before they even exist.
The pupils have no choice in the matter, they have no opportunity for
initiative, and there is nothing for them to cooperate about.   The election of a chairman, or the invitation to a free expression of opinion
become merely farcical.   They are screens for autocratic management,
not departures from it.   In the same way, any proper and reasonable
use of positive incentives as a matter of policy is frustrated.   An
answer is either right or it is wrong.   In the one case it receives credit,
and in the other it does not, and that is that.   To advise a teacher
operating in terms of such a pattern consistently to praise success and
to avoid blaming failure seems absurd.   It is almost like asking him to
notice only white, even though he knows only too well that there is a
great deal of black in the picture.

But the moment meaningful learning has been organized and established, everything is different.   Meaningful learning, as we have
already seen in several connections and shall see in several more, occurs
when the determining motives and values of the learner's living are
engaged.   Put more simply, meaningful learning occurs, and only
occurs, when the learner wants to learn.   And when one has 1 learner,
or 20 learners, or 40 learners who really want to learn, then democratic
cooperation and responsibility become the most natural things in the
world.   All can benefit from the intimations, the discoveries, the
endeavours of each, and each individual can feel that he is contributing
to the joint achievement of all.   The whole group can concern itself to
find and bring in vital and illuminating contextual material, and can
work together to clarify intelligible focuses.   The whole learning situation is transformed from a routine memorizing and reciting of factual
data to an active process of group thinking.   This immediately lends
itself to a reasonable and sensible use of positive incentives, because
now instead of an exclusive alternative between black and white—
between the incorrect and correct answer—there are innumerable
shades of gray.   There is not just light and darkness, but many intimations, nascent discoveries, emerging insights—many partial and broken
lights, all of them worth something, and all of them properly to be
recognized as worthy.

Thus the social management of learning is not a sort of extra, or a
series of trick arrangements which can be applied without reference to
what is being learned, how it is being learned, or why it is being learned.

It arises out of the very essence of the learning situation itself.   To put the matter in another way, the principle of socialization is integrally related to all the other psychological principles of successful teaching.   This is so because, properly understood, it does not refer to any external devices or methodological techniques, but is simply one aspect of the general organization of meaningful learning.[4]

### Notes and References

1. The research studies on social facilitation are summarized well in Floyd H. Allport, *Social Psychology*, Chaps. 11 and 12, Houghton Mifflin Company, Boston, 1924.

2. For basic primary material on incentives see Elizabeth Hurlock, "The Psychology of Incentives," *Journal of Social Psychology*, Vol. 2 (1931), pp. 261–289; also M. W. Johnson, *Verbal Influences on Children's Behavior*, University of Michigan Monographs on Education, No. 1, 1939.   For a summary of the material with suggested applications, see James L. Mursell, *Educational Psychology*, Chap. 11, W. W. Norton & Company, Inc., New York, 1939.

3. Two influential reports upon the effects of democratic and autocratic group management are R. Lippett, "An Experimental Study of the Effect of Democratic and Authoritarian Group Atmospheres," *University of Iowa Studies in Child Welfare*, Vol. 16, No. 3 (1940); and Kurt Lewin, "Experiments in Autocratic and Democratic Atmospheres," *Social Frontier*, Vol. 4 (1938), pp. 316–319.   As to democracy in industry, the basic study is F. J. Dickson and H. A. Wright, *Management and the Worker*, Harvard University Press, Cambridge, Mass., 1939.   This is excellently reported by Goodwin Watson, "The Surprising Discovery of Morale," *Progressive Education*, Vol. 19 (1942), pp. 33–41.   Common classroom attitudes are treated in two studies which have attracted considerable attention and some controversy, namely, E. K. Wickman, *Children's Behavior and Teachers' Attitudes*, Commonwealth Fund, Division of Publication, New York, 1928; and N. W. Campbell, *The Elementary School Teacher's Treatment of Classroom Behavior Problems*, Teachers College, Columbia University, Bureau of Publications, New York, 1935.

4. For an interesting study of the practical problems involved in classroom "democracy" see Arthur T. Jersild, Robert L. Thorndike, B. Goldman, and J. J. Loftus, "An Evaluation of Aspects of the Activity Program in the New York City Elementary Schools," *Journal of Experimental Education*, Vol. 8 (1939), pp. 166–207; also Arthur T. Jersild, B. Goldman, C. L. Jersild, and J. J. Loftus, "Elementary School Classes in Action: II. A Study of Pupil Participation and of Aspects of Pupil-Teacher Relations," *Journal of Experimental Education*, Vol. 10 (1941), pp. 295–302.   The very interesting and repaying report on utilizing friendship relations is Merle H. Eliott, "Patterns of Friendship in the Classroom," *Progressive Education*, Vol. 18 (1941), pp. 383–390.

### Items for Dicussion and Study

*Refer to the two opening suggestions for discussion and study in connection with Chap. 5.   Follow them out in connection with the principle of socialization.   You should consider particularly the relationship between a genuine sense of a problem and group cooperation.   Retain the outcomes in your notebook or card file.*

1. Describe with concrete illustrations how social contacts affect your own learning.

2. How does the social atmosphere and life of the school affect the learning that goes on? Is it more influential in some curricular fields than in others? Why?

3. Discuss instances from observation or personal experience of the effect of social facilitation on learning. How were the situations handled to get the social increment?

4. Can you recall, from your own experience, cases where learning was hindered by negative incentives such as scolding, sarcasm, penalties, etc.? Is there any place for such incentives in well-organized learning?

5. Does the established superiority of positive incentives mean that a teacher should be lavish with indiscriminate praise; that he should never criticize or blame?

6. Why is it bad to fail to give any recognition of work done? Has such a failure on the part of any teacher ever adversely affected your own learning? Particularize.

7. From a careful and detailed reading and study of the discussion of democratic group organization and action presented in the chapter, make a list of specific and definite points showing exactly what such organization and action means. By what ways and means and specific procedures would you go about establishing such a situation?

8. Could we define good discipline as good working morale? Does this conflict with the conventional conception of discipline?

9. Suggest ways of preventing the "big talkers" from wrecking the group morale without snubbing them to such an extent as to kill all discussion and participation.

10. What values and what disadvantages do you see in recognizing the friendship relations in a class? How might this be done?

# CHAPTER 10

## THE PRINCIPLE OF SOCIALIZATION AND THE APPRAISAL OF TEACHING

### HIERARCHY OF APPLICATIONS

Here a three-step hierarchy or scale is suggested for the evaluation of teaching situations with reference to the principle of socialization. As always, the steps on the scale are neither wholly clear cut nor mutually exclusive. Not seldom one can find all three clearly exemplified in a single class period. Nevertheless, the classification is serviceable for it brings out the essential differences among teaching situations in terms of their utilization of the social dynamics and social-psychological factors involved.

### PRINCIPLE OF SOCIALIZATION: HIERARCHY

I    Social pattern characterized chiefly by submission: function of the group is to respond to questions and directions from the teacher; imposed discipline

II    Social pattern characterized typically by contribution: members of the group allowed and encouraged to volunteer suggestions, raise issues, etc. Discipline still imposed, but sympathetic

III    Social pattern characterized chiefly by cooperation: group function is to carry through common undertaking in which all have responsible share; self-generated discipline

### THE FIRST LEVEL

First we have the type of situation chiefly marked by *submission* on the part of the group of learners. This is the most commonly found pattern of teaching, even at the present day. Stimuli originate from the teacher, either directly through the questions he asks and the words he speaks or writes, or indirectly through the assignments he makes. The business of the group of learners is simply to respond to these stimuli. Volunteering is either discouraged or held to a minimum, or so undirected and unsystematized that it amounts to very little. Discipline is chiefly negative, and has for its purpose either to check unconventional or disturbing behavior or, better, to forestall it. One finds this type of social arrangement and functioning in a great many classrooms.

170

The authors of *Middletown* have given a vivid description of this kind of teaching.

The school, like the factory, is a thoroughly regimented world.  Immovable seats in orderly rows fix the sphere of activity for each child.  For all, from the timid six-year-old entering for the first time, to the most assured high-school senior, the general routine is much the same.  Bells divide the day into periods.  For the six-year-olds the periods are short (fifteen to twenty-five minutes) and in some they leave their seats, play games, and act out make-believe stories, although in recitation periods all movement is prohibited.  As they grow older the taboo on physical movement grows stricter, until by the third or fourth grade practically all movement is forbidden except the marching from one set of seats to another between periods, a brief interval of prescribed exercise daily, and periods of manual training or home economics once or twice a week.  There are study periods in which children learn lessons from textbooks, prescribed by the state, and recitation periods in which they tell an adult teacher what the books have said; one hears children reciting the battles of the Civil War in one recitation period, the rivers of Africa in another, the parts of speech in a third; and the method is much the same.  With high school some differences come; more vocational and laboratory work varies the periods.  But here again the lesson-textbook-recitation method is the chief characteristic of education.  For nearly an hour a teacher asks questions and pupils answer, then a bell rings, on the instant books bang, powder and mirrors come out, and there is a buzz of talk and laughter as all the urgent business of living resumes momentarily for the children, notes and dates are exhanged, five minutes pass, another bell, gradual sliding into seats, a final giggle, a last vanity case snapped shut.  "In our last lesson we had just finished . . . " and another class is begun.*

It is revealing to compare this conventional and familiar pattern with another which, superficially considered, seems very different. This is the situation as found in schools which are organized partially or completely for individualized instruction.  Here the recitation, if not completely abandoned, at any rate ceases to be the staple procedure.   Instead, the children, at arranged times, go to one of the study rooms or "laboratories" where there is a teacher in charge, and proceed to study assignments which have been laid out very carefully, often a month in advance.

A child describes his experience under the so-called "unit laboratory plan" as follows:

I went into the room.  First I asked John if he had remembered to bring the book he promised.  He had, so I took it and went to my desk after I had got my papers and pencil from the drawer.  For the first half of the period I read from the book and took notes as we had been taught.  Then I arranged

* Robert S. Lynd and Helen Merrell Lynd, *Middletown*, p. 252, Harcourt, Brace and Company, New York, 1929.

my notes and combined them with the notes I had from the radio talk and the magazine articles I had read.   Once I had to go to the book shelf and search for a magazine because I had forgotten to put down the name of the article from which I had made some notes.   At the end of the period I had all my notes in shape so that tomorrow during the history period I can begin writing my theme on the Real Causes of the War.*

On the surface this looks like the cleanest possible break with the recitation routine, and it is probable that an appreciable change in the functional organization of learning may really be involved.   But the difference which is most conspicuous, and which the unanalytic observer is almost sure to find the most striking, is in fact the least important, and may even be to a considerable extent spurious.   For socially the two situations are very much alike.   The routines are different.   Under the unit laboratory plan the child goes to his seat of his own accord, is allowed to seek out another child and ask him a question, and can leave his seat to look something up from the book-shelf.   Moreover he is not expected to listen to a string of questions propounded by the teacher, and to try to answer a few that come his way.   But these are externals only.   He is still responding to stimuli emanating from the teacher, although these now take the form chiefly of mimeographed assignment sheets rather elaborately prepared.   The discipline remains chiefly negative and turns on the avoidance of disturbing or unconventional conduct, although conventionality is less rigidly defined.   And there is certainly no more and perhaps even less give and take between members of the group of learners present in the room.

It should be clearly understood that this is by no manner of means a complete appraisal of the type of individualized instruction which has become fairly familiar in recent years, owing particularly to the influence of Helen Parkhurst and the Dalton School.   A full evaluation of any teaching setup, including the unit laboratory plan, requires the application of all the psychological principles here under explanation. But from the standpoint of socialization the plan differs very much less from the conventional and hidebound recitation procedure than one might easily suppose.   Here, as so frequently, one sees the great advantage of an analysis of teaching in terms of the psychological factors operating instead of the superficial procedures and arrangements.†

To make another illuminating and less-than-obvious comparison,

---

* Robert W. Frederick, Clarence E. Ragsdale, and Rachel Salisbury, *Directing Learning*, p. 182, D. Appleton-Century Company, Inc., New York, 1938.

† Lest the reader become confused by a semitechnical jargon it may be said that the unit laboratory plan is a lineal descendant and close relative of the Dalton laboratory plan.

the functional social aspects of a lecture given to immature students are closely similar to those displayed in the conventional recitation and in the unit laboratory arrangement. Superficially, again, there is a great apparent contrast. A group of children listening to a lecture and taking notes looks very different from a group responding as a teacher asks questions round the class, or quietly working on assignments in a laboratory or study room under the general supervision of a teacher. Also it is true that in certain respects there may be important differences in the three situations. But as phenomena of the social psychology of learning they are not far apart. Response chiefly to the stimuli put out by the teacher, lack of voluntary activity, lack of give and take within the group, and behavior negatively controlled to avoid disturbance—such are the essential characteristics of all three.

Now it is evident that whatever virtues the unit laboratory plan or the lecture method may have, they share with the conventional recitation procedure one great weakness. They simply do not exploit the dynamic potential of the social situation. A group is present but it is not used to forward or further the learning process. A certain measure of social facilitation may be possible, although it is not very likely to occur. As a matter of fact, if this is the best we can do, and if we really are going to operate on this rudimentary level of socialization, it would probably be better to abandon group teaching entirely. The real argument for the recitation is not that it organizes learning well, but that it conveniently brings a considerable number of learners together to receive assignments and have their work checked up. But that great invention, the mimeograph, can do the job even better, as Helen Parkhurst and the proponents of the unit laboratory plan discovered. One can make out elaborate assignments, including practice materials and tests, and give them on a monthly basis. Teaching then can go on without the nuisance of trying to handle groups of learners who cannot keep abreast of one another, and without the impossible technical problem of asking enough oral questions in a 45-minute period to check up properly on the work of 30 to 60 pupils. What we have in the lecture method and also in the unit laboratory plan and similar plans for individualization is the almost complete neglect of the psychodynamic possibilities of the group. The conventional recitation displays the same neglect but .it retains the group as the basis of operations.[1]

## THE SECOND LEVEL

The second level of the hierarchy is by no means sharply separable from the foregoing, and yet a significant distinction exists. The distinctive characteristic is that, although stimuli still emanate chiefly from the teacher, the situation is more or less deliberately organized to allow and encourage pupils to respond with questions, suggestions, voluntary comments, and suchlike, directed mainly to the teacher, but to some extent to one another. The specific psychological point is that whereas at the first level social facilitation is about the only psychodynamic resource, now positive incentives are systematically used.

A comparison and contrast which has been made between 47 good and 47 poor teachers, selected as good and poor on numerous criteria, will help to clarify the point. For some of the most significant differences turn precisely upon the distinction between the first and second levels of the hierarchy. The good teacher was found to ask a large proportion of thought questions (i.e., questions which tend to elicit variable and extensive answers, original suggestions, discussion, etc.), to conduct the class conversationally with a good deal of give and take between himself and the pupils, to draw out the experiences of the pupils, to pay careful attention to what they say, and to comment widely and variously and in an interesting fashion on their remarks. The poor teacher, on the other hand, tends to ask few thought questions, 78 per cent of all questions noted in the investigation as emanating from poor teachers turning out to be mere interrogations. He talks most of the time himself. He elicits only very brief responses from the pupils with 14 seconds being the average time for such responses. He appraises them briefly as right or wrong, and has few comments to offer on what the pupils say, and dull ones at that.

If one asks how good were the good teachers, it is a perfectly fair question. The only answer is that they were so judged by local and state supervisory officers and by experienced observers who visited their classrooms. Presumably, then, they exemplified a type of practice which, in the opinion of experienced judges, must be considered superior and desirable. And the report hits off with great precision the essential distinction between the first and second levels of the hierarchy. There was a marked and palpable contrast between the poor and the good teachers in their handling of the social situation. The good teachers still retained the essential stereotype under which the individual in charge of the class is originator and controller of everything that happens. But they used it with a difference. They encouraged volunteering and initiative by the questions they asked and the comments they made and by their whole relationship to their pupils. Thus, apparently, it was a matter of policy. The contrast with poor teaching was not radical. It did not go down to fundamentals. But it was appreciable. And it points toward something else, and something more extensive.

Teaching of this kind is often found. For instance, an observed eleventh-grade class in physics spent almost an entire period in discussing problems at the end of the chapter which had been assigned for homework on the previous day. (The balance of the time was devoted to announcements, school business, and the like.) The teacher took up the problems one by one, and asked in each case whether anybody had run into difficulties. In every instance somebody had! When a difficulty was brought to light in this way, the teacher asked for volunteers, and one or more pupils would offer help and would proceed to do so, sometimes by dint of verbal discussion, sometimes by going to the board and developing demonstrations. The teacher kept remarkably in the background, offering few and sparse comments, but continually promoting group thinking. To be sure the material had been assigned, and everything remained very firmly under the teacher's control. But the situation, and its basic psychology, was definitely different indeed from the conventional hidebound recitation with its drumfire of interrogations. In fact it tended toward the emergence of true and full group responsibility for the learning process. The case is of particular interest, because it shows how much can be done in shaping up a functional social situation in the classroom, even under the limitations of a conventionally organized school and a standardized course of study.

Once again, a fourth grade devoted about half an hour to free silent reading by the pupils of material which they themselves individually chose. The question may well arise why this was done in school at all. Was there any teaching whatsoever? The answer is, decidedly yes. The teacher herself set up the pattern, and during the half hour she made it her business to go around the group, asking them what they were reading and how they liked it, and offering many interesting and well-chosen comments. There could be no doubt that a genuine social situation and stimulation was created, and that it had a considerable effect. Here again the teacher was in immediate and constant control. She constituted herself the mainspring of the proceedings. But she organized considerable freedom of action.

One important characteristic of all cases which belong in this general category is that discipline is sympathetic and positive rather than minatory and negative, although a pattern of imposed good order still prevails.

A very beautiful exemplification of the essential nature of the psychological and dynamic factors determining discipline in such instances was furnished by a happening in a third-grade classroom. The previous day the teacher had been called away from the room in order to attend an emergency committee, and the children had been extremely unruly. In fact they had managed to disturb several other classes, and had called much unfavorable attention to themselves. The teacher handled the situation most constructively and skillfully. She entered into a discussion with them of yesterday's unfortunate happenings, the class being seated around a square of tables, with the teacher sitting in as one of the group. The exchanges were remarkably free and earnest. The children themselves mentioned one or two individuals who had been conspicuously out of order. The teacher said that she herself enjoyed good fun as much as anybody, and was sorry to have missed some remarkable doings. She pointed out, however, that what troubled her was the thought of their doing things with her away which they would not do with her present. Needless to say there was a strong and evident relationship of mutual confidence and sincerity. She then raised the question as to why yesterday's behavior had been bad. The class talked, discussed, considered, and suggested that their behavior had been undesirable because it violated safety provisions, because it disturbed other people and other classes, and because school was not the place for such doings.

This instance is interesting and instructive both for what was emphasized, and what was not emphasized. The appeal consistently was to friendliness, considerateness, good feeling, and respect for the rights and convenience of others. There were no threats, no scoldings, no punishments. So far so good. It was, however, very noticeable that among the reasons the children gave for blaming their own conduct one never mentioned was that it intruded upon other things that they wanted to do, or that it broke into any group undertaking for which they felt responsible and which they wished to see through.

There, precisely, lie both the limitations and the values of teaching situations on this level of social organization. Positive incentives and encouragement are used as a matter of policy. Negative incentives and blame are avoided. The children are allowed and encouraged to use very considerable freedom. The behavior patterns of the conventional recitation are to a large extent dissolved. It is no longer necessary to speak only when one is spoken to, to avoid so much as a whisper to a classmate, never under any circumstances to move from one's seat. The whole situation, including the seating arrangements, the physical equipment of the room, and the kind of questions that are asked, is manipulated and organized for the sake of greater freedom. Praise instead of blame, encouragement instead of strictures, conversation instead of quizzing, the working assumption that pupils are civilized human beings amenable to reason—these are the earmarks of the situation. However, the basic control is still very definitely,

very immediately with the teacher. There is very little true delegation of authority in making essential decisions. Thus one cannot say
that, as yet, there is a true participant democratic morale.

Teachers working in any reasonably organized school will not find
it difficult to go as far as this. And when they have gone so far, the
next step, which often seems so overwhelming, so formidable, even so
preposterous to those familiar with nothing better than the conventional rigid controls, will begin to seem not merely possible, but even
feasible and inviting.[2]

## THE THIRD LEVEL

The decisive and crucial feature of the third type of social learning
situation is that it goes beyond friendliness, sympathy, encouragement,
a considerable measure of freedom, and the consistent use of positive
incentives generally, and involves the prevailing sense of a joint undertaking responsibly chosen and accepted.

An ambitious and instructive instance of such organization is provided by a yearlong study of architecture carried on in a sixth grade.
Immediately after the opening of school the proposed study was
initiated and "sold" to the pupils informally, by conversation about
their vacation experiences, about the apartment houses in which most
of them lived, and about the architecture of New York City, where
the school was located. The entire enterprise was built around the
central idea of architecture as expressing the lives and ideals of human
beings. This clearly established an over-all focus, which was not
clearly or explicitly stated at first but which was present from the
start. As good focalization always does, it coordinated the entire
business of learning and made possible a wide diversity within a
functional unity. The work proceeded with a great wealth of coordinated and related activities. At an early stage, pupils brought to
class crude sketches of architectural detail which were displayed on
the bulletin board. This soon grew more systematic, purposeful,
and meaningful, as the items were classified for period and style,
carefully mounted, arranged and collated to bring out relationships
and contrasts, and so on. This phase of the work led to a division
of the class into small groups based on the special interest expressed
by different pupils in this or that architectural period. These groups
were held together by a joint organizing committee which developed
a common working scheme for all of them, and a common plan for
collating their findings and reporting them to the class as a whole.

Two activities which developed in the course of this study very
strikingly illustrate the establishment of a sense of participant group

responsibility, and a working morale. The first began with a request made by a number of the pupils that they be allowed to work together to construct a stained glass rose window. The idea caught on, and was enthusiastically adopted by the entire group. Facilities were made available by the school, and the work was carried through with great energy and pride as a cooperative venture, and finally written up in the school paper under the title The History of Our Rose Window. The teacher had blocked out in advance many developments which she foresaw in connection with the year's study, but this came as a completely new suggestion.

The second instance was another unforeseen innovation on the part of one of the pupils. The child in question was one of the less mature members of the group, who had for a time shown little leadership. He chanced, however, to come across piles of old magazines in a secondhand bookstore, including files of the *Architectural Record*. He saw that they contained a great many pictures and diagrams which would be of interest in connection with what was going on at school. So he proceeded to buy them with his own pocket money, clipped and mounted the illustrations, and went into business selling them to his classmates.

It is clear that situations of this sort go definitely beyond the social patterns indicated in the second level of the hierarchy. The teacher moves further into the background. He still functions as an organizer, but in a less direct, more skillful, more sophisticated fashion. The situation itself takes charge. The group is led to assume a responsibility for its own doings and its own achievement. Pride in good work and a positive team spirit become controlling influences. The basis of discipline shifts, and the problem encountered by the teacher whose class ran wild in her absence is not likely to occur, for the group is so taken up in its own chosen undertaking that destructive disturbances are pretty well ruled out.

Another example, less elaborately worked out but similar in kind, occurred in an eighth-grade course in English composition. The class had for a time studied different types of composition, and was then divided into four subgroups, each of which was to spend most of the rest of the term producing a magazine which was to be mimeographed and distributed. There was to be a lead topic for each magazine. Each was to contain instances of all the types of composition studied, and was to be as good as possible in style, format, spelling, and so on. School time was spent partly in groupwise meetings, partly in committee of the whole, the latter being devoted to clearing common problems, and in discussions among the class members and also with the teacher on the merits and demerits of submitted pieces of writing.

A somewhat analogous plan was followed in a seventh-grade class in science. Some of the work was done in and by the class as a whole, but experiments were carried through by subgroups which reported back to the class, considered past, present, and prospective problems and difficulties, and staged a number of demonstrations.

Two general comments should be made with regard to these sample cases, and the general ideas they illustrate.

1. It will be noted at once that many situations of the second or contributory type merge into situations of the third or cooperative type. The geometry lesson described on pages 119–120, the furious discussion of "isms" described on page 153, even the period given over to a discussion of the problems in physics assigned the previous day described on page 175, are not easy to discriminate from the fully cooperative, fully responsible group pattern. Nevertheless the distinction, although subtle and in borderline cases hard to establish, is genuine and crucial. It involves a change in attitude on the part of the teacher toward his work, toward his pupils, and toward himself. Both the similarity and the difference call for consideration; the first because full democratization in the classroom often looks like an utter departure from all pedagogical conventions although it is not; the second because no teacher should mistake amiability and friendliness for the conscious organization of responsibility in the group of pupils.

2. In the second place it should be noted that true cooperative situations, although they are usually ambitious and far-reaching when fully developed, can certainly be established without any tremendous fanfare, and without giving the impression that one wishes to shatter the sorry scheme of things and then remold it nearer to the heart's desire. There can be no doubt that many practical teachers, confronting accounts of sweeping cooperative schemes such as the study of architecture just mentioned, or the study of textiles previously described, are apt to be afflicted with a feeling akin to despair. If these are the kind of things that ought to be done, they tell themselves, then one might as well give up at the start, for they are only possible in the most favored and enlightened of schools and school systems. Moreover, such pessimism is first cousin to hostility, and after one has decided that such measures are impracticable the next step is to persuade oneself that they are fantastic and undesirable. Well, there can be little doubt that the unit on architecture and the unit on textiles do foreshadow and, at least in part, indicate what education ought to be like, if we accept the implications of our understanding of the learning

process and its conditions.    And even they do not go nearly all the way. There is no doubt that the ultimate implications of the conception of meaningful learning do involve a far-reaching transformation of the existing framework of the class and of the school.   On the other hand, it is perfectly possible to apply the principle of socialization at a high level, and to establish true cooperative situations with surprisingly little disturbance of the aforesaid framework, and without shocking even a conservative constituency, as the work cited in eighth-grade English composition and seventh-grade science clearly shows.

One final word should perhaps be said as to the value of cooperative situations such as those described.   This lies in the fact that they fully exploit the group potential in the interest of effective learning. With them both social facilitation and the use of positive incentives are possible.   But above all they involve a positive participant group morale which, as we have reason to know, is an important factor in bringing about good learning and effective achievement.[3]

## PRACTICAL PROBLEMS IN APPLYING THE PRINCIPLE OF SOCIALIZATION

1. In all attempts to apply the principle of socialization at a high level, and particularly in organizing any kind of genuinely cooperative situation, an important measure is *cooperative planning*.  This is because, as a matter of obvious common sense, one is likely to get a better working morale and a more genuine sense of joint responsibility by planning with the pupils instead of merely planning for them.   It is a wise policy to take the pupils into confidence as much as possible about all aspects of what they are going to do.   Also one should remember that if such a policy is to amount to anything and to do any good it must be honest and sincere, and the pupils must know that they are not merely being manipulated, and that their wishes and choices will have real weight in shaping the conduct of events.   Time spent on such cooperative planning—and if it is done properly it takes time—will be well spent, and will prove a repaying investment in better learning.

By way of illustration, a teacher of junior-high-school science spent some time at the beginning of the course in a group discussion with her pupils of the question: What would you like to get out of this year's experience in science?   A large number of problems, prevailingly factual, were quickly assembled, such as Why are some people color-blind? and How does a photoelectric cell work?   A pupil committee then classified them as having to do with physics, chemistry, biology, and so forth.   Then the class went to work on them, although they were by no means exactly what the teacher wanted to secure.   A little later on, the basic question was raised again, and now the pupils saw values other than those of factual subject matter, and tended to emphasize study skills, various personal qualities, and similar outcomes.   Still later on the question was discussed for a third time, and now the emphasis had evolved into one upon various factors of personal growth.

The idea of taking pupils into confidence, and of giving them a real share in the planning of their own education is a very sound one.   It tends to maintain a close liaison between teachers and learners.   It often gives rise to some excellent suggestions which might otherwise never be brought up.   And above all, it promotes that sense of a shared and responsibly accepted undertaking which is the essential characteristic of the democratically functioning group.   Such cooperative planning need not be made formal.   It need not all come at the beginning, or at any fixed point in the work.   It should, in fact, permeate all the relationships and activities of the group.   And naturally it need not be confined to discussing objectives and outcomes, but can very well touch every phase of the activities in and through which learning goes on.[4]

2. Such cooperative planning obviously involves the problem of a teacher's relationship to the pupils as, indeed, does the whole issue of the socialization of the learning process.   As we have seen, that relationship can best be expressed by saying that the teacher is an organizer.   As such there are always two extremes for him to avoid.   On the one hand he should not center all decisions and the shaping up of all action entirely in himself.   On the other he should not refuse on principle to exercise any kind of control, or function simply as a member of the group on a level with every other member.   The essence of good organization is proper delegation of authority and the steady encouragement of freedom and initiative combined with a sense of shared responsibility.   This is true in any administrative setup, including the classroom.   The primary business of the teacher, like that of any other organizer, is to keep the group functioning at the highest possible level.   Since the whole question has already been discussed in these pages, no more need be said here.

3. One of the most important lessons any teacher can learn is how to function effectively as an organizer of learning *in terms of his own qualities and characteristics*.   An observer visiting a school which could be named here, can, if he knows his way about, spend three periods watching three first-rate teachers who seem, superficially at least, to work in three very different ways.   The first is a highly extroverted

social organizer.  He prods, he sometimes scolds, he pounces on some back-seat pupil who has had nothing to say for quite a while, he centers class thinking by the use of the blackboard, raising his voice, gesticulating, almost pulling ideas out of the group.  The second is extremely quiet and subdued.  Most of the time he talks hardly above a whisper. His method always is to get other people functioning conspicuously. One might almost get the impression that he is doing nothing, and letting the social situation roll on as it will.  But in many of his lessons the group builds up a focalization and a shared impulsion that is almost hypnotic in its power.  The third is a self-dramatizing aesthete, who reads and speaks brilliantly, who is lightning quick on the comeback, and whose periods in English literature often turn into most impressive one-man shows.  To differentiate between these three in terms of methodology would be stupid.  Yet stenographic reports of their work would certainly reveal what would look like great differences in procedure—great difference, for instance, in relative percentages of "teacher talk" and "pupil talk," in comments on remarks made by pupils, and so on and so forth.  None of these things get down to essentials.  For as one comes to know these teachers, one finds them men of great ability and mature judgment who have learned by long experience how to organize a cooperative learning situation, and to do so in the only way it ever can be well done—in and through the use of their own personal characteristics.

Similarly the expert teacher will not handle every group similarly or by similar routines and techniques.  A first-rate teacher was observed dealing first with a "rapid advance" eighth-grade class, and then immediately afterwards with an "adjustment" eighth-grade class (a polite name for a group of slow learners).  In the first the theme was transportation.  The boys in the class constantly tended to go off into the intricacies of airplane construction, and had to be constantly pulled back.  One boy kept popping up to volunteer and had to be popped back so that somebody else might have a chance.  The teacher behaved quite aggressively, and yet it was evident that he did so without discouraging anybody or shattering morale.  As one neat instance of technique, the boy who was the embarrassingly eager talker was held in line by the promise that at the end of the period he should have five minutes to say whatever he might want to say.

When this same teacher faced the slow-learning pupils he was like a different person.  Whereas before he had been a leader holding an extremely spirited discussion group to its direction, he now became almost a monitor.  He checked up on homework very carefully.  He accepted and praised almost any answer that was made, and never once discouraged or cut short the response of a pupil. By comment and attitude he constantly made it clear that effort rather than achievement would be recognized. He never once lost patience, or seemed nervous or annoyed.

This contrast was a remarkable display of virtuosity, and of applied psychological insight. The teacher was wholeheartedly himself with both groups, but different because they were different. In each case he seemed to relish what he was doing. He set up in both instances, situations which must probably be classed as contributory, although they merge closely toward the full cooperative pattern. In both instances he systematically used positive incentives and sympathetic discipline—yet how differently. In the first, barbed remarks, much frankness, no little "shutting up"; in the other nothing but smooth words and praise. Yet both had the same effect, because both were enjoyed and understood.

4. An important administrative implication of all that has been said is that the controlling factor in classification and grouping in the school should be *social homogeneity*.

Suppose we ask why an institution whose *raison d'être* is the promotion of learning should divide learners into groups and handle them as classes at all. The question may seem surprising because the class-wise organization is so completely taken for granted, but it is intelligent and pertinent just the same, and a little reflection upon it makes many things clear. The ordinary reason for having classes is that it seems efficient and economical to arrange for considerable numbers of learners to be studying the same material at the same time. If this is the controlling idea, then the nearer each class can come to being made up of learners all able to learn equally well the better. There are very serious objections and difficulties here which will be considered in connection with the principle of individualization. But the weakness relevant at this point is that such an arrangement almost certainly means a failure to use the social dynamics of learning. The class consists of perhaps 30 individuals, all supposed to be moving along parallel lines. The job is to keep them steadily working, and to prevent them from disturbing each other. About the only psychosocial factors that can be utilized are social facilitation and positive incentives, and this is poor socialization.

But it is possible also to see in the existence of a class an opportunity for something far more constructive, far more potent, far more effective in promoting good learning. When the principle of socialization is applied at a high level, the basic assumption of group teaching is not that everyone shall perform identical tasks, or move forward at a uniform rate of speed, but that the social dynamics of the situation shall be utilized to the full for the sake of good learning. Therefore the ideally teachable class is one whose members are able to function well together in the sharing of joint responsibilities and the discharge of joint enterprises. It is, of course, quite true that too great a spread of mentality or of educational age within the group will create difficulties and tend to disrupt its effectiveness as a working unit. These are decidedly factors to be considered in setting up groupings, and the general testing and guidance program of the school should reveal them and take them into account. But in and of themselves they are not decisive, and their bearing upon the situation is indirect rather than direct, since it is their effect upon social homogeneity that is important. It has been well said that " . . . the purpose of classification is to bring together a group of children with common interests and common needs who can work together and play together happily and successfully irrespective of school achievement, intelligence, or probable rate of learning."*[5]

5. There are certain particular aspects of the social scene presented by the classroom of which the teacher does well to be aware.

*a.* As a usual thing any well-handled class, during a 50-minute period will present a social kaleidoscope. At one time the pupils constitute an audience for the teacher; then they become an audience for a pupil; then they function in attending to questions asked by the teacher; then they shift into a group concerned with mutual discussion; then into a group concerned with mutual criticism; then they break up into a disparate set of individual entities working separately for the time being; then they come together for mutual drill. So it goes, endlessly and fascinatingly. Many a teacher is sublimely unconscious of these continual shifts in the pattern taking place under his very nose, and forming and reforming itself with the fluidity of clouds in the sky. But an important element in the art of teaching consists in handling them expertly and with insight Very often a class drags and learning falters because the kaleidoscope ceases to turn, and a pattern is held too long. In a certain review lesson summarizing the causes of the Civil War, a mild discussion pattern was inaugurated, with pupils offering suggestions which were noted on the board by the teacher, followed by desultory chat on each one At first there was a reasonable measure of attention, but after half an hour it began to flag. One felt that if only the teacher had possessed the resourcefulness to throw the class quickly into a sharply contrasting pattern of group action,

* Robert M. Lane, *The Teacher in the Modern Elementary School*, p. 83, Houghton Mifflin Company, Boston, 1941.

the situation could have been saved. But no! The lesson jogged along to its finale, with reproofs becoming more and more frequent and languidness more and more evident.

Whatever particular pattern of group action is going forward, however, the essential consideration is always the same. It must be as genuinely and highly participant as possible. And here is another reason why the teacher needs to be keenly aware of the kaleidoscopic social shifts he is eliciting. One finds a class spending its time individually reading around successive stanzas of a long poem, or successive speeches in a play. This may be perfectly justifiable and satisfactory. But when the reading is poorly done, and the nonreaders condemned merely to the function of sitting and suffering, it is neither justifiable nor satisfactory. Under many circumstances, again, a class may work very fruitfully in developing and expressing constructive criticisms of the offerings of some of its individual members, but not if the criticisms are so languid, so pointless, so hit-or-miss that they amount merely to somebody saying something while the silent majority are simply and justifiably bored. By all means social patterns should vary, and it is hard to mention any which are essentially inadmissible. But also, by all means, they should be pointed and functional, and should involve active participation by all concerned.

*b.* This leads to the second point. An effective social pattern in the classroom is *inclusive*, it involves all the members of the group concerned, though they need not be, and usually are not, identically engaged. For instance, a class in third-year French was engaged in discussing group letters which they planned to write to children in France and in French Canada. Most of them were absorbed, though some had a great deal to say, and others little or nothing. Still, even most of the nontalkers were visibly drawn in. But in the back of the room three pupils were doodling and chatting, and at last the teacher, after numerous glances in their direction, cracked down with a scolding. What this clearly indicated was a failure in the group pattern. No doubt the ideal is easier to talk about than to achieve, but that is no reason for not recognizing what it is. And the ideal social situation is so skillfully handled that everybody is pulled into it, and no one needs to be scolded for inattention.

*c.* A social pattern in the classroom which is handled in first-rate fashion has the quality of *resiliency*. It is held together not by the teacher's presence and insistence but by its own intrinsic vitality. This is one of the surest of all signs that a true cooperative and functional situation has been established. Can the teacher go out of the room without the pattern falling to pieces? Can he come ten minutes late and find that the class undertaking is already under way? If visitors or latecomers arrive, is the fragile crystal shattered? These are all very searching, very revealing psychological tests. Moreover, the more resilient, the more participant, the more autonomous, the more democratic the social pattern, the less the necessity for insisting on conventional classroom behavior. In a very active working committee there may well be an occasional conversational exchange outside the line of business, and there is certainly no prohibition on leaving one's seat in case of necessity. The same with the actively working class. The minutiae of behavior only loom up as very important when the situation itself lacks life and compelling power. Discipline, in other words, should not be understood or judged negatively, as the absence of disturbance. It should be judged positively, in terms of an active and responsible and participant group morale, a joint desire to accomplish something, which at once means that small disturbances simply cease to disturb.

## REVIEW AND INTERPRETATION

A valuable formulation of the process in which a learner may engage in living and interacting, and through which he may learn, affords a pregnant review and interpretation of the argument of this chapter.

(1) *Adventuring*, exploring, trying, finding out, experimenting, investigating, searching, reaching, inquiring, extending, contemplating, collecting, examining, questioning, proving, asking, studying. (2) *Creating*, contriving, devising, proposing, constructing, imagining, planning, organizing, thinking, initiating. (3) *Cooperating*, pooling, suggesting, helping, contributing, out-giving, discussing, refuting, talking, reporting, proposing, sharing, participating, communicating. (4) *Judging*, evaluating, deciding, considering, concluding, forming an opinion, summarizing, formulating. (5) *Consuming*, enjoying, receiving, accepting, intaking, being affected, depending upon, listening. (6) *Recreating*, resting, renewing, playing, singing, dancing, relaxing. (7) *Recording*, drawing, writing, expressing, painting, sculpturing. (8) *Repeating*, reciting, practicing, drilling. (9) *Obeying*, accepting, following, conforming, submitting. (10) *Dictating*, controlling, ordering, forcing.*

Mrs. Mossman points out that the conventional school tends to emphasize the last three of these processes, but that modern education, while recognizing the importance of all of them, seeks in particular to elicit the first seven.

Now it is evident that the first seven processes are characteristically and essentially those involved in meaningful learning, whereas a learn-

* Lois Coffey Mossman, *The Activity Concept*, pp. 54–55, The Macmillan Company, New York, 1938.

ing process which utilizes chiefly or entirely the last three is meager and limited in meaning, although to be sure it cannot lack it altogether. Also it is evident that the first seven processes are essentially and characteristically those involved in cooperative, participant, mutually responsible, democratic social situations, whereas the last three taken by themselves involve social situations marked by submission and dictation.   Thus once more we see that there is an integral relationship between the democratically conducted class and meaningful learning.   One cannot make imposed and relatively meaningless learning good and effective by placing it in a democratic social setting, for the reason that such a setting essentially involves an accepted joint responsibility for an enterprise which is itself significant because it is undertaken as an act of choice and will.   In teaching and learning, as in all living, everything goes together.   The full and adequate application of the principle of socialization is simply one aspect of the unitary task of organizing meaningful learning.[6]

### Notes and References

1. For an exposition of the unit laboratory plan see Robert W. Frederick, Clarence E. Ragsdale, and Rachel Salisbury, *Directing Learning*, pp. 180–198, D. Appleton-Century Company, Inc., New York, 1938.

2. The source of comparison between good and poor teachers, interesting and instructive if interpreted in terms of principles, but as it stands definitely externalistic, is A. S. Barr, *Characteristic Differences in the Teaching Performance of Good and Poor Teachers in the Social Studies*, Public School Publishing Company, Bloomington, Ill., 1929.   The monograph is a short one.

3. The study of architecture is ably and interestingly reported, with many interpretive comments, by Emily Ann Barnes and Bess M. Young, *Children and Architecture*, Teachers College, Columbia University, Bureau of Publications, New York, 1932.   The entire report repays careful reading.

4. For numerous excellent and practical illustrations of cooperative planning see H. H. Giles, *Teacher-Pupil Planning*, Part V, pp. 90–123, Harper & Brothers, New York, 1941.

5. For a good discussion of grouping from the point of view of social value see Robert M. Lane, *The Teacher in the Modern Elementary School*, Chap. 3, Houghton Mifflin Company, Boston, 1941.

6. Lois Coffey Mossman, *The Activity Concept*, The Macmillan Company, New York, 1938, presents a brief but important formulation of modern educational ideas with practical references, and on a historical basis.

### Items for Discussion and Study

*Refer to the opening suggestion for discussion and study in connection with Chap. 6. Follow it out in connection with the principle of socialization, of course substituting Chap. 9 for Chap 5.   Retain the outcomes in your notebook or card file.*

1. In what respects is individual teaching better than poor group teaching of the routine recitation type?   Would this apply to the "backing one's book" type of individual teaching?

2. On the basis of reflection, observation, and experience in and out of school, suggest ways in which a group can and does stimulate and further the learning and achievement of its members. Do committee situations, team situations, staff situations, etc., suggest possibilities that might be used in teaching? Is it possible to get things in discussing a matter with a group that might not appear in private discussions with its individual members?

3. Is it possible to organize learning in a large class otherwise than by using the group for the uniform consideration and study of uniform topics? In other words, does a large class make a lockstep organization inevitable?

4. Consider the general problem of class size in relationship to the principle of socialization. How might social organization and action differ as the size of the group changed? Is good teaching possible with a large class?

5. As you compare the "poor" and the "good" teachers contrasted on p. 174 would you expect pupils actually to learn better with the latter? Is this really the acid test of a good teacher?

6. Is the concept of discipline implied in the illustration on pp. 175–176 still of the negative type, in spite of the kindness, consideration, sympathy, and fine human relationships manifested?

7. Do teachers in general tend to use positive or negative incentives? What is your own experience?

8. Is it possible for the teacher to establish a fully cooperative group situation if he himself does all the planning? Are there any fundamental objections to letting the pupils share the planning? Must this mean that the teacher loses essential control?

9. Write up a few case studies of teachers who have succeeded partly because they learned to make a wise use of their own characteristics, and of teachers who have failed because they never really learned to be themselves.

10. What concrete problems of the social organization of learning are likely to arise in a class with a very wide range of ability or age? Consider the problems along this line in a one-room, one-teacher rural school.

11. Observe two or three classes, each for a whole period, concentrating entirely on the shifting social patterns that occur. Try to identify and note down these sequentially appearing patterns. Is there any evidence of a conscious management of these shifts?

12. Compile for discussion a list of instances showing resiliency or the lack of it in the group attitudes of classes.

13. What general inferences for his own improvement should a teacher draw from noticing that certain pupils in a class are out of the picture, not attending, not participating, etc.?

## CHAPTER 11

# THE PRINCIPLE OF INDIVIDUALIZATION AND THE ORGANIZATION OF LEARNING

### THE PRINCIPLE OF INDIVIDUALIZATION

A boy had reached the sixth grade with a school record somewhat less than mediocre. None of his studies had gone well. He had repeated one year's work without beneficial effects. He was quiet and shy, and seemed immature for his age. Soon after the session opened, his sixth-grade group undertook to make a study of the American Indians, and more particularly of the campaign of Custer against Sitting Bull. Subgroups and individuals were to take responsibility for various aspects of the work, all of which were to be brought together by the class as a whole. As culminating activities there were to be a pageant and an exhibit, both dealing with aspects of the life of the Indians, and their clashes with the whites.

In organizing her situation the teacher had in mind this boy's poor previous showing, and made an effort tactfully to sound him out to discover what he might be able to do best. Following some hints which he very diffidently let fall, she suggested that he might like to try to prepare some pictures and illustrations which the class could use. The proposal was remarkably successful and tapped a hitherto hidden spring of talent, energy, and self-assurance. The child followed up the commission with growing enthusiasm. He read up on Indian customs, life, dress, and habitat, produced a series of sketches which stimulated much lively class discussion and opened unexpected avenues of investigation, and for the final exhibit worked out an elaborate, illustrated map showing the location of the tribes, the chief routes and areas of white penetration, and the scenes of striking events, including of course Custer's famous "last stand."

Here is a revealing case history in which the effectiveness of a pupil's learning and the value of his year's school experience turned on finding the opportunity suited to him as an individual. Clearly the success of the teacher in dealing with him depended on their mutual discovery of this opportunity. So, in general, meaningful learning must proceed in terms of the learner's own purposes, aptitudes, abilities, and experimental procedures. This is the *principle of individualization,*

189

the fourth of the guiding generalizations in terms of which learning must be organized if it is to be effective.

## CHARACTERISTICS OF GOOD INDIVIDUALIZATION

No general psychological proposition is better attested than that individuals differ from one another. The bulk of material turned up by almost innumerable investigations in support of this statement is nothing less than overwhelming. Of course it has always been a truism, but only since tests of various kinds began to be widely used— and this means only since about 1900—have psychologists and educators fully realized the magnitude and variety of individual differences. This is not the place to summarize the evidence, and the reader who wishes to study it can readily do so by consulting the references at the end of the present chapter. The specific question here before us is this: How does our knowledge about individual differences bear upon the organization of learning?[1]

It is perfectly obvious that learning is and must be an individual matter, for the simple reason that every person has to do his own learning. From a practical point of view, however, the valuable thing to know is in what important respects one person's learning is likely to differ from that of another person. The sixth-grade boy whose story has been briefly told learned badly in an alien way, and quite well in his own way. But how many children were there in the same class whose particular way of learning was never discovered and who got comparatively little out of their year's work chiefly for this reason? How many such children are there in most of the classes one visits, or teaches, or hears about? What should be done about it? What can be done about it? What guiding ideas ought to be kept in mind if one hopes to do anything intelligent about it at all? These, clearly, are the practical issues; and the immense and impressive mass of research data on individual differences must be boiled down and brought to bear upon them.

This may look like a very large order, and of course it is. But the problem is more manageable than it might seem. For although details are endlessly complicated, there is a broad and really quite simple distinction which takes us to the very heart of the practical issue. Differences between people, as they affect learning and achievement, are of two kinds. First there are those which are vertical, or one-dimensional, or quantitative. Second there are those which are qualitative. Well-organized learning must take care of both.

**1. Vertical Differences.** It is possible to arrange human beings in ascending and descending order in respect to some single characteristic or trait. The basis of classification may be physical, as when people are shown to differ in height, or weight, or muscular strength. Or the basis may be mental. So far as the practical organization of learning is concerned, by far the most important vertical or one-dimensional differences among human beings seem to be those in what is called general intelligence. At least we know far more about these than about any others, and have far better means of getting at them.

The nature of intelligence and the problems involved in its measurement are still in the realm of controversy, although many of the disputes have died down a great deal over the past 20 to 25 years. So, although we are still far from a stage in which everything is settled, yet it is fair to say that many conclusions have been reached which seem reasonable and tenable, and which would probably be accepted by a majority of competent experts. This is of great importance for the practical teacher, because there are certain things he needs to know about the intelligence of his pupils if he is going to make a good job of teaching them. So long as these matters are wrapped in a fog of technical and often quite violent argument he has nothing to go upon. But a stage has been reached at which many points of importance to him have been greatly and very helpfully clarified, if not settled once and for all.

There seems good reason to believe that what an intelligence test actually measures is ability with the kind of abstract, academic, verbal learning which is the staple fare of the conventional school, and particularly the conventional high school or college. A great deal of discussion has centered on this point. If it is proposed to call an instrument an intelligence test, then the question as to what intelligence really is becomes obviously pertinent. Much active debate has been carried on about it and many definitions have been proposed, but for the most part they seem too vague and also too liable to various objections to be as helpful as they might be to practical people. There has even been a suggestion in responsible quarters to drop the term "intelligence tests" altogether, and to speak of "classification tests" instead.

A sensible way to seek for enlightenment is to ask how intelligence tests are made, and particularly how they are validated. The maker of such a test assembles a large number of problems involving language arrangements such as completions, numbers and numerical problems, codes and symbols, geometrical figures, and the like. From these he selects a smaller number which he has reason to consider particularly suitable. These he arranges in a determinate order. It is this final selection and arrangement which constitutes his test. But when he has finished making it, how does he know that it is any good? How does he know that it will measure something of importance—something that might reasonably be called "general intelligence"? Clearly he must check it up against some outside criterion or standard in order to make sure that an achieved score on his test really indicates something beyond itself. Binet, who was the original author of what is still the best of all intelligence tests, used precisely this procedure.* He tried out innumerable items that might go into his scale, sifted them down, and made sure that he picked out those with which bright children would do well and dull children poorly. This is the process known as test validation, or at least one type of it.

Now the prevailing criterion used in validating intelligence tests and in picking out items to go into them has been performance in school. It is not the only one, but it is the most common. The assumption has been that, taken on the average, children who do well in school are more intelligent than those who do badly. One may build up a speculative structure on this foundation. One may say that children who succeed in school possess certain general qualities partially or wholly lacking in those who do badly. One may debate at great length about the nature of these qualities, about whether they are inherited or acquired, and so on and so forth. Such questions are of undeniable importance. But as a matter of concrete, common-sense, practical fact, the best of our intelligence tests are specifically designed to measure not some abstract attribute of human nature called general intelligence, but in the main a very real and recognizable quality that may be called "success in school."

A good intelligence test, then, is a very useful tool. It can be given, probably in less than an hour, to a large number of people, and it can yield some very important information about every last one of them which would be almost impossible to get in any other way. It can arrange them in a vertical, one-dimensional scale in respect to their ability to do certain kinds of mental tasks. Of course even the best of intelligence tests is fallible and limited. This is quite obvious to common sense, for human personality is far too complex to be rated with complete accuracy even in respect to a single trait in 30 to 60 minutes. So a child's intelligence test score always needs to be supplemented with other information about him before a dependable judgment as to his place on the scale can be reached. His previous school record and

* The Binet Scale in its first form was published in France in 1905 and has gone through many revisions and improvements in this and other countries. Its use is limited because it must be given individually by a trained person, which makes it expensive and time consuming to administer.

his showing on so-called "educational tests" (that is, tests in the special subject areas) are among the other factors to be considered. But the assumption is that when everything is properly taken into account, a child can be placed on a vertical, one-dimensional scale in respect to his ability to handle "academic" tasks. There are some who would dispute this proposition, and of course as knowledge advances it may turn out that they are right. But as matters now stand it is widely believed by competent persons, and may, with reservations, be accepted.

Among important educators, Carleton Washburne has conspicuously stressed the importance of this idea. He has insisted that in any class group there will be children at many different levels of readiness to learn. Readiness to learn is revealed partly by mental age as determined by an intelligence test, and partly by other and more intimate information about the individual child. What it means is that different children in the same class cannot possibly handle the same material in arithmetic, or in reading, or in spelling, or indeed in any other subject-matter area. This puts the matter in a more concrete and cogently practical way than saying that children in the fourth grade have been found to vary in mental age from 6 years and 8 months to 12 years and 1 month, which is one typical item from an enormous mass of similar findings. The mental age score, together with suitable supplementary data, is supposed to reveal what kind of intellectual tasks the child is now able (or ready) to attack. If this is correct, as it well may be, and if there are enormous differences of this kind within each class, which is certainly true, then something has to be done about it if learning is to be properly organized.

But beyond this it is believed that intelligence tests, again suitably supplemented, can show us not only what a child is now ready to do, but his future possibilities and limitations as well. For instance there is much evidence that if a child's I.Q. (which is the ratio of mental to chronological age, or the so-called "measure of brightness") falls much below 110, he is never likely to get much out of a conventional course in ninth-grade algebra, although he may make a passing mark. To be sure, children whose I.Q.'s ran as low as 93 or even less have been taught the subject with some success, but only by very time-consuming individual treatment; but when children below the indicated level who have failed once with the course repeat it, the only result is usually a second failure. Any technical device which can prevent children from being steered into disaster and frustration is certainly well justified.

But a much wider issue is involved. It must be remembered that a substantial majority of all children in school have I.Q.'s well below

110, and that about half of them or slightly more will fall below 100. Now we definitely know that for all such the system of learning conventionally organized under the title ninth-grade algebra is sure to be meaningless and defeating. As to other subjects we are not so sure, but it probably holds true of geometry, Latin, modern foreign languages, physics, and chemistry. This either means that these subjects should be excluded from the general curriculum, or that they should be reorganized. The latter is almost certainly the answer. The content itself is not unmanageable. After all, many Roman children with I.Q.'s far less than 100 managed to speak Latin. But the educational cooks have done such a bad job of preparing their material that when it comes to table it is unfit for normal human consumption.

Would such a reorganization ruin the value of these subjects for the bright, able, intelligent individuals who seem able to learn them more or less effectively in their present form? Why should it? Little can be said for setting up a body of material so awkwardly that only a genius with a very strong character can make head or tail of it. There are no dividends in this, even for a genius, for he can surely find more repaying things to do than beating his brains on the stupidities of his teacher.

Although the classification of individuals on a vertical or one-dimensional scale seems a reasonable and useful thing to do, such classification must always be conservatively and cautiously interpreted. It can never tell us nearly all about that person, although it may tell us something very important about him. This is a point to bear in mind in organizing learning with reference to the principle of individualization.

The idea that intelligence tests reveal general hereditary ability has been the basis for great exaggerations of the importance of vertical classification. Twenty to 25 years ago a great many psychologists believed this to be the case. The I.Q., it was claimed, was virtually unchangeable during a person's whole life, except of course for sheer errors in measurement. Within the limits of accuracy of the measuring instrument, however, the individual's intelligence was believed to be fixed and unalterable. It would remain the same no matter what his circumstances, for as long as he lived, for it was a gift of nature which the environment could not alter.

Cautious workers always knew these claims were extreme, and this has grown steadily clearer. It is no longer possible to doubt that under certain circumstances the intelligence quotient can be changed materially. It cannot be done always or easily, as by putting a child into a somewhat better home or a somewhat better school, or by bringing about some improvement in his general health. But if he is brought under specific influences quite young, as in a fine nursery school, or if he can go on with his formal education until he is through college or even further, something beneficial may well happen.   To be sure, extravagant miracles are not possible.   One cannot take a child with an I.Q. of 60 and build it up to 120; but one may be able to bring about a change of 15, 20, or 25 points, which is a good deal.

The practical implication of all this is the unwisdom of narrow and rigid classifications on a one-dimensional basis.   Some time ago it was recommended that schools should be run on a five-track system, with pupils classified chiefly on intelligence test results.   If the intelligence quotient really did reveal general innate ability there might be something to say for such a plan.   But it varies a great deal more than was once generally realized.   So an arrangement of this kind would lead to an enormous amount of overlapping and misclassification, and would be very unlikely indeed to improve learning.

Vertical classification, then, has its uses.   But it also has its limitations.   And both uses and limitations need to be borne in mind when we set out to individualize learning properly.[2]

**2. Qualitative Differences.**   People differ from one another in special aptitudes and interests, and in methods of working.   Thus one person may be definitely intellectual in his tendencies, another definitely aesthetic, another definitely mechanical, and another definitely social.   Such differences cannot be arranged in a straight-line, one-dimensional sequence of more or less, because they are distinctions in kind or type rather than in degree.   For the purposes of education in general and of the organization of learning in particular they are probably quite as important as vertical, one-dimensional differences, if indeed not more so.

Vastly less is known about special abilities than about general intelligence.   It is most improbable that human beings can be classified into clear-cut, definite psychological types.   Special aptitudes are not as highly specialized or as rigidly determined as that.   We do not even know how much they depend on inborn nature, and how much on opportunity, influence, chance, and circumstance.   A great many special aptitude tests have been published from time to time, but very few of them can be considered as more than experimental, none of them compare to the best intelligence tests, and they have not been widely used in the schools.   Nevertheless qualitative differences of this kind undoubtedly exist and are very important—far too important to be overlooked by any teacher who wants to succeed.

Probably the best practical way to get at this problem is in terms of interest, for a person's interest-pattern has a definite relationship to his

achievement and learning.  A declared interest, even though strong
and lasting, is in itself no guarantee of superior ability.  A youngster
may work hard of his own volition at some manual pursuit, or at art,
or at music, or at mathematics.  He may sacrifice other occupations
and doings for the sake of his choice.  But still he may be excelled by
some other person who seems to have no particular interest in the line
of activity in question but who is in general better equipped.  This,
however, is very far from meaning that a declared interest should be
considered trivial.  For what it does indicate is that the person concerned will probably do better in that respect than in others.  This is
particularly probable if the interest is of long standing.  When a child
presents a history of a continuous and stable interest-pattern, running
through the lower grades, the upper grades, and high school, this
reveals very little as to his possibilities in comparison with other people.
But it is a highly significant sign of the pattern of his own possibilities.
It tends strongly to indicate what he himself can do best, although how
good that best may be is another question altogether.

The reason for this is to be found in our account of the nature and
conditions of meaningful learning.  A strong and continuous interest
is a strong and continuous purpose.  It may easily be strong enough to
lead the youngster to save up his pocket money to buy equipment, to
be reluctant about doing other things that might be thought intriguing
if they interrupt his chosen pursuit.  Such an interest—such a purpose
—fulfills one of the most basic and essential conditions of meaningful
learning.  It means that the individual is ready and able to learn with
all the effectiveness of which he is capable.  This is why a powerful
and continuing interest is a very significant sign, and an important
determiner of the learning process.  But even an ephemeral interest,
often called a "mere whim," is by no means to be despised.  At least
it indicates an autonomous purpose, although perhaps trivial and
fleeting.  And this is a great deal better than none at all.  Moreover
ephemeral interests can often coalesce and deepen into significant ones,
which latter do not usually manifest themselves full-fledged.

The following is one simple and useful classification of interests
which has been employed for guidance purposes, and which the practical teacher may find helpful.

1.  Physical interests: liking work involving bodily exertion
2.  Outdoor interests: liking outdoor life and doings
3.  Mechanical interests: liking to repair and make machinery, etc.
4.  Skilled manual interests: liking to use one's hands, manipulate, etc.
5.  Fine manual interests: liking to use one's fingers, make fine adjustments
6.  Social interests: liking for group activities, preference not to work alone
7.  Domestic interests: liking to care for a house, run a household

8. Interest in children: liking to play with, teach, care for them
9. Leadership interests: preference to lead rather than follow
10. Commercial interests: liking to deal with people in business
11. Interest in order: liking to have things arranged systematically
12. Mathematical interests: liking to work with figures and symbols
13. Scientific interests: in physical phenomena
14. Aesthetic interests: liking for art and beauty
15. Interests in drawing: liking for representing objects
16. Interest in music: liking various forms of musical expression and appreciation
17. Literary interests: liking to express ideas in written form
18. Interest in vocal expression: liking to talk to people, argue, explain
19. Interest in study: liking to dig into a subject and know all about it
20. Interest in experimentation: liking to try things out and watch results
21. Interest in observation: liking to notice how people or things act
22. Interest in creative imagination: tendency to picture things vividly in one's
mind

This classification, of course, is crude and quite empirical, and its subdivisions are not too well defined and certainly not mutually exclusive. But it is based on a good deal of experience and observation. It can be used to construct an interest profile that is by no means without significance. It can give a teacher a fairly good idea of the sort of things to look for. So it is not without its uses. There are many others of more or less the same kind.

One very important point to notice about this or any other realistic catalogue of human interests is that it coincides only here and there with the subdivisions of the conventional school curriculum. Thus we could not take care of interests simply by assigning pupils to appropriate courses even if we wanted to, and even if we knew enough to handle the job in this way. The only thing to do is for the individual teacher to shape up his work with reference to the declared interests of the pupils with whom he is dealing. What this means in practice is strikingly shown by the following account of experience.

. . . I was assigned late in the term to a public school in a slum area in the Williamsburg district of Brooklyn. The principal was an iron disciplinarian. Pupils and teachers stood in equal fear of her. Discipline problems were so acute that police cars were always cruising around the school. The principal looked me over rather dubiously and gave me a 6-A opportunity class with the gruff injunction, "I don't expect you to teach them anything, but I do expect you to keep them quiet." When I saw the class, my heart sank. It was composed mainly of overage huskies sitting out the school term until they were old enough to get their working papers. They were tough.

One stout youngster sat before me with a freshly stitched knife slash that ran from each ear to mouth.

"How did you get that?" I asked, during a friendly interlude in the course of the day.

Summoning all his tact and linguistic resources, he replied, "Oh! Some guy insulted me mudder."

Another student always signaled his future absence by building up a preliminary alibi in class.  One day he raised both hands, fingers hanging limp from his wrists.  With a woebegone look on his mobile face he exclaimed, "Teacher, my pawses hurt me."  He was a native American boy of immigrant stock who had not learned the word for "wrist" or the plural of "paw."  That was my class.

After a few false starts and lively scraps, I rediscovered for myself the truths of progressive education.  I could keep that class from running amok—which was what the principal meant by keeping them quiet—only by teaching them.  I could teach them only by arousing their interest.  And the most effective ways of arousing their interest were the use of their own experiences as a starting point, to let them participate in setting up the teaching goals for the week and the day, and abandoning the set syllabus for the grade.  For example, I believe that the syllabus called for teaching the geography of South America.  But I taught that class the geography of the United States of which they had only the vaguest notions.

It came about in this way.  The boys had easy opportunities for making money and I soon learned that they were betting heavily outside on baseball games.  Baseball was their religion.  It was not difficult to get them to figure out the standing of the clubs, percentages, errors, batting averages; to induce them to write up baseball games and read with growing discrimination some good newapaper stories; to follow on the map the travels of the teams, the cities they visited, their histories and environments; to read about and discuss the sport of other times and countries; and, crowning triumph, to make them see the necessity of establishing rules of the game in class.  A different pair of boys acted as umpires every day to arbitrate disputes.  I taught them all the subjects of the curriculum—arithmetic, composition, geography, history, reading, penmanship—on the basis of their existing interests.  I succeeded thereby in building up new interests in things that previously had seemed to be utterly academic.  I worked as hard preparing for class as I ever did for any subsequent class.  Material conditions were very bad.  But there were two advantages I enjoyed which contributed enormously to my success.  The group was considered so hopeless that I was given complete freedom in my teaching approaches.  More important still, the class was small enough for me to get to know intimately every boy in it.[*3]

Differences in methods of work and learning are also of great importance and must be properly handled if teaching is to succeed.  The psychological considerations involved and the bearing of the whole

* Sidney Hook, "The Case for Progressive Education," *Saturday Evening Post*, Vol. 217 (1945), June 30, pp. 28–29.

issue upon the organization of learning can be formulated in the following propositions:

1. Trial and error is a universal characteristic of all types of learning. It occurs in problem solving, and indeed plays an essential part. In one of the earliest pieces of research on this subject, the learners were given wire puzzles in which a key was to be taken off a complicated frame. The experimenter knew how each problem could be solved, and sometimes he gave the learners either hints or full directions. But even then they had to fumble and try and make their own mistakes, although the process could be considerably shortened by the right kind of help. The same point has been established with many other kinds of problem material in which manipulation was not nearly so prominent. Trial and error also occurs in memorizing, and here it takes the form of trying once in a while to recite what one is learning, instead of merely repeating it again and again. This has the effect of showing from time to time how the job is coming along, and is definitely a beneficial procedure. Trial and error even occurs in the establishment of the conditioned reflex. Just before the reflex is tied up to the new stimulus—the knee jerk to the sound of a bell for instance—there will be changes in respiration, as though the organism were gathering itself together and casting about within the narrow and rigid limits prescribed, and getting ready to set up the new relationship of stimulus and response.

Such facts have long been familiar and are mentioned in most standard textbooks on psychology. But their practical significance has not been generally recognized. What they mean is that every learner puts through every job of learning to some extent in his own individual way. Two pupils will not acquire a physical skill, or the ability to solve problems, or indeed anything else, and will not even memorize a given body of content by precisely the same method. In the case of memorizing they will not intersperse recitations at just the same points, and other learning sequences will show similar variations. Even if they are given quite careful instructions, their methods of learning will not be reduced to an absolute uniformity. Everyone has to do his own learning in his own way, and this needs to be recognized and provided for. Everyone must learn by his own direct experience and experimentation. To give a very simple and familiar illustration, a person may be given careful verbal directions about what turnings to take to drive from one town to another. But in order to be sure of the route he must actually drive over it, and even if he makes no overt mistakes he is very likely to hesitate, wonder, and anxiously watch every once in a while.

There can be no manner of doubt that individualization shaped up as guidance of the trial-and-error experimentation peculiar to the learner who is attacking a genuine and compelling problem is a most potent agency for securing authentic results.[4]

## Notes and References

*General References on Individualization*

Two references dealing with individual differences with emphasis on the educational inferences to be drawn are A. M. Jordan, *Educational Psychology*, Chap. 10, Henry Holt and Company, Inc., New York, rev. ed., 1935; and James L. Mursell, *Educational Psychology*, Chap. 4, W. W. Norton & Company, Inc., New York, 1939.

*References in the Text*

1. For a good though partial summary of work on individual differences, in addition to the sources above, see Gertrude Hildreth, "Individual Differences," *Encyclopaedia of Educational Research*, pp. 596–602, The Macmillan Company, New York, 1941.

2. Material on the intelligence levels required by school subjects is summed up by James L. Mursell, *The Psychology of Secondary School Teaching*, pp. 325–330, W. W. Norton & Company, Inc., New York, rev. ed., 1939. For the special problem of algebra see C. A. Woods, "A Failure Class in Algebra," *School Review*, Vol. 28 (1928), pp. 41–49; and C. N. Stokes, "Comparing the Effect of Arithmetic and General Mathematics in the Seventh and Eighth Grades upon Achievement in Ninth Grade General Mathematics," *School Science and Mathematics*, Vol. 30 (1939), pp. 852–857. The relationship of individual differences to various high-school subjects is treated by Homer T. Reed, *Psychology and Teaching of Secondary-School Subjects*, Chaps. 4, 7, 11, 16, 20, and 24, Prentice-Hall, Inc., New York, 1939.

Various definitions of intelligence are discussed by Rudolph Pintner, *Intelligence Testing*, Chap. 4, Henry Holt and Company, Inc., New York, new ed., 1931. Pintner also gives an account of the Binet Scale in Chaps. 2 and 3. For material on the constancy of the intelligence quotient see James L. Mursell, *Psychology of Secondary School Teaching*, pp. 269–271, W. W. Norton & Company, Inc., New York, rev. ed., 1939. For a report on a recent and very striking study showing that continued schooling raises the I.Q. see Irving Lorge, "Schooling Makes a Difference," *Teachers College Record*, Vol. 46 (1945), May, pp. 483–492.

3. The most important items on the relation of interest to ability are E. L. Thorndike, "Early Interests, Their Permanence and Relation to Abilities," *School and Society*, Vol. 5 (1917), pp. 359–360; J. W. Bridges and V. M. Dollinger, "The Correlation between Interests and Abilities in College Courses," *Psychological Review*, Vol. 27 (1920), pp. 308–314; E. L. Thorndike, "The Correlation between Interests and Abilities in College Courses," *Psychological Review*, Vol. 28 (1921), pp. 374–376; Richard S. Uhrbrock, "Interests as an Indication of Ability," *Journal of Applied Psychology*, Vol. 10 (1926), pp. 487–501; O. K. Garretson, *Relationship between Expressed Preference and Curricular Abilities in Ninth Grade Boys*, Teachers College, Columbia University, Bureau of Publications, New York, 1930. The items are arranged in the order in which they can probably be read with most profit.

4. J. F. Dashiell, "A Survey and Synthesis of Learning Theories," *Psychological Bulletin*, Vol. 32 (1935), pp. 261–275, heavily documents the claim that trial and error occurs universally in learning.   A good general account of trial and error from the organismic viewpoint is given by Raymond H. Wheeler and Francis T. Perkins, *Principles of Mental Developments*, pp. 82–105, The Thomas Y. Crowell Company, New York, 1932.   See A. I. Gates, "Recitation as a Factor in Memorizing," *Archives of Psychology*, No. 40 (1917), for its place in memorizing.   The wire puzzle study is Henry A. Ruger, *The Psychology of Efficiency*, Teachers College, Columbia University, Bureau of Publications, New York, 1926; also in *Archives of Psychology*, No. 15 (1910).

### Items for Discussion and Study

*Refer to the two opening suggestions for discussion and study in connection with Chap. 5. Follow them out in connection with the principle of individualization. Retain the outcomes in your notebook or card file.*

1. What is the significance of the suggestion that intelligence tests be called classification tests?

2. What are the practical advantages for the teacher in having intelligence test scores for all members of his class?

3. If large numbers of children cannot handle the learning setup in school as ordinarily organized, what should be done about it?   Consider the point in connection with specific school subjects.

4. Would you think it likely that children could be classified as possessing or lacking definite inborn "gifts" for this or that school subject?   Consider the implications of your answer for the organization of learning.

5. Apply the interest inventory on pp. 196–197 to a few individuals, and consider what the interest patterns revealed seem to indicate as to probable ability, and as to possible choice of career, school studies, hobbies, etc.

6. Are there any revisions, extensions, or reductions that you think might improve the inventory?   Any items that might be consolidated or further subdivided?

7. Have you ever known anyone who had a strong and lasting interest, but apparently little corresponding ability?   Would this mean that the interest in question was of no importance?

8. How can a teacher discover the interests of his pupils?   Would some of the interests on the inventory be harder for him to discover than others?   Is the discovery of interests hampered by the conventional instructional organization? How might the organization of learning be changed to help in the discovery of interests?

9. Is there always one "best" way of doing everything—writing a theme, reading and understanding a passage, preparing a speech, solving a problem, etc.? Consider the implications of your answer for the organization of learning.

10. Why is it better for a teacher to let a learner attack a task in his own way and help him when trouble arises than to impose an efficient procedure from the first?

# CHAPTER 12

# THE PRINCIPLE OF INDIVIDUALIZATION AND THE APPRAISAL OF TEACHING

## HIERARCHY OF APPLICATIONS

As with all the other principles of teaching discussed in this book, so in the case of individualization, a scale or hierarchy is presented which brings it into touch with teaching situations and practices. Here once more the levels are not rigid categories or classifications but are set up for the purpose of analysis and appraisal. And again, individualization like all the other principles is unavoidably recognized somehow and to some extent in all teaching, even though at the lowest level this amounts to no more than the acceptance of differential results from uniform procedure. So in all teaching from the most poorly organized to the best, there is a continuous gradation in the application of this principle rather than a point at which it is suddenly introduced and below which it is completely ignored.

### PRINCIPLE OF INDIVIDUALIZATION: HIERARCHY

I  Uniform tasks on uniform schedule with individualization showing in differential performance

II  Homogeneous grouping on two or more levels on I.Q., M.A., E.A. combined in some formula: differences in level between groups, differential performance within them

III  Contract plans on two or more levels: allows some choice and so more flexible than the above.

IV  Individual instruction: Dalton and Winnetka plans as typical

V  Large units with optional related activities and experiences

VI  Individual undertakings stemming from and contributing to the joint undertaking of the group of learners.

## THE FIRST LEVEL

**1. Appraisal.** Instances of teaching which belong to the first and lowest level of the hierarchy are so numerous and familiar that it is hardly necessary to cite specific instances. This, in fact, is the conventional and accepted pattern. A sequence of items to be learned is set up in the syllabus in terms of a prearranged time schedule. These items are presented by some variant of the assignment-recitation routine to an unclassified group of learners who certainly vary widely in capacity and background, and indeed in every important respect. It is not quite true to say that the timing of the items has no reference at all to the abilities of the learners, but the relationship is very vague and remote. On the basis of uncriticized experience, those who plan the work believe that the sequence can in some sense be covered in a term by the average child in the group, who is taken as the representative or prototype of all the rest—the "sixth-grade child," the "average tenth grader," etc. Materials, textbooks, and classroom procedures, too, are very roughly adapted to the average child in the grade or class. Thus the course, as an organized pattern of learning, is supposed to be suitable to the third grade, the tenth grade, or what not.

No precise adaptation of learning to the learner is possible in terms of this scheme, for the simple reason that within each grade or class there is always an immense range of variation, as has already been pointed out. This obviously means that the average child is merely a statistical concept and not an individual person. And statistical concepts cannot learn and cannot be taught. Moreover there is no precision in determining whether the learning as organized is really suited to the hypothetical average member of the group. But even allowing that this might be so, and supposing further that quite a number of children were precisely at the average or close enough to it to make no matter, what would happen to the others? Under the very best of conditions some of them would be bored because they found the work going too slowly, and others would be bewildered because it went too fast. The only way in which individual differences can express themselves at all is in the record, the bright children making high marks and the dull ones low marks, and both being tolerated.

Clearly, then, this whole plan of operation completely ignores the principle of individualization as far as the process is concerned. That anyone could be found to take it seriously, or to defend it for an instant as an effective organization of learning is astounding. It establishes the certainty that at least half the class will learn badly and in a superficial way, and the extreme probability that many of those whose record is satisfactory to good will not be called on for anything like the full use of their powers. To argue, as some do, that this reproduces the conditions of actual life which we all must face, in which many will fail while some succeed with ease, is simply preposterous. Teaching, like the practice of medicine, is a meliorative activity. Its whole point and purpose is to make matters better than they are in unregulated and uncontrolled living. A doctor who let half his patients die, and defended himself by saying that they would be bound to die sometime, would be run out of business. The same thing should happen to a teacher who consciously and deliberately maintains conditions under which large numbers of his pupils are sure not to learn well. It is his business to get these people to learn, and to establish the conditions and organization which will make this possible. Thus the conventional scheme, in spite of its very wide occurrence, not only mishandles the principle of individualization but also amounts to a repudiation of the whole conception of successful teaching.

**2. Attempts at Improved Practice.** It is noteworthy that the good sense and sound instincts of multitudes of practical teachers make it impossible for them to operate this scheme in accordance with its strict logic. In rating pupils they nearly always take account of effort, cooperativeness, amiability, good behavior, and so on. Often they do this quite informally by manipulating and modifying their marks or adding some sort of evaluative comment to the record. Sometimes a dual system of marking is used in which these general values are officially recognized. Sometimes, though much less commonly, there is a system under which marks indicate a relationship between the child's educational achievement and his supposed ability as indicated by mental tests or otherwise. Under this plan a dull student may do poor work and still get a good mark, because he is doing as well as he can, while a bright student may do much better work and still be marked low because he is not performing up to capacity.

These are, indeed, alleviations. As to their real effectiveness in bringing about better learning, it is impossible to say. A teacher operating under this scheme should always remember that its strong tendency is to condemn part of the class to bewilderment and another part to boredom. Anything within reason that he can do to mitigate and modify the impact of its influence is probably legitimate. However there is no denying that it is so basically bad that it cannot be much improved without being transformed, and to persuade the authorities to permit such a transformation the conscientious teacher should steadily work.

### THE SECOND LEVEL

Various plans for homogeneous grouping have been adopted in the attempt to rectify the above defects. Classes are subdivided on some criterion, usually a combination of educational and mental test scores and school record, into sections in which the range of differences is reduced. For a time the plan was very widely used, but today it is considerably less emphasized than previously. There have been numerous variations of the scheme. Sometimes two classifications are set up, and sometimes more. Sometimes a child is held in the same classification for all his studies, and sometimes he shifts from one to another. The most ambitious and rigid proposal of the kind has been to divide the whole grade sequence from first to twelfth into five sections or "tracks," to place the pupil in the appropriate one at the time of school entry by means of mental tests, and to keep him there throughout his entire school career.

**1. Appraisal.** The plan is at least an explicit recognition of the principle of individualization, and of the very serious teaching problem to which it refers. But it takes into consideration only one of the various psychological factors upon which an adequate individualization of instruction depends. It proposes merely to reduce the range of vertical differences in mentality and achievement. It makes the basic assumption that every section will move along the same pathway, but that the slower section or sections will not go so far or so fast as the abler. There may be some differences in methodology and in mode of handling the different sections, but each of them is supposed to advance along the selfsame road. Homogeneous grouping organizes a learning situation which differs from one the first level only in the fact that the extreme range of differences within the group which a teacher must handle has been lessened.

There has been a great deal of theoretical argument about this plan. It has been called undemocratic because it relegates some pupils to a position of inferiority and gives others a superior status. On the other hand, the reply has been made that such a classification is essentially democratic because it recognizes the true potentialities of individuals. There has been a great deal of speculation, accompanied by the comments of experienced teachers, as to whether dull pupils in an unsectioned class are encouraged or discouraged by the presence and performance of brighter fellow pupils, and about whether the bright are seriously impeded by the dull. On points such as these there has been no decisive answer, and indeed one can hardly expect that this would be possible because so much depends on how the social situation is handled.

A much more serious criticism is that the alleged homogeneity of homogeneous grouping is pretty much of a myth. A slow section may be made up of pupils who rate low on a combination of mental age and reading age, but these, after all, are only two out of a very large number of individual characteristics. The section will contain no pupils whose mental ages or reading ages are very high for their grade, and in that respect the range of individual differences will have been reduced. But what of other factors and abilities? The group will still almost surely contain pupils whose arithmetical, artistic, or musical capacities range from very high to very low. The point is that it is not possible to bring together a group of human beings fairly homogeneous in respect to one or two characteristics without having them differ as much as ever in others. And the school has to do not with one or two of a person's characteristics but with them all. In particular, it is inadmissible to section pupils entirely on intelligence tests. The assumption that these tests reveal basic hereditary capacity or quality and thus provide the master criterion in dealing with human beings belongs to a period of early and naïve enthusiasm overpassed these many years. Intelligence tests properly used have great value. But they certainly cannot tell us once and for all just where a person belongs in the educational scheme of things.

But all such considerations, although not without interest and importance, are in a certain sense beside the point. The vital practical question is whether homogeneous grouping gets better results. It is a scheme for the organization of learning, and here as always the decisive proof of the pudding is the eating. Does it in fact bring about better learning, or does it not? Apparently it does not. The evidence, admittedly, is slender—indeed quite surprisingly so, considering the obvious importance of the issue. But such comparisons as have been made clearly indicate that there is very little difference in the achievement of pupils in homogeneous sections and in heterogeneous or unclassified groups. There may be some recognizable advantage sometimes one way and sometimes another in different subjects, but it is so slight that the plan is not worth the energy and trouble needed to operate it if what is wanted is the better learning of subject matter. To be sure it may often be necessary and desirable to reduce the size of classes by subdividing them, but there seems no particular point in doing this by dint of an elaborate scheme of testing and record keeping for the sake of putative gain in efficiency which does not seem to accrue.

**2. Steps to Improved Practice.** Homogeneous grouping as such has no particular virtue. Its whole value depends on what teachers do with their groups after they have been sectioned. The usual assumption is that a teacher dealing with a slow section must be patient, tactful, helpful, and kind, and must be content to bring them along at a comparatively gradual pace. Moreover it is pointed out that some teachers are temperamentally suited to deal with slow learners and some better fitted to deal with fast ones. All this is indubitably true, and it indicates some of the things that can be done to make homogeneous grouping effective in the organization of learning.

But one can go a great deal further. What if the whole underlying conception of differential progress along a single track is abandoned? What if we think that the organization of learning might mean the establishment of a joint undertaking in which all may have a part? Homogeneous grouping gives an admirable opportunity for putting this doctrine into practice. Indeed it establishes a condition that is highly favorable to it. If the spread of age and ability in a group is too great, any coordinated social enterprises in which individuals may freely make their own contributions and play their own parts become very difficult. It will be hard to get the pupils at the extremes into the undertakings. Such undertakings, it has been said, become hard to handle if there is a spread of more than two years in grade scores on standard mental and educational tests. This condition is not met in the heterogeneous group; but in the homogeneous group it may be. So the teacher with a reasonably compact and closely classified group of pupils has an opportunity. However, he should remember that the advantage is not automatically created by the sectioning, but by his management of a potentially fruitful social situation.[1]

## THE THIRD LEVEL

**1. Appraisal.** A further step toward adequate individualization is the contract plan, an instance being the following "Contract for Fourth Grade Reading."

Text: *Study Reader*, by Walker and Parkman
Types of learning: pure practice
What we want to learn from this lesson

1. The meaning of some new hard words
2. The history of matches
3. To read quickly and understand what we read

The story about the lesson

Just pretend for one whole day that no one could find, buy, or make a match. What a time everyone would have. How would mother light the fire? How would father build a fire in the furnace? We would have cold food and cold houses. We would find it hard to live without matches, but a hundred years ago people had to get along without them. These long-ago people had fires, but they made them in another way. This lesson tells how these people made their fires.

How to study this lesson

(C level, minimum essentials)

1. Open your *Study Readers* to page 113.
2. Our new words for this week are given at the beginning of the lesson, study them and their meanings.
3. Read Part I of the Story (pages 113–127)
4. How did George Washington "strike a light" when he could not get a light from the fireplace?
5. Who was the inventor of the match?
6. What hard thing did the inventor succeed in doing?
7. Of what are matches made?

(B level, average material)

1. What is it that makes a match light?
2. Be able to tell why safety matches are safer than other kinds.
3. What three things about phosphorus do you learn from this lesson?

(A level, enriched material)

1. Try to make a picture of a fire drill (page 124, second paragraph)
2. Can you find something in this lesson which will explain what is meant by the saying, "Necessity is the mother of invention"?

Study the following words for meaning and pronunciation

C. Autumn, tale, repair, bloom

B. Coin, cloak, anxious, courage

A. Acre, vain, compass, tower*

It is interesting and instructive to evaluate this lesson plan somewhat more broadly than with reference to the particular principle now under consideration. As an attempt to organize learning it has numerous and manifest defects. The context in which the learning is to go on is almost entirely verbalistic, and is confined to a single book. There is some suggestion of a broader, more concrete, and presumably more compelling area of reference in the instruction to the pupil to imagine a day without matches, and probably an imaginative teacher would exploit it. That is to say, instead of the purely imaginary situation, a real one, or a series of such, might be set up. The instruction to try to make a picture of a fire drill also suggests possibilities, although this has the look of an adventitious item dragged in for no particular reason, and unrelated to the principal learnings. Beyond these two rather vague hints and intimations, however, the principle of context is applied at its lowest and least effective level.

From the standpoint of focalization, too, the scheme is open to the most drastic criticism. Perhaps the very most that can be said is that an attempt is made to establish some kind of working focuses, which

* G. A. Yoakam, *The Improvement of the Assignment*, pp. 70–71, The Macmillan Company, New York, 1933.

is more than one frequently finds in plans for the organization of learning. But the focuses are very inept and ineffective. To inform children that one of the things "we want" to learn in this lesson is the meaning of "some new hard words" is almost grotesque. The "history of matches," too, is a purely topical focus, without any essential unity or promise of intelligibility. And "to read quickly and understand what we read" is an objective far too remote to control the immediate learning activities of most fourth graders. Furthermore, the questions and study suggestions which should transform these generalities into plans for specific activity do not help matters appreciably. The questions are all of them quite hit-or-miss, and belong to the quiz-query type, rather than striking at essential and central intelligibilities or indicating relationships which the learner should clarify. All in all, the lesson violates every one of the basic criteria for effective focalization.

It is worth while to take up these criticisms before considering the lesson as an exemplification of the principle of individualization because they enable us to see the very close interrelationship of the various principles of successful teaching. As a scheme for the individualization of learning, the contract plan in general suffers from one great defect which is very clearly shown in the present instance. The proposed levels from which the pupil is invited to make his choice are usually quite arbitrary and lack any intrinsic significance. This is certainly so in the present case which is typical enough. The pupil who makes up his mind to do a B or an A contract finds that he is simply called upon for some more work, pretty much of the same kind as that involved in the minimum essentials that presumably must be covered by everybody. So far as actual achievement or insight, or any kind of actual educational returns are concerned, there seems no particular reason for adopting any one of these contractual levels, and the only incentive is the offer of a higher mark, which of course is an entirely extraneous reward. But how could anything else be possible with a learning unit which is a loosely coordinated collection of material, lacking structure, unity, and central intelligibility—lacking, that is to say, any effective and genuine focus? Once grant that pupils are to learn an arbitrarily determined amount of material held together by nothing more determining than a vague topical designation, and the only way one can establish higher levels is by adding more material.

Again, consider the A-level contract, which involves what is described as "enriched material." There is, perhaps, some justification for the term in this particular instance. To tell the children to look for something in the lesson which explains the proverb about necessity being the mother of invention is not a bad instruction, as such things go. It calls for analysis, reflection, and the clarification of meaning, and is probably the closest approach in the whole assignment to a really acceptable focus for learning. Also the making of a fire-drill picture involves a concrete and compelling context, although its relevance is open to doubt, and although the instruction to *try* to do it seems to bring in a sardonic undertone which is decidedly out of place. But what strikes one as most peculiar is that these psychological tidbits should be reserved for the favored few who have the nerve to tackle a contract at the top level. Apparently the idea is that the staples of learning should be the dry bread and potatoes of routine, and that the good children who clean up their plates should be allowed a chance to deal with something meaningful as a special treat. This, of course, is an exact inversion of the proper arrangement. The persons best able to benefit from facts, verbalizations, and generalizations are those who have already grasped essential meanings in terms of a rich, concrete, compelling context, and the clarification through understanding of an intelligible focus. "Minimum essentials" therefore, if the term is to be retained at all, should consist of items calculated to convey and evoke meaningful learning. And "enrichment" should certainly not be the ice cream at the end of the meal, withheld from all save the specially deserving; for if real results are wanted, the context of learning cannot be too much "enriched" from start to finish.

Thus the various principles of teaching are closely interrelated. A misapplication of the principles of context and focus leads to a distorted individualization. Not only are the various levels arbitrary and meaningless, they are actually destructive as well, for the worst learning materials are imposed on everybody, and the best are, in effect, made available only to a few courageous souls.

**2. Steps toward Improved Practice.** From this analysis it clearly appears that the effectiveness of the contract plan as an instrument for individualization depends upon the entire organization of learning. One might work out better, more careful, more sensible contract levels, and yet not do much to improve the psychological conditions of learning. It is the pattern as a whole that needs transforming. Above all one must avoid having contract levels which are merely more of the same for the sake of a better mark. This is spurious individualization, since it has virtually nothing to do with individual interest, differential methods of work or even differential capacity of the vertical kind, since the pupil chooses his contract pretty much in the dark.

There is just one way to obviate this. Build the unit or lesson round an intelligible focus. Consider again the unit mentioned on page 127 which was built around the issue of whether insects or human beings are to control the earth. This very readily lends itself to differential tasks which are really different—collecting, exploring, reading, making notes, summarizing class discussions, making sketches and photographs and models, interviewing experts, and so on at length. Yet all these diverse activities can be related to a centralizing idea, and contribute to a job of group thinking and group learning. If, on the other hand, a unit or lesson is simply a block of material, differential assignments can be set up only in terms of more or less, which means that they do not give opportunities for individuality to function and express itself. The idea of the differential task is sound. Without it individualization is impossible But the mechanical contract, differentiating only in terms of more or less, does not apply it soundly. What is necessary is to organize learning as a quest for insight, and then set up a division of labor which is natural and reasonable, so that each may make his own contribution to the benefit and enlightenment of all.

### THE FOURTH LEVEL

Next come applications of the principle of individualization which take the form of plans for purely individual instruction. The idea was first made prominent by Frederick Burke. The earliest widely known plan was that of Helen Parkhurst at Dalton, Mass. The scheme has been quite widely applied in various forms. Many of its characteristic features are excellently exemplified at Winnetka, Ill., under Carleton Washburne.

The Winnetka plan for reading above the second grade shows how it works out. After the primary reading adjustment has been established every child in the schools is tested to establish his actual grade level in reading ability. Then he is given opportunity, during school time, to read plenty of books fitted to his ability level. These appropriate books are chosen from *What Children Like to Read—the Winnetka Graded Book List*, prepared by Carleton Washburne and Mabel Vogel, Rand McNally & Company, Chicago, 1926. This book list was compiled from the choices of thirty-seven thousand children who were tested by eight hundred teachers throughout the United States. The children turned in ballots on how well they liked the books they read. One hundred thousand ballots were obtained from children of known reading ability. Thus it was possible to grade any given book for difficulty and interest. The fifteen hundred most important books were selected from the total list by librarians expert in children's literature, and these again were divided into three lots of five hundred each in descending order of importance, so that the final report might be of service in selecting school libraries.* The child at Winnetka, using the book list selected for him, does considerable oral reading to the teacher, because this is considered an important process. Moreover he reads to the teacher rather than in class, so that a poor performance does not embarrass him unduly or disturb or delay the learning processes of others. The comprehension with which the child reads is tested at irregular intervals, whenever deemed advisable, either by regular reading tests, or by oral reports, or simply by watching the eagerness and application of the learner. After 15 books have been read, which is the minimum number for each grade, a reading test is given. If his performance is adequate, the child goes on immediately to the next grade, the transfer taking place at whatever time during the year he is ready for it. If his performance on the test is not adequate, he proceeds to do some more reading of additional books on the same grade level. The same general procedure is followed for all the knowledge and skill subjects, such as arithmetic, social studies, spelling, and English. All these subjects are taught on a purely individual basis, without the use of class situations, the pupil reporting individually to the teacher, and doing his assignments at his own speed and moving through the grades at his own tempo. Afternoons at Winnetka are devoted to "social," "expressive," or "creative" undertakings, which are not related to the subject-matter learnings which occupy the mornings.

The Dalton laboratory plan is similar in principle, although there are various special elaborations and arrangements for the orderly management of the school. Simply stated, Miss Parkhurst's idea has been that students should receive assignments or "contracts" in each of their subjects on a monthly basis, and should plan and allocate their time in working on them individually in the so-called "laboratories," which are subject-matter study rooms, each with appropriate books, equipment, and other materials, and each in the charge of a teacher who is there to assist the pupils with their work. Besides the Winnetka and Dalton plans of individualized instruction there have been many less elaborate and ambitious variants. Essentially what is involved is the more or less complete abandonment of class teaching

---

\* There is no doubt that such an elaborately selected and classified list is a very useful instrumentality. It is rich with practical suggestions for teachers and school authorities. One must not, however, suppose that it automatically determines that such a book will be of interest to such and such a child, because interest is such a highly individual matter that no statistical determination of it, arising out of the study of average trends and the judgment of juries of experts, can ever be decisive.

situations and techniques, and the transformation of the school into an institution for individual tutoring on a large scale.  It has been demonstrated that this is well within practicable administrative possibility, without increasing costs unduly, and without large increases in staff. Clearly it introduces a very considerable change away from convention in the basic organization of learning.  Instead of the ordinary group recitation, with everyone theoretically but not actually moving abreast, each pupil works at his own speed and his own level, and the whole school is held together by carefully prepared assignments, practice materials, reading lists, tests, and records.*

How, then, should it be appraised?  It offers very great advantages.  The contact between teacher and learner is far more fruitful than in the conventional recitation.  The pupil's capacity can be evaluated and diagnosed.  He can be given tasks suitable to his level. He can receive individual assistance.  He can work at his own speed. Under the Dalton plan he can go a long way toward controlling his own time, for he may clean up his month's assignment in a single subject by a continuous week's work, or subdivide his working day among several subjects.  So much for the positive values of the plan, which are very far indeed from negligible.

There is, however, a negative side to the picture.  It seems fair to say that individual instruction carries homogeneous grouping and the contract idea to their ultimate logical conclusion.  That is to say, it recognizes and deals with vertical differences between individuals.  If these were all, then class teaching would be irrelevant and impeding, and a clumsy way of working for good results, except perhaps for social facilitation.  Each person should be free to do what he is able to do and to go ahead at his own pace without reference to anybody else. And the teacher's job would be to assign the right tasks at the right time, to chart the learner's course, to help him on his way, to show him how to overcome obstacles, and to find out from time to time how far he had gotten.  Compared to the lock-step class a plan which does all this is enormously superior.

But qualitative differences also are important, and these, individualized instruction as ordinarily conducted does not recognize.  The point of properly handled group work is that it permits differences in purpose, interest, and type of achievement to express themselves in such a way as to benefit the learning of the individual while still contributing to the focalized thinking and learning of the group.  Within the setting of the group undertaking plenty of individualized learning

* Perhaps, indeed, the basic physical instrumentality of the scheme is the mimeograph.

will go on. There will be skills to acquire and practice to be done, and much of this should be on an individual basis. But it will not be uniform or one-dimensional, although it will be related to the group undertaking. All such individualized learning will express the purpose of the individual as related to the over-all purpose of the group.

Where there is an individual purpose, individual learning is indicated. That seems to be the basic principle. If the over-all purpose is to get through the College Entrance Board examinations, the best answer is probably tutorial instruction, which is why so many college preparatory schools are leaning towards it. But if the over-all purpose is to get the most authentic possible grasp of a problem, then there should be as many different approaches as there are different interests in the group, these approaches should be handled so that they enrich and illuminate each other and contribute to a common understanding, and each pupil should do whatever individual learning is necessary to make his own best contribution.[2]

### THE FIFTH LEVEL

**1. Appraisal.** Another type of organization designed with specific reference to the principle of individualization is the unit in connection with which optional related activities are set up. The following ninth-grade unit on immigration is a typical instance.

*The Unit.*

The United States has developed from a small weak nation at the close of the Revolutionary War to a strong world power. Without a great deal of immigration this would have been impossible. Early immigrants to America were easily assimilated, and early immigration laws were passed merely to exclude undesirable persons. Later immigrants have been harder to assimilate, partly because of their ideals and customs, but largely because they came over, particularly after the World War, in such numbers that it was impossible to assimilate them. To protect the American way of living, drastic restrictions have been placed on immigration from all countries.

*Delimitation of the Unit.*

(1) The United States is a nation of immigrants. (2) Immigrants came to America in the hope of bettering their living conditions, of finding an opportunity for success in business and industry, and to escape religious and civic persecution. (3) Until 1880 most immigrants came from the Northern and Western part of Europe. They accepted the American language, customs, and government. (4) Since 1880 a flood of immigrants has entered the United States mostly from Central, Southern, and Eastern Europe and from Asia. They settled largely in crowded areas in large cities. Each group kept much

to itself, spoke its own language, and followed its own customs. Consequently, these later immigrants have not been so thoroughly assimilated as the early immigrants. (5) The restriction of immigration has become a major governmental problem. A Bureau of Naturalization and Immigration has been established in the Department of Labor, to handle this problem. (6) We closed our doors to the Chinese in 1882, and to the Japanese in 1907. (7) Our present National Origins Quota Plan of controlling immigration was adopted in 1929. Under the quota plan the number of aliens who may enter the United States from any country in a single year shall be a number which bears the same ratio to 150,000 as the number of inhabitants of continental United States in 1920 having the national origin bears to the total number of inhabitants in continental United States in 1920; but the minimum quota of any nationality shall be 100. (8) Under the present immigration laws, contract laborers, Mongolians, anarchists, convicts, epileptics, the insane, the feeble minded, and persons likely to become public charges are not admitted. (9) American consuls in European ports give preliminary physical examinations to immigrants, so that they will not need to be sent back from our ports of entry. (10) The immigrant pays a head tax of $8 and passes a literacy test. (11) If the present foreign-born population of the United States is to be assimilated, the barriers of distrust and intolerance which now exist between American-born and foreign-born Americans must somehow be broken down. (12) A sense of civic responsibility must be promoted in the foreign-born and the American-born.

*Indirect Learning Products.*

*A.* Appreciation (1) of the actual and potential contributions of various nationalities to the American way of living, and (2) of the necessity of a common language and common laws, customs, and system of education as a basis for mutual help and understanding. *B.* Attitudes of sympathetic understanding toward the unassimilated foreigners in the United States, and of friendliness toward all portions of the population as a means of begetting friendliness.

*The Unit Assignment.*

*A.* An introductory talk and discussion centering around the following. Suppose you and your family were to take all your belongings and move several thousand miles to a new land where you intended to spend the rest of your lives. What problems would you face as to (1) getting a job? (2) a home in which to live? (3) food to eat? (4) clothing? (5) language? (6) further education? What would happen if you tried to keep on living in the new country just as you had lived in the old country?

*B.* Individual and small group work. (1) Why is a person fond of his home and country? (2) Why would anyone leave his home and country and go to live in a foreign land for the rest of his life? If you have a friend whose family came to make America their home, be prepared to tell why the family came. (Reading references given here and on each following question from list at the end of unit.) (3) Make a list of the main reasons why foreigners have come to make the United States their country. (4) Before the year 1880, from what countries did most of our immigrants come? What languages did they speak? Were their customs and ideals like the customs and ideals of most of the people already here? To what form of government had each group of immigrants been accustomed in the country from which they came? Where did they settle? Have they fitted easily into the American way of living? (5) After the year 1880, from what countries did most of our immigrants come? What languages did they speak? Were their customs and ideals like the customs and ideals of most of the people already here? Where did they settle? Have they fitted into the American way of living? (6) Is it true that the United States is a nation of immigrants? Explain. (7) What proportion of the population of the United States is white? Mexican? Indian? Oriental? Negro? What proportion of the white population came originally from Northern and Western Europe? From Southern and Eastern Europe? (8) Find out the years, if any, in each of which we have admitted more than a million immigrants. Where did most of them come from in those years and why did they come here? In what year did we have the largest number of immigrants? Why was the immigration rate so high that year? (9) Where is Chinatown? Little Italy? Little Russia? Ghetto? Are they good or bad for the United States as a whole? If bad, why do they exist? What can be done about it? (10) When were Japanese and Chinese denied the right to immigrate into the United States? Is it fair to refuse this privilege to the Japanese and Chinese? In any event, is it necessary? (11) Study the present quota plan to limit immigration to the United States. Is the plan fair? Is it necessary? (12) Who has the power to restrict immigration to the United States? What department of our government has charge of immigration? How do American consuls in foreign countries help to solve the immigration problem? (13) Make a graph to show the number of immigrants that may enter from each leading European country under the existing law. (14) What immigrants are not subject to the quota? What country sends us the greatest number of non-quota immigrants? (15) List the names of famous Americans who came here as immigrants. What have immigrants contributed to the development of the United States? (16) Prepare to tell why immigrants should learn English as soon as possible. Should English be spoken in the home of the immigrant? Why? Are there any schools where adult immigrants can learn to speak English? How can the church, radio, and movies help them in this respect? (17) If you think many immigrants have not become good Americans, try to find out why. What could they do to improve the situation? What could others do to help them? (18) Name the agencies and organizations which now exist to help immigrants become good Americans. What does each agency or organization do? Make a dictionary of words connected with the problem of immigration. Try to find pictures to illustrate each word.

*Optional Related Activities.*

1. Prepare to tell the class what some famous immigrant has done for the United States. Consider whether he could have done in the land of his birth what he did in the United States. If not, be prepared to tell why not. Perhaps you will want to take one of the following: Louis Agassiz; Mary Antin; Konrad Bercovici; Edward Bok; Andrew Carnegie; Walter Damrosch; Morris Gest; Victor Herbert; Franklin K. Lane; Ludwig Lewissohn; Henry Morganthau Sr.; John Muir; Michael Pupin; Jacob Riis; Carl Schurz; Edward Steiner; Charles Steinmetz; Oscar Straus. Instead of making an oral report, you can prepare and exhibit pictures, or you can use selected pictures with or without the opaque projector to illustrate your talk. (Here again suggested readings are listed from the bibliography at the end of the unit, as also in connection with the following points.)

2. Prepare to tell the class about Ellis Island. This also may be done in the form of an exhibit or illustrated talk.

3. Make an outline map of the United States and show as many cities as you can which have names of foreign origin other than English. Be prepared to tell how each city got its name. Serve on a committee to prepare an illustrated dictionary of words connected with the problem of immigration. The committee will select and arrange the best materials from the dictionaries prepared by individual pupils. If you are interested in this, consult your teacher.

4. Describe in any way that you think best what is meant by calling the United States the "Melting Pot."

5. Find out how many nationalities are represented in your class. In your city. Can you show these facts by means of graphs?

6. What evidence of foreign modes of life can you find in your own city?

7. In the three largest schools of Manchester, N.H., nine tenths of the pupils come from homes where a foreign language is spoken. Is this desirable or undesirable? What can be done about it, if it is undesirable?

8. Read one of the following books that you find interesting. (Here follows a list of books by famous immigrants.) When you have finished reading a book ask your teacher for a short objective test on the book.

9. See if two or three other pupils would like to work with you in an effort to show the class what immigrants have done for the United States in any one of the following fields: (a) art, (b) literature, (c) music, (d) science, (e) food, (f) clothing, and (g) games and recreations. To do this you may want to prepare and give a dramatic sketch, or to do something else. Talk with the teacher, and get your plan approved.

10. Prepare to show the class what the Negro has contributed to American life.

11. Make a chart showing the countries sending immigrants to the United States in 1800, 1880, 1920.

12. Make a graph to show what proportion of our population is native born; foreign-born.

13. Plan a pageant on some phase of immigration. Have your plan approved by the teacher.

14. Write a short play to show how native-born Americans and immigrants should regard the process of naturalization.

15. With the teacher's approval, prepare to dramatize before the class or in assembly the pageant or play written in optional related activity 12 or 13 above.

16. Prepare an exhibit of newspaper clippings bearing on the problem of immigration.

17. Prepare an exhibit of pictures pertaining to the participation of some country in the New York or San Francisco World's Fair.

*List of Readings.*

(21 books in all)*

As an instance of the organization of learning, this unit is exceedingly instructive and will repay careful examination. It is careful, thorough, exhaustive. Moreover it exemplifies one of the most important points in all good pedagogical planning, namely that the teacher should prepare a much larger number of alternatives and possibilities than he will be able to use on any one occasion. This unit might be quite differently taught in two successive years, or with two different ninth-grade groups. There is a considerable latitude of choice within the Unit Assignment, which is the material to be studied in common by all the pupils. Certain of the items might be included and others omitted on different occasions. The same, of course, is even more evidently the case with the Optional Related Activities. The comprehensive consideration of such a wide range of possibilities is always eminently sound procedure. Compare it with the crude, awkward, meager contract lesson discussed above, and its indubitable values become immediately clear.

Nevertheless, it has certain serious limitations. The common context consists entirely of extensive reading, and an examination of the list of books appended to the unit (not here reproduced) reveals them to be prevailingly academic in character. Superior types of context are indeed introduced in some of the Optional Related Activities, but they are not intended for the class as a whole—only for those who might wish to undertake them. The focalization, too, is prevailingly upon information rather than upon understanding and insight. What is chiefly contemplated is clearly memory knowledge, and there is a really formidable mass of verbalization, as for instance such terms as

---

* Roy O. Billett, *Fundamentals of Secondary School Teaching*, pp. 527–533, Houghton Mifflin Company, Boston, 1940.

"consul," "Department of Labor," "Quota," or again the intricate detail of the quota scheme. The unit as a whole is essentially a collection of information, carefully assembled, well put together, but still lacking in vital and functional unity.

These limitations are reflected once again in the scheme for individualization, which is the plan of Optional Related Activities. They are in many cases ingenious, and they have an undeniable relationship to the subject in general. Moreover they are not set up as a series of levels as in the contract plan, which is all to the good. But they are, after all, more or less tacked on as so much additional work. They cannot be considered elucidations of a basic meaning which can be fed back into a job of coordinated group thinking. In some cases one can see that they might effectively engage the purpose of the learner, but they are laid out as carefully planned appendices, and lack the character of spontaneous or on-the-spot generation. And one finds the same trouble with them as with the A-level items of the contract lesson, for some of them contain the best and most promising educational materials in the unit, and yet these materials are made available only to a few selected pupils who happen to choose the activities in question.

**2. Steps toward Improved Practice.** It would take only a comparatively little reorganization radically to transform such a unit as this. Instead of an introduction by means of the general lecture and discussion as suggested, it could be introduced by some actual, current, local problem of immigration well within the range of the pupils' sympathy and understanding, if possible discovered and presented by members of the class. The primary focalization could shift to the present Indirect Learning Products, somewhat reformulated, because these are presumably the important educational outcomes, because they involve the processes of insight and appreciation rather than memorization, and because they tend to give unity to the whole undertaking. The material listed under the headings The Unit Assignment, and Optional Related Activities, somewhat reorganized, can be used as a source of suggestions for activities by individuals and subgroups, and other activities involving concrete and compelling local contacts could be set up, partly suggested by the teacher and partly originating from the pupils. The common core of the unit could consist, not of a body of material prevailingly verbalistic in character about which everyone is supposed to inform himself, but of the pooled result of the individual enterprises and contributions, perhaps brought to a head by some kind of effective joint culminating activity. This would bring about a deep psychological transformation, and in particular a superior application of the principle of individualization, because now each pupil would be enabled and encouraged to contribute to a common enterprise in terms of his own choices, interests, methods, and capacities.

### THE SIXTH LEVEL

Many instances of individual variation within a common scheme have already been described. One such is the unit on architecture already mentioned. At an early stage the children were encouraged to bring to class crude sketches of architectural detail which were put on the bulletin board. This activity soon became more systematic, purposeful, and meaningful, with certain children finding scope for their artistic capabilities and concerning themselves with the mounting and collating of contributions and the classification of them into periods. This led to the formation of small groups each selecting for intensive study a period of special interest to them, and making reports to class on an orderly schedule worked out in discussion. This in turn led to the making of blueprints, with one boy offering to make them at home if he could have tracing paper and sensitive blue paper. Some children again developed special interest in making plaster casts of architectural ornaments. Also it will be remembered that one of the less mature "followers" developed a remarkable scheme for clipping architectural illustrations from magazines, and selling them to his classmates. All these are pertinent examples of individual variations within a common scheme which recognize both vertical and qualitative differences.

Again, the following account of two days' experience with an interest center on Lumbering with an eleven- to twelve-year-old group is a case in point.

This interest center grew out of the reading of an article on the General Grant Sequoia. The class was greatly interested in the article, and had many questions to ask when it was finished. One boy wished to know, "What kind of a tree is a sequoia?"

A girl explained that she had just been reading a story about the big trees of California, and gave the following answer, "A sequoia is a great big tree. It has branches like a fir tree. Some sequoias have such large trunks that a roadway can be built through them." She ended by showing a picture of a big tree and its roadway.

Then came the statement, "That is a redwood tree. I've been up in the redwoods, and I saw all those big trees."

Someone said, "Maybe a redwood and a sequoia are the same thing." Since no one seemed to be certain, the teacher suggested that one of the boys look up the word "sequoia" in his dictionary. He soon reported the following: "Sequoia is the name of either of two big trees in California. The redwood is one of these. They both belong to the same family."

A girl wanted to know, "Where do redwood trees grow?"

Immediately the answer came, "In northern California."

One of the boys corroborated this by stating that his father had worked in a lumber camp and had brought home pieces of pine and fir trees from this northern area.

A girl added, "My dad works on a lumber boat. He unloads lumber and he brings home scrap boards of Oregon pine and white pine. I can bring pieces of different kinds of wood. My dad will bring them home to me."

"What could we do with pieces of wood?" came the question.

"We can make a chart and see how many different kinds of wood we can find," was the answer.

The class approved of this idea and several children said that they would bring small pieces of wood next day. This they did and along with them came bark, leaves, and seeds from trees.

The next day one boy began our discussion by telling about a lumber camp he had visited. He told how the logs were floated downstream to the mill. He explained how the big logs were sent into the huge saws; how three- and five-ply wood was made; and how the newly sawed lumber was taken away from the mill to be sent to various parts of the world.

Someone suggested, "It would be fun to build a lumber camp."

Another added, "We could build it on a big table."

"How could we get trees for it?" was asked.

Another added, "We could use sand for the ground and stick the twigs in the sand."

Still another said, "We can make rivers in the sand and show logs in the rivers."

Some of the girls offered immediately to make little dolls for the camp. These, they said, would represent the lumberjacks. One girl said, "I have a little doll at home I made out of crepe paper and pipe cleaners. I can make a lumberjack out of pipe cleaners. The other girls can help, I'll show them how."

Our discussion and plans for two days had aroused much enthusiasm over lumbering. The following day children came with articles about trees and samples of leaves, wood, bark, and seeds, together with a supply of pipe cleaners. Plans were then begun for books and charts to display the leaves, seeds, bark, and wood. In the afternoon a table was covered with oilcloth; then came the question, "How can we keep the sand on the table?"

After several suggestions had been made, someone said, "Why not build a frame of lath around the table and line it with a bottom to keep the sand in.?"

"What can we line it with?" was asked.

We had had a large roll of wrapping paper across the hall, and one of the girls suggested that the frame be lined with wrapping paper.

The lumber camp grew. Another table was drawn into use and another group began an old-fashioned scene of early lumbering methods. The children had fun comparing early and modern pioneer camps, leading to a brief study of forest conservation and reforestation method.

Throughout this study the teacher supplied the class with many books, pictures, movies, and slides on forests, lumbering, and forest conservation. Interest in the work continued over a period of three months. Much was learned and accomplished. During this time minor centers developed along hobby lines, consisting of shell collections, rocks and minerals, stamps, old coins, and petrified wood, affording the class a variety of minor experiences along with the major experiences.*

Or again, the seventh grade in the Montclair Academy became interested in the use and history of the town banks. All of them had seen bank buildings. The fathers of some of the children were bankers or bank employees. Some of the children had bank accounts. Also bank problems arose in their arithmetic. Various questions about the organization, functions, and types of banks, and the numbers of them came up in discussion. Answers were contributed by various children from reference books, visits, interviews, and information which they could secure at home from members of their families. Finally, after a good deal of consideration and clarification, a class bank was set up, a company was organized, deposits were taken, and checks were cashed for the purchase of school supplies. This went on for a period of a month, during which each child had two days' experience as cashier and as bookkeeper.

In all these and many similar cases, the underlying psychological structure and dynamics are the same. First there is a coordinated, unified, meaningful enterprise, undertaken jointly by the group. This immediately opens up numerous avenues for contributions and intrinsically related activities which stem from and are built into the central undertaking, and which are still highly varied. Psychologically these are very different from the rather arbitrary Optional Related Activities, which are simply a list of things that might be done, and which are more or less germane to the central topic. Children determine upon their activities and contributions by a combination of their own initiative and the suggestion and stimulation of the teacher. They are able to work in terms of their own interests and purposes. They are able to work and learn in their own way. And their own capacities are exemplified and utilized in what they do. It should be noted, moreover, that such effective individualization can be remarkably informal and seemingly casual, although it actually depends on a highly skillful and imaginative organization of the learning situation. The core of the situation may be regarded as a focalization which emerges out of the individual lines of activity and contribution, or as a social

* Robert Hill Lane, *The Teacher in the Modern Elementary School*, pp. 216–218, Houghton Mifflin Company, Boston, 1941.

unity which integrates the individual endeavours ramifying out of and returning back to it.[3]

## Notes and References*

1. Three broad treatments of homogeneous grouping, important beyond the immediate topic are Luther T. Purdom, *The Value of Homogeneous Grouping*, Warwick and York, Baltimore, 1929; Marvin Y. Burr, *A Study of Homogeneous Grouping*, Teachers College, Columbia University, Bureau of Publications, New York, 1931; A. V. Keliher, *A Critical Study of Homogeneous Grouping*, Teachers College, Columbia University, Bureau of Publications, New York, 1931. Analyses bearing on the results achieved are R. R. Cook, "A Study of the Results of Homogeneous Grouping in High School Classes," *National Society for the Study of Education; 23rd Yearbook* Part I, pp. 301–312, 1924; W. S. Miller and Henry J. Otto, "Analysis of Experimental Studies in Homogeneous Grouping," *Journal of Educational Research*, Vol. 21 (1930), pp. 95–102. These are all pertinent and selected items from a very large literature.

2. Excellent accounts of individualized instruction are Helen Parkhurst, *Education on the Dalton Plan*, E. P. Dutton & Company, Inc., New York, 1922; Carleton Washburne, *Adjusting the School to the Child*, World Book Company, Yonkers-on-Hudson, New York, 1932; Carleton Washburne, *A Living Philosophy of Education*, Chap. 21, The John Day Company, New York, 1940, Also see the *National Society for the Study of Education, 24th Yearbook*, Part II, 1925, which is devoted to the subject.

3. Many further accounts of such teaching are available. See A. Gordon Melvin, *Methods for New Schools*, The John Day Company, New York, 1941; James S. Tippett, *Schools for a Growing Democracy*, Ginn and Company, Boston, 1936; Inga Olla Helseth, *Living in the Classroom*, Edwards Bros., Inc., Ann Arbor, Mich., 1939.

## Items for Discussion and Study

*Refer to the opening suggestion for discussion and study in connection with Chap. 6, of course substituting Chap. 11 for Chap. 5. Follow it out in connection with the principle of individualization. Retain your outcomes in your notebook or card file.*

1. Teaching situations, usually bad ones, are sometimes defended as reproducing the conditions one must face in life, *e.g.*, submitting to hard and meaningless toil, etc. What is the fallacy?

2. Why is the contract organization indicated in the hierarchy as superior to homogeneous grouping?

3. Is it justifiable for a teacher in a conventional situation, in rating or marking pupils, to consider anything but pure achievement? Should he consider attitude, ability, interest, hard work? What are the objections to his doing so? What are the implications for the organization of learning if he thinks he should?

4. If you were teaching in a school which used homogeneous grouping and had a dull section, would you be satisfied simply to go more slowly, or would you want to introduce more fundamental changes in the organization of learning? If so, what changes?

5. Can one set up really homogeneous groups on the basis of test scores?

* For general references on individualization see Chap. 11.

6. What difficulties in the constructive organization of learning might be reduced by homogeneous grouping? Could they be handled without it?

7. Why is a contract plan which merely offers a choice of "more of the same," or promises better marks for more work, very unlikely to bring about better and more authentic results?

8. How does a contract arrangement differ from a cooperative situation in which different individuals make different contributions to a joint undertaking?

9. If all that we want is progress towards a uniform goal, *e.g.*, the passing of an examination, would purely individual instruction be best? Would it mean failing to use any factors which might make for better learning?

10. Are there any values which can come from group experience and learning which cannot come from individual instruction?

11. Study with care the unit cited on pp. 216–220. It contains a wealth of valuable material and suggestions. It could be "slanted" and taught in many ways. Work out a few of them. See how far you can go in grouping everything round good focuses, and then see how this affects the Optional Related Activities.

12. Show in detail how a good focus is essential in such teaching patterns as those on the sixth level, to secure unity even though there may be no uniformity.

# CHAPTER 13

# THE PRINCIPLE OF SEQUENCE AND THE ORGANIZATION OF LEARNING

## THE PRINCIPLE OF SEQUENCE

Up to this point our attention has been devoted to the separate job of learning and its proper organization in terms of the principles of context, focalization, socialization, and individualization. This is an altogether necessary practical concern for every teacher, for if the separate job of learning is not richly meaningful, if the separate lesson or undertaking is not handled so that it roots itself in the learner's mind, everything fails.

But there is another consideration, implied in everything that has been said so far, but not yet made explicit. For the teacher must concern himself not only with the effectiveness of the separate job of learning but also with the effectiveness of a series of learnings arranged in time. He is teaching not only multiplication but also arithmetic, not only the theorem of Pythagoras but also geometry, not only the rise of slavery but also American history, not only *Hamlet* but also English literature. Indeed he must go still further in his thinking and planning, for he is not only teaching this or that subject, or organizing this or that project or activity, such as the studies of architecture or of textiles which have been described. Also he is trying to bring about certain changes in human beings—certain insights, outlooks, attitudes, and ways of action—which transcend any subject or any determinate activity, although subjects and activities contribute to their formation. The cumulative impact and effect of a series of learnings is a vital concern for every educational institution because this is the only means whereby the objectives of its curriculum can be attained, whatever those objectives are—and they may range all the way from the ability to typewrite a hundred words a minute to the achievement of the democratic outlook upon life. Also this cumulative impact and effect is a vital concern for the individual teacher, and in fact he always does think about it more or less, even if he gets no further than supposing that when a lesson has been taught some item of knowledge is added to a lasting mental store.

To draw a line between the separate learnings and their sequence is, of course, an abstraction. Like all abstractions, it can be a convenience and a help for clear thinking, but it involves a danger which we must be at pains to avoid. Let us suppose that a course in physics contains twenty units. Each unit is a separate job of learning. But the course as a whole must also be considered as a job of learning, of which the units are the parts. It is larger, longer, more elaborate, to be sure, but a job of learning just the same. Exactly the same is true of the organization of instruction in reading in the primary grades, although here the separate jobs, or units, or parts are not nearly so clear-cut. Surely then, it would be very foolish to organize the units in terms of one orientation, and the large total learning in terms of another—to make the units meaningful and the sequence mechanical, let us say. Indeed, as we shall see, we could not do this even if we wanted to, for a mechanical sequence will do much to destroy the meaningfulness of the units, and one cannot build a meaningful sequence out of mechanical units. The controlling orientation, both in the separate learnings and in their sequence, which latter is learning on a larger scale, must be the same.

The implication, then, is clear. *The sequence of meaningful learnings must itself be meaningful, if authentic results are to be obtained.* Here we have the *principle of sequence.*

## SEQUENCE AND MENTAL GROWTH

The long-time sequences here under consideration, which we have spoken of as processes of learning, are more ordinarily called processes of *mental growth.* The distinction is very far from clear-cut, but it no doubt has its uses and significance, and since the term "growth" has come to be used in this connection in psychological and educational literature, and indicates a fairly well-defined area of research from which we must draw, it will be employed in what follows here. *The sequence of learnings, then must be regarded and in practice treated as a process of mental growth.*

This proposition has emerged out of many years of investigation and practical experimentation. The problem of sequence has been recognized from time immemorial. Textbooks, courses, and curriculums have been organized with a view to introducing the learner first to the rudiments, or elements, or fundamentals of a subject, and then leading him to the more advanced and presumably more difficult parts of it. Herbart, who made the first serious and systematic attempt to psychologize education, used the concept of apperception in his approach to the question. One never, he insisted, apprehends anything in isolation, but always in terms of one's background of previous experience and learning. So the first consideration in properly organized learning would be to make sure that the learner had the right background. This was to be assured partly by the way the curriculum was set up and partly by the step of preparation in the inductive development lesson which has already been described. And since Herbart's day the problem of sequence has been persistently attacked, and more and more broadly treated. Many changes have been advocated and tried out in the order and placement of topics in most school subjects. In some schools the teaching of formal arithmetic has been postponed to the sixth grade. In learning to read a foreign language, extensive reading has been introduced very early and grammar cut to a minimum. In learning to read English far less time than previously is spent on the alphabet. And many different arrangements for teaching history have been suggested, including beginning with the child's immediate interests instead of with ancient history or the history of his own country. These are just a few of many possible examples of attempts to reorganize sequence, and they have culminated in the contention that the controlling idea must be that of mental growth.

What this means may be seen, in principle, from a couple of instances. The first has to do with the development of the character trait of responsibility, certainly one of the major educational concerns of human life  In the latter part of the afternoon the mother of a small child about five-years old sent him out to play with his companions. She told him that he must be home by six, because his father and mother had an evening engagement, and supper must be prompt. Also she had an educational purpose. It was the general family policy to encourage the children to make responsible choices for themselves as fully as possible, and here she thought was an opportunity. Also the parents had been trying to teach the child, who was unusually precocious and could already read, to tell the time, and they thought they had succeeded. There was a large church clock visible for many blocks around. The mother called the child's attention to it, and then let him go, thinking that here was a chance to apply what he seemed to have learned. But it did not work out. Supper time arrived, but no child! At last, some 45 minutes late and with the evening shadows gathering, he sauntered in, and was questioned, reprimanded, and penalized. This mother was demanding something which the child was not mature enough to fulfill—that all through his play he should glance at the very visible clock, that he should understand its warning, that about ten minutes before six he should break off from his doings and start home. But his apparent ability to read and judge time was spurious.   In an applied situation it was not there.   And so the pattern of responsible action broke down.

The second instance is that of a graduate student who, as part of his advanced work, undertook a study of the *Passion According to St. Matthew* by John Sebastian Bach in order to study the master's use of musical color, his tonal painting, so to speak.   It was a superbly focalized piece of learning, centering upon a novel and most challenging problem.   The student set it up on his own initiative.   It gripped and thrilled him for many weeks.   It not only gave him a remarkable knowledge of the *St. Matthew Passion,* but widened and deepened his understanding of music in particular and creative art in general, and opened up new vistas for study of which he would otherwise never have dreamed, and which he followed to his own great advantage.

In these two instances, the one of failure, the other of success, one can clearly see what is involved in a sequence of learnings which is also a sequence of growth.

1. The specific learnings and experiences are always necessary. The graduate student's growth took place in and through the specific study of a specific problem and a specific body of material.   Without this it could not have taken place.   The child's experience did not help him toward the development of responsibility because a specific learning had not been achieved.

2. The more richly meaningful the learning, in the sense already explained of being an intelligible attack upon a problem which the learner is deeply motivated to solve, the more it becomes an agency and means of growth.   If the graduate student had been given a cut-and-dried assignment on the *St. Matthew Passion,* and been told to make a report on its history, setting, and formal structure, and done so perfunctorily or unwillingly, this would never have yielded the values that were actually forthcoming.   If the child had really been able to learn to tell time in a meaningful way, there would have been a good chance of his using this ability in a situation requiring responsible action.

3. No specific job of learning can be meaningful if the learner is so immature that it defeats him.   This was the trouble with the child. His mental development was such that he could only *seem* to learn to tell the time, so that the result he achieved was spurious, although his parents did not know it.   The graduate student's undertaking was meaningful because he was mature enough to catch a glimpse of its possibilities and challenge when it first dawned upon him.   The Pearl Harbor disaster was one of the most pregnant lessons ever taught the American people, yet when the news broke a certain ten-year-old child

brushed it off as a dull adult concern, although its consequences were bound to affect his entire life.

Such, in general, are the characteristics of a sequence of learnings which is a sequence of mental growth. It can be divided into parts, but these are only high points in an evolving whole, not separate and self-bounded entities. Such a sequence is in the sharpest possible contrast to one determined by addition, in which a series of separate learnings is dealt with one by one, with the idea that their outcomes will form a sum-total in the mind of the learner. The contrast is that between the growth of a tree, in which the development of the whole organism penetrates all its members and reciprocally is affected by them, and the fabrication of a brick wall. Since the mind, like the tree, is a living thing, we cannot expect it to perform otherwise than disappointingly if we treat it like a brick wall.

## CHARACTERISTICS OF GOOD SEQUENCE

The characteristics of a properly organized sequence are those of mental growth, and here we shall consider seven of them.

**1. Growth is Continuous.** This is perhaps the most important of all, theoretically and practically. According to the time-honored theory of recapitulation, which was that the development of the individual paralleled that of the race, a person passed through the stages of savagery, barbarism, and civilization, and his education ought to be built in terms of them. This failed to stand analysis, and it was then suggested that he was dominated successively by sensation, imagination, memory, and finally reason. The memory stage was supposed to be reached about the age of 12, and was thought to be particularly suitable for the study of foreign language with its heavy load of vocabulary, and of history with its numerous dates. No responsible psychologist maintains this position today. All the powers the child will ever have are present from the first, albeit in nascent form, and they develop together and not in series. Growth, then, is a continuous process. It cannot be broken down into stages. Above all, it cannot be broken down into stages determined by the learnings included in the school curriculum.

This point of view is full of momentous practical consequences for the organization of learning, and all teachers should be aware of what they are. The only way in which growth can be brought about at all is by means of specific experiences and specific learnings. But these specific experiences, or learnings, or lessons should never be thought of or treated as self-bounded units, each one complete and independent. Their relationship to and influence upon the long-time continuous sequence of growth is like that of the specific episodes in a novel to the development of its plot. The plot cannot be chopped up into a number of disconnected episodes, and growth cannot be chopped up into a number of specific learnings, for both are continuous, although the episodes and the specific learnings are still essential. This is the central consideration to keep in mind.

How strongly teachers tend to think and plan in terms of the specific lesson is very well shown in the example given on page 209 where one of the stated purposes of the assignment was "to read quickly and to understand what we read." This was criticized as being quite an impossible focus for learning, particularly with grade-school children. But as a developmental trend to which the particular job of learning might well contribute it would be quite defensible. This would mean that a pupil's work on the specific lesson should not be thought of as something to be set up, carried through, rated, and then put into the record of his educational achievement, but rather as an influence leading him to grow in the desired direction. Again, one of the mental capacities which might well be expected to come from science teaching would be the ability to recognize personal bias and to guard against it in making judgments. But this would not be suitable as the focus of a specific lesson which would be presented, learned, and finished. Many lessons, many learnings, many experiences would contribute to the developing of it. And none of them should be treated as self-contained units to be mastered one by one and put into storage, but as influences promoting a general line of growth. This would affect the way they were chosen, and arranged in time, and taught, and the way their results would be evaluated. Or to return to the illustration of the tardy child, his ability to control his behavior with respect to time would evolve as a result of many learnings and experiences. Each one of them would no doubt be specific, but none of them would be self-bounded or segregated in their psychological effect, like separate lessons, each one rounded out and completed when the next is undertaken.

**2. Growth Depends on Purpose.** Sometimes the purpose is established by the physical ripening or maturation of the organism. Thus, in acquiring an erect posture, maturation plays a far greater part than practice. The first signs and attempts come when the baby is very young. If one raises a baby a few months old from a supine to a sitting position, he is likely to press both feet to the floor and momentarily rise erect. Gradually he begins to push himself upward of his own accord, and to balance alone. There is a definite sequence which, so far as we know, cannot be greatly altered or modified. It is often suggested that maturation is purely mechanical because there seems to be nothing much we can do about controlling it, and because it goes on just about so in spite of circumstances. As a matter of fact it is a process directed toward and shaped up by a goal which becomes clearer and clearer. The individual, no doubt, is not fully conscious of what he is trying to do. But he is striving to do a definite something just the same, and nature enables him to come steadily closer and closer to his objective. If a child or a young animal is put under some kind of physical restraint which prevents him from making these crude but purposive efforts until after the behavior pattern has had time to ripen, and then released, it is likely to establish itself almost at once. Maturation has done its work without practice. The purpose is fully defined, and the new behavior appears forthwith.

So far as schools and teachers are concerned, however, the purposes on which growth depends are established chiefly by circumstance and environment. One of the most revealing of all studies on growth shows how this happens. The experimental subjects were two identical twin boys, Johnny and Jimmy. Johnny was given all kinds of special opportunities and incentives to learn, and Jimmy was given none. Johnny was started in at rollerskating when he was 350 days old, and he made very surprisingly rapid progress. Clearly there had to be an artificially introduced opportunity. He would never have simply grown into the ability to rollerskate if nature had been allowed to take its course. As it was, he learned much more slowly than a twelve year-old child would do. But the reason why he learned at all—and many people found it highly sensational that he could—was that rollerskating was within the scope and compass of his purpose at the age of less than a year. He could not, for instance, have learned to play the violin, or to do fractions. These activities would have meant precisely nothing at all to him, and so they would have been impossible. But skating did mean something, and so the growth of his mentality or his behavior (whichever expression one prefers) could flow in this direction just as a stream flows in a certain direction when a gap is made in the bank.

So the most important requirement of good sequence is that all learning shall be within the scope of the learner's purpose. When is a person teachable? Chiefly when he wants to learn! What is the most promising characteristic an entering college freshman can have? Eagerness for study and enlightenment! Why do pupils go through three sequential years of English composition or American history with hardly any improvement? Chiefly because they do not care! It is the first business of a well-planned sequence of learning in school to promote appetite, to kindle interest, to strengthen purpose. Purpose, to be sure, is not the only characteristic of good sequence, or the only feature of the process of mental growth, but it is absolutely essential. Without purpose there is no growth. Apart from growth there cannot be good sequence. Without good sequence there cannot be good learning.[1]

**3. Growth Depends on the Emergence of Meaning.**    For growth to take place it is not enough to have a number of sporadic experiences and learnings, however purposeful and compelling each of them may be.    These experiences and learnings must contribute to the emergence of a pattern of intelligible behavior, or insight, or understanding—to the emergence of meaning.    Erect posture does not develop out of sporadic meaningless squirmings, no matter how impassioned.    It develops out of sequential tries which are at first very vague and far afield, but which steadily approach the goal.    Again, when Johnny first had roller skates on his feet, he cried, struggled, flopped, and did his best to get rid of them.    This was certainly a purposive performance, but it contributed nothing to his development as a skater.    That development began to manifest itself when, instead of struggling and protesting, he started to slide his feet on the floor.    In both these cases purpose was necessary.    But it was also necessary that the series of endeavors, experiences, and learnings should make more and more explicit a pattern of intelligible action.

Exactly the same is true of the types of mental growth in which we are interested in school.    Consider, by way of illustration, what this means for the teaching of mathematics.    The whole sequence of mathematics from beginning arithmetic to the most advanced levels can be organized about a single thread or clue of meaning.    The very heart of mathematics is the concept of relationship or functionality, and all the learner's endeavors, experiences, and learnings from start to finish should be pointed toward helping him to grasp it more clearly and completely.    At the start the concept of relationship must be understood in a very concrete and immediate context, by the sort of activities which were partially catalogued in Chap. 6.    As the child comes to use symbols the emphasis must be upon grasping relationships rather than doing sums, for instance by finding out what happens when one adds 1 to all digits, or 2 to all digits, by experimenting with doubling and halving, and in general by manipulating the symbols to see how they hang together and affect one another.    It has been found that arithmetic so taught brings about much improved accuracy and retention. When the youngster comes to algebra, he should not be taking up a new subject, but expanding and deepening his understanding of relationship or functionality.    Algebra, in fact, should be handled as the organized study of relational thinking. It has been pointed out that the whole of first-year algebra can center upon an understanding of the proposition $y = ax + b$. If $a$, $x$, and $b$ are given all possible positive and negative values, the laws of signs can be related to the problem of finding the values of $ax + b$. If $b = 0$, $y$ varies directly as $x$, which leads to the study of direct variation. By transposing the expression into the form $\frac{y}{x} = a$ one gets ratio, reduction of fractions, and some factoring. Fractional values of $a$ bring in the topic of proportion. Tables of corresponding values of $x$ and $y$ involve graphs. With $y = 0$ we get the solution of linear equations with one variable. Also we can get into the solution of equations with two unknowns. Thus all the conventional topics arise, and yet they are held together by a single emerging line of meaning. And as for second-year algebra, it can center on the proposition $y = ax^2 + bx + c$.

There are several things to notice immediately about this scheme.

1. It looks like a highly abstract treatment. As a matter of fact it is not. One of the great troubles with mathematics teaching is to find concrete applications and real life problems. This is due to the way the subject is set up. There are very few real life applications to the topics of the conventional textbook. But ordinary experience is crammed to the bursting point with relationships, and offers endless concrete material for the progressive illumination of the concept of functionality. Relationships of cost to weight, of price to profit, of gallons of gas to mileage are a few meager suggestions which may set the reader's mind to working. When learning is organized for meaning it is both intelligible and also related to concrete experience.

2. Mathematics, like everything else, should be organized for teaching in a setting of compelling and concrete problems and experiences. On this mathematical growth depends. But these experiences and problems cannot be merely sporadic and disjointed. They must be interrelated. They must be agencies by which a central understanding is being brought to the birth.

3. This pattern of mathematics teaching is entirely different from the ordinary organization which consists of a series of topics without any over-all relationship or central idea becoming progressively clearer to the learner. The ordinary organization is a sequence brought about by building one thing upon another, each item being almost as self-contained and independent as a separate brick in a wall. If anyone imagines that this is a good plan, one look at the results achieved should disillusion him. The described organization is a sequence determined by mental growth.

4. Explicit logical understanding and complete and well-grounded insight is something towards which the learner grows. It is not something with which he starts. The idea that a child must master everything completely or round out every aspect of a subject as far as he goes is a prime fallacy. He cannot do it. We know that until children are about eight years old they are remarkably insensitive to the contradictions that might trouble adults. They do not stick to any one opinion on any subject, and although they may not hold two opposite ones at the same moment, they are very ready successively to adopt entirely inconsistent ideas. Inconsistency, of course, is not a monopoly of children, but they carry it so far as to disallow the notion that they are capable of highly systematic thinking. What the child is capable of, however, is experience and learning with a core of meaning which later experiences and learnings can make increasingly explicit. The attempt to put across a systematic structure of ideas because it is supposed to contain the "fundamentals" or the "rudiments" of a subject is hopeless and can only lead to minimally meaningful learning and so to sheer verbalization. One starts with experiences and learnings which contain the seed of future systematic insight, and one proceeds to encourage that seed to sprout and grow

We have spent a good deal of time on mathematics because it so beautifully illustrates the relationship between growth and emerging meaning. But the same considerations apply to any field of study. The trouble with sequence in history is that it simply amounts to a bunch of topics, whereas everything should be centered about a germinal idea. In English composition, again, the whole emphasis is often placed on separate, isolated techniques and skills, whereas the whole sequence should be shaped up as growth in the power to express oneself linguistically with precision and point. Art, once more, should be a sequence of development in the power to project one's feelings and intimations in a visual medium. In these cases and all others the pattern of a good sequence is the development of erect posture from vague though still meaningful and purposive fumbling to final achievement.[2]

**4. Growth Is an Evolution from Immediate toward Remote Controls.** In the rhythm of physiological growth the proprioceptors (the organs of touch, temperature, hunger, pain, etc.) come into full function first, then the ears, and then the eyes. The baby's first adequate response is to what is in immediate contact with his body, and as the organism ripens he comes to respond adequately to objects farther and farther away. This also is the characteristic rhythm of mental growth.

Geographic concepts, such as bay, island, peninsula, trade, and so on must first be immediately and concretely experienced if they are to be securely grasped. If this is not done, then children in the upper grades may be found able to recite on them satisfactorily, but when some kind of test is given to ascertain if their meaning has been understood, it is not. Children will not be able to identify instances of these concepts when they see them before their very eyes. What this obviously indicates is sand-tray work, the use and construction of model towns, the use of large-scale clear maps and good pictures, the exploration and mapping of the school grounds and the immediate neighborhood.

There is reason to believe that the capacity to deal with historic time does not develop much before the age of ten. First the child comes to think of the past as different from the present. Then the large historic divisions begin to establish themselves in his mind. Then later on he is able to apprehend the smaller divisions of historic time. So far as we can tell, the use of time lines, time charts, and similar devices in the lower grades does not help much, because the basic idea itself is beyond the range of the learner. The answer is to teach history at an early level simply as stories, and to emphasize temporal relationships in terms of concrete and immediate experiences. Particularly absurd is the persistent practice of the premature teaching of historic dates. Surely a child must have some notion of the long sweep of historical events before the concept "eighteenth century" can mean anything much, and some notion of the concept "eighteenth century" before the specific date 1776 can mean anything much. Anyone who remembers how hopelessly foggy he was as a child about the ages of adults should have a few reflections about the sense of trying to get children to grasp the meaning of hundreds and thousands of years.

Social behavior and social concepts, too, are at first related only to the very small, intimate, face-to-face group. The immediate family, the small play group, the class, the team, the school, the larger society beyond the school—that is the approximate sequence. To attempt anything like a systematic teaching of the concepts of the social studies to children whose social horizons are inevitably limited to their own class companions is not to invite verbalizations and spurious results, but to make them absolutely certain. Such ideas as democracy, justice, dictatorship, and cooperation are in fact nascent in the smallest and simplest face-to-face group. And the business of a well-organized sequence is to use the experiences and contacts which are significant to the learner at his present stage of development for the purpose of securing a growth toward a wider-ranging understanding.

Emotional response, again, is at first very closely tied to the imme-

diate situation. The child can learn to exercise prudence and fore-
sight, but always within exceedingly narrow limits. What is going to
happen a week from now or a year from now does not affect him at all,
because it is too remote. It has been shown that even in high school
the life career motive is not particularly strong or influential, and that
children who say they have decided on a career do not seem to work any
harder at studies closely related to it.[3]

Thus any good sequence must begin with immediate and compelling
experience, even if it seems fragmentary. But it moves toward interrelatedness, completeness, and an awareness of remote issues.

**5. Growth Is a Movement from the Concrete toward the Symbolic.**
The extreme practical value of a sequence rooted in adequate concrete
experience is admirably shown in an experimental project in arithmetic
carried out in the schools of Lawrence, Mass. and involving 475 children. During the period of the first two grades there was no systematization and no drill. All the work was set up as informational or social
arithmetic, with the use of projects such as play stores, games, and so
forth, whose reality to the children was the essential point. Highly
sensational results were achieved. By the end of the second grade the
children knew the addition facts better than others who had been in
conventional formal programs, although these facts had not been
emphasized at all. In the third grade the social arithmetic was continued, combined with drill in which the motivation already generated
was applied. At the end of this year a standard test was run in which
the normal third-grade score was 60 per cent. But the average score
of the 475 children concerned was 97.8 per cent. This is an exceedingly
striking and clear-cut demonstration of what good sequence can do.

The provision of adequate concrete experience is time consuming,
and many teachers tend to consider it time wasting. The class does
not seem to move along very fast, and the number of topics covered
during the year is not that indicated in the syllabus. But one can
hardly consider a measure which enables children to raise their scores
on a standard test by nearly 40 per cent much of a waste of time.
What does waste time is a premature systematization which the learner
cannot assimilate, and a remorseless covering of topics which leaves
him dragging in the dust. Early learning should most assuredly be in
a compelling, concrete, copious setting. If out of this context a thread
of vital meaning is emerging, even though as yet very partially understood, systematic grasp will establish itself later on, and it will be
authentic and not spurious.[4]

**6. Growth Is a Movement from the Crude to the Discriminating.**
When Johnny became able to rollerskate, even his first successes were

awkward and full of irrelevancies. He used one foot as a pusher, was bothered by irregularities on the floor, could only manage rather stiff nonball-bearing skates. His development as a skater meant the evolution of a more and more finely adjusted pattern of response. He became able to adapt himself to skating on a thick mat instead of the bare floor, to manage tricky ball-bearing skates; and he gave up pushing himself around with one foot. Crudeness gave place to discrimination. This again is one of the universal aspects of the characteristic rhythm of growth.

Exactly the same sequence is discernible in the improvement of English style. Here is a typical piece of high-school English.

One of the head men of the village sat opposite me. He was smoking, and a few women and children gathered to look at the "foreign devil." I made them understand that I wanted something to drink, and I said I wanted it hot, so they sent someone to heat water. I felt a little soft touch on my arm while we waited. I turned, and saw a little girl scuttle off. She hid behind her mother.

Now for the revision and improvement.

Opposite me sat one of the head men of the village, smoking, while a few women and children gathered to look at the "foreign devil." I made them understand that I wanted something to drink, and that I wanted it hot, so they sent someone to heat water. While we waited I felt a little soft touch on my arm, and turning, saw a little girl scuttling off to hide behind her mother.

The changes deserve close scrutiny. (1) "Opposite me" is pulled out from behind the word "sat" for the sake of a clearer arrangement and a better emphasis. (2) The grammatical relationship between "smoking," and "one of the head-men . . . " is very close, and so the words are juxtaposed. (3) "While" defines the sense more discriminatingly and precisely than "and." (4) The pair of "that" clauses in the improved version carry an added emphasis. (5) Because of this, the shaded meaning of the word "so" is altered in the second version.*

The whole purport of these changes is to bring out and throw into finer relief the balance and relationships of the sense. It is a movement from relative crudity to relative discrimination similar in principle to that achieved by Johnny as his rollerskating progressed.

Again, a child undertakes to paint a picture which will project his impression of a fire that he has witnessed. He uses crude masses of scarlet and black. For the time being he is satisfied. The powerful, harsh colors correspond roughly to what he has seen and to the feelings

* Adapted from C. H. Ward, *What Is English?*, Scott, Foresman and Company, Chicago, rev. ed., 1925.

it has aroused.   But later on he will wish to make clear both to himself
and to others that this is not a scene of war or murder but of conflagra-
tion, and then more refined indications become necessary.   This is
how growth in art takes place.   If the teacher had tried to convey
abstract color relationships, or the laws of linear perspective, or—to
sink to the lowest depths—the technique of the freehand drawing of a
straight line, the sequence would have been hopelessly bad.   The
child's intentions must evolve, and discriminating choices, reactions, and insights must establish themselves within the scope of this
evolution.

It needs to be understood clearly that a premature attempt to force
discriminating insights or reactions can inhibit the whole process of
growth.   The reason is that the learner's concern and trouble over the
fine adjustment prevents him from attending to anything else.   He
loses sight of meaning in a dust storm of detail.   This very often happens in the laboratory teaching of science in the secondary school, for
the sheer job of manipulation may be so difficult that the pupil has
no mind left for the scientific principles.   It happens when a foreign
language is approached by an elaborate and detailed study of its
grammar, because everything is concentrated on rules and procedures
and nothing on the core task of saying things somehow or other in the
medium.   In music, again, it has been said on high authority backed
by wide experience that a child need lose absolutely nothing and on the
contrary may gain a great deal if he postpones the study of an instrument until he is at least twelve years old, so long as his musical insights
and enthusiasms are being built up in the meantime.   The instrument
is extremely restrictive, and strings, fingerings, black and white notes,
and scales usurp the place which music itself must have in the learner's
mind if authentic growth is to be promoted.

No doubt it would be nice if human beings could grasp the finest
discriminations of action and insight from the very start.   Crudeness
and blundering can never be extolled for their own sake.   But they
undoubtedly belong in the rhythm of growth; for growth depends on
getting hold of meaning and hanging onto it in despite of everything
else.   When this happens, crudeness and blundering slough away and
discrimination authentically emerges.   But if we set up a sequence
which attempts to force discrimination from the first, then a few hardy
souls may push through the sand dunes and reach the promised land
half dead, but most of them will certainly be buried in the desert and
never heard from again.[5]

**7.  Growth Is a Process of Transformation.**   It is a process in which
earlier levels are overpassed and assimilated.   When a group of experi-

mental subjects were set to learning the Morse code on the telegraph key, their first business was to learn the separate letters. Then for a long time they formed each word letterwise, spelling it out. So long as they continued on this level they made almost no progress. At last, however, and quite suddenly, letters coalesced into words, so that instead of having to form such an entity as "the" by spelling out the letters t-h-e, it became a single rhythmic pulse of effort. Speed and accuracy at once dramatically improved. Then again there was a long period virtually without progress while they worked wordwise. Advance came about not by an improvement in word skill, but when words coalesced into whole phrases which now became the units of response. Thus the development of the telegraphic skill was shown to be an affair of transformed control.

This is true of typewriting, where the learner moves very fast from concern for the separate letters to a wordwise and later a phrasewise type of response. It is true of chess where the learner gets away from concern about the separate pieces and their individual moves towards an awareness of the total situation on the board. It is true of reading, where progress depends on coming to grasp larger and larger phrase units on the page. It is true of mathematics, where one comes to apprehend more and more inclusive generalizations, and so to be able to use more and more potent techniques. The expert does not perform as the beginner performs, only a little more smoothly and efficiently. He performs quite differently. Always the sequence of growth is a sequence of transformation.

This has a most profound bearing upon the organization of learning. *The sequence of learning should not be set up with the idea that earlier material will be retained, but with the idea that it will be assimilated.* Any retention that takes place will be due to assimilation, and not vice versa. The beginner in arithmetic, English, social studies, or natural science is in a chrysalis stage, and the whole point is that he ought to get out of it. Teachers constantly maintain that the only way to build a solid foundation for learning is to pound the fundamentals into the learner's head so hard that he will never forget them as long as he lives. Then when he manages to forget them with the greatest of ease, they are nonplussed and say that there must be something wrong with his character. But the vital point in all learning, from the earliest to the latest, is not to remember but to understand. Is the learner getting a glimmer, even a very dim and partial one? That is the crucial question. For a glimmer can grow brighter. If it is encouraged and followed up it will grow brighter. To try to pound the "scientifically selected important facts" about American history into the heads of grade-school children is to invite the process of forgetting to take charge, which it ineluctably will.   To convey even some tiny fragment of American history in such a way that it is impressive, compelling, and understandable is to plant a seed that can grow.   The understanding may be crude, limited, even in some respects partly mistaken.   If it is the genuine article this does not matter, any more than the chrysalis matters to the dragon fly, or the tadpole's tail to the frog.   For the limited understanding expands, enters into relationships, and corrects itself because it has within it the principle of life, whereas a mere block of information is as dead as a number in a telephone book.[6]

So the characteristic nature of properly planned sequence is an emerging thread of intelligibility, made increasingly explicit by purpose, and arising out of concrete, immediate, compelling experiences and learnings which are not so exacting as to confuse and deflect the learner.   The conventional program, with its set arrangement of block topics whose interconnection could only be apparent to a youthful genius, completely falsifies this condition.   The most common defect of the so-called "activity program" or "progressive program" is that it organizes plenty of rich experience but fails to establish any emerging thread of meaning.

### SOME COMMON FALLACIES

1. The proposition that the sequence of learning should be determined by the characteristics and rhythms of mental growth contrasts with the commonly held idea that it should be determined by preparation as ordinarily understood.   The practice of setting up certain courses as required prerequisites for others is very familiar.   Again it has been contended that the study of ancient history should precede that of mediaeval history, and that this again should precede the study of modern history.   And certain designated studies are supposed to be particularly important in getting a person ready for college.

If what is meant is that earlier studies furnish the mind with a body of information and knowledge which is retained and used in later studies, then these preparatory sequences are certainly built on a fallacy. It is known that the amount of transfer between a prerequisite study and one that succeeds it is usually very low.   High-school physics is supposed to be built on high-school algebra, but pupils are found to have far less command of their algebraic techniques when they enter physics than the arrangement assumes.   Even when a series of very similar courses is given, each one dealing with much the same content, and the chief difference being a slight advance in difficulty, the carry-over from the lower to the higher levels is surprisingly meager.   The chronological sequence in the teaching of history looks very reasonable in the abstract, but no one has ever undertaken to show that it produces better learning and more authentic results, and there are no grounds whatsoever for believing that it does. As to the college entrance studies, every investigation that has ever been made has shown that the preparatory advantage they are supposed to yield is a myth. So far as we can tell, almost any pattern of subjects would equip a student for college work about equally well.

As the schools are currently operated, the real significance of certain studies lies in their selective rather than their preparatory effect. Classes in Latin or geometry and suchlike academic subjects have a distinctly higher average level of intelligence than classes in cooking and typewriting and the practical or vocational subjects generally. As one goes on to second- and third-year Latin or mathematics, the selective effect, and the consequent difference, becomes still greater. This is why the academic studies are the best recruiting ground for college candidates. If preparation in the literal sense of the retention and carrying forward of content were the determining factor there would not be a great deal of point in any organized sequence at all, except as an administrative device, and a very good case could be made for a pure elective system and the selection of students by means of adequate mental testing.

For the qualities which really carry over into new studies or more advanced studies are interest, purpose, eagerness to work, good methods of work, and a broadening awareness of interrelationships. These qualities are in fact often generated by the ordinary preparatory sequences, but only indirectly and of course inefficiently and with many needless obstacles. They are the typical outcomes of mental growth, and so the clear conclusion is that sequence ought to be determined not by the myth of preliminary preparation but by the authentic characteristics of the growth process.[7]

2. Recent discussions of mental growth have much of the concept of readiness. To call this concept an out-and-out fallacy would be decidedly questionable, but there is no doubt that it needs to be qualified and defined with great care unless it is to lead to the gravest errors in thought and practice.

Essentially the idea is that a general process of growth makes a person ready for specific learnings. By the use of proper and sufficient diagnostic techniques one can tell when this condition of readiness has been reached, and that is the moment when the learning in question can be fruitfully introduced. It is possible to ascertain the arrival of readiness to begin reading and to begin formal arithmetic with considerable certainty, because there are sufficient good tests and other instruments of analysis. With most other learnings we cannot be so sure. But it is believed that when enough research has been done it may be possible to diagnose readiness for most of the important learnings with which the school is concerned, so that we shall know just when they ought to be introduced. Needless to say, this would call for considerable individualization of instruction, because a number of people are not likely to reach the same stage of readiness all at the same time. Such, then, is the claim.

While the idea of readiness as thus interpreted contains much truth, there are two interrelated objections which must be urged against it.

A. It seems to treat certain learnings—beginning reading, beginning arithmetic, beginning algebra, beginning Latin, and so on—as definite stages in the process of development. Now one of the chief points that has already been emphasized in this chapter is that growth is continuous, and that it is not marked by definite stages. Yet the reality and practical importance of such stages is exactly what the proponents of readiness appear to assume.

The conception of readiness has been most extensively applied in connection with reading. In the mental development of the child there is supposed to be a watershed separating the periods before and after he begins to read. It is contended that the existence of this watershed ought to determine the entire organization of learning. Everything on one side of it is to be geared to getting him across it, and culminates when he does so. Tests and techniques of observation have been devised with the purpose of charting his approach to it, and ascertaining the arrival of the moment when he may profitably be introduced to printed language. Furthermore it is assumed that every important learning in school constitutes just such a psychological watershed, and that sufficient research will enable us to know just how close any child is getting to it and what kind of learnings and experiences will best help him to cross it.

This is a very dubious proposition, for the idea of specific readiness seems to amount to the doctrine of stages of growth in a new form. Its adherents admit that only a few types of readiness—chiefly those in reading and arithmetic—are at all well understood, but claim that research will throw light on the rest. But if growth is essentially continuous, then the basic assumption is unsound, and this will frustrate the best and most arduous research. Enormous efforts have been made to find out the optimum timing of practice periods in various skills, but the findings are a mass of confusions and inconsistencies. The reason is that the length and distribution of practice depend on extremely complicated interlocking factors, and are impossible to determine by the clock, so that the basic question posed in the research is unanswerable. The same with attempts to find out how to diagnose readiness for many kinds of jobs of learning. What if there is no such thing as specific readiness? If not, all the research in the world will never discover it.

*B.* Another objection, closely connected with the foregoing, is that the concept of readiness as understood and applied seems to interpret wrongly, or at least very partially, the relation between the specific learning and the total process of growth. A sharp line of distinction is drawn between the process of getting ready to learn, and the learning itself. Informal arithmetic, or social arithmetic, which means a wide variety of informal experiences and activities, is introduced to get the child ready for number work itself. Then number work is begun, and it is called "formal" arithmetic, which obviously suggests that from now on everything is to be different. The objection is that the emergence of number concepts is neither more nor less than a moment in a continuous process of development, which has exactly the same character throughout. A compelling and concrete context out of which problematic focuses arise, the stimulation of a participating group, and the sense of individual contribution to joint enterprises—all these are just as important after as before. There is no abrupt watershed beyond which the scenery changes. The study of mathematics is always the study of relationship, and psychologically it has the same character and requires the same conditions from the first moment when the child realizes that one thing is bigger than another up to the most abstruse analysis. The only essential change is that insight becomes deeper, broader, and clearer, and control more precise and expert.

In the same way, a child learns best to read when he is in a physical and social environment which is rich and stimulating and which constantly suggests reading as a desirable achievement—an environment, be it said, which both the home and the school should cooperate in establishing. In such an environment he grows into reading. There will need to be a certain amount of special help here and there, including the use of specially adapted materials, so that the right focuses may be set up. But quite likely, as he looks back, he will never remember being definitely introduced to reading, any more than he will remember the big moment in his life when his height went beyond exactly four feet. And after he can read, exactly the same conditions are necessary to keep his reading ability growing.

The truth of the concept of readiness is that the only effective preparation for any specific learning is to grow into it. This is why the plan of social arithmetic described above worked out so well. But it is only half the truth. The error of the concept of readiness is to treat growth simply as preparation for learning and as no more than this. For the learning itself is a factor in the continuous growth, and an integral element in it, and must be treated as such. It must be treated, that is, as a developmental experience which brings wider insight, deeper understanding, surer control, and thus opens vistas of further growth. The concept of readiness centers attention on what happens before the learning, which is indeed important. But what happens during, after, and because of the learning is just as important. And what should happen is more growth! The plan for preceding formal arithmetic with social arithmetic was admirable as far as it went, but if the school authorities and teachers of Lawrence had been endued with the courage and the skill to continue doing in all their mathematics the same kind of things they did in their social arithmetic, at higher and higher levels and with constantly wider and deeper focuses right up to the end of high school, they would have been able to announce results which would have astounded the educators of the nation.[8]

3. The two most fatal errors in the management of sequence are postponement and prematurity. Some years ago considerable stir was caused by a scheme for the teaching of arithmetic which put it off until the sixth grade. Apparently this caused no disaster—unless the ordinary results of arithmetic teaching are considered disastrous. In rebuttal, however, the point has been made that much younger children are perfectly capable of handling symbolic number work. The answer is, of course, that the early phases of a sequence of learning should have the character of promotion, the arousal of interest and purpose, and the application of meanings in a concrete and copious setting. This is what gets results later on. The claim is supported by the investigation on the effects of social or informational arithmetic cited above. It is further buttressed from quite a different source. Emil Jaques-Dalcroze has consistently reported that if children are given a year of experience with bodily rhythm before starting in on the piano they will make 400 per cent normal progress in their first year of piano study. This, however, is not postponement. It is the intelligent and effective promotion of growth

A much more common and even more serious fallacy is that of prematurity. It has been definitely established that formal arithmetical drill in the first two grades is not an effective mode of organizing arithmetical learning. The reason is that it persistently forces routine on the child when the emphasis should be on quantitative or relational thinking. In the same way and for the same reason premature systematization, premature symbolization, and premature attempts to make everything logical and complete and perfectly rounded out defeat their own purpose. It is perfectly true that the omnibus project does make for fragmentary and incomplete learning. But this is not necessarily bad. To be sure, such projects may institute purely haphazard undertakings which get nowhere—although even then they could hardly be as futile as the conventional recitation lesson. But if they institute purposive learnings in which there is a thread of emerging meaning, then they will lead onward toward increasing power and their momentary fragmentariness does not amount to anything at all.[9]

### Notes and References

*General References on Growth*

Myrtle McGraw, *Growth, A Study of Johnny and Jimmy*, Chap. 10, "General Principles of Growth," D. Appleton-Century Company, Inc., New York, 1935; James L. Mursell, "Growth," in Charles E. Skinner, *Readings in Educational Psychology*, Chap. 4, Farrar & Rinehart, Inc., New York, 1937.

*References in the Text*

1. Myrtle McGraw, *op. cit.*, pp. 94–47, 160–165.

2. Jean Piaget, *Judgment and Reasoning of the Child*, Harcourt, Brace and Company, New York, 1928, emphasizes the inconsistency of children's opinions. A rebuttal is presented by T. M. Abel, "Unsynthetic Modes of Thinking Among Adults: A Discussion of Piaget's Concepts," *American Journal of Psychology*, Vol. 44 (1932), pp. 123–132.

3. T. G. Eskridge, *Growth in Understanding of Geographic Terms in Grades IV to VII*, Duke University Press, Durham, N. C., 1939, deals with the development of geographic concepts. The child's awareness of historic time is considered by E. C. Oakden and Mary Stuart, "The Development of the Knowledge of Time in Children," *British Journal of Psychology*, Vol. 12 (1922), pp. 309–336; and by F. Pistor, "How Time Concepts Are Acquired by Children," *Educational Method*, Vol. 20 (1940), pp. 107–112. The social concepts of children are discussed by Hyman Meltzer, *Children's Social Concepts; A Study of Their Nature and Development*, Teachers College, Columbia University, Bureau of Publications, New York, 1925; and by Joy Muchmore Lacey, *Social Studies Concepts of Children in the First Three Grades*, Teachers College, Columbia University, Bureau of Publications, New York, 1932. The influence of remote motives is discussed by Grayson H. Kefauver, "The Life-Career Motive and Its Effect on High School Work," *School Review*, Vol. 34 (1926), pp. 426–430.

4. The report of the arithmetic project is Guy M. Wilson, "New Standards in Arithmetic: A Controlled Experiment in Supervision," *Journal of Educational Research*, Vol. 20 (1930), pp. 351–360.

5. For a very well-treated account of artistic development see Polly Ames, "Children and the Teaching of Painting," *Progressive Education*, Vol. 16 (1939), pp. 535–542. For an admirable treatment of the developmental approach to instrumental performance see Carl E. Seashore, "A Symposium: Music and the Child," *Child Study*, Vol. 5 (1928), May, pp. 1–18.

# CHAPTER 14

## THE PRINCIPLE OF SEQUENCE AND THE APPRAISAL OF TEACHING

### HIERARCHY OF APPLICATIONS

Every curriculum, which is of course a comprehensive, long-term organized plan for learning, has some kind of sequence built into it. These arrangements, however, like all the rest with which we have dealt, vary all the way from extreme crudity and ineffectiveness to high and judicious skillfulness. So once more a hierarchy or scale is presented, to be used as a tool of analysis in appraising teaching situations.

The principle of sequence and the hierarchy of applications here presented have an obvious bearing upon the curriculum. But their bearing upon the specific jobs of learning, or the lessons, within the curriculum or the course is just as important and inescapable. No one will deny that an intelligent teacher ought to be aware of the structure and aims of the whole curriculum, but the relationship of that awareness to his daily work in the classroom is often not as clear as it might be in his mind. A proper understanding of the principle of sequence should make this relationship very evident. For the sequential organization of the curriculum and the course has a profound effect on the handling of the specific learning. At one end of the hierarchy each specific learning is a self-contained unit, or lesson, or block, to be taken up, covered, and passed by. At the other end of the hierarchy it is treated as a developmental influence much of whose value turns upon its effect on a continuous line of growth.

### PRINCIPLE OF SEQUENCE: HIERARCHY OF APPLICATIONS

Sequential blocks of content: (lessons; courses)

I     Held together chiefly by requirements, prerequisites and logical order: Basic assumption, additive accumulation of knowledge and skill

II     Attempts to knit learnings (lessons; courses) more closely together by introductions, previews, pretests, and the rearrangement of the order of material: Basic assumption, apperception

III     Sequence organized in terms of readiness

IV     Sequence organized in terms of lines of emerging meaning

## THE FIRST LEVEL

The conventional sequence is simply a succession of blocks of content. The larger ones are called courses. The smaller ones are called lessons or units. The movement of the pupil through the succession is determined largely by requirements, to a considerably less extent by course prerequisites, and to a degree which cannot be exactly determined and which varies in different schools, by his own choice.

The arrangement is by no means arbitrary. In fact it is often called "logical" par excellence. In a sense this is undoubtedly so, but it is well worth while to consider just what this sense is. If one examines any elementary-school or high-school syllabus or textbook, one can see clearly that it has a plan. The sequence of topics is determined by some sort of organizing idea, whether original with the author or derived from conventional practice. However it is very far indeed from being the only possible plan or arrangement. The content might very well be revamped and reshuffled into many different patterns, each one of which would probably be as coherent and intelligible as another, and each one equally defensible in the abstract. This becomes quite clear if one examines a number of different textbooks or syllabuses, and more especially if one compares those prepared several decades ago with modern examples. Even in such a tightly organized subject as mathematics, school textbooks present a wide range of different topical patterns.

Furthermore the plan of the textbook or the syllabus, while it may be feasible and understandable, never presents the basic intrinsic logic of the subject itself, and indeed never so much as undertakes to do so. Rigoristic mathematicians have developed a field of study dealing with the basic logical principles of mathematics. But with these the axioms, postulates, definitions, and rules of procedure found in school textbooks have almost nothing to do. Indeed the two are usually quite inconsistent, so that from the standpoint of mathematical rigor the ordinary school text is an atrocity. So also in language study and in science, school textbooks are never built up on the ultimate logical principles of linguistics or physics. This may be perfectly proper, but it certainly means that we must be on our guard when calling the ordinary sequence "logical."

When we pass beyond the separate course and consider the curriculum as a whole, the evidences of any sort of intelligible order are much feebler. The various courses usually hang together very loosely indeed. If one looks at their titles one can sometimes see a sort of reason for their arrangement, but not always. But if one goes below since the Herbartian inductive-development lesson attracted wide attention, attempts of this kind have been common. All of them seem based ultimately upon the concept of apperception.

The inductive development lesson, it will be remembered, opened with a step called preparation, in which the past relevant experiences and knowledge of the learner were called to mind before anything new was introduced. A closely similar idea appears in Morrison's mastery-unit technique. It was, however, much more narrowly conceived and handled, for each mastery unit is supposed to open with a summary preview or synopsis of what is to be covered, usually presented in lecture form by the teacher, and immediately following a pretest designed to find out how much of the material of the unit the pupils already know. Then, after the introductory synopsis or summary, the study phase of the work commences, with the pupils learning the materials set out from books or other sources.

Later attempts at stage setting are a good deal more flexible and less tied down to a definite formula than in the mastery unit. The concept of apperception is more loosely and effectively applied, but still it seems to control. Thus an extensive secondary unit on agriculture opens with an account presented in the text, of two boys, one of whom decides to take agriculture courses, while the other proposes to prepare himself for something "that will count in the world." The pupils are intended to read the story and talk about it for a while, before plunging *in medias res*. This is supposed to lead to a consideration of the true importance of farming, its universality, its recognition, and of sources of information about it. A unit in French opens by distributing to the pupils mimeographed copies of a story they are to read, carefully graded to the desired level of difficulty. They are told that many French words have the same meaning as similar English words, warned of the pronunciation problem, and urged to try to read in sentences and to infer the meanings of unknown words from the context. Again, a third-grade unit took off from the interest aroused in the class when a postman arrived with a registered letter. The pupils were encouraged to ask questions centering on this experience—how long the postman works, when he collects mail from the box, what happens on the railway mail car, what happens at the post office, who pays the postman, and so forth. These questions were sifted and organized into an effective unit on the post office, which was one of a series on the local community. These are fair illustrative samples of the technique of psychological stage setting, one effect of which is to make the transitions less abrupt between lessons or units.

Preparatory stage setting of this kind often goes along with a more or less formal pretest at the beginning of each unit or lesson.   At its most restrictive, the purpose of the pretest is to find out how much of the content of the unit the pupils already know, so that it can be reduced or expanded, and so that individual adaptations can be made. More effectively used, the written pretest is a device employed in combination with class discussion to reveal what relevant experience and knowledge the pupils possess, so that the unit can be more meaningfully organized in terms of their actual background.

Besides such preparatory measures in handling the lessons or units, many efforts have been made to smooth out the sequence of learnings. by rearranging the order of topics.   The old practice of starting history with ancient history has been very strongly criticized, because of its remoteness and because of the many strange and difficult terms and ideas involved.   In algebra it has been recommended that the study of polynomial fractions precede that of monomials.   Very often a child introduced to polynomials make such an error as the following:

$$\frac{x^2 + 8x + 15}{x^2 + 4x + 3} = \frac{x^2 + 8x + 15}{x^2 + 4x + 3} = 2 + 5$$

The reason is the literalistic carry-over of the rules for monomials.   In arithmetic it has been found that long division is often easier than short division, and that the usual order here may profitably be reversed. These are merely illustrative selections from a very large number of cases.

The general effect of measures of this kind seems to be to make the separate units more meaningful and effective, and to establish some liaison between them here and there.   But attention is still fixed upon the separate units or lessons, and not upon the sequential evolution of understanding and purpose which they ought to exemplify.   One might say that the attempt is to glue them together rather than to treat them as living members of an evolving organic unity.   Certainly these and similar techniques are valuable.   Certainly they should not be discouraged.   But it is necessary to go beyond them, and to go deeper, if the problem of sequence is to be solved.[1]

### THE THIRD LEVEL

The attempt to organize sequence in terms of readiness belongs to the realms of hope rather than of actual accomplishment, except in a few areas.   To understand it, let us see what is proposed and done under the most favorable circumstances.   One such favorable instance is the introduction of so-called "formal" or "symbolic" arithmetic.

out in one situation over a period of time. (1) During the first week of school the children bought and ate animal crackers. The teacher recited to them Morley's "Animal Crackers." It was familiar to some, but all enjoyed it. Thus they *listened readily*. (2) Several days later the teacher repeated the poem once more. One child asked her to say it again, and all listened. Here the significant point is the *request for repetition*. (3) A week later a child asked for "Animal Crackers," and when the teacher began it several children said part of it with her. Then she remarked about a child who was home with a cold, asked if they would like to hear a poem about him, and repeated Milne's "Sneezles and Wheezles" to an accompaniment of chuckles. Here we have the children *entering actively into repetition*. (4) A boy found the book containing "Sneezles and Wheezles" and brought it to the teacher to read. A girl asked to say "Animal Crackers" herself, and did so with most of the others following along softly. Here we have *preparation for participation*. (5) A week later the teacher brought to class a book of children's poems, and talked about it. The children examined it, commented on it, and asked for the reading of selections interestingly illustrated. The *examination of a book of poetry* is clearly a step in advance. (6) Next day the children asked for several poems from the book, giving various reasons. Here the *element of choice* begins to appear. (7) Some time later a child who had been unresponsive came to the teacher and said that she used not to like poetry much, but now she did.*

This is a very revealing illustration. The new experiences which the teacher introduced could not possibly be meaningful and appealing in themselves unless the children grew into them. Yet they were not treated as predetermined stages toward which the growth process was to be oriented and for which it must bring about readiness. Furthermore there was a nice balance between planning and extemporization. The teacher certainly did not decide far in advance just what she was going to do or what she was going to present or how she was going to present it on such and such a date. Nevertheless she had a coordinated plan, but it allowed much flexibility. She was promoting a certain line of growth and she did so when and as the occasion seemed to indicate. This is exactly how sequence should be handled.

How a properly planned sequence of learnings and experiences can foster a developing insight is well shown by a study of generalization in science teaching. The general proposition set up as a line of growth was: The Sun Is the Chief Source of Energy for the Earth. A concrete context consisting of the reaction of the plants to light was organized.

* Adapted from Inga Olla Helseth, *Living in the Classroom*, pp. 213–215, Edwards Bros., Inc., Ann Arbor, Mich., 1939.

In the first grade typical responses were, "Plants bend to the window to get light," and "Light makes plants strong." In the third grade a typical response was, "In the dark a plant would lose all the food in it and then get yellow and die." In the sixth grade a typical response was, "The chlorophyll in the leaves acts like a machine and through the energy of the sun makes food which is stored in the stem and leaves." Here is a typical picture of mental growth, with advancing complexity, precision, logical adequacy, breadth, and depth.

1. The plotted line of growth must never be allowed to degenerate into a series of separated and self-contained lessons. When this happens, we are right back on the first level of the hierarchy, and the integrity and effectiveness of the sequence are destroyed. Each learning must be treated as integrally and vitally related to what went before and what comes after. To revert to a comparison already made, it must be treated as a novelist treats an episode which is to carry his plot along. This is a very practical consideration indeed. Among other things, it means that it cannot be completely and finally planned long in advance, although the teacher should certainly have an idea, or better still a number of alternative ideas, about how to handle it in the setting of development. But the details, and even the general plan adopted, must clearly depend to a great extent upon the nature of the actual development that has taken place in the minds of the learners. This will be, to a considerable degree, unpredictable, because it depends on many unforeseen conditions and circumstances. Experiences may occur, and suggestions may arise of which advantage should be taken, and which may greatly modify the treatment of the learning under consideration. The teacher may become aware of a need for delay, or of the advisability of speeding things up.

Or again, the level of proficiency or the standard to which the specific learning should be taken at a given time cannot be wholly predetermined. It depends a great deal on what has happened before and on what is to come later—on the effect of the learning in question upon the total developmental line. So one cannot map out a series of lessons and decide ahead of time just how well each one of them must be done as an independent unit. For the lesson is not an independent unit, and the level of thoroughness and competency which it ought properly to achieve depends on its relationship to continuous growth, just as an author's development and elaboration of any episode depends on its relationship to his plot.

2. The second error to avoid is the making of a program out of merely haphazard experiences and activities that for some vague reason are considered "worth while," perhaps only because they are suggested by the children rather than by the teacher. A very cogent criticism

# CHAPTER 15

## THE PRINCIPLE OF EVALUATION AND THE ORGANIZATION OF LEARNING

### THE PRINCIPLE OF EVALUATION

An observer was visiting a grade-school classroom in connection with an investigation that was being made. The teacher, who seemed considerable of a martinet, was conducting practice exercises in subtraction, with the children individually occupied with their workbooks. While they worked she went round the group observing what they were doing and making comments here and there. Finally she paused beside a boy who gave numerous signs that he was having trouble. She peered at the sheet on his desk, frowned, shook her head. "No," she said, "that's all wrong." And with that she gave him a sharp rap with her ruler and passed on. Then, coming to the front of the room where the observer was standing, she sighed and murmured to him, "That's the stupidest boy I have."

After the class was dismissed the observer managed to have a little conference with the child. They worked out a few subtraction exercises together, and soon the case became perfectly clear. The pupil was entirely able to handle subtraction so long as there was no carrying over to be done, but the moment this came in he was helpless. He simply did not understand the process at all. So the mystery was readily solved. The trouble was not stupidity or the lack of an arithmetical bump. The child had never gotten the hang of a definite technique which he could see through very quickly when it was explained to him.

This is an instance of what in modern educational practice has come to be called "evaluation." Evaluation is the scrutiny of a job of learning for the sake of picking out its crucial features. An ordinary school test has this purpose. It is a means of scrutinizing a job of learning, and it usually picks out certain results as the crucial element—the feature of the situation which has the paramount value. The score or mark given on the test is a record of how the learning in question has been evaluated. Evaluation, then, is a business familiar to all teachers and all pupils, and it has been since schools began. Indeed, it is familiar to all learners both in and out of school, for one rarely learns anything at all without at least wondering from time to time how well he is doing, what he is getting out of it, and perhaps considering how to do better.

So common sense makes it quite clear that evaluation is inseparable from learning. But it may be done either well or badly. In the instance just considered, two of the people concerned evaluated badly, and one did so well. The pupil knew all too certainly that there was something wrong but had no notion what it was. The teacher also was aware that there was something wrong, because the child was falling down on his subtraction sums; and she placed a high enough value on this to be annoyed about it. Unlike the pupil, she had her own idea as to what the trouble was, but the idea was wrong. The observer, however, went straight to the root of the difficulty and did a good job of evaluation because he picked out the crucial feature of this particular piece of learning.

Another instance is suggestive and instructive because it plays up certain aspects of evaluation which teachers need to consider, and which will be discussed in what follows. A grade-school class was returning from a trip downtown where they had been buying food for the cafeteria they were running that year in their small campus school. The college student who had chaperoned them on their trip overheard the following during the walk back to school. "Don't let that substitute teacher waste our time when we get back. We've got to find out about that division." The children had discovered that in order to compute the cost of something to be served soon, a type of division unfamiliar to them was necessary. They had decided that this was the crucial feature, the high point, the outstanding value of the situation, and they proposed to concentrate on it.

Many other instances of evaluation will be given as we proceed, but it hardly seems necessary to go any further to show its great and obvious importance. Learning is a purposive, conscious process. It is something that the learner does for himself, not something that merely happens to him, like the effect of a drug. So the better both he and those who are trying to help him understand what he is about, and what the crucial aspects of it are, the better the learning is likely to go.

*The effectiveness and success of any job of learning is heightened by a valid and discriminating appraisal of all its aspects.* This, in its simplest and most general form, is the *principle of evaluation*. Its soundness is so self-evident that nobody who has ever learned anything at all is likely to question it.

his own endeavors.  They wonder whether such a policy may not let them in for they know not what—working out all marks in the public view, for instance, and thus bringing down avalanches of complaints from pupils and parents.   What really is involved we shall see later on. But the point here is that all teachers, in spite of doubts and hesitations which come chiefly from misunderstanding, in effect accept the proposition.   Teachers very often urge their pupils not to work for marks.   That is to say, they invite their pupils to adopt for themselves standards of evaluation different from those of the marking system. Also, there is not a teacher in the business who does not think well of a pupil who shows good judgment in his work, who sets up a job intelligently, who knows when it is well and truly done, who tackles his own difficulties with resolution and insight, and who can go ahead without constant instructions.   This is the capacity for independence which is always so highly regarded.   What it amounts to is that the pupil is good at evaluating his own learning situations and problems.

The conclusion, then, from both these implications is clear.  *To be effective, learning must be organized in such a way that all concerned, and particularly the learner himself, achieve a valid and discriminating appraisal of all its aspects.*   This is the sixth working psychological principle of successful teaching.

## CHARACTERISTICS OF GOOD EVALUATION

Teachers and learners can evaluate well, or they can do so badly. The difference turns upon discrimination, upon what is noticed and played up and emphasized, upon what is considered important.   So, in order to find out what good evaluation is, one must decide upon the crucial features of learning situations.

It has been consistently argued throughout this book that by far the most important aspect of all learning is the purpose of the learner. Learning starts with a sense of need, or a compelling problem, of a situation which one wishes to control by skill or understanding or discriminating appreciation.   When it succeeds it goes on to a progressive fulfillment of this purpose in the face of difficulties and obstacles. It can be regarded either as the emergence of insight or the realization and definition of purpose, for these are two sides of the same process. Thus any good scheme of evaluation must be directly related to and must help along the progressive realization of purpose which is the essence of learning.   Let us consider a number of approaches with this criterion in mind.

**1. Evaluation and Direct Results.**  The feature of the learning process by far the most commonly emphasized in evaluation is its direct result. How much history, or algebra, or science does a person know at a given time? What degree of mastery has he achieved in French or Latin? What is a child's showing on a standard test in reading or arithmetic? These are the kind of questions on which evaluation very largely centers, and they all play up the direct result.

This emphasis is perfectly understandable. Everybody learns for the sake of getting results. It is in fact, the essential purpose which animates the process. Indeed the attainment of them is the most decisive sign that learning has gone well and that teaching has succeeded. So the question is what an emphasis upon direct results in evaluation on the part of teachers, and consequently on the part of learners, does to the learning, and also why it does it. Here, fortunately, we have some very illuminating findings accumulated by extensive research over a good many years.

It has been known and established for a long time that in a laboratory situation a knowledge of results is a potent influence in stepping up achievement and expediting learning. Also, the reason why this effect is produced has been made clear in a series of investigations, so that the proper bearing of the idea upon schoolwork and the practical organization of learning is now apparent.

In the first important experiment, the subjects worked on the ergograph which is an instrument requiring a stated output of muscular energy to operate. Some were told at frequent intervals how much work they were doing and others were not. It was found that those given the information consistently surpassed the others both in rate of work and in total amount accomplished. A little later another experiment was conducted along similar lines, this time using four simple jobs of learning—acquiring skill in crossing out all the small a's on a page, in crossing out certain designated letters in Spanish, in making certain substitutions in a code, and in two-place mental multiplication. The subjects were divided into two sections. The first section was kept informed of and interested in the results of its work, and the second section was not. And the first gained much more rapidly and extensively in speed and accuracy. As a check the crucial condition was reversed two thirds of the way through the experiment, the first section now being kept in the dark and the second section informed and interested. With this change the effect upon the learning was also reversed. Still later, in another investigation, 126 college students were divided into three groups and given practice in substitutions three times a week for four weeks. The first section was left to its own devices. The members of the second section were incited to compete against each other. The members of the third were as much to the creator himself as to any outside critic or teacher. But often the interim evaluation of results can be managed readily enough. For instance, pupils may graph their progress in a specific skill, or they may keep folders containing successive samples of their own work. There is, however, a serious danger to be avoided. Teachers, in their zeal to make pupils continuously aware of the results of their learning, may give a great many closely spaced tests. Or they set up a whole series of specific steps for the writing of a paper—suggested topic, revised topic, bibliography, proposed outline, revised outline, first draft, final draft is one actual case—each step to be completed and handed in for criticism on an assigned date. Teachers should understand clearly and definitely that arid routines of this sort positively do not help. They keep pupils busy. They probably make them unhappy. But they do not make them learn better. The point has been established in quite a number of investigations to which reference has been made in this book. This leads directly to the third consideration which must be taken up.

3. The results of which the pupil is made aware must be results that he wants to attain, or his awareness of them will have very little effect of any kind. That is exactly the trouble with the kind of well-meant and conscientious schemes just described, which certainly make plenty of labor not only for the pupils but also for the teacher. They substitute a set of mechanical devices for a living purpose, and so they waste the time and energies of all concerned. The children who went back to school eagerly planning to study a new type of long division which they found they needed would certainly benefit from knowing their results as they went along with the job. But if the long division had been set up as a topic in a sequence of formal lessons without any purpose being aroused, a series of practice tests intended to reveal progress would have had the effect simply of so much busy work. In the same way, a child who comes up with pencil and pad and says, "Please give me some sentences like those I had trouble with in my letter today, I'll try them at home," is all set to benefit by an awareness of how he is doing as he works, because a specific and authentic purpose is present. It constantly happens in school situations that pupils do not care very much whether they learn or not. All they really want is to get by, which is not too difficult, and if the announced results indicate that they have done so they are satisfied, and the information has no effect at all upon learning. To put the point in a somewhat different and more general way, *results must be meaningful in terms of the learner's purpose if a knowledge of them is to have a beneficial effect.*

**2. Evaluation and Transfer.** The crucial test of all learning is transferability, and particularly transferability to a functional situation. This is good psychology and good sense. One has not learned to multiply until one knows when to multiply instead of adding when confronted with a challenge in ordinary living, without any textbook to tip one off. One has not learned a grammatical principle unless one can apply it in writing a letter to a friend, instead of merely being able to recite it, or to use it in certain carefully selected cases in class. One has not learned a motor skill such as the golf swing until one can use it in all the varied, and trying, and unexpected situations on the course instead of merely at the practice net. A result which will not transfer, and which can be delivered only in one single, special setting is spurious. A result which transfers to actual use is authentic.

So good evaluation must play up authentic results, and the test of such results is transferability. This was brought out more than seventy years ago, in the reorganization of the schools at Quincy, Mass., which was described earlier in this book. It was found that results were being obtained which looked good but which were actually spurious. The children could recite in the words of their textbooks, but any new application immediately defeated them. The same point has appeared innumerable times since then. In one striking investigation it was found that children could name two explorers but could not tell what an explorer was; could name one member of Washington's cabinet, but did not know what a presidential cabinet was; could tell that New Hampshire produces granite and that Massachusetts has many textile mills, but had no notion of what either granite or textiles might be; and so on at length. Obviously this can only mean parrot mastery. Evaluation which stresses spurious results either for the information of the learner or for any other purpose cannot be other than spurious.

Careful and thorough investigation has convincingly shown that the possession of information in no way guarantees understanding or insight. Tests of three kinds were developed in chemistry, biology, home economics, statistics, social science and zoology. One type showed the recall of information; another type showed power to recall and apply principles; a third type showed power to draw inferences from data. It was found that a great many students who did well on the first type of test were conspicuously weak on the other two. Thus an emphasis on information does not produce thinking. As the investigator remarks: "If the higher mental processes of application of principles and inference are really to be cultivated, learning conditions appropriate for their cultivation are necessary."*　And among the most important of these conditions is a scheme of evaluation which consistently emphasizes understanding and insight rather than routine memory.

Such a scheme of evaluation will constantly raise the issue of transferability, for transfer is brought about by understanding, and is the one sure sign that understanding is being achieved.　Thus in properly organized learning, manifestations of achievement in situations which call for application will be played up and given careful and systematic attention.　This means, among other things, a shift away from the kind of test calling for a reproduction of material just as it has been studied.　In geometry there may be sketches of mechanical or woodworking problems that call for geometrical analysis.　In science there may be descriptions of experiments or assemblages of data calling for conclusions arising from the application of scientific laws.　In the social sciences there may be accounts of social or economic events which provide opportunities for discussion and explanation.　In history, comparisons, contrasts, and analogies between different periods, and particularly between the past and the present, may be set up.　Current material, such as news stories, advertising, popular books including fiction, government and trade brochures are exceedingly rich sources for the kind of applications clearly desirable.　And after all, if school learning does not bear on such matters, just what is it good for?

But the organization of learning and the conduct of evaluation to emphasize transfer goes far beyond the use of tests as ordinarily understood.　Field trips, the planning of parties and assembly programs, the writing of letters, the management of an experimental school garden, the mapping of the local community and the writing up of its history, its economics, its terrain conditions, will do far more to reveal the realities of the child's learning and the authenticity of his grasp of science, arithmetic, art, music, English expression, and so forth than anything he is likely to do with a pencil and paper in the classroom. The practical difficulty, of course, is that an evaluation of the child's responses on such occasions cannot usually be expressed in anything that looks like a test score.　But it is rather absurd to let statistical conventions get in the way of significant judgments.　Some kind of a record can certainly be made, and it can be far more important and revealing, even though it comes from a shaggy natural situation, than a neat score based on the tidy convenience of a paper-and-pencil test.

* Ralph W. Tyler, "The Relation Between Recall and the Higher Mental Processes" in Charles H. Judd, *Education as the Cultivation of the Higher Mental Processes*, p. 17, The Macmillan Company, New York, 1936.

There are two reasons why results involving transfer are particularly important in evaluation. First they reveal to the teacher with peculiar and sometimes devastating clarity what is really going on or not going on, and to what extent meaningful and authentic learning is really being achieved. Second, they are very closely related to the learner's purpose, so that an awareness of them has a very powerful effect in shaping up his learning. It is true that we always learn for results. But it is not true that we usually learn simply to accumulate a stock of information, or to build up a skill that will only work in a few carefully regulated situations. We learn for results that will transfer, results that can be freely and flexibly used and applied. When a child tries to produce a legible page for a class magazine, or to plan an exhibit with a proper arrangement of shapes and colors, or to figure out how the cost of a gift may be divided among a group of donors, or to explain a geological fault that he sees on an expedition, or to compute calories in a diet, he finds out a great deal about the realities of his own competence. He is up against something which is a genuine challenge and which is likely to enlist some pretty deep-going motives. He is dealing with a richly meaningful situation so that his successes and failures are richly meaningful too, and can serve as highly influential guide lines by which to steer his learning.

It may be that some people will find in this discussion cause for a certain misgiving. Are exact and copious information and precise and demonstrable skills not important? Are they to be disparaged, perhaps neglected? Certainly they are important. Certainly they are not to be neglected. What was established by Tyler, in the investigation to which reference was made, was that the way to understanding is not through information. On the contrary, the surest way to information is through understanding. A student may display quite a knowledge of the facts in some field but be lacking in any authentic grasp of it. In this case his information is not likely to do him much good, and almost for a certainty it will be temporary and transient and soon forgotten. But a student who has a real grasp of a given field is also likely to be well informed about it and to remember his information for a long time. Facts stick well in a vital pattern of comprehension, but when they are grooved into the mind for their own sake they are written on the sand.

What this means for the practical organization of learning is that evaluation on direct results is important, but only in a meaningful setting. A child finds that he is helpless in a class undertaking involving multiplication. Under the guidance of the teacher he drills himself on the multiplication combinations, and it is important for him to be aware of the direct results he is achieving in his drill. Another child finds that he cannot read the interesting and challenging material provided for the fifth grade. On investigation it turns out that he can handle the fifth-grade vocabulary all right, but that much simpler words defeat him because he has skipped the second and third grades. He willingly and intensively practices himself on second- and third-grade material which is much below his level of maturity so far as content and interest are concerned, and which for him is relatively formal. And once more it is important both for his teacher and for him to know how well the drill is coming along. A whole group of children willingly routinize themselves on spelling lists because certain difficulties in preparing a class book have revealed to them the importance of such work. All this is simply a repetition of the proposition already made, that an awareness of direct results is beneficial to learning when it is germane to the purpose of the learner, and not otherwise.[2]

**3. Direct Evaluation of the Learning Process.** The beneficial effect of evaluation which emphasizes results, whether direct or involving transfer, is due to the influence of a knowledge of such results upon the process of learning. It is always the process that must be controlled, and there can be no doubt that a properly organized and administered awareness on the part of the pupil and the teacher of the results being achieved will be a constructive factor in so doing. Clearly, however, its effect although important is indirect, and good evaluation will also deal directly with the learning process while it is going on rather than being confined to a consideration of the results forthcoming.

Just what this means may be made clear by the following excerpts from a teacher's folder, comparing the processes of two children, one doing poorly, the other doing well.

STUDYING PROBLEMS IN CIVICS, HISTORY, GEOGRAPHY, AND SCIENCE

| | |
|---|---|
| Could not find questions to investigate in his study. Said he had read "some." | Proposed two large problems and two subquestions to class. |
| Sorted over books. Read here and there. Had no good references nor any data to report. | Brought article from home. Reported summary from encyclopaedia. Added two good references to list. |
| In laboratory today ruined beaver board by cutting without measuring. Bothered Fred so much that he complained. | In laboratory prepared excellent exhibit of process of manufacturing about which question had been raised. Got several other pupils interested in making exhibits. |

### Writing an Account of a Trip Taken by Class

Had lost questions set up before going. Took no notes during trip.

Had fitted questions together before trip and notes together. Wanted data on certain questions if others had it.

Read the pages that the teacher insisted on for further ideas. Wrote a paragraph.

Got into such interesting material that his whole plan for story had to be revised.

Said he'd make some copies of the stores and maps for the class book.

Suggested that class could plan a book from stories, take best out of each, and rework for good book.

### Problem Solving in Arithmetic

Played with pencil unless teacher personally helped him decide processes needed.

Tried to write parts given in problem and parts wanted in problem; found and tried processes.

Could not think of any home processes in fractions until teacher had asked many questions.

Wrote up five realistic home situations involving fractions and solved them. Used diagrams to illustrate.

Listened indifferently to class arguments. Worked on drill examples whenever free.

Started discussion on whether pupils needed arithmetic; got into arguments over expenses of recent trip.

Appeared bored when class discussed how to work at a story problem. Teacher later tried to help him apply his ideas.

Contributed to a teacher-led discussion on how to study a problem. Proposed they try it on certain problems in text.*

It is clear that such a direct scrutiny of the learning process is of great value in many respects. It suggests many searching questions for the teacher. For one of these pupils the organization is succeeding, and for the other it is not. Therefore to that extent it is defective. If the teacher can ascertain why, it can lead to an improvement of his work not only for these particular individuals but for other pupils later on as well. It is by dint of such realistic analysis, and not merely by year after year of repetitive experience, that a teacher becomes more expert, discriminating, and resourceful. Also such a scrutiny can put the teacher on the trail of the trouble with the pupil who is not doing well. What is wrong? What can be done about it? Can the teacher clear matters up by some changes in dealing with him? Can his parents be drawn into cooperation to explain and rectify the difficulty? One cannot always answer these questions out of hand, but it is always

* Selected and adapted from Inga Olla Helseth, *Living in the Classroom*, pp. 240–242, Edwards Bros., Inc., Ann Arbor, Mich., 1939.

intelligent to raise them on the basis of observed and pertinent facts.
Finally, a scrutiny of this kind can be valuable for the pupils themselves
—just as valuable as a knowledge of the results of their work, if not
more so.    It should certainly not be kept concealed from them.    Nor
should it be presented to them as an objective impersonal record.    On
the contrary, it should be handled as something to be discussed,
understood, and heeded.    And as far as possible and as fast as possible
they should be led to share in the making of it.    Such self-knowledge
can make success more beneficial because one sees how and why one is
succeeding and is thus helped to succeed in the future.    And it can lead
toward the correction and remedying of failure because one sees how
and why one fails.

It should perhaps be emphasized that nothing can be said against
the proper recognition of results in a scheme of evaluation.    In the
cases just partially described it is perfectly legitimate to make a record
of how much civics, history, geography, science, and arithmetic these
two children manage to learn.    Also, and even more obviously, it is
legitimate to record the extent to which they seem able to transfer and
apply what they have learned.    Indeed not to make such a record
would be preposterous for many reasons, one of which is that an awareness of achievement is a primary stimulus to purposive learning.    The
achievement of results is a highly important feature of learning and
should certainly be recognized.    But a scheme of evaluation which
recognizes nothing else omits matters which are also of the highest
importance, and is a defective instrumentality for shaping up the process of learning towards greater effectiveness.

The question of how to systematize a direct scrutiny of the learning
process—how to pick out its really significant and activating features
and how to discriminate between them and trivialities—is an important one.    Learning is an exceedingly complex affair, involving everything in the personality of the learner, and the reasons why people
sometimes succeed and sometimes fail are often by no means obvious.
This should be clear from the case material just cited, and indeed from
everything contained in these pages.    So one needs some kind of working plan or guide for the direct evaluation of learning.

There is certainly no one best plan or method, recognized as such.
In fact the literature of teaching is remarkably deficient in practical
and systematic plans of any kind for this particular purpose.    What is
wanted is a schematic account of learning, bringing out its determining
aspects, which can be used as a guide.    The analysis presented in this
book is in effect just such a schematic account, and it sets up categories—context, focalization, socialization, individualization, and

sequence—in terms of which the direct evaluation of the process of learning can be carried on.

For instance, in the paired cases cited above there are several examples of the good and bad use of context. One child had no good references and reported no data, whereas the other brought an article from home and reported a summary from an encyclopaedia. One child read the assigned pages, whereas the other assembled a great quantity of interesting material which transformed his treatment of the undertaking. One child could think of no home situations involving fractions, while the other presented five realistic situations of this kind.

Again there are several examples of effective and ineffective focalization. One child could not find questions to investigate in his study and simply read some, whereas the other proposed two large problems and two subquestions. One child lost the questions set up before going on a trip and made no notes, whereas the other had fitted the questions and the notes together. One was bored during a class discussion of how to work at a story problem, whereas the other contributed to a teacher-led discussion on how to study a problem. The general importance of considering focalization in any appraisal of a learning process is indicated by the following incident. A boy failed badly in an arithmetic test and was punished for it by his father. In the next test he did quite well, which seemed to indicate that punishment was the remedy. But then in still the next test he failed again. It turned out that in the first and third tests there were numerous zeros, but none in the second, and that he had never really understood the concept of zero and the method of dealing with it. The two failures were due, not to lack of seriousness or effort, but to a defect in focalized comprehension.

Once again, the principle of individualization is illustrated in the two contrasting cases. One child played with his pencil until the teacher personally showed him what techniques to use, whereas the other set up a purposive process of trial and error to discover an effective methodology. In fact, the impression throughout is of one person whose attitude is passive and whose reactions are stereotyped, and another who is actively discovering interests and techniques peculiarly his own. Also the differences in social attitude and reaction are equally clear cut, one person being a contributing member of a democratic group, and the other pretty much of a dead spot in the social pattern.

The only one of our categories or principles not exemplified in these two cases is that of sequence or growth, and the reason is that the record is not designed to bring it out. To do this the evaluation must be made continuously over a period of time, and changes in reactions and traits must be noted. One must ask whether the children are developing interests which become deeper and are followed up; whether their command of thought processes is becoming more precise and broadly inclusive; whether they show gains in the power of enjoyment; whether their activities tend to become more and more self-chosen and self-directed; whether their capacities for social action become more responsible and foresighted; whether their ability to work harmoniously and constructively with a group improves.

It should, perhaps, be pointed out that in a scrutiny of learning, all these five categories may very well be exemplified in a single reaction or observation. Thus, when a child ruins some beaverboard in the laboratory because he cuts it without measuring, one may say that the context lacks a compelling appeal so far as he is concerned, or that there is an insufficiently focalized understanding of what he is about so that he is only going through an unintelligible routine, or that he lacks a sense of responsibility to the group, or that he is working at something for which he is individually unfit, or that he is immature. All are principles that apply because they are simply different aspects of the same thing—meaningful learning.

Once again, it is not suggested that this systematization is the best to use in making young learners aware of the excellences and deficiencies of their own working processes. The categories or principles offer a set of guide lines for the direct evaluation of learning, and indicate the important respects in which it needs to go well and often goes badly.

Alternative schemes are perfectly possible, and often work out very well. For instance, it is often suggested that a teacher might well isolate certain traits of personality, such as initiative, responsibility, creativeness, the power to see broad relationships, the power to enjoy, cooperativeness, and so forth, and take note of their manifestation and development. The traits need to be carefully defined as actual and observable characteristics of behavior. When this is done they afford a very good and revealing set of categories for direct evaluation. Also they have the advantage of being, or seeming to be, understandable to pupils and parents. From the standpoint of the teacher they have the disadvantage of being less clearly and closely related to the process of meaningful learning and its problems than those just suggested. Of course these categories, like the foregoing and indeed like any that can be proposed, always overlap. A given success or failure in learning is sure to involve all of them and cannot be considered due to only one.

Some such systematic frame of reference for direct evaluation of the learning process is always desirable and useful. It is particularly helpful to the teacher, who whether consciously or not, has always gone on the assumption that the only thing to be noted in connection with learning is the result. Simply to tell such a teacher to scrutinize the process without making as clear as possible to him how to set about doing so is apt not to get very far. He needs something definite to start on, and something to work on. In the terminology of this book, he needs a focus in order to get under way toward acquiring this complex and unfamiliar new ability. As he gains in experience and insight he can cut loose more and more from any specific scheme of categories, and can make significant appraisals with increasing freedom and confidence. But no matter how expert or how sure of himself he becomes, a specific and defined frame of reference will still be useful, and he ought to make a point of returning to it from time to time, to correct one-sidedness and an unconscious tendency to notice only certain aspects of learning while forgetting others.

Whatever scheme he uses, however, he must always keep in the forefront of his mind one controlling consideration. Learning is essentially a purposive process. It stems from a conscious need or desire to control a situation through skill or insight or appreciation. It realizes this purpose or desire by integrating the situation about an intelligible focus. This purpose or desire is reinforced by proper socialization, conserved by proper individualization, and given increasing depth and spread by a sequence controlled by growth. This is how any job of learning must be understood if it is to be correctly and justly evaluated, and the relationship of just evaluation to it is to support, direct, and intensify the purpose in which its vitality resides.

### Notes and References

*General References on Evaluation*

Two excellent general references on evaluation are L. Thomas Hopkins, "Exploring New Avenues of Measurement," *Curriculum Journal*, Vol. 6 (1935) pp. 22–25; and L. Thoma Hopkins, *Interaction*, Chap. 10, "How Should Educational Outcomes Be Measured and Evaluated?," D. C. Heath and Company, Boston, 1941.

*References in the Text*

1. The general studies on the effect of knowledge of results in laboratory learning are G. F. Arps, "Work with Knowledge of Results versus Work without Knowledge of Results," *Psychological Monographs*, Vol. 28 No. 3, whole No. 41 (1920); William F. Book and Lee Norvel, "The Will to Learn," *Pedagogical Seminary*, Vol. 29 (1922), pp. 305–362; Verna M. Sims, "The Relative Influence of Two Types of Motivation on Improvement," *Journal of Educational Psychology*,

Vol. 19 (1928), pp. 480–484. The last of these compares competition with the records of others and competition with the learner's own record.

The studies dealing with the effect of knowledge of results in school learning are C. C. Ross, "The Influence upon Achievement of a Knowledge of Progress," *Journal of Educational Psychology*, Vol. 24 (1933), pp. 609–619; E. C. Deputy, "Knowledge of Success as a Motivating Factor in College Work," *Journal of Educational Research*, Vol. 20 (1929), pp. 327–334; Francis K. Brown, "Knowledge of Results as an Incentive in Schoolroom Practice," *Journal of Educational Psychology*, Vol. 23 (1932), pp. 532–552.

The study indicating the slight effect of very frequent testing is Vicor H. Noll, "The Effect of Written Tests upon Achievement," *Journal of Educational Research*, Vol. 22 (1939), pp. 345–348.

2. In regard to the problem of transferability, the reader is referred to note number 13, Chap. 4. The material on "parrot mastery" and general meaninglessness is from Flora Scott and Garry C. Myers, "Children's Empty and Erroneous Concepts of the Commonplace," *Journal of Educational Research*, Vol. 8 (1923), pp. 327–335, which is full of items both entertaining and arresting. Also the case is excellently presented by Ralph W. Tyler, "The Relation between Recall and the Higher Mental Processes," in Chalres H. Judd, *Education as Cultivation of the Higher Mental Processes*, Chap. 2, The Macmillan Company, New York, 1936.

### Items and Discussion and Study

*Refer to the two opening suggestions for discussion and study in connection with Chap. 5. Follow them out in connection with the principle of evaluation. Retain the outcomes in your notebook or card file.*

1. Do you agree that no test is good unless it has a good effect on learning? Should the same be true of the marking system?

2. It is often said that a good teacher makes his pupils independent of him. Is this the same as saying that he promotes self-evaluation? Is the idea sound?

3. Why is it that a series of objective tests in a course often does not, as investigation shows, have a very beneficial effect on learning?

4. When it is said that a knowledge of results is helpful only if the learner wants to attain them, is this the same as saying that the meaningful aspects of learning should be stressed in evaluation?

5. Would you agree that transferability is the acid test of learning? If so, devise ways and means of testing transfer in connection with the learnings in any school subject you choose.

6. Show how a pupil's discovery that what he has learned out of a book helps him in a practical situation, *i.e.*, transfers, may be expected favorably to affect his learning.

7. Apply the scheme for evaluating the learning process suggested in this chapter to some instances of your own learning. Is the plan helpful? Can you suggest modifications, improvements, better alternatives?

# CHAPTER 16

## THE PRINCIPLE OF EVALUATION AND THE APPRAISAL OF TEACHING

### PRINCIPLE OF EVALUATION: HIERARCHY

I  Evaluation on results only: chiefly direct results

II  Evaluation chiefly on results, emphasizing transferability and objectives: some attention paid to process

III  Evaluation on total learning process, including results

Evaluation, as we have seen, is the conscious and discriminating appraisal of learning for the sake of its improvement. This appraisal needs to be carried on by everybody concerned with the job of learning. But the learner's share in it is of primary and outstanding importance, because it bears upon the improvement of his own work.

An immediate consequence of this position is that evaluation must be considered and studied as a single, unitary function if the problems connected with it are to be intelligently approached. The proper techniques for the construction and administration of tests, the statistical methods for handling test results, the conversion of direct or "raw" test scores into a system of symbols which indicate their practical significance, and the recording and reporting of findings are all parts of the total process of evaluation. Since elaborate procedures are often involved, it is both proper and inevitable that specialized study should be given to all these matters. A specialized consideration of them is beyond the province of this book. What is here undertaken is to deal with evaluation as a whole, for procedures such as those just mentioned are only parts of it. No one of them constitutes its essence. It is of great practical importance for teachers to see the relationship of these parts to the whole. How should the single, unitary function of evaluation be managed if it is to fill its proper place in the economy of learning? That is the question here to be considered. And the hierarchy of applications shows how the principle of evaluation as stated is brought to bear with varying degrees of adequacy in actual working situations.

281

### THE FIRST LEVEL

The conventional marking system represents the first level of the hierarchy.   It is a scheme of evaluation which emphasizes nothing but results, and chiefly direct results.

The logic of the system is simple, clear, and unmistakable, although a great many teachers do not understand it as well as they might. Such an understanding, however, is very worth while.   For one thing, the system is very widely used, and so everybody in the business of education should know exactly how it operates and what its possibilities and limitations are.   For another thing, even experienced teachers often make extraordinarily crude blunders in connection with marking and entertain quite untenable ideas about it, all of which could be avoided if they understood its real nature.   Thirdly, if one feels dissatisfied with the conventional marking system, as many people do, one should know just what steps need to be taken to bring about an improvement and what changes are merely superficial and trivial.

The marking system is built on three definite postulates.   First, learners should be subjected to a uniform testing program.   This may contain written tests, oral tests, or both.   The essential point, however, is that it should be uniform for everybody.   Thus the testing program reveals the relative standing of the individuals in a group on a criterion of achievement which is the same for all of them.   This feature of relative standing on a uniform criterion is the first crucial aspect of the marking system.   Second, the differential relative standings revealed by the tests are converted into a system of symbols known as grades or marks.   This may be done by a stated formula, as for instance when the top 5 per cent are rated A, the next 20 per cent B, the next 50 per cent C, the next 20 per cent D, and the lowest 5 per cent F.   There are many such formulas in practical use, and not all of them require a symmetrical distribution of marks.   Or the conversion of differential test results into grade symbols may be done without any formula at all, on an impressionistic basis, in terms of the judgment or the whim of the teacher.   But whatever formula is used, or even if none at all is employed, the point is that there must be some way of deriving grades or marks from the test showings.   This is the second crucial feature of the marking system.   Then thirdly, these symbols or grades or marks are recorded and used for administrative and educational purposes, to determine promotions, awards, privileges, eligibilities, recommendations to other institutions, and so forth.

All in all it is a very clear-cut system, very understandable, very businesslike, and within its limits very workable.   In fact it is so clear and intelligible that there can hardly be much doubt when we come to appraise its values and limitations and its effect upon learning.

**1. Appraisal.** This type of evaluation orients learning expressly and entirely toward achievement on tests, oral or written, formal or informal. Teachers very often urge their pupils not to work merely for marks, and no doubt this is excellent advice. But the whole influence of the system is against it. Tests and marks are made decisively important in the pedagogical scheme of things, and the words of the teacher, by comparison, have very little weight. Anyone who may from time to time feel moved to give a group of pupils advice of this kind should understand that, although he may be quite right, he is in effect criticizing the system of evaluation itself. For if marks are not worth working for, it is hard to see why they should be given at all, and not only given but made extremely important, if we want well-organized learning.

Closely connected with this is the point that marking should be on tested achievement and on nothing else. Here is something upon which every important writer on the subject has insisted. There is no doubt that it is inescapably implied in the logic of the system. Effort, attitude, good and bad behavior, differences in ability, personal pleasantness or unpleasantness, cooperativeness or noncooperativeness, and all similar factors should be disregarded. The reason is that the marking system cannot take care of them. It provides no means whatever, systematic or otherwise, by which they can show up, be examined, considered, assessed, and recorded. It is an organized plan for dealing with just one thing—differential achievement on uniform testing—and within its limits and when properly used it does so very well.

It is interesting that while all students of the theory of marking insist that the only proper basis for it is tested achievement, teachers usually refuse to stick to any such limitation. They let all sorts of considerations influence their decision on a pupil's mark—their annoyance or pleasure over the way he acts, their sympathy for his sickness or dullness or earnest effort, even their fear of the influence of his parents. In terms of the strict rigor of the game, what this actually means is that the mark they assign is a falsification. It is as though one decided to put a small orange in with the big ones because one was sorry for it, or a big one in with the little ones because one felt annoyed. The marking system, like a thermometer, can register one thing. It can register achievement. And when one lets other influences enter in, it is as though one breathed on the thermometer or dipped it for a moment into cold water. Obvious though this seems to be, investigations have shown that there are something like forty factors other than achievement which teachers deliberately and consciously consider in making out grades.

In a wider sense, however, the refusal of practical teachers to stick to the criterion of achievement without any modification whatsoever is an implied criticism of the marking system itself, and just as genuinely so as telling pupils not to work for marks. One may properly classify oranges by size, and to be hard-boiled in such a matter is also to be honest. But human beings are not oranges, and there is much more to learning than its direct results. Teachers are perfectly right in wishing to take account of more than tested achievement. Where they are wrong is in trying to make a system of measurement and evaluation serve purposes for which it was never designed and which it cannot fulfill. It may be beyond their power to change the marking system, and perhaps the best they can do is to shade it. But they should never be in any doubt about the significance of their own actions. They are not marking correctly, for this can only be done on a basis of tested achievement, pure, simple, and unmodified. They are in effect sabotaging the system itself, perhaps justifiably.

2. The second point to make in appraising the current and conventional system of evaluation is that it orients learning towards relative standing. By the inescapable necessity of its logic this is all a mark expresses or can express. A mark of A in algebra tells nothing about how much algebra the pupil knows or ever has known. All that it can indicate is that he is in the upper 5 per cent or 3 per cent, or whatever the formula requires, of the group. A passing mark in a subject does not indicate that the pupil has a satisfactory mastery of it but only that he does not rate so low in the comparative scale that the teacher feels compelled to refuse him credit on the course. A very favorite practice in old-time schools was the spelldown. The class lined up, and tried to spell out words dictated by the teacher. If a word was missed by the first ten children, and was successfully spelled by the eleventh, he went to the top of the line. The marking system is a statistical sophistication and refinement of this procedure. Teachers often do not realize clearly just what it involves, because the children do not line up and shift places before their very eyes. The job is done by figures on paper which, like so many verbalizations, are apt to be more or less meaningless. But the computations do exactly the same thing as the changing order in the spelldown. If at the end of each course pupils were lined up in the classroom in the order of their total tested achievement, and then subdivided into groups to be designated A, B, C, and so forth, the true nature of the marking system would be better understood.

As a statistical technique the practice of rating on relative achievement is perfectly allowable. Many of our most important judgments in everyday life are made on a relative basis. Seven feet is tall for a man but short for a telephone pole. Seven hundred pounds is heavy for a pony but light for a Percheron. A hundred dollars is a lot of money for a teacher, but a bagatelle for a millionaire. So a fairly good showing on a test on quadratic equations is refreshingly creditable in a mediocre class in algebra, nothing remarkable in a very able class, and quite negligible in a group of graduate students specializing in mathematics. There is nothing wrong with the logic of judgments which use a certain group of people or other phenomena as a base line for relative determination.

The weakness of the practice, however, becomes evident in the light of the psychology of learning. It does not emphasize the learner's awareness of his own performance as such—its excellence, its limitations. It does not set up his own record as something for him to compete against. It throws him into conscious competition with the records of other people. It does not tell him how well he is himself doing in French, or algebra, or spelling. It merely tells him where he ranks in relation to how well other people are doing. There is an actual reported case which brings out excellently and absurdly this aspect of the marking system. A certain professor was known always to fail 5 per cent of all his classes. When a group of students came together for the first time in one of his courses, they counted noses and found that there were 19 enrolled. One, therefore, was doomed to fail no matter what happened. So they chipped in and paid the fees of one additional student, who entered the course on the understanding that he was to fail it. He did so, and the other 19 passed. Undoubtedly these students managed to learn something in the situation, but it was not at all what the professor intended. Nevertheless it was just what the organization of learning played up and suggested.

It need hardly be said, in the light of the psychological data discussed in the preceding chapter, that a scheme of evaluation which stresses intragroup competition and comparative standing, and which actually conceals the realities of the learner's own performance, is not likely to have a beneficial effect upon learning. That a knowledge of results can have a good effect upon learning is well established. But the sort of knowledge of results played up by the marking system is a travesty on the idea.

3. A third important aspect of the conventional system of evaluation is that it tends very strongly to orient the learner toward mechanical routines. This is not a logical necessity, but it is a practical con-

sequence. The reason is that technically sound tests are easiest to make when they deal with routine outcomes.

This is particularly true of "objective tests," so-called. The term "objective" is a misnomer because no test of any kind is any good, and does not even deserve to be called a test, if its result depends upon the subjective personal whim or feeling of the person who rates it. Every test, that is, must be within reason objective if it is to be a test at all. The term however, has become attached to a type of test calling for short answers or responses, such as filling in words, underlining of rearranging statements, indicating the truth or falsity of propositions, and so on.

The defense of objective tests has turned almost entirely on considerations arising from the theory of measurement. They can cover a great deal of ground in a given time, and thus make a good and representative sampling of the student's knowledge. The likelihood of hitting by chance upon matters that he knows or does not know and disregarding everything else is greatly reduced. This tends to bring about better reliability. Also a number of people rating a set of such tests will come out with the same scores, except for sheer errors in marking or counting; and this is the technical definition of objectivity.* But an instrument of evaluation stands or falls by its net effect upon learning, and here the objective test is open to most drastic criticism. It has been shown that in practice they lead to the most mechanical types of study—underlining, taking random notes, making lists of disconnected names, dates, facts, and words, and desperate attempts at routine memorization. There is no doubt that objective tests of a superior kind, calling for reflection, comparison, and judgment, can be made, and that their effect upon learning is very different. But there is equally no doubt that most teachers never make such tests whether they could or not, and that to do so calls for more time, thought, and ingenuity than the average teacher can find the energy to display.

It is known that the essay test has, on the whole, a much more favorable effect on study than the objective test as used in actual practice. Moreover many of the technical weaknesses of the essay test can be overcome. If one wants to use this instrumentality properly, the thing to do is to be very clear indeed about the values and standards on which the rating will be made. These values and stand-

---

* One sometimes suspects that the popularity of objective tests among teachers is due not to their technical superiority but to the fact that once made up they can be rated with a minimum of trouble, perhaps even by an assistant, and that students dissatisfied with their standing find it hard to argue against them.

ards should be actually written down, and the students also should understand what they are. Then the test papers must be read and reread with care, with the list of standards always at hand, so that one does not surreptitiously change one's values during the laborious process of marking, perhaps without even knowing it. When such common-sense precautions are taken, the essay test has a reliability about as high as that of ordinary objective tests, and a satisfactory objectivity as well. And one can feel some confidence that it will lead to better study procedures.

Even when technically well handled, however, the essay test is a limited instrument of evaluation. This is not a matter merely of opinion, but of well-attested demonstration. The essay test has a much better influence on learning than the objective test, stressing memory and routine as it usually does. But still it leaves much to be desired. One significant study investigated the choices made by college students when given a chance to select from a number of alternative essay questions in a final examination. It appeared that these students were not able to choose the best questions for them to answer, in the light of their preparation and actual knowledge. They had studied. They had studied in more than a merely routine and mechanical way. But they had not studied intelligently enough to know what they knew and what they did not know. No scheme or instrument of evaluation can be considered psychologically adequate unless it makes the learner aware of his own strengths and weaknesses.

**2. Steps toward Improved Practice.** Measures looking toward the improvement of the conventional system of evaluation are of two kinds: those looking toward an improvement in its technical efficiency without changing its character and those looking in the direction of a change in its essential nature.

Let us first consider improvements limited to increasing technical efficiency. These consist simply in realizing the essential logic of the marking system more completely, and putting it into operation more consistently. Attempts of this kind are numerous, and within limits they are no doubt desirable, for if a system is to be used at all it should presumably be used as correctly as possible.

1. First there are various proposals about the number and kinds of marks or grades to be given. Some schools use a numerical system running from 0 to 100, with a passing mark usually set somewhere in the neighborhood of 70. Others use an unmodified letter system, A, B, C, D, F with perhaps E included. Others again use a letter system modified by plus and minus signs. The point of the difference is not always very well understood. It turns upon the number of marks,

or steps, or categories in terms of which achievement is to be classified. Otherwise there is no difference at all, for the letters could just as well give place to numerals and the effect would be precisely the same. A numerical system with a passing mark set at 70 recognizes 31 kinds of passing work (70 to 100 inclusive) and an indefinite number of kinds of failing work, for most of the symbols from 0 to 69 are never used. An unmodified letter system recognizes four kinds of passing work, one kind of unconditional failure, and often one kind of conditional failure (E). From the technical standpoint there is no doubt that five categories are altogether more manageable than 31 plus. It is far harder to discriminate accurately between 70 and 71 on a 100-point numerical scale than between B and C on a five-point scale. Again technically speaking there seems no particular point in a letter system modified by plus and minus signs. It is no more than a sop to convention, and it gives rise to absurd controversies, for instance as to whether an A— is or is not a "kind of A," whereas it is neither more nor less than the third level of classification in a thirteen point system (A+, A, A—, B+, B, B—, C+, C, C—, D+, D, D—, F).

2. There is a wide variety of practice and much debate in regard to determining the statistical meaning of grades. Most teachers have heard about "grading on the curve," though apparently many of them do not really understand what it involves. To adhere to the normal probability distribution does not indicate what percentage of each grade shall be given, but only that the distribution shall be symmetrical about its central axis. Five per cent A, 25 per cent B, 50 per cent C, 25 per cent D, 5 per cent F, or 3 per cent A, 17 per cent B, 60 per cent C, 17 per cent D, 3 per cent F are both normal probability distributions. Theoretically the use of the probability curve in grading is impossible to defend. It is true that pure chance aggregates of events do so distribute themselves. But there is always selection of some kind at work in any school situation. And of course the whole point and effect of teaching is to disturb pure chance. Practically the idea of having some agreed values for the symbols of the marking systems seems sound, for otherwise there will be the wildest of vagaries. It must be understood that the whole meaning of a mark is determined by the proportion of people who are able to get it, and by nothing else. There is no such thing as "A work," or "C work" as such. There is only work better than that of 90, 95, or 97 per cent of all work evaluated, which is usually worth an A, or work better than 25 per cent of all that is evaluated but excelled by 25 per cent, which is usually worth a C. The school has a perfect right to legislate the value of its grades precisely as it chooses, for there

are no national standards and few regional or city-wide ones. All that can be said is that although a rigid adherence to the normal distribution is indefensible, it seems well to have some agreed standards if the system is to operate reasonably at all.

3. It is recognized as sound statistical practice to compute a grade only on the total showing of the pupil as revealed by the entire testing program of the course. That is, instead of thinking of a series of oral and written tests on each of which a mark is worked out, one should think of one complete block of testing running throughout the entire course, and one should compute the grades only when all test results are in. Interim grades at the end of six weeks or at mid-term are very commonly given, and of course the idea of letting the pupil know how his work is going is very sound, although this is rather a feeble way of doing it. But such interim grades should be rough, perhaps no more than statements that matters are going well, acceptably, or unacceptably, and they should be entirely tentative. It is definitely unsound to work out grades day by day and test by test, and then average them. All the raw scores of all tests should be assembled for a total picture, and then converted into grades.

4. Practice as to the announcement of grades differs greatly in different schools. In some institutions a mark is given every day in every subject, and entered in a ledger which is open to the inspection of anyone who may be interested. In others, all information about marks is withheld until the term is over. It would seem on principle that pupils ought to know what marks they are getting whenever the information is available and the marks have been computed. There is a good deal to be said for this as a matter of right and justice. But as a matter of psychology there is not so much to be claimed on its behalf. No doubt a knowledge of results stimulates learning. But as we have seen, a grade does not convey a true or direct knowledge of results but merely a knowledge of relative standing, which is a horse of quite another color.

These are the principal measures and proposals for the improvement of marking, although there are almost endless variants and details, to study which the reader must turn to treatises on educational measurement. They add up to improved efficiency. But they do not modify in the least the net effect of this system of evaluation upon the processes of learning. It remains a system which emphasizes direct results only, and which has the very grave defect of expressing those results in terms of relative standing rather than of actual personal achievement.

If one wants to improve the conventional system, not merely in the sense of making it more efficient within the limits of its logic, but in the wider sense of bringing to bear a more helpful and constructive influence upon learning, the steps which must be contemplated are very different.

1. One should work for a reduction of the number of different grades or marks in the system. A modified letter system (13 points), is better than a number system (31 points plus). An unmodified letter system (five or six points) is better still. And overlooking such administrative problems as the transfer of credit and taking a stand on purely psychological grounds, a three-point system is again still better (distinction, pass, fail). The reason is that the fewer the classifications the less testing it takes to get a student's work into the right pigeonhole. The ordinary numerical system, with its very numerous and fine classifications, is an incubus because it tends to transform every reaction the student makes into what is in effect a test, and concentrates attention with almost pathological fixity upon nothing but direct results.

2. One should work for an abandonment of all marking below the senior-high-school level, where the question of transfer of credit does not arise. This has been done successfully in a good many school systems, and the roof has not fallen, and pupils have continued to work and study at least as well as they ever did. For although grading may be abandoned, evaluation is not abandoned. And as it is hoped that the reader who has continued thus far with the present book is able to realize, there is more to teaching than evaluation.

3. One should, in any case, refrain from marking every day, or on every response that a pupil makes. Every response that a pupil makes is significant, and an ideal scheme of evaluation will take proper account of it. But not every such response by any manner of means is related to direct results, and it should not be so considered. The teacher with the omnipresent classbook, always watching and wondering what symbol to put down, applies a straitjacket to learning, and is himself failing to learn one of his own most important professional lessons, which is that pupils, when properly handled, really will work hard and learn well for something else than grades.

4. In making interim and short-term reports to pupils, one should as far as possible use direct records of achievement rather than marks which express achievement in terms of relative standing. The important thing for a pupil to know is how well he himself has done and how much better he might do, not how much worse or better he has done than Bobby Smith. There is no reason why this direct awareness of results cannot be cultivated and promoted, or for the matter of that

why pupils cannot have a large share in ascertaining and determining the results of their own efforts by cooperating in the setting up and scoring of tests, even in schools where the marking system is the prevailing official means of evaluation.

5. This leads directly to the last point to be mentioned, which is that the cooperation of pupils in the business of evaluation should be encouraged and built up in every possible manner. When a test is set it should be discussed carefully beforehand, its bearing on proper preparation and study brought out, and the character of the standards which it should legitimately involve considered by all concerned. After it has been given, its return should be treated as an important educative experience and event. A teacher who studies the question of evaluation in cooperation with his students not only brings to bear influences likely to benefit their learning but will almost certainly find himself steadily led away from evaluation based on direct results only, and toward practices which stand higher in our hierarchy of applications.[1]

### THE SECOND LEVEL

A major and fairly widespread attempt to improve evaluation has been made in recent years, by bringing it much more closely into relationship with the stated objectives of teaching, and by emphasizing such processes as analytic thinking, drawing inferences from data, applying principles, and the like, rather than routine memory. The most conspicuous instance here is the Eight Year Experiment in which 30 participating schools in various parts of the country were freed from rigid college entrance requirements, and so enabled to try out new practices in curriculum, instruction, guidance, and also evaluation. But the attempt to bring about improvement on the indicated lines has by no means been limited to this particular undertaking.

1. The crucial change has been an improvement in the construction of tests. Ordinary classroom tests made by teachers, it is pointed out, are usually very defective and crude. They often have many technical defects, such as debatable true-false statements, ambiguous completions, extreme brevity, and the like. Besides this they tend to center pretty exclusively on memory outcomes, because these are always easiest to handle in test form, particularly when short-response tests are being used. Thus it is very often found that they have low reliabilities and that they do not measure the desired objectives of the course with any reasonable approach to validity. This is probably just as true of the so-called "objective tests" that teachers make as it is of their essay tests.

As a corrective, a new procedure has been worked out. Groups of teachers, in which supervisors and administrative officers may or may not be included, begin by formulating very carefully the objectives or desired outcomes of the courses or teaching sequences for which they are responsible. These objectives are first stated in general terms— "To develop the capacity to draw inferences from data," "To develop the capacity to observe discriminatingly," and so on. Then they are defined still further in terms of actual concrete recognizable modes of behavior which such generalizations indicate. When this stage has been satisfactorily completed, technical experts in test construction are called in, and instruments of measurement are built by utilizing the types of behavior in which the objectives of the course realize themselves.

An actual instance or two will make clear just what is involved. The zoology department of The Ohio State University formulated goals for the elementary course as

(1) A fund of information about animal activities and structures. (2) An understanding of technical terminology. (3) An ability to draw inferences from facts, that is to propose hypotheses. (4) An ability to propose ways of testing hypotheses. (5) An ability to apply principles in concrete situations. (6) Accuracy of observation. (7) Skill in the use of the microscope and other essential tools. (8) An ability to express effectively ideas relating to zoology.

Test materials for 1, 2, and 8 already existed. Others needed to be worked out. In connection with constructing the test for Objective 3, lists of facts and findings from recent experimental work in zoology were assembled, and the test was made from selections from them. The general instruction to the student taking the test was as follows.

Suppose in each of the exercises which follow that the facts given were observed or known to be true. Write in the space below the facts, the one inference which seems to you most reasonable in attempting to interpret the facts. The sample illustrates this procedure. SAMPLE. *Facts*—starch when treated with iodine solution gives a blue color. When saliva is mixed with the starch and left for a time the mixture no longer turns iodine solution blue. *Inference*—Saliva produces a change in the starch.*

Another closely related test was the following:

In each of the following exercises several facts are given. After the facts are suggested a number of inferences. Supposing these facts are true, select the inference which seems to you the most reasonable and place a check mark in front of it as in the following sample. SAMPLE. Starch when treated with iodine solution gives a blue color. When saliva is mixed with the starch and

* Ralph W. Tyler, *Constructing Achievement Tests*, pp. 33–34, The Ohio State University Press, Columbus, Ohio, 1934.

left for a time the mixture no longer turns iodine solution blue. (a) Saliva turns starch to sugar. (b) Saliva turns iodine blue. (c) Saliva produces a change in the starch. (d) The color of saliva destroys the blue color. (e) Saliva has no effect on grape sugar.*

It is interesting to know that the correlations between scores on the two tests just described are low. This indicates that the process of proposing an inference is by no means the same as that of selecting one. Here also we see how sharply and realistically such tests can define the exact objectives contemplated by a group of teachers, and usually stated in language so general that it has little effect either on evaluation or on the emphasis of the teaching.

2. A second major point to notice about this type of evaluation is that it takes express cognizance of the transferability of what the student has learned. Indeed one of the essential ideas in developing the tests is to set up new situations which call for the application of the student's knowledge, or insight, or skill. This should already be evident from the examples just given, but another may serve to make it even clearer.

In a test designed for secondary school use, and aiming to measure the ability to apply scientific principles, the following typical examples occurred:

1. *A farmer grafted a Jonathan apple twig on a small Baldwin apple tree from which he had first removed all the branches. The graft was successful. If a new branch develops from a bud below the point of the graft and produces apples, what kind of apple will it be?* Here the student is asked to make a prediction about a situation in which presumably he has had no actual experience. It is presumed that if he understands certain laws of heredity, he will be able to make a valid prediction.

2. *All the leaves of a growing plant were observed to be facing in the same direction. Under what conditions of lighting was the plant probably grown?* This explanation requires that the student offer an explanation of observed phenomena. Some knowledge of the principles of photosynthesis, growth, and tropiatic responses of plants would be required for the solution of this problem.

3. *The rear of an automobile on a wet pavement is skidding toward a ditch. If you were the driver of the car, what would you do to bring the car out of the skid?* This problem requires the student to choose a course of action. A knowledge of the principles of centrifugal force and Newton's laws of motion would enable the student to choose a satisfactory course of action.†

* *Ibid.*, p. 34.
† Eugene E. Smith and Ralph W. Tyler, *Appraising and Recording Student Progress*, "Adventures in American Education," Vol. 3, pp. 81–82, Harper & Brothers, New York, 1942.

These and many similar problems were assembled, and worked over into the form of an objective test by an elaborate technique which may be studied by those interested if they refer to the indicated source. In connection with the Eight Year Experiment, for which the above was one of the instruments of measurement, a great wealth of such tests and items was accumulated. Clearly one of the important ideas behind such tests is to call for the application to new problems and situations of what the student has learned. Thus they take express cognizance of transferability.

The same kind of thing has been done from time to time on a much less ambitious scale, and as a matter of fact it is by no means beyond the capacity of any serious teacher who wishes to give thorough and proper attention to the very important matter of constructing the best possible tests. An instance is a final examination in geometry worked out by the teacher in charge of the course. It consisted of (1) sentence completions for testing knowledge of definitions, axioms, postulates, and a few theorems; (2) a number of statements about diagrams which were shown on the examination paper, these to be marked true or false; (3) a series of more general geometrical statements to be marked true or false with reasons being given for the choice of a response; (4) sets of data presented from which inferences were to be drawn; (5) formulas applied in specific computations; (6) analysis of the geometrical relationships in drawings of construction in carpentry, etc. Here again transferability is given strong and explicit emphasis.

3. A third noticeable feature of evaluation at this level is that, although it stresses chiefly results, it does to some extent reveal the process itself, or at any rate it is capable of so doing. Many of the tests expressly call for a statement of reasons for reaching a given decision or making a given statement. The following is a good and characteristic example.

A motorist driving a new car at night at the rate of 30 miles per hour saw a warning sign beside the road indicating a "through highway" intersection 200 feet ahead. He applied his brakes when he was opposite the sign and brought his car to a stop 65 feet beyond the sign. Suppose this motorist had been travelling at the rate of 60 miles per hour and had applied his brakes precisely as he did before. *He would have been unable to stop his car before reaching the "through highway" intersection.*

Below this statement a space was provided in which the student could place an A if he was uncertain about the italicized proposition, a B if he though it quite likely to be true, or a C if he disagreed. Then reasons for the response were requested. If a student put down A, indicating that he was uncertain, he was given ten reasons from which to choose in explaining his uncertainty—lack of experience in driving at 60 miles per hour, length of the run might depend on condition of the road, reaction time of the driver might enter in, mechanical efficiency of the brakes might be important, whether the brakes were mechanical or hydraulic might affect the result, the situation has too many variable factors for prediction to be possible, mathematical formula for the problem not known, distance run depends on the mass of the car as well as the speed, depends on the skill of the driver, condition of the tires a factor.

It may strike the reader that some of the alleged reasons for uncertainty listed in connection with this test item are somewhat foolish. But the idea itself is excellent. A test which not only emphasizes a result, but to some extent at least brings out the process by which that result has been achieved, has a genuine and undeniable value.

4. A final consideration in connection with this type of evaluative procedure is that it takes cognizance of a wide range of important factors. Instruments of measurement have been constructed which deal with thinking of various types, with social sensitivity, with aesthetic appreciation in many of its aspects, with interests, and with many factors of personal and social adjustment. There can be no manner of doubt that a program of evaluation which is tied closely to stated objectives, and which assumes that the large generalizations which adorn so many courses of study actually have a concrete and definite meaning and should be used as criteria, offers many advantages. Not the least of those advantages is the forcing of attention to a wide range of desired outcomes and a broadening of the whole basis away from the conventional narrow preoccupation with memory routines.

By way of general appraisal one may say that up to a point the scheme has incontestable values, but that it still leaves much undone. It requires teachers to think hard about the outcomes they desire, and to define those outcomes realistically. Also it tends to establish a meaningful and intelligible focalization in the working processes of the learners. Just what influence it has upon their study activities we do not know, but in all probability it is a favorable one. The plan undoubtedly has its uses.

But also it has its limitations. One might be inclined to criticize it because it demands a great deal of effort and skill on the part of the teacher, which it certainly does. But this cannot properly be considered a defect, for good teaching in general and good evaluation in particular can never be easily and automatically done, and both require thought and hard work. The true criticism is that as actually put into operation it gives the learner himself almost no share in establishing the values toward which he works and in terms of which his work is to be judged. Everything is determined for him, and virtually nothing by him. The scheme of evaluation is not set up in such a way as to embody and express his own working purposes. This is a very serious and vitiating limitation indeed, and it affects the plan adversely at every point. For instance, a real attempt is made to recognize transferability, but it is always transfer to predigested and described situations, not to real ones. The assumption is that the test of learning is to transfer it to a situation verbally presented, whether one is concerned with it or has a sense of participating in it or not. This, to say the least, is questionable. A child's grasp of biological principles would be far more convincingly revealed if he had to cooperate in the actual grafting of an apple tree in a school garden or a neighbor's orchard than by a paper-and-pencil response to a described problem about grafting. And the difference is not merely that one situation is concrete and the other verbal, but that one situation engages purpose far more effectively than the other.

So the suggestion would be to informalize the whole procedure, to enlist the active cooperation of the pupils in the actual making of the tests, and above all to rely on a multiplicity of situations in which learning and achievement can naturally manifest themselves even though they do not lend themselves to exact statistical appraisal, rather than confining evaluation chiefly to written tests however thoughtfully and skillfully constructed.[2]

## THE THIRD LEVEL

Evaluation which adequately meets the psychological conditions discussed in the preceding chapter points steadily toward understanding the pupil as a learner as completely as possible, and toward enabling him to understand himself in the same way. This, of course, means understanding him as a person, for the pupil is precisely a person who learns, and must be so considered and so handled.

Evaluation of this kind involves a great deal more than a system of making records and keeping educational accounts. It requires the development, both in the teacher and the learner, of a discriminating sense of the relative importance of things. Nevertheless, the bookkeeping scheme has a great influence upon the minds both of teachers and pupils. It may constantly tend to narrow down their attention to a few factors, an instance being the conventional marking system which so strongly features direct results expressed in comparative standings or rankings that nothing else is apt to be considered. On the other hand, it may constantly tend to throw into relief the many other factors in a learning situation which are of at least equal importance. Then too, the scheme of recording and accounting constitutes a concrete starting point for teachers who want to know what to do if they are to apply the principle of evaluation at the highest level of adequacy. So we shall begin by describing a workable plan for the making and keeping of records which can be satisfactory, although it is by no manner of means the only possible good one. Then we shall consider the kind of questions about the learner and his learning for which this or any other working scheme must be capable of furnishing answers if it is to be good. Finally we shall consider what effect evaluation as so conceived and described has upon the total organization of learning.

**1. A Working Plan.** Many attempts are being made today to improve evaluation by devising better systems of records. Various educational agencies, including some important school systems, are putting out record blanks and report blanks to be filled in for individual pupils. They vary a good deal in layout and detail, and many of them are useful and in any case well worth examining. However, they tend to have the rather serious defect of rigidity, which means that teachers will often find them at least partially inapplicable. Moreover they sometimes include rather elaborate and finely divided listings of traits, personal qualities, types of achievement, and so forth, and this can constitute a very marked difficulty. Not only is it often hard to classify the responses of pupils as the blank requires, but the kind of statements which one makes when this classification has been done can seem less significant and helpful than what one could say without such detailed directions. So, in the scheme here described, it is recommended that instead of using one or other of the published blanks for rating and recording the responses of pupils, the teacher set up a folder for each member of the class, and proceed to assemble relevant information in it. This is much more flexible, and has the advantage of calling for a minimum of clerical work.

What should go into the folder? That, of course, is the crucial question. The recommendation is that as it builds up it should contain nine chief types of material.

1. The pupil's folder should contain his entire scholastic record. This should be available at any time to any teacher who is dealing with him. In most cases this means simply a record of marks in various subjects, which is far from satisfactory. As evaluation improves throughout a school or a school system, the available

scholastic record itself naturally tends to become more significant and adequate. Nevertheless it would be a great mistake to ignore the pupil's marks in the various subjects, as they furnish at least a starting point in understanding and helping him. They are very indirect and imperfect symbols of achievement, and as the marking system is actually used it is often impossible to say exactly what they mean. But they indicate strength and weakness and the location of trouble spots, and they suggest many questions in dealing with a child.

2. The pupil's folder may very well contain an autobiography. It has been found successful, early in the term, to have the members of the class write autobiographical statements, the teacher explaining that this is one good way to get acquainted, and offering to tell about himself and his concerns when they have told him about theirs. It is nearly always necessary to set up some organized plan for the writing of these autobiographies, and this can be done by putting sets of questions on the board or dictating them, although of course the pupil should be free to mention anything he likes even if the questions do not touch upon it. Himself, his family, his home, his education up to date and educational plans, his interests, his occupational preferences, his group contacts and memberships are more or less the chief points to be considered, although they will need a good deal of breaking down and specific definition if some of the pupils are to give any helpful account of themselves.

3. The folder should by all means contain material which throws as much light as possible upon the child's capacity to learn. If general tests of intelligence and aptitude are given in connection with the guidance program, the results for each individual child should be transcribed in suitable form and placed in his folder so that they may be readily available at all times. But even if no such general tests are given there is still much that the teacher can do to ascertain the learning capacity of his pupils; and no matter how adequate the testing may be, it always needs to be supplemented by data from firsthand observation and personal contact.

There are two indications of general capacity to learn which are definitely significant and which can readily be noted by the teacher. First there is the relationship between diligence and achievement. The child who consistently works hard and faithfully and whose attendance record is good, but whose attainment is only mediocre is quite probably a scholastically limited person. If, however, he seems to get places with comparatively little toil and trouble, the reverse is probably the case. The second indication is the child's vocabulary, which is usually considered the most important single sign of academic aptitude. It is well within the capacity of the teacher to take both these indications into account. Furthermore, attention should be paid to the attack made by the pupil upon the work and activities of the grade or class in which he is placed. This is a further indication of general capacity, and it should also do much to reveal his special individual trends and strengths and weaknesses. The more the work is routine, uniform, and exactly the same for all, the less it will reveal special capacities. The more it consists of diversified undertakings organized about a core of group thinking and contribution, the better it will do so, because then initiative, interest, choice, and differential methods of work are given a chance to display themselves.

It should always be remembered that capacity to learn is not an abstract and isolated faculty, unaffected by circumstance and background. Thus the material under this heading should include environmental factors which affect learning. The kind of cultural and intellectual stimulus furnished by the home is very important. So are the child's social and personal relationships with his classmates and his teacher. So is his general emotional adjustment, as is shown by the case of a boy who began to fail hopelessly in fourth-grade arithmetic because of a violent antipathy built up in the second grade. In this connection, attention should always be paid to the child's physique, for physical defects, and particularly concealed and unsuspected difficulties in sight and hearing, and concealed malnutrition and fatigue are often primary causes of failure in school.

4. The folder should contain samples of the pupil's work and records of his activities. This is one of the easiest points at which to begin developing an active cooperation between pupil and teacher, because the pupil and his parents are readily interested in placing on file concrete evidence of his improvement and growth. Besides schoolwork, a record of outside activities such as voluntary reading, hobbies, club memberships, and the like can well be included. The pupil can readily be led to cooperate in keeping material of this kind up to date.

5. The folder should contain reports of interviews and conferences with parents and pupils. Such interviews and contacts are often far more important to the pupil than the teacher easily realizes. In them a mutuality of understanding can sometimes be created in a matter of minutes which might never build up at all in ordinary classroom relationships.

6. The folder should contain reports of the doings and reactions of the pupil in natural situations. Such "anecdotal records," so-called, must of course center on significant aspects of the pupil's behavior.

It has been suggested that happenings most worthy of the teacher's attention are those which reveal fortitude, responsibility, open-mindedness, originality and initiative, influence or leadership, self-control, self-direction, fair play, consideration for others, cooperation, persistence, and ability to face failure objectively. Here again cooperation between teacher and pupil can readily be developed, for the child's own comments on his behavior are often highly significant and well worth eliciting and recording. It may be remarked that in recording all behavior episodes a standard form should be used so that the name of the child, the name of the observer, the date, and an indication of whether the recorded behavior is typical of the individual always are written down.

7. The folder should contain records of all physical and medical examinations. The importance of physical condition for successful work in school has already been pointed out.

8. The folder should contain a record of group achievement which shows the standing of the child in the group. The reason is that in general the child's adjustment as an individual is greatly influenced by the kind of group with which he is associated. A slow reader in a fast reading group presents quite a different problem from what he does in a slow reading group. As a matter of clerical practice, the general group record may perhaps best be mimeographed, so that a copy can be inserted in each individual folder.

9. From time to time, and at approximately set dates which act as a check to negligence and forgetting, the teacher should make cumulative summaries and appraisals of all the material accumulated in the pupil's folder. The summary should give as full a picture as possible of the personality and present development of the pupil, indicating his strong and weak points and his needs, and suggesting desirable goals and the next steps to be taken in achieving them.\*

What has been presented is by no manner of means the only possible good plan. It may not even be the best plan. In some small and specially favored schools recording and educational accounting are made considerably more elaborate, and presumably yield better information. But it is typical procedure in evaluation at the third level of our scale.

**2. Questions That the Record Should Answer.** The important consideration is not the form in which records are made and kept but the questions which they are capable of helping to answer. Evalua-

---

\* The above recommendations are a condensation of the working plan presented by Ruth Strang, *Every Teachers' Records*, pp. 13–43, Teachers College, Columbia University, Bureau of Publications, New York, 1936.

tion is far more than a set of clerical techniques, necessary though they may be. It calls for skillful discrimination and a recognition of what matters and what does not matter. An adequate set of evaluative records should be built up with a view to throwing light at any time on the following questions about the pupil.

1. To what extent are his own authentic purposes being elicited, encouraged, carried forward, and realized? This, of course, is basic, because without purpose effective learning and authentic results are impossible. Is there evidence in the total pattern of the pupil's behavior that he is learning because he wants to learn? Are strong and definite interests manifesting themselves? Do they carry forward and realize themselves in achievement? If not, why not? Is it because the context or setting of the learning has no dynamic appeal because it is very meager and limited, or too purely verbal? Is it because of some defect in focalization which makes achievement impossible and thus defeats and negates interest and purpose? Instances would be a failure to progress in arithmetic because the child never gets away from counting on his fingers or never grasps the meaning of zero, failure to progress in algebra because the true significance of variability (the symbol $x$) is never grasped, failure to progress in reading because of persistent lip movement, failure to master punctuation because of concentration on unintelligible rules, and so on. It is no use advocating interest and purpose and then frustrating them by impossibilities. Is it due to some failure in social relations and contacts, or to some unfortunate and frustrating social or personal experience? Before everything else a good set of evaluative records should reveal the authenticity of purpose, and the factors which tend to support or to nullify it.

2. Is the child showing evidences of mental and personal growth? Are his activities becoming more self-chosen and self-directed? Is he making more and richer thought connections in his work? Does he show gains in his power of enjoyment in literature, the arts, and other studies? Is he moving toward an increasing acceptance of responsibility in a free group situation? Is he coming gradually to be aware of and to seek larger social ends?

3. Is he developing capacity for self-evaluation? Does he react to failure by analysis and experimental readjustment? By seeking help on his own initiative? Does he react to success by showing interest in how it was attained and how it may be continued? Does he tend to plan and organize his own practice and study? Does he select and use suitable practice materials? Does he show signs of being aware of his own needs in the matter of practice, and of doing

something about those needs? Does he plan, work, and study with his fellow students, seeking help from them and in turn helping them when so desired?

4. Is it possible to derive from the records, or at least with their help, a fairly complete picture of the pupil as a person and a learner? Anything in the personality can affect learning, and thus in ideal everything should be considered. The whole program of evaluation should build up toward a cooperatively developed picture of the learner, including his health and physical characteristics, his mental and emotional traits, his home relationships, his relationships with his fellows, his interests and hobbies and actuating goals, and his reactions to school situations. It must be emphasized once more that learning is not an isolated process but an activity which engages the whole personality, so that a scheme of evaluation which is to have maximum effect must take into consideration the entire range of personal factors.

**3. Implications for the Pattern of Teaching.** Clearly a scheme of evaluation which undertakes to scrutinize crucial aspects of the learning process implies a situation in which those aspects can really manifest themselves. It is a farce to tell a teacher to look for initiative and cooperation if he has established a situation which calls only for uniform obedience and subservience. The statement has been made that when high-school students study they hardly ever do anything except follow specific directions. But the answer may very well be that no organized effort is made to give them much chance to do anything else. If it is true that effective learning has certain crucial aspects upon which evaluation should concentrate, then the whole organization of learning which is teaching should be built around them. For evaluation is not a process independent of teaching but, rather, one of the principles which must determine its proper operation.

To be specific, consider what is involved in saying that good evaluation will determine the extent to which self-evaluation is manifesting itself. This necessarily implies that self-evaluation will be consciously promoted in the organized plan of operation. The following procedures for doing so have been suggested:

1. Recognizing the free oral expressions which are helping the class to do good work.
   a. Thoughtful remarks and questions by pupils.
   b. Materials found and reported by pupils.
   c. Suggestions and plans for self and class.
   d. Leadership in organizing the thinking the class does together in class periods.
2. Recognizing the writings and other graphic expressions having creative tendencies.

    *a.* Guiding individuals to use in class discussions the illustrative material made by themselves—maps, charts, drawings, constructions, and demonstrations.

    *b.* Connecting classwork with songs, poems, dramas, or descriptive bits produced by individual members.

    *c.* At times, bringing teacher's creative work to share with pupils.

    *d.* Practicing the habit of encouraging spontaneous constructive and appreciative comments when work of others is seen or heard.

    *e.* Exhibiting with sympathy and cordiality, pieces of creative adult work or accounts of such.

    *f.* Arranging opportunities for pupils to express informally their own judgments on various types of products.

    *g.* Arranging for carefully planned class analyses of products and processes.

    *h.* Encouraging in pupils the freedom to call together a group of pupils for the purpose of getting the judgment of their peers on a certain type of work while in the process of doing the work.

3. When making required assignments, teacher and class suggesting concrete possibilities of further free contributions of members in the field of the assignment.

    *a.* Until habit is formed in pupils, the teacher specifying times and occasions when a pupil may, in place of routine performance, substitute work according to his own judgment and taste in working in a field if he has the initiative to substitute.

    *b.* Steadily encouraging pupils to propose variations for self and others.

4. Setting up the form by which pupils may express judgments on certain types of products on which all are working or on a process in which all are at the moment occupied.

    *a.* The class setting up standards and analyzing their processes and the results of their efforts against these standards.

    *b.* Teacher making charts to indicate lines of growth and concrete steps up in each line and leading pupils to watch their own process in light of these steps.

    *c.* Pupils compiling successive samples of their own work for the purpose of studying growth concretely.

5. Keeping an analytical private file which any given pupil may see only so far as it concerns himself.

    *a.* Teacher or pupil listing successful struggles of the pupil.

    *b.* Teacher or pupil listing what he needs to work to overcome.

    *c.* Teacher or pupil recording diagrammatically pupil's weekly march of conquest.

6. Pupils and teachers making and using various objective forms for studying processes and results.

    *a.* Pupils checking and recording results after teacher has made objective practice exercises with keys.

    *b.* Pupils making objective exercises for each other's use.

    *c.* Pupils making and using games whose score records are really test scores.

    *d.* Pupils comparing their products with those in commercial scales.

    *e.* Pupils making scales from their own products.

    *f.* Pupils, with teacher guidance, expressing criteria and other forms, and analyzing by their use.

**7.** Pupils participating in using standard tests.

   *a.* Bringing their own money for purchase of tests.

   *b.* Joining teacher in scoring tests and interpreting results.

   *c.* Cooperating in proposing remedial efforts and further testing for themselves.

8. Teacher and class informally making comparative analyses of similar pieces of work that all pupils have done.

   *a.* Making summaries at critical points.

   *b.* Developing plans for next step in classwork.

   *c.* Reviewing plans for pupil's individual work on a class project.

   *d.* Organizing conclusions from class study of a problem.

   *e.* Recording results from long continued studies.

   *f.* Expressing ideas for a written organization of ideas.*

This illustration seems ample to establish and explain the point at issue. If learning is to be properly evaluated it must be properly organized. If certain aspects of learning are worth noticing they are also worth emphasizing. For here, just as much as at the lower levels of the hierarchy, the effect of evaluation upon learning is the paramount consideration.[3]

### Notes and References

1. The following general references deal with the marking system, and explain its logic and its practical operation. F. W. Johnson, *The Administration and Supervision of the High School*, Chap. 15, "The Marking System," Ginn and Company, Boston, 1925; James L. Mursell, *The Psychology of Secondary School Teaching*, Chap. 15, "How to Construct and Use Examinations," W. W. Norton & Company, Inc., New York, rev. ed., 1939; C. W. Odell, "Marks and Marking Systems," *Encyclopaedia of Educational Research*, pp. 697–703, The Macmillan Company, New York, 1941. The general effect of the marking system upon learning is discussed by R. A. Norsted, "To Mark or Not to Mark," *Journal of Education*, Vol. 121 (1938), pp. 81–84. The more specific effect of various types of tests upon learning is discussed in the following: George Meyer, "An Experimental Study of the Old and New Types of Examinations. I. The Effect of the Examination Set on Memory," *Journal of Educational Psychology*, Vol. 25 (1934), pp. 641–661; George Meyer, "An Experimental Study of the Old and New Types of Examinations. II. Methods of Study," *Journal of Educational Psychology*, Vol. 26 (1935), pp. 30–40; George Meyer, "The Effect on Recall and Recognition of the Examination Set in Classroom Situations," *Journal of Educational Psychology*, Vol. 27 (1936), pp. 81–99; Paul Terry, "How Students Study for Objective and Essay Tests," *Elementary School Journal*, Vol. 33 (1933), pp. 592–603; Paul Terry, "How Students Study for Three Types of Tests," *Journal of Educational Research*, Vol. 27 (1934), pp. 333–343; Harl Douglass and M. Talmadge, "How University Students Prepare for New Type Examinations," *School and Society*, Vol. 39 (1934), pp. 318–320. The responses of students to a choice of questions are discussed by George Meyer, "The Choice of Questions in Essay Examinations," *Journal of Educational Psychology*, Vol. 30 (1939), pp. 161–171.

   * Inga Olla Helseth, *Living in the Classroom*, pp. 226–229, Edwards Bros., Inc., Ann Arbor, Mich., 1939.

2. The following references on the cooperative preparation of tests closely related to the objectives of the course and stressing higher mental processes are particularly valuable. Manley E. Irwin and Paul T. Rankin, "The Cooperative Preparation of Improved Examinations," *School Review*, Vol. 39 (1931), pp. 112–122 (an early study which presents the total idea very clearly); Eugene E. Smith and Ralph W. Tyler, *Appraising and Recording Student Progress*, Harper & Brothers, New York, 1942 (one of the volumes of the report on the Eight Year Study and the most important source on the whole topic); Ralph W. Tyler, *Constructing Achievement Tests*, Ohio State University Press, Columbus, Ohio, 1934 (a concrete report on earlier work of the same kind); L. E. Raths, "Evaluating the Program of a School," *Educational Research Bulletin*, The Ohio State University, Vol. 17 (1938), pp. 60–84 (a revealing account of the application of these techniques in the "Lakeshore School"); L. E. Raths, "Techniques for Test Construction," *Educational Research Bulletin*, Ohio State University, Vol. 17 (1938), pp. 85–114. Vera Sanford, "A New Type Final Geometry Examination," *Mathematics Teacher*, Vol. 18 (1925), pp. 22–36, uses essentially the same ideas and has much to report and suggest that is of value to the working teacher. Ralph W. Tyler, "The Relation between Recall and the Higher Mental Processes," in Charles H. Judd, *Education as Cultivation of the Higher Mental Processes*, Chap. 2, The Macmillan Company, New York, 1936, stresses transferability and the measurement of meaning in tests of this type.

3. For treatments of evaluation at the highest level see Ruth Strang, *Every Teacher's Records*, Teachers College, Columbia University, Bureau of Publications, New York, 1936; Inga Olla Helseth, *Living in the Classroom*, Edwards Bros., Inc., Ann Arbor, Mich., 1939, particularly from p. 185 on; Carleton Washburne, *A Living Philosophy of Education*, Chap. 6, "The Function of the Psychologist, Pediatrician and Consellor," The John Day Company, New York, 1940; Wendell Cranston Allen, *Cumulative Pupil Records*, Teachers College, Columbia University, Bureau of Publications, New York, 1943; Anna B. Foreman, "Report Card for Evaluating Progress of the Whole Child," *Elementary School Journal*, Vol. 40 (1940), (pp. 195–205; Ida Grace Ball, "An Evolutionary Report Card," *Progressive Education*, Vol. 12 (1935), pp. 89–94; A. E. Hammalainen, "Existing Practices in the Evaluation of Pupil Growth in the Elementary School," *Elementary School Journal*, Vol. 40 (1941), pp. 175–183. These, taken together with the general references given at the opening of the preceding chapter, should give the reader a good idea of what is being proposed and attempted.

## Items for Discussion and Study

*Refer to the opening suggestion for discussion and study in connection with Chap. 6, of course substituting Chap. 15 for Chap. 5. Follow it out in connection with the principle of evaluation. Retain the outcomes in your notebook or card file.*

1. Discuss the commonly given advice not to work for marks.

2. Why should marking be only on tested achievement? What does the very common violation of this rule imply?

3. Why does the marking system make it difficult to organize cooperative situations?

4. Does our discussion of marking show why such failures to learn as those indicated in Chap. 2 may be common, and yet most pupils pass their courses? What does this imply about the marking system as an instrument for the organization of learning?

5. Would it be possible to have a good examination in which pupils were perfectly free to use notes and references, and even to discuss their answers with others? Could it still be a real and stringent test? What would it do to the problem of cheating? What would be its probable effect on learning?

6. Does your own experience with the effects of objective and essay tests on learning correspond with the research results cited in the chapter?

7. Would the various proposals for the merely "businesslike" improvement of the marking system discussed on pp. 287–289 make marking "fairer"? Would this mean an improvement in its influence on learning?

8. If the more fundamental type of changes discussed on pp. 289–291 were made in the marking system, would this mean that pupils would cease to study hard?

9. How satisfactorily and completely do such tests as those described on pp. 293–295 take care of the problem of transferability, and show whether or not transfer is being attained? Of the evaluation of one's own processes? Can you suggest the limitations of such tests and also better ways of getting at the two factors mentioned?

10. Check over the items recommended on pp. 297–300 as desirable to include in a pupil's folder. How would you rate their relative importance? If you could not include them all, which would you discontinue first? Which would you retain to the very last?

11. Consider the specific kind of evidence you would want to throw light on the various questions about a pupil which his record folder should reveal.

# CHAPTER 17

## SYNTHESIS AND APPLICATION OF THE PRINCIPLES OF TEACHING

### THE INTERRELATIONSHIP OF THE PRINCIPLES

Up to this point the organization of learning has, in the main, been considered analytically. Its various aspects have been separated out from one another, defined, and explained. The effectiveness of teaching—its success in producing authentic results—depends upon context, focalization, socialization, individualization, sequence, and evaluation. These are the determining considerations both in the appraisal of teaching situations and in the planning of them. To be sure, they are all branches springing from the same trunk. *The effectiveness of learning depends upon its meaningfulness.* If one asks how to go about organizing learning for maximum meaningfulness, and so for maximum effectiveness and the best and most authentic results, these are the six practical aspects of the problem, not one of which can be neglected. So the six principles of successful teaching are in fact very intimately interrelated. Indeed they merge into one another continually, for they are simply different ways of looking at the same process—the process of meaningful learning. But so far, each one of them has been examined more or less in isolation from the others, although attention has from time to time been called to their mutual bearings.

If, however, one wants to appraise a job of teaching that has been described, or observed, or conducted by oneself, then all the six principles are involved. In the same way they are the guide lines for good and intelligent planning. One cannot give thought to a few aspects of the situation and ignore the rest without coming out with a misleading appraisal, or an unbalanced and disappointing plan. So the unity whose theoretical basis in the psychology of learning was set forth in the four opening chapters of this book is clearly a vital, practical consideration. Having derived the principles of successful teaching from a single, central idea, and having examined each of them one by one, it now becomes necessary to show how they come together in practical applications.

307

## THE ANALYSIS OF PROPOSALS, METHODS, AND DESCRIBED SITUATIONS

Teachers in service and students preparing to teach are often presented with verbal accounts of proposed procedures, methods, types of organization, and model situations. They are told about the individual laboratory method or the lecture demonstration method in science, the direct method or the reading method in foreign language, the syllable method of teaching music reading, the project method, and a whole variety of unit methods. Sometimes words like "approach" or "idea" are used in preference to the word "method," because they seem less rigid and restricting and cut-and-dried, as when we read of the phonic approach in elementary reading, or the creative approach in art, or the activity idea in general. The terminology does not matter a great deal, for to a large extent it is a matter of fashion, and it should not be allowed to become a cause of confusion. For essentially what is conveyed is some sort of operating scheme or proposal for organization, often worked out in considerable detail with suggestions for specific steps and other procedures, and presented with the thought that teachers and intending teachers will examine it for the benefit of their own work.

If they are to do this repayingly, however, they must proceed in terms of some well-founded plan. A vague, over-all examination of some scheme for the organization of learning is not likely to yield very worth-while opinions as to its excellences and defects, its possibilities and limitations. One is apt to come out with nothing more helpful than a general feeling that one likes or dislikes it, that it is good or bad, or perhaps that it is modern and progressive or old-fashioned and conservative. This does not touch the real question, which is its promise as a plan for bringing about effective learning and authentic results. Even to begin to get a valid answer to this question, an intelligently directed analysis is necessary. The six principles which have been discussed provide a working method for precisely such an analysis. And when they are brought to bear on the very practical problem of analyzing a described scheme for the organization of learning, their unity and essential interdependence at once become apparent. These two interrelated points, that our six principles provide an illuminating method for the analysis of teaching proposals, and that in such analysis their unity becomes apparent, will be borne out by a few illustrations.

Consider first a classic proposal that is still influential and also interesting and instructive for its own sake, the inductive development lesson already characterized in these pages. To be specific, let us deal with a lesson of this type devoted to developing the definition of the adverb. The plan calls for a series of steps or stages, fairly clearly characterized.

(1) First comes *preparation*, in which the already available relevant knowledge and experience of the learners is called to mind. The suggestion here is to review other parts of speech already studied, emphasizing particularly the verb and the adjective. (2) Out of preparation comes the *statement of aim*, which sets up the problem for what follows. It consists characteristically of a question, preferably asked by the pupils, but at any rate provoked by conversation and discussion. Here the suggested question runs, "The adjective makes clearer the meaning of the noun; is there a class of words that will help the verb in a similar manner?" (3) With the third step, that of *presentation*, the learners deal with new experiences and materials in and through which they may move toward an answer to the question which has already been raised. Here the new material consists of sentences written on the blackboard or otherwise conveyed, and handled in such a way as to highlight the adverbs. (4) Next comes *comparison and abstraction*, in which the presented adverbs are isolated and scrutinized for common characteristics and differences. (5) Next comes *generalization*, which here takes the form of an achieved definition: "An adverb is a word used to modify a verb by answering one of the questions, How? When? Where?." (6) Finally there must be *application*, *i.e.*, the use of the achieved generalization in new situations—in this case the identification of adverbs in new sentences.*

The first reaction, perhaps, is to say that the method is extremely old-fashioned and that it has gone largely out of use, at least in its standard form. This would, however, be highly unintelligent. The plan is just as good and just as bad as ever it was, and we can learn just as much from it today as people could when it was first proposed. Indeed the purpose in selecting it for treatment was partly to bring out this very point. Obviously what is indicated is a correct analysis, not an appraisal on the basis of convention.

The essence of the plan is the emergence and establishment of a generalization in a setting or context. The focus appears in the second step, the statement of aim. It is in the form of a question, which leads to a process of exploration and discovery moving towards an answer. This is perfectly sound so far. But if the context is not concrete, dynamic, simple, and copious, the focus itself will not have the aspect of a genuine and compelling problem which challenges curiosity and mobilizes powerful motives. It will be merely a verbal-

* This example is adapted from William C. Bagley, *The Educative Process*, Chap. 19, The Macmillan Company, New York, 1917.

ized question with a minimum of meaningfulness, and the succeeding process will fail of its intent. This is just about what seems apt to happen in the light of the context proposed for the preparation and the presentation. The fourth and fifth steps of the lesson, which carry through the focalization to a solution, are very likely to be verbal exercises and little more. Socialization, again, is explicitly recognized only in the first two steps, where the statement of aim or focus is evoked by conversation and discussion calling up existing knowledge. Little else, however, seems feasible, because of the prevailingly verbal character of the context and focus. If the whole organization were transformed into a group attempt to clarify and perfect some statement which it was urgently desired to make as good as possible, with particular attention for the time being to adverbs, context and focus would become highly meaningful, and social discussion and cooperation would naturally and readily facilitate the whole process of discovery. So too, in such an organization, different individuals would naturally make their own contributions to the group clarification, which means proper recognition of the principle of individualization. Once again, the whole pattern is that of a tightly bounded unit, a lesson to be learned, an insight to be achieved once and for all. It is tied to the following lesson simply by the step of application. This again flows from the verbal character of context and focus. If, as has been suggested, the children were attending to adverbs for the purpose of improving a written statement (perhaps for the school magazine) which they wished to make as effective as possible, it would be immediately transformed into an experience of advancing a step toward the control of significant action. Thus the principle of sequence, as well as those of socialization and individualization, is relevant. Evaluation, also, is involved. As the scheme now stands, evaluation hardly amounts to more than having the teacher tell the children when they are right. Under the transformed scheme it could and probably would become a process of self-discovered success organized by the teacher in a setting of social discussion and collaboration and individual contribution.

From this analysis certain very important points emerge. (1) The effectiveness of the inductive-development lesson does not depend on its formal steps. It depends on the meaningfulness of the learning that is organized. This is universally true of all such methods. (2) Its effectiveness does not even depend on what is ordinarily considered its chief characteristic, namely the evocation of the insight from particulars without any previous hint as to what that generalization is. There is no sound psychological reason why at least a gleam of light should not break through the clouds quite early in the game, and the children will not learn worse if it does. (3) The point to concentrate on in connection with this, or any other proposed scheme, is not a stated series of pedagogical maneuvers but the regulative principles of meaningful learning. And those principles intertwine. A good context permits a good focus. These again permit a good socialization which in turn opens the way to good individualization. And all these together open the way for proper operating conceptions of sequence and evaluation. Any orderly plan which facilitates the application of these principles, taken all together, at a high level, adds up to good teaching. But it is the applied principles of meaningful learning, and not the skeleton of the plan, that does the business.

Another example of this method of analysis is furnished by a comprehensive scheme for teaching English composition at the secondary level. The plan is presented under four main headings, each dealing with an important aspect of it. They are Objectives and Organization, Practice, Individual Differences, and Motivation and Materials.

In considering *Objectives and Organization* it is pointed out that the controlling aim in the study of English composition is the development of clearly expressed thought in writing and speech. This general aim analyzes into five more specific objectives. (1) Developing a pattern of thought. (2) Developing the idea of the sentence. (3) Developing patterns of thought out of the individual's own experience. (4) Effective presentation of patterns of thought. (5) Presenting the desirable qualities of a given pattern, such as the letter, the essay, the short story, etc.

As to *Practice*, its function is said to be simply to develop habits of correct expression, not to develop the ability to think, or to give the pupil something to say. This should be the controlling consideration. Practice should make much of properly directed drills on correct usage, on the elimination of errors, on special phases of language such as connectives or personal pronouns, and drills applied at the point of error as it manifests itself. Theme-grading is recommended rather than detailed theme-correction. The value of the study of grammar is considered doubtful in connection with English composition. In all practice it is important that the learner be aware of the results of his work and be clear about the goal at which he is aiming.

In connection with *Individual Differences* the findings of a good many studies are epitomized to show that work in English composition is affected by a wide range and variety of such differences. The attention of teachers is called to a number of devices for dealing with them, such as homogeneous grouping, group teaching with individualized drills, various plans of individualized instruction, and individual diagnosis.

As to *Motivation*, it is said that the chief types of motives relevant to English composition are mastery motives, social motives, the selection of interesting topics, and the selection of socially useful language activities.

This classification of motives clearly suggests the choice of certain types of materials.*

This, of course, is a far broader set of recommendations than the inductive development lesson, or any similar set method. It has, however, fairly well-defined characteristics, and the question is how effectively and adequately it calls the teacher's attention to the pertinent aspects of the successful organization of learning in English composition.

At the outset it places considerable emphasis upon the principle of sequence, interpreted at a high level. English composition must be thought of and planned as a long-time development in a defined direction. Five more specific developmental lines are indicated, although their validity may be open to doubt and they would seem to need much further analysis before they would be of much use in planning instruction. So far so good. In connection with practice, however, there is much stress on purely systematic focalization with a minimal concern for meaningful context. Definitely directed drills are to be set up to build certain well-defined skills without reference to the content of thought. Such focuses are not likely to be effective for the reason discussed in dealing with the inductive lesson. Language skills certainly call for sharp focalization, and indeed often for drill; but this focalization is likely to work well only in a setting of endeavor to say something or to think through something worth while. Moreover systematization of this kind is almost sure to break the organization down into a series of more or less self-contained lessons, so that the long-time developmental sequences are honored only in word and not in fact. Consistently with this, individualization is handled as a problem of classification, whereas English composition offers very rich opportunities for individual contributions to group undertakings— but only if those undertakings are meaningful and compelling. Similarly, socialization is almost entirely neglected, except for the recommendation of social motives as one type of incentive. There is no strong emphasis on the great importance and valuable possibilities of cooperative group experience as a developmental influence in English composition. Evaluation, too, stops short with a knowledge of results, which may or may not have an important effect, but which is a very limited conception. And it is peculiarly significant that motivation is

* Adapted from Homer B. Reed, *Psychology and Teaching of Secondary-School Subjects*, Chaps. 2–5, Prentice-Hall, Inc., New York, 1939. This is the characteristic organization recommended by Reed, with some modifications, for all school subjects, both on the secondary and elementary levels. See also his *Psychology of Elementary School Subjects*, Ginn and Company, Boston, 1938.

treated separately, as a sort of extra, instead of as something that arises from the total organization of learning.

All in all, then, what this plan seems to indicate is a systematization of the teaching of English composition. The consideration of context, *i.e.*, the choice of topics and content and of situations in which the writings of pupils are actually used, is consistently slighted. This means that the focuses tend to become empty and verbalistic. The group becomes a problem, almost a handicap, because the prevailing conception is that of more or less uniform skills to be learned, whereas with a rich context and compelling focuses, social experiences can be highly constructive. In the same way individualization is conceived chiefly in terms of differential vertical progress. Very little emphasis is placed upon flexible and continuous self-evaluation, which is surely one of the strongest influences in learning to write well, and again this is inevitable because of the poverty of the context and the formalism of the focuses which leave nothing to evaluate except results in predetermined lessons. And although a good deal is said about the principle of sequence, the ideas do not penetrate into and permeate the organized pattern.

To point up and summarize the contrast, people young and old learn to write best by dealing with real issues in real situations, by having someone show them where and how they need to improve, by cooperative discussion with others concerned in the same undertaking, by discovering through such contacts the peculiar quality and quantity of their own abilities and needs vis-à-vis other people, and by continuous self-evaluation helped by contact with fellow workers and an experienced guide. The long-time result of such experiences and learnings is a developing power to express oneself, which may fruitfully be analyzed into a number of aspects. This is what is indicated by the principles of context, focalization, socialization, individualization, sequence, and evaluation.

The so-called "reading approach" in foreign language offers a very interesting case for analysis. The student is presented with very large amounts of material, linguistically simple, but of a content likely to be of interest and significance to him. He is urged to keep moving ahead, and to try to read at all costs, disregarding difficulties and obscurities as far as he can. Grammar is cut down to an absolute minimum. The aspects of this plan are very clear in the light of our principles. A sharply defined developmental line—ability to read—is plotted, and it is pursued at all costs. A dynamically compelling, simple, copious context is provided. The problem of focalization is handled by helping the learner to find and use some technique for building vocabulary, and by introducing such grammatical concepts and skills as may be essential. This treatment of context and focus makes possible a sequence determined by continuous growth in the indicated function, *i.e.*, in better and better reading, rather than by a series of separate lessons or units. Also the progressive emergence of this ability, in the whole setting of its personality concomitants, is something of which both the learner and the teacher can be continuously aware. The chief omission is the lack of emphasis upon socialization, but this could readily be supplied by encouraging group discussions of difficulties and procedures and materials, by having members of the group read and translate aloud to one another, and so forth. This would probably improve what is already a very effective plan, and also it would open up favorable possibilities for better evaluation.

The individual laboratory method in science, about which a great deal has been written, offers another instructive opportunity for our method of analysis. Context here, consisting of laboratory equipment and condensed instructions, is extremely limited, and it usually creates quite refractory problems of its own. The focalization is very definite and clear cut, and has the appearance of centering on genuine problems and insights. But the limitations of the context make this an illusion, and what the student is actually doing is not thinking through a scientific problem, but following a set of instructions. There is very little socialization because with undertakings so defined there is nothing in particular for group cooperation to take hold of. Individualization means simply the differential performance of assigned tasks. The real sequence is a discrete series of experiments rather than a continuous growth in scientific insight, and evaluation can mean little beyond a record of getting predetermined results in a given time.

In most of the cases so far considered, the primary weakness lies in the context, following upon which the application of all the other principles is vitiated. But in some project or activity teaching the defect is in the focalization, and the same is often true in the creative approach to the arts. There is an admirable, promising, and provocative context, but somehow nothing is ever brought to a head. A happy social time may be had by all, but there is no core around which cooperative group work can be organized, so both socialization and individualization fail. And there cannot be good evaluation, because there is nothing in particular to evaluate. All this need not be so, of course, but it often is.

Numerous other examples could be given to show how the principles of teaching here formulated can be used as tools to analyze and reveal the significant aspects of described teaching situations as patterns for the organization of meaningful learning. And when they are so utilized they must be taken in conjunction. for each reciprocally influences and is influenced by all the rest.

## THE OBSERVATION OF TEACHING

There are two chief purposes which are served by classroom observation. For teachers and intending teachers it is an opportunity to learn how to improve their own work and how the job is done, by the study and consideration of actual situations. For critic teachers, supervisors, and administrative officers it is an opportunity to appraise the work of a teacher by watching him in action, and to understand what suggestions may be helpful and constructive for his betterment.

If these two purposes are to be fulfilled, however, it is altogether necessary that observation be discriminating and intelligent. Nothing is easier than to watch a class for a period and to come away with no more than a rough, vague, general impression from which very little is learned, and which leads to a thoroughly faulty judgment as to the excellence or the defectiveness of what has gone on. Good and repaying observation must have the following four characteristics.

1. The observer must be able to discriminate between the essential and the unessential. This is by no means easy. The spectacle of a class in action is very complicated and confusing. A great many things are happening, and they happen fast. Some of these things matter a great deal, some of them hardly at all, and very often the latter are the more conspicuous and easy to notice. This is why observation reports so often make much of inconsequential detail and omit vitally important aspects of the situation. The observer notices the tidiness of the room, the cuteness and cleanliness of the pupils, the attire and general demeanor of the teacher, the routines of seating, passing papers, asking questions, using the blackboard, and comments on them at some length, often to the neglect of other things. These and similar matters may be important, but only on one condition. They are important, not in themselves, but only insofar as they make for good learning. *For the essentials in any teaching situation are the factors which make for good learning, and the evidences of it.* Anyone who wishes to observe well, either for the sake of improving his own work or of helping the teacher whom he watches, must learn to discriminate these crucial aspects of the business.

2. The observer must be able to see the general and universal in the particular and accidental. He may be watching a teacher who is

dealing with a small class, or an advanced class, or a bright section. The particular problem is, of course, interesting and important. But the observer should be able to pick out the factors which make learning go well in this specific situation, and which could be applied, *mutatis mutandis*, to quite a different one. What can one learn about handling a class of a hundred from watching a class of ten? About handling a class of beginners from watching a class of advanced students? About teaching a large heterogeneous group from watching a highly selected group of brilliant pupils? These are the sort of considerations he ought to have in mind. And there is a positive answer to all such questions, for anyone who has discovered how to see the general in the particular can learn much about the conduct of a nursery-school group from watching a graduate seminar.

Or again, the observer may be watching a class in a subject outside his own specialty. His chief professional interest may be in English literature, and the class he is visiting may be in mathematics. But it would be a very great mistake indeed for him to consider this a waste of time. What makes learning go well in mathematics also makes it go well in English literature, and it is on this that he should concentrate. A person who once grasps this truth will find any teaching, anywhere, in any field, a fascinating phenomenon which richly repays observation and reflective study.

3. The observer should consider it repaying to watch bad teaching as well as good teaching—perhaps equally repaying, though not equally enjoyable. Perhaps if he is a student preparing for the profession he will be sent to some school where he will see a harsh, narrow, unimaginative, obviously very limited routine, entirely different from what his training institution recommends. Here again he should by no means feel that he is wasting his time. He should ask himself which of the factors making for good learning are being neglected, and how they are being neglected, and why. An intelligent approach of this kind will yield valuable dividends, even though he may vow that, with the help of Heaven, he himself will never copy the example he has seen.

Above all, the observer should not allow himself to be controlled by his prejudices, even if those prejudices are well founded. He may like and appreciate a certain kind of teaching and a certain kind of teacher, because of his own background and experience in school, or because of the influence of his training institution. He may dislike other kinds of teaching, and other kinds of teachers. But these likes and dislikes should not stand in the way of intelligent analysis. Indeed it may be a very good thing for him to watch, study, and reflect about examples of teaching which he is inclined to condemn out of hand.

It is often admirable medicine for a convinced progressive to visit some very orderly classrooms, and for a convinced conventionalist to observe situations where there is a great deal of group freedom. When these persons have recovered from their initial shock they will do well to ask themselves, as objectively as they can, whether and to what extent the conditions of good learning are being fulfilled or nullified in the teaching they have watched. For always the issue is not between progressivism and conservatism but between good and bad learning.

4. All this comes to a head by saying that an observer must have the proper orientation if he is to observe well. First he must know what to look for. Second he must know how to look.

The orientation of many observers is at fault because they concentrate their attention on only part of the picture. They center almost entirely upon the activities of the teacher—how he asks questions, responds to replies, meets problems of disorder, uses the blackboard, introduces the lesson, makes the assignment, and so forth. Clearly, however, what the pupils do is altogether more important than what the teacher does, because they are the learners on whose learning the entire success of failure of the undertaking depends. To be sure, the observer cannot read their minds or know for certain what is going on there. But he can form a fairly good idea just the same. So he should pay attention primarily to the behavior of the learners in response to stimuli which come in part from the activities, including of course the words, of the teacher, and in part from the general organization of the situation. This is the only way in which he can hope to decide whether good learning is going on, which is always the essential question.

The orientation of many observers is faulty because it is not reflective. They visit a class, make copious notes, and then transcribe those notes into a running account of what they have seen. To do no more than this, however, is to minimize the value of observation. If one is to get at the essential and universal factors of a teaching situation, what one notices while watching must be food for thought afterwards. Sufficient notes should be taken so that one does not forget. Suggestions and ideas that come to mind should be jotted down so that they will not be lost. But all such notes are merely for the purpose of supporting memory, and above all they should be regarded simply as raw material for the fashioning of an answer to the question whether good learning is going on and why.

If these general lines of advice are to be followed out effectively, they must be translated into a working plan. Classroom observation cannot be done well at haphazard. On the other hand, it cannot be done well in the straitjacket of rigid uniformity. Both propositions are directly and evidently implied in the four points just discussed. The practical answer, then, seems to be that the observer should be guided by general principles which call his attention to the salient features on which good learning depends, which are sufficiently flexible to apply to any teaching situation, and which are sufficiently inclusive to cover all its essential aspects.

By way of showing how classroom observation may be organized and pointed up by controlling principles, there is presented here a report by a student observer as it was handed in, and an account of a critical discussion of it afterward. The student in question was a person of excellent ability who was one of a group of visitors, including the instructor of the teacher-training seminar, who observed and reported on a twelfth-grade class in world literature. The various reports by the students were actively discussed in the seminar group on the following day. The report as first turned in reads as follows:

It is pretty close to impossible to report on a class of Mr. X's without giving perhaps undue emphasis to the teacher himself. I feel myself capable of reporting from the point of view of a learning student member of the class, since what I gained in actual subject matter made a more lasting impression than an almost necessarily subservient study of student reactions to it. The fact is, that whatever his methods, Mr. X actually does teach "poetry," that most nebulous of forms, and more specifically techniques and feelings for distinguishing poetic words, poetic phrases, and poetic ideas, from the non-poetic, with all his examples found within a set of five excerpts from as many different "poetic translations" of Homer. This is a job quite as difficult, it seems to me, as teaching correctly and effectively, techniques of painting or judging art, or music, and in my long career of lit. courses I have studied under only one college instructor who may be said to have done a better job of it.

My personal opinion, however, is not necessarily valid as an evaluation of a teaching job in high school; certainly an objective treatment of Mr. X's methods reveals many flaws from the point of view of established practices of "modern education." In the main, he follows quite consistently and admirably his own prospectus for the best teaching of world literature . . . with the general aim of arousing a real and vital interest in the supposedly dead classics in his student body. In actual practice, however, he makes liberal use of short sarcastic comment without allowing any explanation from the student thus excoriated; and he is apt to sweep over student opinion, asking, do you like this?, receive a tentative hesitant reply, y-e-e-s, or n-o-o-o, and go on as if unhearing, declaring "Well, I don't," or "I do too," generally an opinion exactly opposite to the one elicited from the hapless student. In an entire class period, probably four fifths of the talking was done by the teacher, if not more.

Mr. X is an excellent example of the triumph of personality over technical errors; he is a masterful teacher and there is very little to attribute his genius to other than his own vibrant and outgoing personality and his own sincere love for and understanding of poetry and all forms of art. Although the students were on the whole repressed and served as mere recipients of facts and opinion thrown at them, they all obviously were content with their quiet role. In few other classes at this school, certainly in no other of this age group, have I seen such real and class inspired discipline, in the strictest sense of the traditionalists. There was next to no fidgeting, vacant stares, preoccupation with other works, whispering, or note passing. The class was not taken up with any exceptionally dramatic readings; it was a rather painstaking analysis word by word of different translations of the same sections of the Odyssey, with Mr. X doing most of the analyzing, as indicated above. The final test of the popularity of the course is, of course, the large attendance, since it is an elective course. It is possible that these numbers are drawn by the legend of Mr. X, by stories of his dramatization and unorthodoxy; but my only answer to that was a feeling I had from just looking at these students at a comparatively dry subject (that is, word by word analysis) that they gained a good deal more from the class than entertainment alone, and that they were aware of this gain too. In the broadest terms, they gained a capacity for entertaining themselves and enriching themselves for the rest of their lives, a capacity for giving themselves rewarding "cultural values," and making their lives the well-rounded ones which should be the aim of all higher education. Reverting again to my own personal evaluation of the class, I close by saying that I wish I had had a teacher and a course like his in my own high-school career, and that I would not, as a matter of fact, object too strenuously to taking it this year.

Here, clearly, is a highly intelligent and revealing report. The student was confronted with a very striking situation, and in the main dealt with it well. Above all, she concentrated upon the effectiveness of the learning evoked, and was considerably helped by her own personal participation in it, which she was not able to avoid. (This by the way, is always likely to make for vitality in an observation, and to assure it of the proper general orientation.) The report centers upon the accidental somewhat to the exclusion of the universal. It shows some failure to understand and rightly appraise what was seen. And its total emphasis is open to question. This student could have learned more for her own betterment as a teacher than she seems to have done, because she was so impressed by the personality of Mr. X that other considerations were somewhat subordinated. The point for her was not that Mr. X is an excellent teacher, or that one must try to copy him, which for most people would be disastrous. The point was to see what makes Mr. X a good teacher—a good organizer of learning—and to understand these causative factors well enough to apply them herself. A reshaping of the observation would make this possible, as appeared very clearly in the later group discussion, whose general outcomes are here presented, without going into a detailed account of what was said.

The first thing that strikes one is the excellent focalization. The work turned on discriminating between "poetic" and "nonpoetic" values as manifested in words and phrases. This at once established a mind-set toward analysis, reflection, attention to relative values, and the use of the higher mental processes generally. It undoubtedly did much to transform what otherwise might, as the student observer remarks, have been a dry lesson on word study into a living experience. Moreover the focus was set in an adequate context, furnished by five translations of the *Odyssey*. One cannot call this a verbal context, because when one is considering words for their aesthetic values in this way, the words themselves in their poetic settings become concrete material, and of course the only kind of material available. When the observer remarks that the students were evidently gaining " . . . a capacity for entertaining themselves and enriching themselves, a rewarding 'cultural sense' . . . ," she was in effect calling attention to the principle of sequence, and saying that this was not so much a lesson as a true developmental experience. She comments on this only in passing, but it deserves much more emphasis for it is one of the most important elements in the situation and suggests the sort of thing that any teacher of any subject at any level might advantageously learn from watching it. Furthermore, the observer remarks that, in her opinion, the students were well aware of what they were getting, so that evidences of evaluation were conspicuous enough to be picked up even by a visitor. Here again is a determining factor of first-rate significance, but the report merely mentions it and then passes on. Such things do not happen by chance, and since every intelligent teacher wants them to happen, it would have been well to consider how they were brought about in this particular instance.

The observer's chief negative criticisms have to do with socialization, and by inference with individualization. She comments on the aggressiveness and talkativeness of Mr. X, and on his partiality for crushing rejoinders, and also on the quietness and orderliness of the class. Her analysis of what she saw, however, and consequently her inferences from it were not correct. The class consisted of twelfth-grade students in a school which strongly and consistently encourages individuality, initiative, and free self-expression (not always wisely); attitudes which are strongly supported by the home life of the pupils. Moreover the personal peculiarities of Mr. X are a prized tradition among generations of students there. So the liaison on which the observer commented at some length was entirely different from the passive submissiveness evident in so many classrooms. Mr. X served up strong and highly spiced meat, but he was dealing with students who could take it. The inference is not that there are two kinds of discipline, both equally good, or that cooperative group freedom is merely a progressive fashion or convention; rather it is that here one has all the realities of a true cooperative situation, albeit in a limiting case. The students really wanted to learn and behaved accordingly, and although that behavior looked superficially like the conventional submissive good discipline, it was really quite a different thing. This is a very good example of the ease of being led astray by surface and unessential appearances, and of the need to penetrate down to the psychological realities of the situation.

Nevertheless the observer's critical comments on the prevailing use of negative incentives by Mr. X seems on the whole justifiable. Taken by itself, this must be considered a defect and a failure in skill— a certain manifestation of self-indulgence in other words, which the expert organizer of learning would do well to avoid. It was not nearly enough to ruin the situation. It was more than amply offset by other values. It did far less harm than it probably would with tamer and more submissive students. It was, no doubt, a consistent expression of the personality of Mr. X, and was understood and accepted as such. But it was not necessary, for the setup of focus and context certainly made possible much more flexible participation and a greater degree of general amiability. This again would have opened the way for a recognition of the principle of individualization, by encouraging differential contributions, something that did not appear at all. So one must conclude that even considering the total setting in which Mr. X and his students were at work, the strong, striking, persistent use of negative incentives did no good and probably did some harm in bringing about better learning and more authentic results, and that to model oneself on this feature of his practice in the absence of its many and potent constructive influences would be a disastrous mistake. He is not a good teacher because of his wisecracks, but in spite of them.

Clearly, then, the lesson which our student observer watched was not merely or chiefly a manifestation of sheer personality. It was a very expert job in organizing learning. Without this expertness the personality would have been quite unavailing, and its manifestations began to be questionable at the points where expert control slipped. The observer's report indicates some feeling on her part that a systematic psychological and pedagogical analysis is likely to be pedestrian, formal, and unimaginative, and to lead the mind away from the vital realities of good teaching.    This is by no means the case.    The lesson to be learned from the spectacle of Mr. X in action is that the effective organization of learning always depends upon the application of definite concepts and principles, that no teacher can afford to ignore any of them, and that a first-rate teacher will assuredly apply them artistically in a manner suited to his own nature and personal idiosyncrasy, but still apply them, and at a high level.    If another and quite different type of person tried slavishly to model himself on what he had seen Mr. X do, he would almost certainly invite disaster, for he would be apt to copy the faults.    This is why it is always necessary to dig down into the realities, the true determining factors of a situation, if observation is to be fruitful.

Thus it is suggested and urged that observation be systematically guided by the principles of teaching set forth in this book, always understood in the light of their relationship to the basic concept of meaningful learning.    To do this calls attention to the crucial factors, and so avoids wasteful concentration on the unessential and the accidental.    Also it calls attention to all relevant determining factors, and so avoids incompleteness.    At first, or in any given single observation, it may be well to concentrate on manifestations of only one or two of the six principles.    This, however, is never finally satisfactory, because they are all interrelated.    It is, however, quite possible to train oneself so that one can visit a classroom, make sufficient jottings to help one's memory, reflect about what one has seen, and then make a systematic, properly oriented, reasonable, balanced and complete appraisal involving, as it must, all of our six principles.    Such an appraisal contains the answers to the questions: Were they really learning?    Were they really growing?    What made them do it?    What prevented them from doing it?    What were the limiting influences?    What suggestions might one offer for improvement?    What can I myself learn from it all for my own work?

## LESSON PLANNING

The planning of lessons is one of the most practical, urgent, and constant concerns of all teachers, whether in service or in training. All the principles discussed in this book converge upon it, and a consideration of their bearing upon it not only shows how this continually recurring problem may be solved to the best advantage, but also throws further light upon the meaning of the principles themselves, and their relationship to one another.

**1. What Planning Means.**    *Planning is thinking.*    It means bringing to bear sound general ideas upon a particular situation.    The better one thinks—the more comprehensively and yet at the same time specifically—the better one plans.

Much of the planning done by teachers, and even recommended by teacher-training institutions and in books on teaching, is exceedingly limited and defective. It amounts to little more than following some fairly orderly scheme for deciding overnight what to do in tomorrow's work. How to get the period started, what questions to ask on the assignment that is coming up, whether to run a written test, what to put in the blackboard, what assignment to set for the following day, what routine business to transact—these are the sort of things that are considered. It always seems very practical to have some orderly system for dealing with such matters, and to draw up a lesson plan which will take care of them; and of course there is not the slightest doubt that they must be handled properly. But a teacher whose planning is of this type is rather like a practical carpenter who undertakes to build a house. He is able to do the job. He plans it after a fashion. He knows more or less what materials and tools he will need, and he has some ideas about location, orientation, drainage, interior arrangements, and so on. But he works pretty much by trial and error. In the end he comes out with a house but it is almost certain to be far less satisfactory than one that a trained architect would produce. The reason is that the architect is able to think about the problem far more comprehensively and discriminatingly, and so he produces a better practical result. The proper example for the teacher is the architect, not the carpenter; and he can model himself on the architect by making his planning equivalent to adequate thinking.

Planning of this kind has two great values. It makes for good teaching, and it makes a good teacher.

1. It makes for good teaching because it enables one to handle a situation flexibly, resourcefully, and at the same time definitely, yet without rigidity. One has decided upon a feasible line of treatment, yet in working it out one has considered many alternatives and possibilities. So if things do not go just as one had expected, one can change one's tactics, perhaps to great advantage and without losing direction. The teacher who organized the unit on architecture which has been described in these pages devoted a great deal of time, thought, and study to what she was going to do. The work started up pretty much as she had anticipated, but before long the suggestion came from the class that they might set to work to make a rose window. She was able to build this novel departure into her plan, with highly constructive results, because she had everything so well and comprehensively

thought out.   The teacher who plans rigidly, because he thinks narrowly and insufficiently, is like a tightrope walker.   He is all right so
long as he can stick to one line of advance, but he cannot deal with
any alternatives.   And in teaching, as in all life, alternatives are very
likely to arise.

2. Besides this, and perhaps even more importantly, such planning
makes a good teacher.   One becomes a good teacher through learning
and growth, and everything that has been said in these pages about
meaningful learning applies precisely to this development.   One
develops resources in handling context and focus, in dealing with
groups and individuals, in shaping up the process of growth, and in
managing evaluation.   But these accumulating resources do not
constitute a mere bag of tricks which grows fatter with the passing
years, because one comes to understand more and more clearly and
deeply the meaning of the principles in terms of which resources are
used.   This development of insight and resourcefulness combined is
the secret of all power—the power of the general who commands a
wealth of tactical alternatives for the realization of a clear strategic
plan, the power of the musician who can present a brilliant extemporization because he has the materials of music at his fingers' ends
and can draw upon them just as they are needed to convey an essentially simple idea.   And it is brought about by doing the best possible
thinking one can do about the practical situations with which one
must cope.   It may be that some who read this book will think that
the task of putting the principles here set forth into practice at the
highest possible level is beyond the capacity of the ordinary teacher.
There is this much truth in such a doubt, that no one should ever
suppose the art of teaching to be easy.   Like every other art, it must
be learned.   And again like every other art, it is learned by a meaningful process, a process of thought, of seeing the general in the particular
and the particular in the general, of making everything one does the
object of the best reflection one can manage.   A teacher can grow into
the power he needs to work on the highest levels of expertness by
making his planning equivalent to thinking.

Some progressive educators are fond of insisting that a teacher
should never plan "in advance of the situation."   Presumably what
they are attacking is rigid planning, narrow planning, trial-and-error
planning, carpenterlike planning.   For not to plan at all is even more
disastrous and destructive than to plan rigidly.   By all means a
teacher needs to be flexible, resourceful—to be able to extemporize.
But extemporization comes from power and not from chance.   When
some creative achievement amazes us by bursting forth on the spur of

the moment and with what seems like utter spontaneity, it is a sure sign that much has gone before. When a teacher confronts some unexpected challenge and in a flash converts it into a golden opportunity to further learning, it is not because he has not planned at all, but because he has planned extremely well. Rigid, *ad hoc*, carpenter-like planning makes for mediocre lessons and chances thrown away. The teacher who never does better than this is headed straight for that professional hardening of the arteries which is his greatest occupational hazard. Against such planning the critics are altogether right in their warnings. But planning which is thinking contains the promise of the specific job well done, and for the teacher it makes each job an advance toward greater power.

**2. The Sequence of Planning.** All good planning—and this is true not only of teaching, but of every human enterprise—is a process of growth; and the more it fulfills the conditions of growth, the better it is likely to be. It begins with the emergence of a general guiding idea, often, and in the best instances usually, far ahead of the event. At this stage there are many irrelevancies, imperfections, omissions, and much that is vague and later turns out to be unworkable. As time goes on, the imperfections are winnowed out, the omissions are filled in, new suggestions and possibilities present themselves, relevant considerations hitherto unnoticed come to mind, vagueness is steadily dissipated, and the working idea gains clarity and feasibility. On the eve of the event everything should be clear enough so that one can commence action with confidence, knowing what one intends to do. But still it is a mistake to try to have everything cut-and-dried, because there should be room for the inspiration that action often brings to the well-prepared, and for those unexpected happenings that should be welcome to the well-prepared, because they so often lead to the happiest of decisions. Then comes the fulfillment of the plan, when everything becomes definite and final, for better or for worse. This, however, is not a brand-new and wholly different stage, but rather a continuation of what has gone before. Nor does the process properly end here, for after action should come reflection, when everything is reviewed, criticized, and evaluated. This kind of planning is highly recommended in working for an examination or writing a term paper, or preparing a speech or a public musical performance, or organizing a military campaign, or putting through a business deal, or any other kind of human undertaking. It is also highly recommended for the planning of lessons.

Let us make this concrete. A teacher is to conduct a course in algebra during the fall session. This course is to include a study of

arithmetical progression.   It is now late June, with the vacation beginning.   Not a bit too soon to start planning that lesson, if the conditions
of growth are to be fulfilled!   He should start turning over the course
in his mind, and although the specific study of arithmetical progression
may still be very hazy, it should be in the picture.   This need not
mean hard work and forced labor, and indeed it probably should not
at the present stage, for such practices can be narrowing, limiting, even
inhibiting if undertaken too soon.   He should be giving free rein to
reflection and imagination, cultivating ideas and suggestions, encouraging the leisurely emergence of clarification.   Probably he should do
a bit of reading, and jot a note down now and then, to start and stimulate the mental flow.   But so far he is engaged in shaping things up, a
business which takes time and is far from incompatible with having a
good summer holiday.

By the time school starts, much should have been accomplished.
He should have a plan well enough formulated to get things moving,
but by no means rigidly set in all details.   When he meets his class
and comes to know them, and watches how they learn and works with
them, the shape of things to come grows clearer still.   His plan for
dealing with arithmetical progression takes on definiteness, and yet
it is a rich, resourceful, flexible plan because of all the thinking that has
gone before.   It is, moreover, still subject to modification, because
what he will do when arithmetical progression comes up depends on
everything that has happened before, and what this everything will
be remains to some extent still an open question.   Then, the night
before the topic is introduced, he takes time out to put a cutting edge
on the whole mass of previous reflection, preparation, and experience,
and on the morrow he takes it up with confidence, enthusiasm, and a
wealth of resource.   Then, when the study is completed, he thinks it
all over, seeking for a discriminating judgment on the strength and
weakness of this particular job, and an advancing insight into the
challenging business of teaching.

Planning of this kind implies the avoidance of three kinds of errors.
(1) First, there is the error of sheer extemporization.   Far from not
planning in advance at all, our teacher starts to plan a very long time
in advance.   But he plans in such a way as to take advantage of everything the situation may suggest or offer, much of it necessarily unfore-
seeable, and of all his own possibilities, which must be gradually
evoked.   (2) Second, there is the error of mere overnight preparation.
Overnight preparation for any challenge is vitally important, but it
should never mean starting from scratch.   It should mean bringing

everything finally to a head, so that one can attack the situation with impact and confidence, and with a whole range of possibilities ready and waiting just below the level of consciousness. (3) Third, there is the error of dehydrated preparation in which the whole course, complete in every detail, is worked out far ahead of time and put away in storage to be revivified bit by bit as the need arises. Such a practice is often considered praiseworthy and systematic, and it is no doubt very convenient to have an assignment and a detailed lesson plan on paper for November 10, and an objective test all ready for December 3, and to go to one's file and pull them out ten minutes before school starts in the morning. Unfortunately, however, the process of revivification mentioned above is not likely to take place, and one is more than apt to have a mummified rather than a vital lesson. For this is a good way to short-circuit and stultify the whole process of growth, which is the very essence of good planning.

**3. The Orientation of Planning.** What should be the focus of a teacher's planning? This is a vital question, for planning must be rightly oriented. Should he plan for the period? Should he plan his material and its arrangement? Both questions are often answered affirmatively, but in neither case is the reply right. If he plans for the period, he is oriented toward filling in a certain amount of time. If he concentrates on his material, his mind is drawn away from the human beings who are supposed to gain some benefit from the material in question. In contrast to these two suggestions it is often urged that the teacher should concentrate on the persons with whom he is to deal—their needs, their interests, their happiness, their growth. This, of course, is very important, but it cannot be considered sufficient, for what these learners are to learn and what they are to do is also relevant.

The solution of the dilemma is clear. The teacher's planning should center upon learning, and its organization in the particular situation, human, institutional, and physical, with which he has to do. Certainly the learners must be considered, because it is they who do the learning. Certainly the period must be considered, because it is one of the determining conditions of organization, and learning must be managed with reference to it. And, quite obviously, material must be considered very seriously indeed. But all these are only phases or aspects of the fundamental and essential job of teaching, which is the organization of learning. To plan a lesson is to organize learning. To plan it well is to organize that job so that the learning will be meaningful and therefore fruitful of authentic results. How to get these learners to learn—that must always be the crucial question, and all planning is a quest for a working answer.   Such is its clearly indicated orientation.

**4. The Scope of Planning.**   Since the intent of planning is to establish an effective organization of learning, it is necessary for the teacher to consider all determining aspects of the problem.   These have already been considered at length in connection with our six principles.   In showing how the principles of teaching bear upon planning, it seems well, for the sake of clear thinking and practical helpfulness, to regroup them under two headings—those having to do with the pattern of learning and those having to do with the human element in learning—and then to show how the two are interrelated, which last is a most important point.

The principles having to do with the pattern of meaningful learning are those of sequence, context, focalization, and evaluation.   At the beginning, however, it should be said with all possible emphasis that these principles cannot be properly applied, and that meaningful learning cannot be properly organized without constant consideration of the learners themselves as human beings.   It must not for a moment be supposed that the problem of the learning pattern can be handled in isolation in a practical situation, and it is here separated out simply for the sake of clarity.

1. *Sequence.*   An essential question to ask about any specific job of learning is: How does it fit into and contribute to the furtherance of the developmental line which should run through the entire course? How does it contribute to the learner's mental growth?   This is the sort of question which a teacher would usually be wise to ask himself far in advance—a sort of summer vacation problem for reflection. One trouble with a great deal of lesson planning undertaken shortly before the event is that it treats the lesson, or the job of learning as a sort of psychologically self-contained and bounded unit.   The acme of such planning is the mastery unit, in which learning is organized for the previously defined mastery of a stated ability, after which one passes on to the next.   A good contrary instance is the study of word values, described in this chapter, which was by no means a self-bounded lesson but was designed to contribute to a growing awareness of poetic and aesthetic values.   Another contrast would be the study of arithmetical progression, treated on the one hand as a single unit in a series of separated lessons, or on the other as a contribution to a growing awareness of relationship, which is the core of mathematics.   Short-term planning almost inevitably obscures the problem of sequence, or deals with it on a low level, merely as a problem of how to relate a

given lesson with what immediately follows and precedes it. This is why so many teachers find the suggestion that work should be determined in relationship to mental growth baffling and even meaningless. They plan in such a way that the problem of growth can hardly be considered. As any lesson emerges in the teacher's thinking from the vague to the definite, he should become clearer and clearer about its bearing upon the desired developmental line. And he should see more and more clearly how it should be shaped up to apply the principle of sequence at a high level.

2. *Context.* A teacher is not ready to handle any lesson with maximum effectiveness unless he approaches it with a vastly richer context at his command than he will be able to use, and yet with a pretty definite idea of what context he actually intends to use. This again suggests long-term planning. Our teacher, during his summer vacation, may get brilliant inspirations from casual contacts and experiences, or from reading a fiction magazine, for admirable context for his lesson on arithmetical progression. Moreover, as the years pass, his command of suitable context should become greater and greater. No teacher should rely for his context on adopted textbooks or assigned courses of study, though he should use these among other sources. He should be constantly on the lookout for pictures, models, readings, possible projects, and material of all sorts that will help to put ideas across. He should systematically accumulate such material, and he should con over his files from time to time, so that what he has may not be merely in the folders but also in his mind. As the time to teach a given lesson approaches, he should have narrowed down alternatives and should decide and be able to state in writing just what context he proposes to use. Also, as a very practical problem, he should take measures in time to see that what he needs will be on hand.

3. *Focalization.* The planning of suitable focuses can often be done best pretty close to the event, although here as everywhere, inspirations can occur at any time, and should by all means be recorded. A focus is intimately associated with its contextual setting, and arises out of it. So a new idea about context may suggest a replanning of the focus. There is a definite danger in first planning a series of focuses in the abstract, and then hunting for suitable context, because this easily leads to a series of disconnected jobs, unsupported by proper experiential material. The key question in connection with focalization is this: Am I creating a situation in which the learners will be challenged to do some genuine thinking? If the focus is purely verbal, and in a verbal setting, this almost certainly will not happen. One needs to be quite close to the situation, and to know pretty clearly what

experiences are to be organized, before one gets a sense of what is likely to be an effective focus. The thing to remember is that a good focus *asks a question which the learners want to answer*.

4. *Evaluation*. Evaluation is not something that takes place at the end of learning. It penetrates all learning, for it is part and parcel of the process. It is not enough to plan a test at the end of the lesson, or review tests at stated intervals during the term. It is not enough to lay out a set of oral questions which will reveal how well the pupils have done their assignments. When learning is well organized, the learners are constantly aware of how well they are doing and why. They may not know this with perfect clarity or completeness, but they are aware of it. Moreover, in well-organized learning, the teacher also will be aware of these things; and as we have seen in connection with the study of word values, even a student observer visiting the class only once can be aware of them too. Oral and written tests and quizzes most assuredly have a place in evaluation. But they are not the whole story, and if they are made the whole story they will fail in much of their effect. When learning is really meaningful the learner may not be able to diagnose himself completely, but he knows plenty about what is going on—about how he is succeeding, how he is failing, and what he needs in order to improve. When the teacher tells him something about his work, he may not have altogether realized it, but he recognizes its truth. Planning for good evaluation means creating situations where such constant self-judgment occurs. It occurs, for instance, in shopwork, or athletics, or the arts. There is no reason why it cannot occur in history or mathematics, or anywhere else. Nor does this necessarily require revolutionary procedures. Set up learning in terms of meaningful problems, and the conditions favoring good evaluation are fulfilled.

The principles that have to do chiefly with the human aspects of learning are those of *socialization* and *individualization*. We shall consider these two in conjunction.

No planning is good unless it considers the persons concerned. No planning is first rate unless the persons concerned have an active and important share in it. This is what those who insist that a teacher should not plan in advance have chiefly in mind, for a great deal of short-term planning concentrates merely on materials and devices, or at the best treats learning as an abstract pattern without reference to any particular learners. Any lesson plan may well begin emerging from the mists long before it is to be used, but it should not take anything like final shape before the teacher gets to know his pupils, and indeed until they themselves have had something to say about it.

The teacher begins to get to know a pupil from the office records which should go into his folder. But a pupil is more than a bunch of test scores. He is also a human being, and one cannot deal with him well until one gets to know him as such. Moreover one will never get to know him very well simply by studying him as a passive phenomenon. It is necessary for him to reveal himself by interaction in which he shares, and a relationship must be established in which he finds himself free to do so. Furthermore, the individual pupil is a member of a group which influences him and which he himself influences reciprocally.

Thus a vital element in all planning is for the teacher to get to know the group and the individuals with whom he is dealing—to find out what they want, how and what they think, and how they react to situations. This calls for an orderly and well-considered scheme, for it does not happen by chance or because of good intentions only. Some people talk as though individual and group initiative came down like fire from Heaven; but as a matter of fact it depends upon skillful organization. One of the professional ambitions of every teacher should be to become clever and resourceful in dealing with individuals and groups, in stimulating them, in getting *en rapport* with them, and in organizing cooperation.

As we have seen, one of the ways of doing this is to discuss extensively with the class from time to time the objectives, procedures, and standards of the course. Time thus spent is not time lost, because it leads to better learning. There is, however, a certain danger of the plan being accepted as a standard procedure, and formalized and therefore killed. The key question in planning is this: How am I organizing the situation so that the whole group will have the largest possible share in cooperatively carrying it through, and so that the individuals concerned will have the best possible chance of making their own contributions? No one should be afraid that this implies the sabotage of standards. Very considerable experience indicates that pupils are apt to be a good deal more optimistic and ambitious than teachers, and that when they are given a free rein and enabled to make genuine cooperative choices they will tackle jobs which few teachers would dare to impose on them, and do astonishingly well. But to repeat, such cooperation and initiative will never amount to much if it is sloppy and haphazard. It must be well planned, well organized, well led.

In the light of everything that has been said in this chapter, and indeed in this entire book, it should be abundantly clear that the two major phases of planning just discussed interpenetrate each other at every point.  But the idea is so vitally important that it must be emphasized once more.  A good focus is good only for a particular learner or group of learners, for otherwise it will not be a genuine problem.   If they can have a share in setting it up, so much the better. A cooperative awareness that a certain line of growth is contemplated is one of the most essential factors in making that growth really happen.   A context that is actually suggested on the initiative of the class or of some of its members may be enormously effective for that very reason.   And there are few situations which make for better, more stringent, and more revealing evaluation than that of working cooperatively with a group of people intent on a joint undertaking. Then on the other hand, the pattern of learning can be organized in such a way that it either kills social and individual values, or strongly fosters them.   If everything is set up in a stereotyped routine of verbal learning, group cooperation and individual contributions become simply and obviously impossible.   If, however, learning is organized for rich meaningfulness, then there is something to cooperate about, and something to which individuals may make their own unique contributions.

In summary, then, planning should be considered as thinking. planning should be considered as growth.   Planning should be rightly oriented.   And it should take within its purview all the determining factors of meaningful learning.   The specific lesson plan should indeed be definite.   But it should not be something hacked out the night before, and then ruthlessly followed through.   It should be a crystallization of wide and long reflection, brought to a head just before the event, liberating the teacher rather than tying him down, and giving him a confident freedom with his resources for the shaping up of the situation to effective ends, no matter what may come.

### THINKING AND MOTIVATION

This whole discussion is brought to a close with a brief consideration of two problems which often trouble the minds of teachers—how to teach pupils to think, and how to motivate them.   Here finally we shall see the vital interrelationship of all our principles in their practical application.

The problem of teaching pupils to think is the problem of organizing meaningful learning.   For meaningful learning is thinking, and thinking is meaningful learning.   There is only one reason why a human being ever thinks—because he wants to solve a problem.   Give him a highly verbalized history assignment, and his problem is how to get by, and so he thinks about that.   Ask him to figure out a way of lining out the football field by using geometrical techniques, and he

thinks about geometry. It is as simple as that. The ideas that thinking comes about by magic, or by a telepathy through which the thought
an author put into his book somehow gets into the mind of a bored and
fumbling reader, or by some special trick or device, are simply pathetic.
To put it brutally, they amount to unmitigated nonsense which the
least reflection on one's own experience should dispel. A person thinks
when he has a context that challenges him, and when a problem arises
in that context. He does his thinking in his own sweet way, because
he has to, although it is quite possible to help him a good deal. He is
stimulated by collaboration with a group of other people who are also
thinking about the problem. He will not be able to think unless he has
grown to the point where the problem means something to him, but on
the other hand his thinking is what makes him grow. And as he thinks
he is aware, at least dimly, of his difficulties and triumphs. Here again
he can be helped, for other people who watch him and know him and
work with him can also be aware of what is going on. This is how
learning must be organized if we want pupils to think. This is how
learning must be organized if we want pupils to learn. For meaningful
learning, whose organizational principles have been the theme of this
book, is equivalent to thinking and is the only way in which human
beings achieve power and attain authentic results.

Motivation, again, is not a separate, isolated consideration—a
coating of sugar quite irrelevant to what it covers. It turns on the
total organization of learning. How can we make pupils want to
learn? Well, what makes you want to learn? Surely the sense of a
problem that you want to solve! What else? To fix up learning so
that the pupils are almost certain not to care about it unless they are a
bunch of precocious highbrows, and then to try to energize them by
playing games, or patting heads, or giving stern reprimands is the height
of futility. A bored pupil—and there are many such—is an indication
not of the lack of some special magic tricks of motivation but of general bad teaching; that is, of badly organized learning. A bored pupil
in a school is just as disastrous a spectacle as a moribund patient in a
hospital—a sign that the organization has failed to do its business.
Perhaps neither institution is altogether to blame, for sometimes
either problem will defy the wit of man. But at least the hospital
tries, and does not sternly blame the patient for being so lost to all
sense of what is fitting as to die on its hands.

The point is that the bored pupil is the pupil who is not learning.
Interest is an absolute condition for authentic results. But interest,
like thinking, does not descend as fire from heaven without human
intervention. Nor is it elicited by tricks of sugar coating, or by for-
ever asking pupils what they think they want to do. Certainly their

choices are important, but those choices are guided and indeed created by the skillful organization of meaningful learning.    To feel that here is a demanding problem in a challenging setting, to be aware that others around one are wrestling with it and that one can still contribute something of one's very own, to watch one's own stumbles and successes, and to be conscious of one's own growth toward repaying power—this is what makes people want to learn.    Here is epitomized the doctrine contained in the discussion of our six principles, whose application is the organization of meaningful learning, in and through which alone teaching can bring about the authentic results which constitute its essential purpose.

### Items for Discussion and Study

1. Take all the material you have assembled in connection with the primary suggestions for discussion and study in Chaps. 5–16 inclusive.   Reappraise it in the light of the interrelationships of the principles as here presented.   Show how the high-level applications of any one principle opens the way for and even requires the high-level application of others.   Show how such a principle as context or focalization applied at a low level makes an effective application of other principles very difficult.   Bring this whole analysis once more into relationship with Wrightstone's statement on p. 37.

2. To what extent can you bring to bear the six principles of teaching, considered together, on the series of contrasts between the new and the old presented on pp. 38–40?   Do these contrasts go beyond and involve more than the principles here formulated?

3. Make analyses of a number of described plans or methods of teaching, similar to those presented in the chapter, in terms of the six principles.

4. Formulate a scheme for observation which would take into consideration all the relevant aspects of good learning as presented in this book.   What are the practical difficulties of such observation?   Would it be better at first to observe for the principles one at a time?   Can one learn to be a good observer?   How?

5. What are the reasons why a lesson plan made the night before without much preliminary preparation is likely to make for rigidity and routine teaching? There are quite a number of such reasons.

6. Is it possible to plan for a flexible approach and treatment?  How? Would this mean that one should not actually write out one's plan?   If one does write it out, should one use a standard form?

7. Collect and discuss illustrations from your own experience or observation which show that good thinking is really meaningful learning.   Does one always learn something when one thinks?   Is this the only way of learning?   Is it the best way?

8. What arguments have you heard indicating that the best way to teach pupils to think is to present them with a well-systematized body of material, like geometry, for instance?   What do you think of them?   Could there be as much thinking in making a table as in learning a geometrical proposition?

9. Do you think that there is any way of motivating pupils so that they will really want to learn a thoroughly dull assignment?   Have you any suggestions?

10. If we organize learning from the ground up so that pupils really want to learn, does this mean cutting standards, or getting rid of the present curriculum?

# INDEX